If our speech

A compelling and troubling work.
Elizabeth Fox-Genovese
author of *Feminism Without Illusions*

has no me

A stimulating tract on freedom of expression . . . a marvelously written, multi-layered, complex, and imaginative work, a veritable möbius strip. Like no other, this book is an aural, visual, and cerebral experience.

Nadine Strossen
ACLU National President & author of
Defending Pornography

aning, nothing

No one has examined more carefully the interrelationships among commerce, culture, and discourse than Collins and Skover. They offer a learned, thought-provoking, and frightening account of what has happened to freedom of expression.

Neil Postman
late author of *Amusing Ourselves to Death*

has meaning.

Camus

Collins and Skover are true pioneers of the trail. They show the best in Platonic eros — the love of ideas and the joy in risk-taking.

Max Lerner
late author of *America as a Civilization*

No other book on the First Amendment even approximates it or rivals its creativity.

David M. O'Brien
author of *Constitutional Law & Politics*

For many, the intellectual turns of the book will be a gut-wrenching experience. For others, the book will provoke recognition; for others anger; for others a genuine curiosity of what to make of our national puzzle.

Steven Shiffrin
author of *The First Amendment, Democracy, & Romance*

The Death

produced by Bruce Mau

# of Discourse

Third Edition

Ronald K.L. Collins & David M. Skover

CAROLINA ACADEMIC PRESS
Durham, North Carolina

Library of Congress Cataloging-in-Publication Data

Names: Collins, Ronald K. L., author. | Skover, David M., author.
Title: The death of discourse / by Ronald K. L. Collins, David M. Skover.
Description: Third edition. | Durham, North Carolina : Carolina Academic Press, 2022. | Includes bibliographical references and index.
Identifiers: LCCN 2022028577 (print) | LCCN 2022028578 (ebook) | ISBN 9781531025267 (paperback) | ISBN 9781531025274 (ebook)
Subjects: LCSH: Freedom of speech—United States—Popular works. | Freedom of speech—Social aspects. | Mass media—United States—Language. | Popular culture—United States—Language.
Classification: LCC KF4772 .C63 2022 (print) | LCC KF4772 (ebook) | DDC 342.7308/53—dc23/eng/20220831
LC record available at https://lccn.loc.gov/2022028577
LC ebook record available at https://lccn.loc.gov/2022028578

Carolina Academic Press
700 Kent Street
Durham, North Carolina 27701
(919) 489-7486
www.cap-press.com

Designed by Bruce Mau Design Inc.

Lead-in quote from Albert Camus, *Notebooks 1942–1951*, trans. Justin O'Brien (New York: Modern Library, 1965) p. 23.

Printed and bound in the United States of America.

To Life

&

Those We Love

Contents

Book I
The Paratroopers' Paradox

Book II
Commerce & Communication

Book III
Discourse & Intercourse

Text of 1791
First Amendment

Amendment I

Congress shall make no law respecting
an establishment of religion,
or prohibiting the free exercise thereof;
or abridging the freedom of speech,
or of the press; or the right
of the people peaceably to assemble,
and to petition the Government for a
redress of grievances.

ISBN 0-02-932271-5
90000>
9 780029 322710

Dramatis Personae*

Stuart Banner	lawyer
Leo Bogart	sociologist & advertising expert
Shadia B. Drury	political scientist
Elizabeth Fox-Genovese	historian
Robert Hariman	communications professor
Sut Jhally	communications professor
Alex Kozinski	federal appellate judge
Max Lerner	syndicated columnist
David Nyberg	philosophy professor
David M. O'Brien	political scientist
Martin Redish	law professor
Edward Rubin	law professor
Loyal Rue	philosophy & religion professor
Herbert I. Schiller	communications professor
Suzanne Singer	rabbi & former public television producer
Rodney A. Smolla	law professor
Richard Stivers	sociologist
Nadine Strossen	law professor & ACLU national president
Cass R. Sunstein	law professor & political scientist
Mark V. Tushnet	law professor

* Books I, II, and III and the Afterword contain "dialogues" in which the people listed above participate.

How to Read This Book

Writings are naturally accessible to all who can read.

— Leo Strauss
Social Research (1941), p. 488.

You do not have to be a jurist, a lawyer, or a scholar to enjoy this book. Of course, familiarity with philosophy helps, knowledge of sociology and psychology cannot hurt, some comprehension of law and government is useful, and an understanding of modern advertising and theories of communication (from Plato to McLuhan and beyond) is indeed helpful. But these are not prerequisites.

Anyone can read any portion of this book (in any order) and walk away with some new view of the First Amendment. At least, that is our hope. In what follows, we occasionally mix media — i.e., print and electronic. Sometimes discounting the traditional print mindset, we invite you, our audience, to read and listen to music, or to read and view videos, or to read and consider advertisements, or even to read while "turned on" to an eroticized imagination.

So relax. Do not be intimidated by the high-sounding law-talk of those few who quarantine the First Amendment in the lifeless wards of lawyers. Rather, visualize this little book in your own way, at your own pace, and for your own particular purpose. And remember: The First Amendment is, above all, what We the People make of it.

Foreword

If one lives long enough, sometimes the obvious remains so even in the face of denial. After all, yesterday's insights occasionally shed enough light through the corridors of time to reveal a momentous fallacy in constitutional and cultural thinking. That fallacy, which we exposed in this book's first edition, still plagues free speech jurisprudence. And so we return to the scene, a quarter century since we first associated the word "death" with "discourse." Today, as we will point out, that death sentence seems more warranted than ever.

There is a cautionary adage in Proverbs: "He who repeats a matter alienates even his friends."[1] Once written, a book is not to be reworked. That, at any rate, may be the Hebrew Scripture's admonition to authors. If so, there is some wisdom in the warning. For what is a text without closure? Its authority depends, in no small part, on its finality; its artistry on its originality; and its authenticity on its timeliness.[2] Moreover, to reopen the four corners of the printed page for revision potentially exposes it to all forms of novel attack, even by its earlier defenders. Challenges to its analysis may be dressed up in today's fashionable theories; critiques of its style may be fed by current aesthetic tastes; and conclusions about its relevancy may be inspired by the ideologies *du jour*. In short, writers who revisit their works risk severe judgments of obsolescence.

Is that not even more the case for authors who have predicted a death? As the Welsh poet Dylan Thomas reminds us, "After the first death, there is no other."[3] It could be an injudicious act to return to the scene of a battle, if only to declare that the mortally wounded are still dying and the recently deceased are still dead. What might we be thinking, then, in writing a third edition of *The Death of Discourse*? Are we, like the war-weary partisans of the Greek hero Ulysses in Alfred Lord Tennyson's famous ode, enchanted by the belief that "Death closes all: but something ere the end, some work of noble note, may yet be done"?[4]

In the face of censure (even by our friends), we revisit yet again the state of American discourse for three important reasons. First, governmental responses to the geopolitical realities of 9/11 appeared to contradict central tenets of our book; accordingly, a resolution of such seeming contradictions reinforces our thesis. Second, post-2016 political events, combined with ever-emerging communications technologies, validates our arguments to a disturbing degree. Third, new facts and figures further support our previous depictions of the nation's popular culture of electronic entertainment, commercial advertising, and pornographic eroticism. Although our earlier portrait remains surprisingly representative of our times, and retains much of its explanatory force, we relish this opportunity to retrace its lines and retouch its colors.

Think about it: More than any other provision of the United States Constitution, the First Amendment brought the idea of the pursuit of truth into the constitutional arena. Of course, it also brought other pursuits into that realm, some ignoble, others farcical. On the one hand, the Framers were the heirs of the Enlightenment; many of them shared the Kantian aspiration that it signaled "the emancipation of the human consciousness from an immature state of ignorance."[5] On the other hand, as the author of *The Age of Reason* (1794) well knew, the Enlightenment had its share of enemies determined to dismiss or subvert it.

If the Enlightenment promised a new self-confidence rooted in reason, the "no law" command of the First Amendment enabled a future in which that confidence might be eclipsed by folly of the most unsettling kinds. The ideal faith of the Founders notwithstanding, from the beginning the First Amendment was situated at the crossroad of reason and unreason, that place where the philosophical signposts proclaimed conflicting messages.

We are not unmindful that such a seemingly bipolar account wars with the idea of the Madisonian First Amendment cast in a quixotic light. Then again, we are all creatures of a post-modern world, the mere specter of which would horrify Enlightenment heroes such as Immanuel Kant, Denis Diderot, and Jean-Baptiste le Rond d'Alembert. That said, do not mistake our philosophic and pragmatic pause for any animus toward elevated notions of the First Amendment. Our admiration for the Madisonian ideal first prompted us to expose the hypocrisy justifying vacuous forms of free speech mouthed in its name. There should be no shame in debunking a culture in which truth has no real value and falsity masquerades as reality. Just such a social order—lionized in America's political and popular cultures and justified in its legal theory—became manifest in the past several years, and in most surreal ways. Thus, what we wrote back in 1996 strikes us as more relevant today than then, if only because free speech continues to thrive while enlightened discwourse continues to die.

The Death of Discourse reveals a "Huxleyan dilemma" operating in America's popular entertainment culture. That is, much of our public talk resembles, in character and form, the distracting pleasures of Aldous Huxley's anti-utopian *Brave New World.* Book I (pp. 1–65) establishes that we are inundated with the fact-free and amusing sound- and eye-bite spectacles of electronic technologies, even for our most important news and information. Book II (pp. 67–135) demonstrates that we are enticed by the fantasy-fulfilling words and images of commercial advertising, even for lifestyle choices beyond our means. And Book III (pp. 137–200) contends that we are tantalized by the lusty lures of pornography, even as our primary source of sexual fulfillment. In all of this, everyday experiences in mass communication dramatically deviate from the more traditional and lofty notions of rational discourse in the service of the civic good. Moreover, as the Epilogue (pp. 201–216) and the Afterword (pp. 217–249) argue, when we consider America's public speech as it is rather than as it should be, our cultural approach to the First Amendment proves that the exalted reasons given for constitutional freedoms of speech and deliberative democracy are little more than noble lies. The modern First Amendment mixes the high and the low, protecting private indulgences in our carnival culture in the name of the political community's constitutive values. Now our free speech system equates electronic self-amusement with enlightened civic education, the marketplace of items with the marketplace of ideas, and passionate self-gratification with political self-realization. In short, eighteenth-century Madisonian principles of discourse seem ill-suited, if not functionally irrelevant, for our practices in twenty-first-century mass communication.

When you read what follows, remember this: Our cultural approach to the First Amendment was crafted at a time and in circumstances that would be unrecognizable by some and perhaps only faintly remembered by others. In significant respects, it was a very different world. Ground-breaking communicative innovations such as Facebook, Instagram, Snapchat, Twitter, and YouTube did not exist; Fox News had just debuted on cable television; the I-Phone was yet on Steve Jobs's drawing board; and you could not read this book on mobile devices. In the political sphere, Bill Clinton was still President; William Rehnquist was still Chief Justice; centrist Republicans still retained seats in the Congress; and legalized gay marriage was still wishful thinking. On the entertainment front, the sit-coms *Seinfeld* and *Cosby* ruled the TV ratings; the first *Mission Impossible* movie was a top box-office seller; and the first volume of J.K. Rowling's *Harry Potter* series had yet to be published. As for the erotic domain, Pornhub and xHampster, two of today's leading porn sites, were a decade away from erogenous zones.

Running from this past to our present, however, a cultural constant remains. Admittedly, and as we note below, the facts and figures have changed. What has not changed is the Huxleyan dilemma: the unending modern assault on the edifice of the Madisonian First Amendment by entertainment pastimes, commercial pursuits, and erotic pleasures—all made possible by technological proliferation. It may be the same story, but its retelling takes on monumental proportions. In the process, Madisonian values struggle to survive in a popular culture largely indifferent to their demise.

Our Huxleyan warning could appear out of sync with the specter of Orwellian threats to our civil liberties in post-9/11 America. The war on terrorism that the United States waged on both foreign and domestic soil since the fateful morning of September 11, 2001, triggered troubling threats to our cherished freedoms of speech, association, press, religion, and privacy, among other civil rights. To mention only a few examples, the Homeland Security Act, passed in 2002 and still operative, seriously curbed press and public access to governmental information through Freedom of Information Act requests, and the ill-named USA Patriot Act of 2001 (that expired in part in 2015) significantly broadened the Executive's criminal inves-

> **EYEBITES: READER SUPPORT BOX**
>
> Orwell v. Huxley: Two Types of Tyranny
>
> Orwellian tyranny = Ruling with an iron fist to create a system of fear and repression. Government squelches political dissent, bans books, invades privacy, censors electronic information, and conceals truth. The governing maxim is: "Big Brother Is Watching."
>
> Source: George Orwell, *1984* (1949)
>
> Huxleyan tyranny = Providing narcotic "soma tablets" and non-stop entertainment to create a system of pleasure and passivity. Government and the corporate sector offer a surfeit of amusement to distract the public from socio-political realities. The governing maxim is: "Everybody's Happy Now."
>
> Sources: Aldous Huxley, *Brave New World* (1946) & *Brave New World Revisited* (1958)

tigatory authority. Exceptional governmental powers originally used for foreign counter-intelligence—including covert searches of homes and offices, seizure of personal belongings, and "roving wiretaps" to capture private e-mail exchanges, telephone calls, and credit card purchases, all without notice until the targets were actually prosecuted—became available for domestic criminal surveillance, as well. Ironically, at the same time that the Bush Administration secured an unprecedented amount of governmental secrecy, it weakened an unprecedented number of individual privacy and speech freedoms.[6]

For vehement critics of these national security policies, George Orwell's ears would be burning. The English novelist who penned *1984*, his famous tract on totalitarian tyranny, no doubt would have been alarmed by such dangers to our speech freedoms. And many a First Amendment advocate lifted the veil of government propaganda and exposed "Big Brother" behind our government's promises of more security for less liberty. To them, the suggestion that the more profound threat to traditional First Amendment ideals may be Huxleyan rather than Orwellian ignored the realities of the time.

Of course, we must always be mindful of Orwell's dark specter, and *The Death of Discourse* is unambiguous on this point: "Let us be clear: The potential for Orwellian governmental censorship should *never* be dismissed, and we do not dismiss it."[7] Indeed, if American free speech history teaches us anything, it is that our expressive liberties are most endangered precisely when they should be most engaged—that is, in periods of war or anticipated war. Tellingly, the first federal Sedition Act was passed by the Congress in 1798, when war with France seemed imminent; galvanized by concerns about German-American sympathizers, Congress passed the second Sedition Act in 1918, shortly after the United States entered World War I; America witnessed the West Coast relocation and internment of Japanese-Americans during World War II; and between 1951 and 1956, during the Cold War, Congressional McCarthyism supported the exaggerated fears of Communist governmental infiltration. In all of those instances, real spies or traitors were rarely discovered, but many political dissenters, pacifists, labor radicals, and innocent bystanders were jailed or silenced.

What do these lessons of history teach us? First, the American government—one ostensibly committed to the First Amendment and other fundamental liberties—is capable of exploiting national hysteria to expand its powers and to equate dissent with disloyalty. To that point, President George W. Bush's then-press secretary, Ari Fleischer, highlighted the "un-American" character in criticizing the administration's war on terrorism, as he cautioned that "Americans . . . need to watch what they say."[8] Second, our fellow citizens—including many who believe themselves to be free speech advocates—often will yield to the government's repressive agenda, ready to trade a full measure of freedom for the illusion of greater security. The ultimate lesson here: fear is the first enemy of freedom.

Though we must take this Orwellian lesson to heart, *The Death of Discourse* encourages us to confront another clear and present danger to traditional First Amendment values. In America, the dissenter is effectively silenced, and a citizenry that should jealously safeguard its constitutional liberties is lulled into passivity, by a commercial entertainment culture too often oblivious to truth. This is the enemy of free speech identified in the Huxleyan dilemma. And it was just as ubiquitous and treacherous in the aftermath of 9/11 as it had been previously. Indeed, to a large extent, the attributes and spirit of public discourse during the war on terrorism resonated noticeably with Huxleyan overtones.

For example, well-informed professors and pundits frequently decried the government's unprecedented power grab, and at the same time bemoaned the public's apparent ignorance of or indifference to the loss of its civil liberties. Typical were the observations of rhetoric professor Sandra Silberstein and civic activist Jeff Milchen: "In post-9/11 America, 'red, white, and blue' was everywhere.... Stores were unable to keep flags in stock.... '[But] while millions of citizens were waving the Stars and Stripes, our constitutional rights were being whittled away by.... legislation that erodes three core protections: freedom of speech, freedom from unreasonable search and seizure, and freedom from deprivation of liberty without due process. And the flag wavers overwhelmingly were silent.'"[9] Similarly, journalist professor Jane Kirtley explained the citizenry's abdication of its rights as the result of its insouciance: "[I]n this climate of escalating secrecy, the public appears content not to know, at least if enthusiastic support of Congress' [new security measures] is any indication." The general public attitude seemed to be: "Information is dangerous. I don't want to take any responsibility for my own security. Keep me safe. And don't tell me how you do it."[10]

In effect, these commentators depicted the Huxleyan dilemma, without explicitly labeling it as such. The public that they described were the millions of amusement-hungry prime-timers who proved that "Friends" were more popular than enemies, as the ratings for repeat episodes of the NBC sitcom topped those for ABC's live-war coverage.[11] They were the star-struck media reporters who stumbled over themselves to publicize body-builder/actor Arnold Schwarzenegger's California gubernatorial campaign, while virtually ignoring former Vice-President Al Gore's challenges to President Bush's distorted rationalizations for the Iraqi war.[12] And they were the evening TV audience, apparently "burned out" on serious news, who sated themselves with pseudo-"reality shows" and other entertainment fare rather than stress out over "real-reality" programs on such crucial issues as the ever-rising "post-war" military casualties in Iraq, the ever-declining national economy, or the ever-present struggle over affirmative action or environmental protection.[13] Should it be any surprise, then, that the American mindset—occupied as it was with Huxleyan pursuits of triviality and pleasure—appeared markedly complacent about withering constitutional liberties, particularly First Amendment rights for the press and political dissenters?

Moreover, the Huxleyan tactics of our imagistic mass media immeasurably assisted the federal government in winning popular consent for its war against terrorism. From the moment that apocalyptic scenes of the imploding New York World Trade Towers were broadcast to a shocked and distressed nation, television programming exploited a form of "terror-tainment." "Out came the graphics and stirring music as coverage became packaged with titles like 'America Under Attack,' 'America Rising,' and 'America Fights Back,'" observed civil libertarian Danny Schecter. "The effects were soon noticeable as patriotism-influenced punditry and jingoism-informed journalism."[14] Prominent TV and cable news media personalities quickly revealed an uncritical penchant for military boosterism. No less a figure than the CBS Evening News anchor Dan Rather supported anti-terrorist war efforts by observing: "George Bush is president, he makes the decisions, and you know, as just one American, if he wants me to line up, just tell me where." Similarly, ABC News anchor Cokie Roberts admitted, "Look, I am, I'll just confess to you, a total sucker for the guys who stand up with all the ribbons on and stuff, and they say it's true and I'm ready to believe it."[15] Rallying round the flag, most television and press reporters gave little serious attention or depth of coverage to worrisome and well-documented abuses of governmental power, running the gamut from illegal detentions to racial profiling to harassment of dissenters. Instead, they manifested "patriochialism," a "dicktat holding that supporting your country means supporting the current administration."[16] The media's emotion-laden, angst-filled, and chauvinistic agenda delivered the popular verdict that enabled the President and the Pentagon to raise appropriations, to wage war, to broaden investigatory authority, and ultimately to undermine constitutional rights.

Consider also the explicitly Huxleyan terms in which the national government popularized its policies against war-time economic recession. A contracting American economy, further crippled by the September 11th terrorist attacks, presented troubling dilemmas for an administration elected in 2000 on a promise to cut federal income taxes. The solution: define consumerism as patriotism, and justify tax cuts as a tonic to stimulate economic growth. Though our citizens already had accumulated the historically highest level of consumer debt, President Bush called on them all to go shopping.[17] And former Treasury Chief Paul O'Neil urged speedy passage of the President's $1.6 trillion tax cut plan to fill the pockets of avid buyers.[18] "Maxing out your credit cards in the mall," *NYT* reviewer Allan Sloan explained, "wasn't self-indulgence, it was a way to get back at Osama bin Laden."[19] Comically reflecting on the hype to stoke the fires of Christmas-time consumption, *Colorado Business Magazine* editor Jeff Rundles wrote: "I am a patriot, not a debtor. Not exactly a firefighter or anything, but a hero of sorts. An American patriot. I went out this Christmas and spent like there was no tomorrow so that I might be responsible for the recession ending earlier than predicted, or the Taliban being defeated, or something else really important to the country."[20]

To the discerning eye, then, We the People expected hassle-free national security without the bother of governmental accountability; we preferred news-lite puff-pieces without the boredom of in-depth study; and we bought into a patriotic duty to consume without the sacrifice of genuine civic participation. In sum, we seemed to exchange the demands of informed judgment and social responsibility for the delights of illusory spectacle and individual self-gratification. As such, Americans were not the cowering citizens of

Orwell's Oceania, suffering under the totalitarian tortures of the Thought Police. They were, rather, the pain-free and pleasure-seeking denizens of Huxley's *Brave New World.*

Book I of this work focused primarily on the relationship between free speech ideals and America's entertainment culture, particularly as expressed through the medium of broadcast television. The conceptual link there demonstrated how amusement and the distractions of the "carnival culture" infect every aspect of modern existence, including political life. By that measure, celebrity figures—be they the governors of California or Wisconsin or the President of the United States—would qualify as model candidates for high office. In the process, the medium guaranteed that their messages, however bizarre, would become pervasive.

When *The Death of Discourse* was first published in 1996, broadcast and cable television were the dominant electronic communications media, although Internet use was becoming more prevalent in the 1990s. Since then, however, other Internet-based media have challenged television's dominance and surpassed its audience size. Nonetheless, the core tenet of our critique of discourse in America remains: "Entertainment is the supra-ideology of all discourse," is how our late colleague Neil Postman put it in his seminal book *Amusing Ourselves to Death: Public Discourse in the Age of Show Business* (1985).[21] We greatly amplified on that argument and applied it to our thinking on free speech freedoms, always emphasizing how the various channels of communication succumb, in one way or another, to the entertainment mandate. Today, those channels include a large variety of new communications technologies. While our original examples are now offered as historical illustrations, the conceptual thread running through them extends both into the present and the future.

One man, more than all the rest, realized that he could exploit the boundless potential of the new technologies to replicate in the political world the success that he had achieved in the entertainment world. That man became the 45th President of the United States. In his pursuit of power, he changed public discourse in America in ways that would have appalled the great Enlightenment figures and shocked James Madison, the father of the First Amendment. Worse still, the media cashed in on the outlandish spectacle and millions of Americans came along for the ride with fanatical fervor. And yet, exalted free speech principles continued to be bandied about by jurists and legal scholars as if the recent past had never happened, as if truth in the marketplace still had currency.

His name was his brand: Donald J. Trump. Literally speaking, his credentials were not those of a carnival barker, but they were akin to it. For some fourteen years, the former real-estate developer reigned as a TV celebrity, starring as the host of the widely popular reality show *The Apprentice*. Each episode concluded with the elimination of one contestant as the domineering Trump bellowed, "You're fired!" According to Nielson ratings, the beguiling program at its seasonal peak drew in 20-plus million viewers. With such name recognition and natural braggadocio, he was ideally fit for presidential politics in our carnival culture.

The TV-savvy artist knew the workings of the media business better than journalists. He had mastered the skills of being a spectacle, the kind that attracts base instincts while constantly captivating audience eyeballs—and all this to ramp up ratings. By linking his carnival to the media's commerce, he guaranteed that the captains of communication would pay homage to him with 24/7 "breaking news" coverage. No one (pope or politician), no group (religious or civic), and no truth (scientific or economic) could eclipse him. He had a lock on that. And the lock remained secure because his eccentricity was consistent with their commerce—that is, the *business* of the mass media.

The SPECTACLE† was on mesmerizing display during the 2015–2016 Republican primary debates. Time and again, and to the great amusement of the television viewing audiences, trite answers, false denunciations, colorful comments, personal insults, and posturing of all preposterous sorts triumphed over sense and substance in the twelve televised debates. Better than a game show and more enjoy-

---

† We need not fully endorse the philosophical underpinnings of Guy Debord to appreciate the importance of the insight that he offered in *Society of the Spectacle* (1967): The spectacle "is the heart of unrealism of the real society. In all its specific forms, as information or propaganda, as advertisement or direct entertainment consumption, the spectacle is the present *model* of socially dominant life." (emphasis in original) Equally important: "The spectacle subjugates living men to itself."

able than a sitcom, the main play was to the camera. The ratings for the SPECTACLE — between 12 and 24 million viewers—revealed that entertainment politics made for lucrative business.

That was the formula, or a main part of it. Keep the media lights on the candidate even in the face of repeated falsehoods and shocking distortions. It is all part of the SPECTACLE and how it works to the candidate's political advantage and to the media's pecuniary gain. The fact is that cable TV has "built an audience on outrage—people go there to get their anger on," Tom Rosenstiel (executive director of the American Press Institute) told the *Post's* media columnist Margaret Sullivan.[22] The cable-news networks, he added, are "birthing centers for polarizing rhetoric." Translated: polarity produces profits . . . the wellbeing of the Republic be damned.

The result was a paradox: On the one hand, journalists must remain faithful to their highest calling; that is, they must be objective and venture to discover and explain the truth as best as they can discern it. On the other hand, they must be beholden to the market forces that maximize their company's revenues. In other words, they must serve two often warring masters, one that favors a Madisonian ideal and the other that favors a Madison Avenue deal. Though truth sells, it does not always sell as well as its counterpart, especially when the latter masquerades as the former.

Objectivity may be the aspiration but profit is the motivation. Journalism operates somewhere between those two goalposts. How closely it leans towards objectivity depends on its proximity to profit. True, the two may sometimes coexist, but given a test between them, profit is a hard master to disobey. The journalistic problem is seriously compounded when news is cast as entertainment and when politics becomes a circus chock full of outlandish acts designed to capture attention. Yet, this is where we are in our post-2016 world.

Retired journalist Ted Koppel highlighted the paradox, though he seemed to be at a loss as how best (if at all) to resolve it. In a 2019 *Washington Post* op-ed,[23] Koppel portrayed the problem in rather Sisyphean terms: "Let the record show that [the current occupant of the White House] has launched the careers of numerous media stars and that expressions of indignant outrage on the left and breathless admiration on the right have resulted in large, entirely nonpartisan profits for the industry of journalism. Why anyone should assume that [the President] and those who cherish or loathe him in the news business will easily surrender such a hugely symbiotic relationship is hard to understand." In another *Washington Post* op-ed,[24] Koppel was equally critical of America's modern commercial media: "Beginning, perhaps, from the reasonable perspective that absolute objectivity is unattainable, Fox News and MSNBC no longer even attempt it. They show us the world not as it is, but as partisans (and loyal viewers) at either end of the political spectrum would like it to be. Audience share determines profits, which means that profits determine truth." And so, Mr. Koppel sadly proclaimed, "that's the way it is."

What was paradoxical for journalists was propitious for Donald Trump. He garnered astounding media attention without having to pay for much of it. Victorious in one primary after another, he needed a relatively meager campaign budget. As of March 2016, the *New York Times* reported: "[Trump] still doesn't have a super PAC. He skimped on ground organization and field offices. Most important, he spent less on television advertising—typically the single biggest expenditure for a campaign—than any other major candidate. . . . But Mr. Trump is hardly absent from the airwaves."[25]

Trump's *modus operandi*? He "earned" media attention by free news and commentary in newspapers and magazines and on television and social media that reported on his bold and boisterous campaign antics. Although he bought only $10 million of political advertising in the primaries, he benefitted by a whopping $1.898 billion of free media attention. By comparison, the next highest Republican "earner" was Jeb Bush, who came in for only $214 million of free media while paying $82 million for advertising. Notably, Trump's earnings were twice the estimated $746 million that Hillary Clinton took in during the same period. "The big difference between Mr. Trump and other candidates," the *New York Times* story concluded, "is that he is far better than any other candidate—maybe than any candidate ever—at earning media."

During his two election campaign bids and his presidency, Donald Trump sustained the unending barrage of message trafficking by his favorite weapons of mass distraction—Internet-based platforms such as YouTube, Facebook, and Twitter. Although he had attained notoriety through the medium of television, he understood all too well that the nation he governed had moved increasingly to online technologies for their news and entertainment.

Why, for example, would YouTube be so vital to Trump's mission? Answer: YouTube had an algorithm-fed audience of "2 billion regular viewers a month [as of January of 2021]—who watch over 1 billion hours of video per day, mostly via mobile apps on their phone."[26] Given YouTube's sensational popularity, Trump maintained a channel that included an extensive collection of campaign advertising, news bits, and original web shows that he and his associates produced. For a long time, YouTube allowed him to glorify and falsify his messages unregulated by pesky media gatekeepers. In this way, his YouTube channel enabled him to compete with the likes of CNN, MSNBC, and broadcast stations for 24 hours a day, 7 days a week.

From April to September of 2016, his YouTube following grew from 320,000 subscribers to more than 1 million. According to *NBC News*, "the Trump campaign was trying to flood YouTube with content and leverage the site as a secret weapon."[27] During his 2020 reelection effort, his campaign pulled back on television advertising and focused on Google's video platform. "The campaign and its joint fund with the Republican National Committee have spent over $65 million on YouTube and Google—about $30 million of it since July."[28]

Even more important to his brand of communication and style of governance, Twitter was the electronic megaphone that best suited his instinctual nature of executive rule. Given their 280-character limit, his tweets—often peppered with grammatical errors and misspellings—were far less important for their substantive content than for the constancy of their frenzied onslaught. Since Trump first joined Twitter in May of 2009 with the handle @realDonaldTrump, he tweeted approximately 57,000 times, with more than 25,000 of these posted during his presidency. Trump tweeted 5.7 times per day on average during his first half-year in the White House, but the frequency grew to 34.8 times a day on average by the second half of 2020. His most active day was June 5, 2020, when he sent 200 tweets or retweets, as he angrily rebuked General Mattis for denouncing him as a threat to the U.S. Constitution. By 2021, Trump enjoyed over 88.9 million subscribers of @realDonaldTrump. When Twitter permanently locked him out of his account after the U.S. Capitol insurrection of January 6, 2021, he lost the primary vehicle for his constant feed of distraction. The same, of course, held true when YouTube and Facebook banned him. Gone were many of the opportunities for incendiary provocations, implausible claims, defamatory statements, outlandish boasts, and startling charges that energized his base, excited his party, enticed media outlets, and dismayed his political adversaries.[29]

The realities of climate change, responses to the coronavirus scourge, reactions to police brutality of minorities, and relations with China, Russia, and North Korea were all essential topics for the White House and the press corps to hash out in press briefings, or daily White House briefings as they were called. But like the fate of the phone booth, such briefings became a thing of the past for the Trump Administration. As press briefings proved contentious and unproductive, the President turned more and more to "Twitter storms" and impromptu news conferences in front of Marine One, the presidential helicopter. Above the raucous clatter of the helicopter's blades, Trump would hold court in some of his 30-minute exchanges with the press. He shouted, they shouted—"chopper talk." They asked tough questions, he ignored them. And then he'd go off on some tangent in whatever direction the passions of the moment took him. In the process, the value of the Press Secretary and the White House briefings diminished to the point that by September of 2019 they were functionally obsolete. The fate of daily briefings was sealed, since its fare—rational discourse—had no place in a SPECTACLE dominated by his impulses.

There was another way that the President punished the press. He attacked its most treasured asset—its integrity. In this regard he was enormously successful in maligning the credibility of any reporter, newspaper, or media outlet. He did so with the use of two words, which became embedded in the American mind: "fake news." In an interview with the *New York Times*,[30] he prided himself on his vernacular triumph: "I do notice that people are declaring more and more fake news. . . . I even see it in other countries. I don't necessarily attribute that to me. I think I can attribute the term to me. I think I was the one that started using it." He then combined those words with five others to further attack his media critics: "enemy of the American people." As NPR's Scott Simon observed, it's "an incendiary phrase . . . [that's] been uttered by some of history's most vicious thugs—Robespierre, Goebbels, Lenin, Stalin, Mao—to vilify their opponents."[31] What is noteworthy here is how the Orwellian threat came to be aligned with its Huxleyan counterpart.

As we proceed, one thing will come into sharper focus: One cannot reason with a person who does not believe in reason. Facts, logic, and the very idea of reason governing our affairs no longer carried much weight in the toss-and-tumble of Trump politics. More and more people tended to situate reality into the frames of their own partisan beliefs—a case of a verdict preceding a trial. When this occurred, the line between facts and falsity blurred to a mind-numbing degree, as if there were no touchstone for truth. Americans seemed indifferent (or largely so) to a meaningless world, one bereft of reason. Perhaps by dint of fatigue they came to accept it, to acknowledge a political world in which the logic of 2+2=4 succumbs to the lie that 2+2=5. As Max Boot put it: If the President says that "2+2=5, he expects his acolytes to nod in zombified acquiescence."[32] Incredibly, Trump's expectations were often honored.

As he ended a tumultuous week in early March of 2019, the President clutched the American flag and then rambled on for more than two hours in his speech at the Conservative Political Action Conference:[33] "You know, I don't know, maybe you know. You know, I'm totally off script right?" he said at the outset of his remarks. "This is how I got elected, by being off script" he told an indulgent crowd at the annual CPAC event. He dismissed investigations of him as "bullshit"; he mocked his former attorney general with a contrived Southern accent; he complained that the media did not accurately report the size of the crowd at his 2017 inauguration; and he tagged the House Intelligence Committee Chairman, Adam B. Schiff (D-Calif.), as "Little Shifty Schiff." His criticism of special counsel Robert S. Mueller III was laced with profanities; and with capricious speed he crisscrossed from the success of his presidential campaign to immigration to free trade to the midterm elections without ever giving his audience a moment to think. Like a raving tent preacher railing against sin, he lashed out at his opponents: "We have people in Congress right now—we have people in Congress that hate our country. And you know that, and we can name every one of them if you want. They hate our country." He took comic delight in deriding the validity of climate change: "When the wind stops blowing, that's the end of your electric," he said as if speaking to his wife. "'Darling, is the wind blowing today? I'd like to watch television, darling.'" He spoke of the government shutdown and the hardships it imposed on him: "I spent my New Year's all by myself. . . . It was me and about

500 men and women outside with machine guns. I never saw so many beautiful-looking machine guns. I'd look at that equipment and I'd say, 'Man'. . . They sit in the trees. They sit on the lawn." Throughout, he veered time and again from talk of "criminal immigrants," to "crooked Hillary," to "socialist Democrats." Despite it all, the crowd expressed its approval with wild applause.

Because it was so bizarre, it made for great spectacle, great TV, and great fare for the evening's talking heads. Yet beyond the amusement appeal there lay a troubling truth: this was madness; it owed no debt to facts or reality or anything verifiable by the human mind. It was government by impulse: His measure was instinct, that unrestrained urge to say anything in any way, however incoherent. Nothing was vulgar; nothing was sacred; nothing was over-the-top; and nothing needed to make sense. It was all a show, the triumph of instinct over intelligence. Stimulated by the crowd, he upped his verbal ante as his admirers lowered their rational expectations. It was as strange as it was true, the President's own admission: "I'm going to regret this speech." But it was no more than a joke, a wink-wink for the audience, his way of saying that it really didn't matter what he said as long as *he* said it. Meanwhile, the statue of James Madison located on Independence Avenue was sullied by this ignominious display of ignorance, deceit, malice, and fury. In the face of Trumpism, Madisonian ideals had no purchase because the American culture no longer appeared to value them.

Much of the same instinct-driven mindset was on perilous display when Trump rambled on during his January 6, 2021, inflammatory remarks before a mob-ready crowd. Alarming as the storming of the Capitol was, equally astounding was the revisionist characterization given to the insurrection and the events related to it. In early February of 2022, the Republican National Committee officially declared that this episode merely involved "ordinary citizens engaged in legitimate political discourse." How astonishing that the very idea of discourse had become so unanchored that even violent property destruction and physical injury could be functionally labeled and legitimated as "political discourse." Notably, the RNC attempted to walk its statement back by claiming that it was not condoning violence; in this respect, it took its "wink-wink" cue from the Master of Deception.

On the one hand, if one were to articulate a First Amendment theory *critical* of all such exploits, what would that theory be? Whatever it is, it would have to denounce all of the components—advanced capitalism, run-away commercialism, unchecked technology, and the public spectacle of amusement—that made Trump-talk triumphant. On the other hand, if a theory were to *defend* such talk, it must be oblivious to Huxleyan tyranny. We ask: Are any of the defenders of the modern First Amendment, in the courts or in the academy, willing to openly concede and embrace the civic cost of unbridled Trumpism? We ask again: Do any First Amendment reformers actually believe that, short of dramatic governmental and societal restructuring, the flood of toxic Trumpism could be abated?

Thus did life in America turn between 2016 and 2022. Uncertainty was widespread. Demagoguery was unbridled. Hyperbole ubiquitous. Objectivity impossible. Facts suspect. And willful ignorance normal. Snap-judgments replaced deliberate decision-making. Science took a back seat to propaganda. Social media spread misinformation with wild abandon. The media, both liberal and conservative, were often too preoccupied with ratings to ferret out a fuller measure of the truth. Many denied responsibility, deceived themselves, and took refuge in a collective lie in order to defend the indefensible. And all of this transpired while a terrifying plague threatened the very lifeblood of a nation. It was the age of the Un-Enlightenment, the death of reasoned discourse in the public realm.

Book II of *The Death of Discourse* explores our nation's inextricable link between private commerce and public communication. America's mass and social media cater to the demands of producers and the desires of consumers, who thrive in a co-dependent and synergistic relationship. Delivering a banquet of commercial advertising, our channels of public expression promote goods to buy; more abstractly, however, they offer lifestyle fantasies to consume. That is the greater meaning of our study of modern commercial advertising. In other words, speech in the service of selling develops the codes of our culture, and we stand to become the sum of what we buy. Moreover, as the values of communication are fused to the market, the law's notions of commercial speech alter even our understanding of First Amendment freedoms.

As we now cast our thoughts into words, we do so against the backdrop of the Supreme Court's First Amendment decision in *Reed v.*

Town of Gilbert[34] and its largely inflexible ruling on the invalidity of content-based discriminatory speech regulations. If *Reed*'s ruling were methodically applied to commercial speech contexts, constitutional protection for commercial expression would be vastly invigorated. In practical effect, commercial speech could be elevated functionally to the same level of constitutional value as political speech.

In a jurisprudential realm in which legal doctrine is unanchored to some overriding free speech principle, the possibility of equating political dissent with commercial puffery is real. As we noted in Book II (pp. 111–115), just such an anchor was provided in the first case in which the Court extended protection to commercial speech. That anchor was the *right to know*: that is, the right of consumers to receive truthful and accurate information in order to make *informed* decisions in the commercial marketplace. That elevated precept has come to offer constitutional protection to every sort of irrational and even non-sensical advertising of the sort exemplified by imagistic commercials. In other words, *rational* advertising has ever-declining currency in the modern American commercial culture.

If *Reed* portends the doctrinal future of commercial speech, that fate is endorsed today by Professor Martin Redish, the intellectual godfather of an expansive constitutional theory safeguarding commercial speech. In his book *Commercial Speech as Free Expression: The Case for First Amendment Protection* (2021), Redish offers bold arguments for "extending full First Amendment protection to commercial speech. . . ." Whatever one may make of such an alliance between judicial doctrine and academic theory, one thing is undeniable: both positions are consistent with communication in a highly capitalist culture. Indeed, it would be most odd if commercial speech actually were devalued in such a culture.

In a technological world of data collection and terms of service contracts, the specter of consumer information being marshalled by algorithms for marketing purposes is real—it is already happening. Consistent with that phenomenon, the tenacles of commercialism reaches all sorts of communication devices and platforms. A new generation of advertising has evolved through insights informed by data collection. Not surprisingly, in 2021 Facebook launched "a new series of expert interviews to help provide more guidance for advertisers on how to respond to key industry shifts. . . . As explained by

Facebook: '[W]e will explore how the marriage of data and creativity is helping to drive the best [results] in class advertising and powering better returns on investment for brands.'"[35] The way James Greaney, the Chief Data Officer at CHE Proximity (a "full service advertising agency"), sizes things up: "By using the tools and technologies we have at our disposal, the advertising industry can create great entertainment and experiences that are genuinely valuable. And since we have the ability to measure its effectiveness, we need to lean in and make sure that we're understanding it properly."[36] Data harvesting, combined with data configuration, combined with personalized consumer-oriented entertainment—it all points to commodity identities in a consumer democracy . . . protected, of course, by the First Amendment. And if Facebook and other communicative platforms can use political ads to spread misinformation, should they not claim a similar right to do so with commercial ads? Would this not be yet further evidence of the foreseeable move to unite the principles of political speech with the practices of commercial speech? Keep that in mind as you read the commercial marketing examples of yesterday as set out in Book II, since they set the stage for what has come to pass today and what will likely occur tomorrow.

Book III of *The Death of Discourse* introduces an allegorical place named "Pornutopia" (pp. 165–177)—not America as we now know it, but a state to which America often appears to aspire. Our society both celebrates and condemns the carnal; but we cannot deny the ever-increasing prominence of sexualized speech in our public arenas and popular amusements, and the ever-powerful influence of eroticized expression over our notions of First Amendment freedoms. This is entirely predictable: since sex appeals and sex sells, our commercial marketplace imagistically transforms and packages it, and sends it out for sale. The capitalist regime of profit wed to pleasure points the way to Pornutopia—a republic erupting with sensual images, a domain where uninhibited, robust and wide-open fantasies dominate. And the capitalist free speech system protects the rise of Pornutopia, as our First Amendment law equates pornographic images with political ideas, self-gratification with self-realization, and the pursuit of private pleasure with the search for the public good.

The story of Pornutopia, however, is not to be told here. Only in the full context of Book III will you come to appreciate the properties and peculiarities of Pornutopia, the hormone-happy state, a no-man's land of sensual indulgence. At this point, we aim only to present the current data that mark the steep ascent of the pornographic state. In this regard, welcome back to Erotic America as it is currently constituted.

It is a sign of our times: literary classes on pornography. Yes, students are learning how to be literate in pornography; they study how to process the erotic. According to a July 2021 *New York Times* article: "Multiple sex educators . . . said there was nothing inappropriate about [such] classes. . . . All of it was in line with current National Sex Education Standards and the World Health Organization's International Technical Guidance on Sexuality Education." The article went on to note that a recent national survey, published in the *Journal of Sexual Medicine*, "found that the average age of first exposure to pornography was just under 14 for males and just under 18 for females."[37]

In keeping with the need for such education, "[p]ornography literacy classes teach students how to critically assess what they see on the screen—for example, how to recognize what is realistic and what is not, how to deconstruct implicit gender roles, and how to identify what types of behavior could be a health or safety risk."[38] Consistent with such public education, the pornographic website Pornhub has produced a "Classic Nudes" guide for "finding eroticism in dozens of major nude works of art exhibited at prestigious museums."[39] Thus, from K-12 schools to art museums to YouTube to cybersex technology and beyond, behold the Renaissance of Pornography!

Of course, when it comes to such sexual mastery, many viewers, including longtime ones, are illiterate. But that does not prevent them from savoring pornography's sexual delights. Though *Playboy* and *Hustler* magazines no longer rule the erotic roost, their more seductive Internet successors (XVideos and Pornhub) alone claim 6.7 billion monthly visits.[40] According to pornography industry sources:

- American children begin consuming hardcore pornography at an average age of 11.
- Four out of five 16-year-olds regularly access pornography online.

- The pornography industry is a $97 billion business worldwide.
- The pornography industry is a $13 billion business in the United States.
- Internet pornography in the United States is a $3 billion industry."[41]

And "every second, $3,075.64 is being spent on pornography, 28,258 Internet viewers are ogling pornography, 372 Internet users are typing adult search terms into search engines, and every 39 minutes a new pornographic video is made in the United States."[42] In Covid times there was a 43% increase in pornographic consumption.[43] In the near future, virtual reality and cybersex porn will be multi-billion-dollar profit-makers. Thanks to landmark First Amendment cases such as *Reno v. ACLU* (1997)[44] and *Ashcroft v. Free Speech Coalition* (2002),[45] such erotic pursuits have become a common feature of American culture. The Internet is, save for child pornography, a bacchanalian paradise of porn.

The ascendancy of Pornutopia represents a key component of free expression in our modern world. To ignore it, to act as if it stood apart from what we consider free speech liberty, is to turn a blind eye to how electronic eroticism shapes our discourse and our lives. By way of a single example, consider the isolating nature of pornographic use. That may well be understood as a preference for the virtual over the real. In that world, freedom of real association is recast as freedom of virtual association. Erotic companions in Pornutopia are always and everywhere ready to associate with the minds and imaginations of those who value the stimulating *virtual* life.

We trade in taboos, and in Pornutopia there are almost no taboos that are beyond the virtual pale. Moral crusaders such as Anthony Comstock (1844–1915) and his Society for the Suppression of Vice no longer have the clout they once enjoyed when they prosecuted and persecuted the "depraved." Moreover, as a result of the Internet and emerging technologies, obscenity laws have functionally gone the way of Victorian values. That past has lost its currency; ours is the age of the uninhibited First Amendment. No less a man than Harvard Law School's Cass Sunstein long ago realized this cultural truth as he explained pornography's vital role in our society and defended it as valuable under a lofty First Amendment theory of autonomy: "Sexually explicit works can be highly relevant to the development of individual capacities. For many, it is an important vehicle for self-discovery and self-definition."[46] In other words, pornographic self-gratification is tantamount to self-realization.

While we certainly do not wish to embrace the Comstockian mindset and thereby endorse any kind of Orwellian tyranny, we wonder if Sunstein and his conceptual fellow travelers have ever paused to ponder exactly where their "vehicle for self-discovery" will take them on the path to Pornutopia. Precisely such concerns informed us when we wrote the section of our book titled "Deliberate Lies and Deliberative Democracy" (pp. 205–210). Deceit, after all, seems to be a strange attribute to champion in any democracy, especially one rooted in Madisonian soil.

I'm probably the most aggressive defender of the First Amendment. Most people might think that doesn't quite fit with my jurisprudence in other areas. . . . People need to know that we're not doing politics. We're doing something different. We're applying the law.

That's how Chief Justice Roberts described his First Amendment voting record when he engaged Belmont Law School Dean Alberto Gonzales in a conversation about his jurisprudence in February of 2019.[47] But apart from a numerical account of free speech claims sustained by the Court, what does it mean to be a defender of the First Amendment? What exactly is being defended? Throughout our book we examine that question time and again. For example, some of the standard answers given are the following: we value speech because it promotes *self-realization* or *self-fulfillment*; we prize speech because it enables *self-governance*; we protect speech because it provides *information*; or we safeguard speech because it *checks the government*. All of these are elevated reasons for securing free speech. But are those the justifications that are advanced today when the Roberts Court renders its decisions in animal abuse video cases, or violent video game cases, or cases involving lying, or campaign finance cases, or commercial speech cases, and so on? We raised such questions decades ago and found that both the Court and legal scholars either proffered elevated purposes for speech that could not easily be defended when applied in the cases under consideration, or they protected speech for its own sake regardless of the values that they could not claim. Then as now, we were less concerned with whether speech should be protected than we were as to *why* it should be protected. When we explored the "why" question in the Epilogue (pp. 205–210), we concluded that hypocrisy best explained their rationalizations—that deliberate lies were being tendered in the name of deliberative democracy.

Have things changed since we first wrote those words? In response, we ask: what does it mean to be the "most aggressive defender of the First Amendment"? For the Chief Justice, who assigns the lead opinions in 96% of the free speech cases decided by his Court, it means upholding the constitutional right to lie. For example, in *United States v. Alvarez* Roberts signed onto Justice Anthony Kennedy's majority opinion that declared: "Our constitutional tradition stands against the idea that we need Oceania's Ministry of Truth. See G. Orwell, *Nineteen Eighty-Four* (1949)."[48] In *Brown v. Entertainment Merchants Association* the Chief Justice voted to affirm the First Amendment right to sell violent video games to minors. He joined Justice Antonin Scalia's majority opinion that proclaimed: "The Free Speech Clause exists principally to protect discourse on public matters, but we have long recognized that it is difficult to distinguish politics from entertainment, and dangerous to try."[49] Roberts's "aggressive" defense of the First Amendment also meant safeguarding the free expression rights of those who trade in images of "horrific acts of animal cruelty—in particular, the creation and commercial exploitation of 'crush videos,' a form of depraved [sexual] entertainment that has no social value." That, at least, is how Justice Samuel Alito depicted it in his dissent in *United States v. Stevens*."[50] The Chief Justice viewed the matter differently. "The First Amendment itself reflects a judgment by the American people that the benefits of its restrictions on the Government outweigh the costs," he wrote in his majority opinion. "Our Constitution forecloses any attempt to revise that judgment simply on the basis that some speech is not worth it."[51]

False speech, violent commercial expression, and erotized visual fare all claimed and received constitutional protection under Madison's First Amendment. Enlightenment principles were bum-rushed out the constitutional door. By the same measure, the Roberts Court has extended considerable protection to monied interests in both campaign contribution and commercial speech cases. In these regards, liberals—both on the Court and in the legal academy—came to view more and more of the Roberts Court's jurisprudence as being motivated by laissez-faire economic considerations. "Adam Smith's First Amendment"[52] is how Professors Amanda Shanor and Robert Post tagged it. By Justice Elena Kagan's measure, the Court was "weaponizing the First Amendment, in a way that unleashes judges, now and in the future, to intervene in economic and regulatory policy."[53]

In the culture we describe in Books I through III ahead, all such forms would certainly merit First Amendment protection, not because they further lofty free speech ideas, but rather because they resonate with our entertainment, commercial, and pornographic cultures. That, then, is what it actually means to be an "aggressive defender of the First Amendment" for a world that abandons the Age of Reason.

All of the foregoing, of course, is but an overture to our work. So, sit back, ladies and gentlemen, and prepare yourselves for the performance that follows.‡ Welcome to the opening act of *The Death of Discourse*, ushered in with a little night music, if you will.

Ev'ry day a little death
On the lips and in the eyes,
In the murmurs, in the pauses,
In the gestures, in the sighs.
Ev'ry day a little dies.

— Stephen Sondheim,
A Little Night Music (1973)

‡ *Trigger Warning*: In the spirit of the day, we think it advisable to caution our readers about what follows. Some of this may offend you in a variety of ways—political, legal, sociological, moral, or philosophical. Nonetheless, we implore you to hold judgment until the very end of our concededly satirical foray into America in Modern Times.

Prologue

*Per voi s'ora**

Scene opens with the Adagietto from Gustav Mahler's Fifth Symphony. Daybreak at the ruins of the Acropolis. The music continues past its first delicate measures to the key change at its passionate bridge. The focus slowly zooms away from the ancient pillars and into the halls of the National Archives in Washington, D.C. Collins and Skover enter, proceed directly to the display of the 1791 Bill of Rights, and reflect silently. With the diminuendo at the end of the musical score, the text below comes boldly into view.

Discourse is dying in America, yet everywhere free speech thrives.

This is difficult to grasp, much less grant. After all, how can something be dying and thriving at once? Grapple with this and you will be prepared for what follows. Believe us, we "speak" to you in the tongue of our times, even in the face of our more rationalist bents.

DISCOURSE. It is a weighty word of classical origin, the sort of utterance that runs to and fro in erudite circles. Something beyond mere talk is implied. Unlike trivial talk, discourse resonates with reason, with method, with purpose. Whether its loftier values were ever entirely realized is, in one sense, of no moment. Discourse is an ancient aspiration. As idealized in the Western culture's vision of classical Greece, expression was valued as a means to some *telos*, some greater end. For Aristotle, expression was not simply for its own sake but, rather, was discourse in the service of the civic good, or *agathon*. Expression, properly understood, was essential to *paideia*, the shaping of character.

This, of course, is all Greek to us as young Americans. Ours is a system of free speech — free from old notions of discourse. For us,

* "For you we are praying." Recited by medieval monks for the souls of those condemned to death.[1]

expression is no more or less than the speech of our daily experiences. The sight, the sound, indeed the feel, of robust expression is a thing of joy in the carnival of life we call modern mass culture. To communicate with uninhibited liberty, to talk in the vernacular of the popular culture, to express that culture's tastes, is the way of free speech in America. It is often speech for its own sake, speech in the service of self-gratification, and speech that is essential to the *raison d'être* of a commercial entertainment culture.

These two cultures of expression -- the old discourse and the new free speech — turn to the FIRST AMENDMENT for constitutional recognition. Ever since 1791, the judicial and scholarly keepers of the Amendment have invoked the high ideals of discourse to define the boundaries of protected expression. They continue to do so even now as they summon the traditional values of enlightened reason, self-government, and self-realization to protect communication in contemporary popular culture. We wonder, however, why they ignore the wide gulf between yesterday's reasons and today's realities. And we question whether the First Amendment is actually what judges and scholars say it is, or rather what the popular culture makes of it.

Know this: The First Amendment is more than law. It is a way of life. Only in a technical, although important, sense is the First Amendment solely the province of law. Its symbolic and functional meanings extend well beyond what pinstripe-suited lawyers proclaim in courtrooms, beyond what black-robed judges pen in case reports, and certainly beyond what cardigan-sweatered professors pronounce in scholarly journals. James Madison's genius cannot be restricted to the cramped quarters of legal doctrine or to the tidy categories of legal theory. To know the Amendment's vital meaning, one need do no more than breathe its air. In sum, the high values of yesterday's First Amendment must be squared with the realities of free speech in today's America. With law as with physics, "a theory must first and foremost reflect the way the world is."[2]

Unfortunately, what the elite few say about the First Amendment does not mirror what the many do with it. Hence, the truer reference point of the free speech guaranty is the unremarkable talk of popular culture rather than the remarkable discourse envisioned by constitutional doctrine and theory. For this reason, the keepers of the First Amendment need to reflect upon the culture of free expression in order to realize the Amendment's practical meaning.

In law, understanding the First Amendment typically proceeds deductively, from the *top down*. Jurists and legal commentators impose the world of theory onto the world of practice. With this aim, they proudly drag out the dead: the likes of Plato, Aristotle, Milton, Locke, Spinoza, Mill, Hume, Jefferson, Madison, Emerson, Whitman, Holmes, and Alexander Meiklejohn, among others. Similarly, they parade a variety of elevated notions ranging from the attainment of truth to moral responsibility in order to justify speech's special status in our democratic regime. Who would not applaud this worthy tradition of aligning the noble purposes of the First Amendment with their noble counterparts in public expression? Who indeed?

It is said that for love of country Niccolò Machiavelli "pissed in many a snow."[3] The great Florentine political philosopher expressed his love of country by calling for a realpolitik. His point: It is "more fitting to go directly to the effectual truth of the thing than to the imagination of it."[4] The First Amendment is in need of a similar love — a willingness to stain the white snow of pure principles in the name of our common reality. To do this we need to develop a *bottom-up* approach to the First Amendment, an approach going directly to our communicative experiences rather than to imaginative theories. Such an approach might represent a real awakening in First Amendment law, a new sort of Machiavellian moment.

If we look at America's free speech as it is, rather than as it should be, what would we find? Having made such a discovery, what then would our notions of the First Amendment be were they premised on that experience? Tellingly, this culture-centered method — what we call a *cultural approach* to the First Amendment — is still a strange concept to those content with never looking too closely at unsullied snows.

Our popular culture is defined by *mass* communication — communication that permeates almost all exchanges in the American culture, including one-on-one and small group conversations. Even the character of private talk cannot be entirely sequestered from the merging forces of mass talk. These forces, which are necessarily related, are identified by *wide* (even global) dissemination, broad (typically entertaining) *appeal*, dynamic (and disconnected) *images*, *ever-changing* (yet often repetitive) themes, commercial (more precisely, capitalistic) *marketability*, and by the *appropriation* (and redefinition) of our most cherished symbols and values. All of this is made possible by *electronic technology*. In fact, the forces of mass communication are so great as to influence the very *logic* of much thought and expression. (Indeed, in our culture this paragraph is turgid to the point of virtual unintelligibility. But do not worry, for we'll bring things down a bit and be more reader-friendly.)

We cannot honestly think about the First Amendment as a way of life without considering the impact of entertainment and commerce on communication. TV talk, for example, is the talk of our times. There is no escaping the fact: ELECTRONIC VISUAL ENTERTAINMENT is an essential part of our modern culture of communication. "[I]t has oozed everywhere."[5] So much of who we are, what we think, how we express ourselves, and how we perceive and react to our world is tied to the entertainment media. Above all, the electronic media frame our world with a surfeit of amusement. This phenomenon is communication in the service of pleasure. Perhaps more than anything else, these media are our cables to consciousness.

Furthermore, virtually every type of expression is dwarfed by another form of popular communication — ADVERTISING. It represents a multi-billion-dollar investment that links commerce with communication. Various types of mass advertising (e.g., product-image and lifestyle advertising, among others) reveal the character and direction of much contemporary expression. In the service of selling, mass advertising frequently seizes on our politics, values, and even identities and translates them into commercial talk. This is the marriage of the marketplace of items to the marketplace of ideas.

Commercial TV is the Rosetta Stone of our times.

Where entertainment and commerce are the paradigms of communication, "discourse" inevitably combines with intercourse. Clearly, sex appeals and sex sells. PORNOGRAPHY (whether the soft porn of television or the hard porn of explicit videos) represents the commodification of sex. Like advertising generally, it trades the essence of the person for a money-making image. It is a form of communication that promises to make the unattainable attainable. The popularity of pornography is an index of the free speech valued in today's culture.

Of course, mass communication in modern America exists in still other arenas. And as we discuss later, it is the general objective of our cultural approach to the First Amendment to identify and evaluate all other such major environments. In the three main arenas we have identified thus far, the operative logic abounds in *contradictions*. For example, a proposition can be at one with its opposite; something can assume the attributes of something else merely by visual association; a point can simultaneously be understood and misunderstood; and a fact can be real and unreal at the same time. Incredible, yet true. In what follows, we wrestle with this logic of contradictions as we develop our cultural approach to the First Amendment.

Warning

Reader beware! We are not entirely what some will paint us to be. Before leaving this prologue, we think it prudent to sketch our own portrait in bold strokes. Without the benefit of elaboration, we thus declare the following:

1. The obvious import of our enterprise is more descriptive than normative. Thus understood, our work is more concerned with depicting and discussing certain forms of expression in contemporary America than it is with promoting any conventional view of the First Amendment. (Bear this in mind as you think about our cultural approach to the First Amendment.)
2. Although our analysis often focuses on the values of the traditional First Amendment, our enterprise does not depend on affirming or denying those values. (Many will forget this admonition.)
3. To the degree that we dwell on the values of the traditional First Amendment, we do so in order to examine the apparent tension between theory and practice. Again, we ask: Can the high values of free expression be squared with the dominant character of mass communication in our popular culture? (Beware of false prophets!)
4. To say that traditional free-speech values cannot always be squared with popular mass expression is *not* to say that such expression automatically should be denied First Amendment protection. It is only to say that the reason(s) for protecting such expression must be other than the traditional norms. (Assuredly, this point will elude many ideological diehards.)
5. We ask, and we invite you to ask: What notion of the First Amendment would be most compatible with popular mass expression as we have come to know it? What candid and honest view of the

First Amendment might countenance a generous measure of protection for such speech? (Once again, our cultural approach has a role to play here.)

6. Having asked the question, we suggest a possible "answer": Constitutional protection of speech linked to pleasure and to commerce is entirely consistent with the values of a highly consumerist and capitalistic culture. Here too, our endeavor does not depend on approving or disapproving this "answer." (Consider the importance of the quotation marks.)
7. This "answer" raises yet another question: What would be the social and legal consequences of signing on to such a view of the First Amendment? (In answering this, think about the relationship between discourse and democracy.)

If today's First Amendment represents a way of life, what kind of life? If it represents freedom, what kind of freedom? And if it represents the triumph of democracy, what kind of democracy? Perhaps some will reply that the First Amendment's way of life is unbridled, its freedom unbound, and its democracy unlimited. If so, its *logos* (speech with direction) tends toward the Absolute in ways heretofore unimagined or unspoken. In this work, we chart various aspects of this tendency toward the Absolute in life and law. Along the way, we invite you to explore the First Amendment's meaning as it intersects our popular culture.

> MONTESQUIEU
>
> I beg one favor of my readers, which I fear will not be granted me; this is, that they will not judge by a few hours' reading, of the labor of [several] years. . . . If they would search into the design of the author, they can do it no other way so completely as by searching into the design of the work.
>
> Preface to *The Spirit of the Laws*, trans. Thomas Nugent (1750), ed. David W. Carrithers (Berkeley: University of California Press, 1977), p. 91.

Our pestering probes may trigger hypersensitive reactions. This is likely to be true because our analysis plays different ideological stances off against each other. Throughout, "[t]he reader is constantly invited to take two opposite views simultaneously," to consider and reconsider a "complexity of conflicting elements."[6] In all of this, some may surmise a hostile First Amendment posture and consequently fear that we will snatch the First Amendment shield away from the most favored forms of mass expression. (No amount of Valium or Xanax can cure such anxiety.) Quite the contrary, we aim to push the First Amendment closer to the contemporary culture, even at the risk of disowning old notions that cannot be easily reconciled with new realities.

This book represents our first take on a novel, culture-centered approach to the First Amendment. Of course, the first take ought not to be the last. So we invite you, our readers, to look at popular culture as you may and join us in this effort. Indeed, our collective efforts may lead some to ask: Does all of this point to the death of discourse? You be the judge.

TO LISTEN
(fragment of poem by C. K. Williams)

In the dream of death where I listen, the voices of the dream keep diminishing, fading away.
The dead are speaking, my dead are speaking, what they say seems urgent . . .

A Dream of Mind (New York: Farrar, Straus & Giroux, 1992), p. 85

Book I
The Paratroopers' Paradox

We cannot hope simply to retain our old prerogatives. Our bridges are gone and the Rubicon is yet to cross? We have either to assume a large new role or to abdicate entirely. It is the age of paratroopers.

— Marshall McLuhan[1]

The Huxleyan Crossing

Scene: Normandy, circa 1944. Paratroopers prepare to leap from Billy Mitchell warplanes amid a barrage of bullets. The camera pulls away slowly to reveal a young man lounging on a sofa, watching actual footage of the wartime events on TV. While eating, the viewer "zaps" his remote control to change the channel to MTV. A gyrating Mick Jagger then appears, belting out a hard-rock version of "Parachute Woman." At unexpected intervals, the viewer zaps back and forth between Normandy and MTV. Feed into text with loud music from the "Voodoo Lounge" tour of the Rolling Stones.

McLuhan's paratrooper metaphor is both an invitation and a warning. It is a call to action, and a question. In the context of the First Amendment, the metaphor is particularly powerful. It challenges us to cross the Rubicon[a] into a territory hostile to old notions of free speech.

Today, the First Amendment is still grounded in eighteenth-century fears of government's tyrannical censorship. It is ill-equipped to deal with a distinct tyranny in contemporary America, a tyranny that plays upon the public's insatiable appetite for amusement. Crossing the Rubicon requires us to understand the differences between the old and new tyrannies. Furthermore, we need to appreciate the complexities of articulating First Amendment principles to suit a new cultural environment. Those who attempt such a venture are the First Amendment paratroopers of our time; they realize that we cannot retain our old constitutional prerogatives in a world transformed.

The forces of capitalism now encourage exploitation of highly advanced electronic technology to accelerate the age-old human drive for self-gratification. The consumptive thrust of unchecked capitalism

a) The Rubicon was a small river that separated ancient Italy from Cisalpine Gaul, the province allotted to Julius Caesar. When Caesar crossed this river in 49 B.C., he passed beyond the limits of his province and became an invader of Italy, thus precipitating war with Pompey and the Senate.

affects all public expression. This phenomenon has long been apparent in the culture of commercial television.[b] Essentially, "the predicament of American television is the predicament of American culture and politics as a whole."[2] Public talk is increasingly taking a distinctive and aestheticized form consistent with the look and feel of commercial television. This transformation of public talk is essential to the effective marketing of images and commercial goods in a highly consumerist culture: After all, marketing often sells pleasing images. The business of television trades in the economy of such images and pulls other expression into that economy, producing a culture in which America's most beloved toy provides endless mass entertainment and profit.

Where amusement and commerce mark the boundaries for much public speech, traditional First Amendment values—which include serious dialogue and civic participation—are overshadowed. Given these core values and the presumption against censorship in First Amendment law, we ask: Is there anything that could (or should) be done to thwart, rather than to feed, an amusement-centered culture?

In answering this question we encounter a paradox: To save itself, the traditional First Amendment must destroy itself. Let us explain by way of an outline of our argument. On the one hand, to guard against censorship, the First Amendment must protect both the old (pre-electronic) and the new (electronic) communication cultures. Accordingly, it must constrain most governmental controls over expression, including those over the commercial use of electronic media. On the other hand, if the First Amendment's protections do not differentiate between the old and new media cultures, the modern obsession with self-amusement can trivialize public expression and thereby undermine the traditional aims of the First Amendment. To treat the two cultures differently requires governmental "abridgment" of expression, particularly in the case of the commercial entertainment media. With such governmental abridgment, First Amendment protection collapses into First Amendment tyranny. Without such abridgment, First Amendment liberty collapses into First Amendment triviality.

b) The word "television" derives from a combination of the Greek word *tele* meaning "far" or "distant" and the Latin word *vision* meaning "view" or "sight." The idea was that television could empower us to "see over distance," or could provide us with a "long view."

Our discussion of contemporary public expression in Book I focuses mainly on the ecology of commercial television, the most pervasive form of electronic visual entertainment to date. In assessing the relationship of popular culture to the First Amendment, we simply cannot ignore the facts:[3]

- 98 percent of all households in America (93.1 million households) own at least one television set, and one-third of these households own three or more TV sets.
- Our people are tuned in to a television set on the average of 50½ hours per week. On average, Americans spend a greater percentage of their spare time watching television than engaging in almost all other activities taken together.
- On average, 1½ hours of every evening are dedicated to watching television during prime-time (8 PM – 11 PM).
- 61.8 percent of all American households subscribe to cable TV.
- MTV boasts some 58 million subscribers.
- 77 percent of all American households are equipped with VCRs.
- Over 12 billion dollars are spent annually on video rentals.
- Advertisers spend nearly 35 billion dollars annually on television commercials.
- Our young consume over 100 commercials daily.
- In the 1992–1993 viewing season alone, situation comedies, sports events, and soap operas dominated the top 10 list of network and syndicated programs.
- And billions of added dollars will soon be spent on new technologies of "television."

The bottom line: Electronic visual entertainment (in all its new and varied forms) enjoys a dominant and almost unchallenged status in our society. As such, mass entertainment media greatly influence the cultural direction of modern First Amendment freedoms.

The high purpose of the traditional First Amendment, by contrast, is often associated with more serious expression. In essence, all First Amendment cases and theories[4] aim in some way to preserve a robust social and political discourse by which the people might best govern themselves. Without this environment, the First Amendment, as we have known it, cannot survive. This lofty purpose renounces any Orwellian rule in which the hand of an omnipresent government squelches political dissent, bans books, invades privacy, censors electronic information, and conceals truth. Triumphantly, America has survived 1984 and is less fearful of Orwell's dark determinism. But our Orwellian perspective hinders us from focusing on an equally menacing and more realistic threat to the First Amendment—the evil identified in Aldous Huxley's anti-utopian *Brave New World* (1946) and later developed in his *Brave New World Revisited* (1958). As Huxley himself contended[5] and as Professor Neil Postman echoed,[6] it is this threat that today looms large. Now, the Huxleyan evil particularly endangers our historical and idealistic commitment to freedom of expression.

Huxley's nightmare is one in which government has no need to censor dissent, no cause to hide truth, and no ground to ban serious discussion. It is a world of pleasure and trivialization, a world whose citizenry euphorically digests narcotic "soma tablets."[c] The brave new world offers a surfeit of entertainment, "non-stop distractions of the most fascinating nature (the feelies, orgy-porgy, centrifugal bumble-puppy)" that ensure a state of perpetual amusement and happiness. The governing maxim is: "Everybody's happy now."[7]

The purpose of all this "happiness" is to numb. The "non-stop distractions . . . [are] used as instruments of policy, for the purpose of preventing people from paying too much attention to the realities of the social and political situation."[8] The problem with all this "happiness" is the servitude that it spawns and the tyranny that a love of such servitude makes possible. The rulers of Huxley's anti-utopia have learned that soma tablets more effectively suppress the critical mind and spirit than the iron fist of Orwell's world.

c) Huxley tells us that soma was a mild drug dispensed by the government to sedate and gratify the populace. According to Huxley, "the soma habit was not a private vice; it was a political institution, it was the very essence of the Life, Liberty and Pursuit of Happiness guaranteed by the Bill of Rights." Aldous Huxley, *Brave New World* and *Brave New World Revisited* (New York: Harper & Row, 1965), pp. 55–56 (BNWR).

The antiquated First Amendment is eclipsed in the brave new world. Its fear of the tyranny of terror — demonstrated, for example, by the Alien and Sedition Acts of 1798, the Espionage Acts of 1917 and 1918, and the McCarthy era — is overshadowed by a tyranny of pleasure. The Orwellian shackles on physical liberty and ideological freedom constituted hands-on tyranny, but the Huxleyan conception is a hands-off tyranny. Huxley understood tyranny as the product of those "great impersonal forces now menacing freedom," the "motivation analyst[s]"[9] who held out the soma tablets.

In an insightful passage particularly applicable to the First Amendment, Huxley questioned the outdated eighteenth-century American constitutional ideal:

> [T]he early advocates of . . . a free press envisaged only two possibilities: the propaganda might be true, or it might be false. They did not foresee what in fact has happened, above all in our Western capitalist democracies — the development of a vast mass communications industry, concerned in the main with neither the true nor the false, but with the unreal, the more or less totally irrelevant. In a word, they failed to take into account man's almost infinite appetite for distractions.[10]

Huxley's depiction of a tyranny of pleasure accurately forecast the contemporary American media culture. He realized the connection between commercial television and his anti-utopia: "That so many of the well-fed young television-watchers in the world's most powerful democracy should be so completely indifferent to the idea of self-government, so blankly uninterested in freedom of thought and the right to dissent, is distressing, but not too surprising."[11]

America's primary information medium is also its most popular source of entertainment, its favorite plaything. Metaphorically, television is the soma tablet of modern society.

Carl Bernstein:

We are in the process of creating a true idiot culture in America . . . For the first time in our history the weird and the stupid and the vulgar are becoming our cultural norm, even our cultural ideal.

"Talk Show Nation," *New Perspectives Quarterly*, Summer 1994, p. 22.

The Soma Medium: Its Mechanics & Messages

Television is not famous for reasoned discourse.

—Walter Goodman[12]

Because television (in all its new and varied forms) is one of the primary media by which we conceptualize reality, its messages profoundly influence the nature of public awareness and discussion of important issues. As communications professor Neil Postman observed: "[T]here is no subject of public interest—politics, news, education, religion, science, sports—that does not find its way to television." Furthermore, television "has made entertainment itself the natural format for the representation of all experience.... To say it still another way: Entertainment is the supraideology of all discourse on television."[13] Obviously, amusement is not the unique product of contemporary television. Entertainment existed before television and expressed itself in oral and print cultures, as the jester's antics and tabloids' sensationalism so patently evidenced. But today, television's phenomenal appeal has placed a markedly new premium on the pursuit of pleasure.

The medium's entertainment biases derive primarily from three combined forces: first, the attributes of television's technology; second, the commercialization of television as a profit-oriented enterprise; and third, the public's incessant yearning for amusement. These three forces create a communicative environment that favors trivial and entertaining programming. Both television's technological nature and its commercial use disfavor sustained concentration as attention is grabbed by a dynamic, fast-moving, and ever-changing series of images. Television, as we have come to know it,[d] loses a key ingredient of its mass appeal when divorced from visually dramatic pleasure

d) Soon the general public may come to know television in new, multidimensional, interactive, and pervasive ways—ways that merge forms of communication and further accentuate their entertainment functions. We turn to this possibility later in Book I.

programs—for example, rock videos, sports events, or "action" news. Where sustained concentration is the concern, neither René Descartes's *Discourse on Method* nor *The Federalist Papers* plays well on commercial television. The same holds true, in television vernacular, for "talking heads" programs. After all, as TV talk-show host Phil Donahue explained, "You can't televise the front page of the *Wall Street Journal* and survive."[14] TV programmers and advertisers fully appreciate that "[t]elevision is where we go to be hooked. It's our carnival. If this exhibit doesn't astonish us, we change channels." Attention must be grabbed and held, for a bored viewer is prone to zap from one channel to another in search of an ever more delectable tidbit or thrilling wave—"video grazing" or "video surfing," as it were.[15] Or our viewer may turn to her program "grid" to bounce back and forth among 500 or so selections—watching comedy one moment, yearning for sports the next.

ZAP

"Zip it, puke breath," admonishes the host. "Mort! Mort! Mort!" exclaims the horde.

ZAP

TV Guide looks back on the 1980s and ranks its "Top 20." Oprah Winfrey trumps Ronald Reagan, Vanna White tops Sam Donaldson, and Hulk Hogan trounces Dan Rather, who narrowly beats out Pee-Wee Herman.

ZAP

In the liberated USSR, *Geraldo* becomes the first American television show to air daily. Tales of "cross-dressing transsexuals from a topless donut shop" find Huxleyan expression where once there was Orwellian terror. Back in the USA, NBC and Geraldo Rivera team up to produce an exposé on devil worship. The result: "the highest Nielsens ever for a two-hour documentary."[16]

ZAP

In a more serious vein, Diane Sawyer, an ABC News journalist on *PrimeTime*, asks the former mistress of entrepreneur Donald Trump: "Tell me, Marla, was it really the best sex you ever had?"[17]

ZAP

A future president, Bill Clinton, decked out in dark hipster glasses, does a mean sax gig on the *Arsenio Hall* show.

ZAP

Race-and-riot-torn Los Angeles fires up while the *Cosby Show* winds down.

ZAP

The 1994 TV spectacles of the O.J. Simpson police chase and murder trial draw such unprecedented interest that they preempt network and cable broadcasts of the historic appearance of Jordan's King Hussein and Israel's Prime Minister Rabin before a joint session of the U.S. Congress. O.J. fever similarly overwhelms news reporting on the unthinkable tragedies of genocide, disease, and famine in Rwanda. Throughout 1995 the mania leveled everything in its path. "[B]y the end of 1995," *Time* art critic Robert Hughes claimed, "the networks [gave] more TV time to the demented rituals surrounding [O.J.] than to the entire history of America."[18]

ZAP

The 217 members of the 1993 graduating class at Maryland's Goucher College hear a commencement address by Mr. Rogers, the TV kiddie personality watched in eight million households, and then join him in a chorus of "Won't You Be My Neighbor?"

OFF

Call it just another day in TV America. These may not be our highest moments, but they certainly are our most common fare. Admittedly, we occasionally suffer cerebral print types like the late Allan Bloom,[e] but in the end there's nothing quite like the lively cartoon character Bart Simpson. MTV, *A Current Affair*, *Entertainment Tonight*, *Cops*, *The Dating Game* reruns, local news, monster truck derbies, docudramas, and Cher hair-product infomercials—they're all a significant part of our daily electronic life. "And the beat goes on,"[19] forever on and on. Like it, loathe it, or just tolerate it, this is characteristic of much of American popular expression.

The imagistic character of television produces a flow of information that is largely framed, context-free, and content-compressed.[20]

e) Allan Bloom (1930–1992) was a professor of political philosophy whose scholarship focused primarily on Plato and Rousseau. His most popular book, *The Closing of the American Mind* (New York: Simon & Schuster, 1987), delivered a trenchant critique of modern democracy and higher education.

A masterful exploitation of these properties occurred in the 1988 presidential campaign. With notable expertise, political media strategists situated then-presidential candidate George Bush in front of a colorful New Jersey flag factory. This framed bit of television "reality" instantaneously communicated patriotism and leadership without the heavy baggage of commentary on the issues of the day. Years later, the blue-blood president associated with country western singers—creating a down-home image of a blue-collar kind of guy. On the same day, the same President Bush introduced a docudrama on the Persian Gulf War that imperceptibly interwove fictional performances with factual footage—creating a larger-than-life image of a statesman. Former National Republican Party chairman Lee Atwater conceded this process of reality-framing when he explained that modern political campaign consultants must "spend an hour and a half [every morning] figuring out what you're going to do to get on the news that night—to get in the news hole. What stunt you can pull that will give you 14 seconds of news hole."[21]

In addition, television frequently conveys information in a discontinuous and nonsequential manner. For example, television programming catalogs a variety of disassociated subjects, placing the national news next to a game show and situating an endless number of disjointed scenes within a single rock video. These commonplace attributes of television's technology and use maximize its potential as a medium for diversion. Indeed, much of the "grammar" of commercial television derives from the unruly juxtaposition of images. Television's visual logic deemphasizes the systematized, controlled, and abstract analysis associated with print and tends more to emphasize the uncontrolled, the personalized, and the emotive. "TV favors a mentality in which certain things no longer matter particularly," explained art critic Robert Hughes. "[S]kills like the ability to enjoy a complex argument, for instance, or to perceive nuances, or to keep in mind large amounts of significant information, or to remember today what someone said last month, or to consider strongly and carefully argued opinions in defiance of what is conventionally called 'balance'" shrivel in a commercial medium of "emotional hyperbole . . . and blandness of opinion."[22] With print logic, experience is "cognized," whereas with visual logic, experience is "re/cognized." The adage "seeing is believing" is the lodestar of visual logic. (Much of this was foretold by media's high priest

Marshall McLuhan decades ago when he wrote *The Gutenberg Galaxy.*)

And then there is the technology of the *new* "television." Just as the industrial revolutions of the eighteenth and nineteenth centuries moved us down the road from an agrarian society to a modern world, so now a communications revolution will soon take us into the future on an "electronic superhighway." Indeed, the signposts are already in place —fiber-optic cables, satellite dishes, DVDs, high-definition TV, electronic bulletin boards, supercomputer networks, program grids, and interactivity and "virtual reality."[f] Where once a handful of networks ruled the airwaves, tomorrow's merger of computer, telephone, and television technologies promises a plethora of choices from interactive classrooms to shopping channels and Golf-TV. If the economic, ownership, regulatory, and uniform standards problems are overcome, interactive technology will spread our popular culture ever faster, ever wider, and ever more. The presumption is that electronic visual media will produce more information, which will produce more knowledge. But does this presumption take into full account the public's enormous appetite for entertainment over knowledge? Communications and marketing expert Leo Bogart answers: "An electronic information highway that's jammed with the likes of Jimmy Swaggart, Madonna and Ice-T can easily be a road to nowhere."[23]

All of this—the new and the post-new—helps to erode a continuous and critical social perspective. Picture stories that capitalize on aesthetics and emotion do not really promote synthesis, analysis, or criticism. They likewise do little to enhance any desire to take a longer and harder second look at our culture and its directions. On this score ABC's Ted Koppel was frank: "[T]here is not much room on television for complexity."[24] We indulge in an outrageous orgy of local crime news rather than focus on the complex and less sensational social causes underlying violent behavior. Although a "live news story" about a lone Montana gunman squaring off with a SWAT team may be "hot," it trades an informed treatment of the problems

f) "Virtual reality" is an artificial world generated by computers in which viewers, today connected by electronic headsets and gear, participate in a three-dimensional environment. The technology aims to take us to a virtual world of our choosing—e.g., an instructional world, a trade world, a movie world, a sports world, a game world, or even a pornographic world.

of crime and justice in our society for "action" pictures. The aesthetic and emotional experience is unquestionably television's standard fare and modus operandi. In short, as veteran reporter Daniel Schorr once put it: "Television allows people to experience more and understand less. It appeals more to the senses than to the intellect."[25]

Out of this picture-centered environment emerged the prototype of the modern public leader: Ronald Reagan. The former president and "former Hollywood movie actor, rarely [spoke] accurately and never precisely, [yet he was] known as the Great Communicator; his telegenic charm [appeared] to be his major asset."[26] Professor James Barber, a leading presidential scholar, captured the essence of the Reagan television image: "He personifies his rhetoric, speaks with filmic grammar, pretends spontaneity, rolls through narrative and translates every blunder and tragedy into an upbeat lesson."[27] (Try as they did, Presidents George Bush and Bill Clinton never successfully rivaled their Hollywood-trained predecessor.)

Ronald Reagan:
Politics is just like show business.

Elizabeth Drew, *Portrait of an Election* (New York: Simon & Schuster, 1981), p. 263.

Prophetically, in 1958, the British-born Huxley anticipated the Reagan and post-Reagan political persona and its vital role in the brave new world:

> In one way or another, as vigorous he-man or kindly father, the candidate must be glamorous. He must also be an entertainer who never bores his audience. Inured to television . . . , that audience is accustomed to being distracted and does not like to be asked to concentrate or make a prolonged intellectual effort. All speeches by the entertainer candidate must therefore be short and snappy. The great issues of the day must be dealt with in five minutes at the most — and preferably . . . in sixty seconds flat.[28]

Beyond the technological attributes of television, the *commercial use* to which it is put significantly determines its entertainment direction.[g] At least two causes are responsible for this direction: the conglomerated and globalized entertainment industry fueled by bottom-

g) Television has even changed our perception of pleasure itself, allowing the aestheti-

line profit margins, and the unsophisticated and undisciplined appetite of the democratic polity for amusement. The merger of all forms of mass media—book publishing, movie producing, radio and television broadcasting, cable TV, interactive TV, and virtual reality—in an oligopoly of diversified conglomerates is vital to the amusement-industrial complex. One of the highest aspirations of the commercial media is captured in a single word: BLOCKBUSTER. Blockbuster hardbacks spawn blockbuster paperbacks that generate blockbuster movies and network television series that culminate in a host of spin-off market ventures—cable television reruns, videos, and endless products and product tie-ins. Add to this the impact of global marketing. "Entertainment products are now our number-two export item, right behind military hardware.... American popular culture, for better or for worse, for richer and not for poorer, is already world culture."[29] Globalization, in turn, maximizes the profit margin by further marginalizing high culture. As American novelist William Styron put it, "The export of our vulgarity is the hallmark of our greatness."[30]

The hunt for the blockbuster is the unceasing search for a lower common denominator predicated on mass appeal. The general concept—think of it as the *Wayne's World* formula[h]—is that profits go up as the denominator in communication comes down. With specific regard to commercial television, a direct correlation exists between the popularity of a program and the generation of commercial advertising revenues. Popularity, of course, is an appeal to mass appetites. The desire for popularity, and in turn, profits, gives rise to television's "predictable entrepreneurial problem": "How do [producers and advertisers] get maximum audience for maximum return?"[31] Television's sitcoms, talk shows, commercials, and even its news reflect the tastes of its viewers as the old network and new cable programmers strive to sell the attention of the largest possible target audiences to advertisers. Because the media often value audience size over narrative plot or news integrity, it is "not by design but by necessity" that the lowest common denominator in expression wins. "If

cized surface—the abstract image—to dominate. Television has thus replaced pleasure with the *image* of pleasure.

h) Originally a *Saturday Night Live* skit mimicking local broadcasting, *Wayne's World* became a popular movie accompanied by books and a multitude of product tie-ins. The skit, like its commercial successors, was known for its "low-brow" appeal.

twelve million people wanted to watch goldfish racing, that is what would be broadcast. [Indeed, Fish TV—the electronic aquarium—caught on.] The only bad show is one not seen. The only bad story is an unpopular one."[32] In this environment, it is no surprise that when the CBS flagship television station in New York had to choose between a game show (*Win, Lose or Draw*) and Dan Rather's evening news for the desirable 7 PM time slot, the game show won.[33] With profit maximization as the governing norm, television distorts traditional First Amendment values by "associating the lowest passions with the highest ideals."[34]

When mass popularity is the maxim, television—even public and cable TV—is hard pressed to fulfill its touted promises of increased quality and real diversity. Perforce, commercial television often favors noncontroversial and uncomplicated programming. From an advertiser's standpoint, serious public affairs programming may prove so volatile or complex as to discourage commercial support. A mass medium heavily dependent on such support will tend to program with a bias to avoiding viewer controversy or perplexity.[35] Indeed, the promise even of cable and public television to diversify content may not be substantially realized. On the one hand, the economics of commercial television may foreclose any other result. As media conglomerates increase their holdings in the network and cable industries, the entrepreneurial chase for advertising revenues and maximum achievable market shares suggests that more and more cable programming will mirror network entertainment shows.[36] On the other hand, and even more important, if the new forms of alternative television succeed in servicing niche audiences with diverse tastes, the predominant net result will likely remain entertainment fare. Call it diverse—"WWF Mania" wrestling matches, comedy hours, "Shop 'Til You Drop" shows, "Vampire on Bikini Beach"-type movie reruns, or even Playboy programming—but it's terribly amusing any way you look at it.

The economics and aesthetics of commercial television have profound influence in the realm of mass political speech. Professor Stanley Rothman observed that "[t]elevision has changed the very structure of political discourse." It tells us, added Professor Roderick P. Hart, "that politics can be reduced to pictures.... It makes political life a weekly insert in the pages of *People* magazine...[and] turns watching the nightly news into another kind of game show rather than into a vibrant lesson in the problems of self-governance."[37] Hence, images displace ideas, personalities replace policies, and fiction merges with fact.

As politicians master the strategies of advertising and entertainment programming, the gulf between important political expression and pure amusement nearly vanishes.[i] Advertising-agency professionals serve as "media consultants" to the candidates and orchestrate campaigns as if they were prime-time commercials. Recall the forklifts, flag factories, tanks, harbor rides, and convict turnstiles that were only a few of the backdrops for the staged 1988 presidential media events. Though not generally perceived as pathetic as its predecessor, the 1992 presidential campaign had its own share of pop politics — TV talk shows, MTV and Comedy Central convention coverage, attacks on the candidates' sexual exploits, Ross Perot's televised democracy, and Madonna's *Rock the Vote* videos. Kathleen Hall Jamieson, dean of the Annenberg School of Communications, detailed "the direction of American democracy" charted in the 1992 presidential election: "[H]ome movies, phony biographies, peppy visuals, softball interviews and easily manipulated call-in shows" substantially overshadowed extended policy analysis. Something of the same can be said of media attempts to report on Congress in any meaningful way. Not only have television news stories on Congress generally declined over the past two decades, but relatively few of them deal with significant or complex legislative policies. This trend is particularly problematic in light of the resurgence of congressional power after the Republican "revolution" of 1994. If today's commercial media cover government more, they tell citizens less — at least about weighty matters of governance.[38]

Vice President Albert Gore:

Thank you, MTV! ... Thank you for winning this election. You did it!

Christopher Georges, "Mock the Vote," *Washington Monthly Magazine*, May 1993.

True to the entertainment-commercial format, "sound bite" political talk regularly replaces more extended and reflective discourse on

i) We further discuss this and related points in Book II.

complex social and political problems. According to Michael Sheehan, the adviser to four democratic presidential aspirants in 1988: "[Politicians] must understand that the [television] time frame is scrunched — [they] need to be able to express a complex idea in about 15 seconds."[39] The more politicians understand this media maxim, the less the viewing public is likely to understand. "Can a complicated public issue be intelligently debated in today's sound-bite culture," asked media reporter Howard Kurtz, "where partisans must play their roles and score their rapid-fire points . . . before the audience starts channel-surfing?" Then-House Speaker Newt Gingrich emphatically answered Kurtz's questions: "Trying to transform a system the size of the United States cannot be intelligently discussed in nine-second sound bites or even on today's version of talk shows." Neither will

Todd Gitlin: In the country of th

the current television formats for news analysis suffice, Gingrich claimed, "because you can't get to a dialogue. You have to stay in some sort of nitpicking argument."[40] Emotions run high in sound-bite talk, if for no other reason than the TV ratings game cannot stomach dispassionate discourse that eats up valuable time.

Empirical studies by Kiku Adatto, formerly of Harvard University, and Daniel Hallin, a political scientist at the University of California at San Diego, established that sound bites (or blocs of uninterrupted speech) shrank from 1968 to 1988 by greater than 75 percent.[41] Analyzing more than 280 weekday network newscasts during that period, Adatto observed:

- The average "sound bite". . . fell from 42.3 seconds in 1968 to only 9.8 seconds in 1988.

- In 1968, almost half of all sound bites were 40 seconds or more, compared with only one percent in 1988.

- In 1968, [political] candidates spoke for a minute without interruption in 21 percent of all newscasts. In 1988, this never happened.[42]

True to form, during the 1992 general election the average sound bite dropped to a mere 8.4 seconds.[43]

Veteran CBS news anchor Walter Cronkite stated the obvious in 1992 when he observed: "Naturally, nothing of any significance is going to be said in 9.8 seconds."[44] Such unilluminating sound bites likewise irked syndicated columnist George Will, who aptly described the 1988 Bush-Dukakis televised debates as "tossed salads of brevity," serving only to "test skills unrelated to the real tasks of governance....[These] debates [were] primarily the regurgitation of market-tested paragraphs. Reflexes, not thinking, [were] crucial."[45] *Think* about it: Sound-bite campaigning is akin to Pavlovian politics.

It would be incredibly ironic if the scientific genius inherited from the Enlightenment produced an electronic commonwealth that

ound bite, the one-liner is king.

The Murder of Albert Einstein (New York: Farrar, Straus & Giroux, 1992), p. 37.

belittles the American mind by degrading discourse. Reflecting on this general deterioration of political discourse in America's media agora, another syndicated columnist, David S. Broder, complained: "[N]o one is well served by what is happening. The public does not get the basic information it needs for citizenship....And the press finds itself drawn into a downward spiral of cheapened values and lost respect."[46] Echoing this assessment, broadcast journalist Bill Moyers forecast a gloomy future for the American polity:

> Running campaigns in a nation on the pleasure principle is wrecking the polity of America, destroying our ability as a cooperative society to face reality and solve our problems.... Behind the charm and smiles, behind the one-liners [and] the pretty pictures,... the government rots, its costs soar, its failures mount.... But, on the bridge of the ship of state, no one's on watch and below deck no one can see the iceberg but everyone's feeling good.[47]

Not only politics but other forms of important public discourse are increasingly packaged as entertainment when touched by television. The old Edward R. Murrow[j] news model yields ever more to

j) Edward R. Murrow, a highly regarded journalist, covered world events for CBS

attractive anchors, staged visuals, lulling music, compressed context, and commercially oriented video news releases. On this point, CBS news correspondent Lesley Stahl admitted with an amazing mixture of pride and embarrassment:

> As a reporter, I like to be able to wallpaper, as we say in television. ... [That is, put] pretty pictures up while I'm talking behind it. Pretty, interesting pictures, pictures with movement. Pictures that will capture the audience's eye. I shouldn't want that, because I know that it's deceptive and the audience won't really hear what I'm saying. But I still like it. I like my pieces to have energy.[48]

When prime-time news must compete with entertainment programming for advertiser dollars, TV reports rely far more heavily on the visually alluring. In this environment, discriminating and in-depth journalism succumbs to viewer ratings. Openly ashamed of such TV news practices, CBS anchor Dan Rather revealed: "They've got us putting more and more fuzz and wuzz on the air, cop-shop stuff, so as to compete not with other news programs but with entertainment programs.... 'Action, Jackson' is the cry. Hire lookers, not writers. Do powder puff, not probing interviews."[49]

Reinforcing the entertainment affinity of today's news, simulated events (e.g., the ABC News dramatization of espionage scenes and the NBC News fabrication of a GM truck explosion) and docudramas mix the authentic with the make-believe. Though unreal, such media moments may be visually convincing as news. Contemptuous of such mind ploys, TV critic Tom Rosenstiel observed: "We [in the media] have lost sight of giving people the news, in terms of its significance. We're giving it to them in terms of what... is the most titillating and the most ratings-grabbing, and in doing so we've lost the distinction between [journalists] and [tabloid artists]."[50] In such a

radio and television, starting with an eyewitness report on Hitler's seizure of Austria and ending with coverage of John F. Kennedy's inauguration. In a 1958 speech deploring commercial television's excesses, Murrow said: "Surely we shall pay for using this most powerful instrument of communication to insulate the citizenry from the hard and demanding realities which must indeed be faced if we are to survive." *In Search of Light: The Broadcasts of Edward R. Murrow 1938–1961*, ed. Edward Bliss (New York: Knopf, 1967), p. 355.

world, as sacrosanct a prospect as Christ's second coming would be packaged for commercial television with all its electronic graven images.[51]

Zap to music from This Week with David Brinkley *and focus on winter scene of tidal basin in Washington, D.C. Fast cut into ongoing discussion of 1988 presidential election campaigns. Close-up on George Will, sporting bow tie and wire-rimmed glasses.*

George Will (syndicated columnist): [comment to James Baker] It's November and the election is still [filled with idle slogans.] Isn't there a danger [as] you come to November 9th, . . . and you say that our mandate is not to have [prison] furloughs; to pledge allegiance to the flag; to stay out of the American Civil Liberties Union. . . . [How then] do you govern on the basis of that?

James A. Baker III (Bush campaign chairman): Well, . . . I really respectfully disagree with you because the fact of the matter is that we have to deal in thirty-second sound bites. That's not our fault, it's not your fault, it happens to be the fault of the fact that the majority of the American people get their news that way. . . . My point about the thirty-second sound bite . . . is that this is the way the American public gets their news and therefore we in campaigns have to take that into account . . . and plan accordingly.

David Brinkley (moderator): James A. Baker, Bush Chairman, made an interesting point: It is difficult to get a program before the American people because he seems to think that the thirty-second commercial is the only vehicle available to them. I don't think that's true. Is it true?

George Will: . . . A study has been done and it is that ten years ago, the average sound bite . . . was forty-five seconds. In 1984 it was down to fifteen seconds. In the preliminary study this year, [it] says it is down to nine seconds. Why?

Sam Donaldson (ABC news correspondent): I'll tell you, yes, it's true. I was doing some research for a book a couple of years ago and I went back and looked at some of the pieces I did on ABC in 1971. And you're right, I ran sound bites of George Meany [that] went forty-three seconds. Now it's something that's called, I call it the Tom Pettit rule. Tom Pettit is a very able NBC correspondent, but somehow he's gotten the sound bite down to two seconds.... There's something like... the dancing pig syndrome in which every four or five or six seconds there must be another pig dancing on the street.

Hodding Carter (PBS commentator; former spokesman for Carter State Department): The devil made me do it is what I heard Mr. Baker say about why they were doing it. We say in the television business, "well, that's the way it is."... It's almost impossible to tell the difference today between a political ad and an evening news spot about the campaign. They are both impelled by the same ethos, the same standards, the same techniques. Make it punchy, make it sharp, make it impactful. And if it doesn't have anything to do with real issues, too bad, it's good television.[52]

The advanced technology and economic workings of commercial television do not, however, entirely explain its preoccupation with entertainment. Importantly, it is the synergy among private technological and commercial forces and the public pleasure principle that gives the popular entertainment culture its play. With his attention sharply focused on television, Professor James Twitchell charged that WE THE PEOPLE are complicit in the "mediaocracy":

> [T]elevision has shown what happens when a free market is let loose on a culture's mythology. Gatekeepers run for cover. Yet, why blame the messenger when so many of us seem to want the message?... Somehow the dreck of the masses is changing the quality of an otherwise benign culture. The concerns of [the] protectors of our high-culture heritage still come through loud and clear: the Philistines are coming.[53]

If the Philistines have invaded America's culture, it is not because television forced open the gates of the popular mind. Rather, as the French aristocrat Alexis de Tocqueville knew, it has everything to do with the nature of popular democracy. Former *New York Times* theater reviewer Clive Barnes agreed: "Television is the first truly democratic culture—the first culture available to everybody and entirely governed by what the people want."[54] If democracy is simply the aggregation of mass tastes, then America's media cater unstintingly to those tastes. "The truth is that people have been getting what they want: a talk-show nation in which public discourse is increasingly reduced to ranting and raving,"[55] lamented investigative newspaper reporter Carl Bernstein.

Before we go any further with our discussion, several caveats are in order. First, although commercial television alone did not create our Huxleyan predicament, it is nevertheless a vital component. The human drive for pleasure, fueled by so many aspects of a highly capitalistic and technological society, is greatly accelerated by the amusement medium. Second, although studies linking commercial television to cognitive and behavioral effects are indeterminate,[56] more than ample experiential evidence supports the conclusion that a medium that is all pervasive must have some telling effect on the structure of individual and cultural communication; that a society that dedicates more than a quarter of every day to television is less likely to embrace the Madisonian ideals of critical discourse and reasoned political participation; and that billion-dollar commercial efforts to institutionalize the pleasure principle have more than a negligible effect on traditional First Amendment values. Third, the ascendancy of the television culture may not affect everyone in the same way. Nonetheless, just as its traditional appeal is mass, so too its effects are typically mass, and increasingly global. Fourth, television is not without its social benefits. For example, it can offer some solace to the old and infirm; it may produce the likes of a Bill Moyers, Ted Koppel, Judy Woodruff, or William F. Buckley Jr.; and it may furnish information (albeit suitably packaged) at electrifying speeds. But the larger point remains that the cultural costs of commercial television may far exceed its benefits. In Professor Stuart Ewen's assessment, a vacuum of serious public discourse has been filled by a television culture of spectacle and a "democracy of images."[57]

Nota Bene

Television, then, represents the democratization of "discourse." In today's commercial America, television is the majoritarian medium that echoes the voice of the masses. Television "became us. It is who we are."[58] So, who are we?

ZAP

We are the folks who would rather indulge in *Cheers* or *M*A*S*H** reruns than ponder the sometimes weighty talk on C-SPAN's coverage of congressional committee mark-ups.

ZAP

We are the mass of viewers who yawned when the Senate Judiciary Committee questioned Supreme Court nominee Clarence Thomas on his constitutional philosophy, but who came alive when TV talk turned to lurid tales of "Long Dong Silver."

ZAP

We are the audience so charmed by the soma medium that we may prefer to evaluate presidential candidates by their performances on TV talk shows. As political cartoonist Jim Borgman satirized: "We can watch Clinton on MTV, Bush on 'Letterman,' Perot on 'Arsenio' . . . or Madonna on 'Meet the Press.'"[59] Talk-show host Phil Donahue found reason in this to rejoice: "The political scientists should relax and celebrate the First Amendment as it is."[60]

ZAP

We are the producers of *CBS Evening News* who, concerned about shrinking sound bites in presidential campaign news accounts, issued a policy that all such televised statements must be thirty seconds or longer. In the end, however, this half-minute proved interminable and the policy intolerable.[61]

ZAP

And we are the ones who by and large agree with the local TV talk-show producer who in 1993 proclaimed: "There's a lot of mundane stuff that needs to be said." "Weird as it may sound," he told the investigative reporters of CBS's *48 Hours*, "I feel that we're upholding the First Amendment."[62]

OFF

If our contemporary popular entertainment culture is indeed tending toward Huxley's antiutopia, what can or should be done? From a First Amendment vantage point, how do we deconstruct or reconstruct our commercial television culture? Is it possible to draw First Amendment lines that will address the distinct harms posed by Orwellian censorship and Huxleyan triviality in our amusement world?

A Rearview Mirror Look at the First Amendment

[T]he challenge posed by the new technologies to the First Amendment is cultural as well as doctrinal.

—M. Ethan Katsh[63]

Back to McLuhan, this time via another metaphor—the "rearview mirror."[64] This metaphor describes how most people approach the present or future by looking at the past. The rearview mirror perspective is commonplace in the law, particularly in First Amendment thinking. Media-law experts attempt to impose the eighteenth-century ideals of freedom of speech and press on the modern world as if no changes have taken place. Today, First Amendment doctrine assumes that governmental censorship still poses a greater and more real threat to our rational self-governing ideal than self-gratification. It assumes that our free speech guaranty, although forged in a revolutionary era, has the same meaning even though the evils against which that law was directed do not haunt us as they once did. A First Amendment doctrine based on such assumptions fails to address the vulnerability of free expression in the current, commercial context of trivialized speech.

Let us be clear: The potential for Orwellian governmental censorship can *never* be dismissed, and we do not dismiss it. Practically speaking, however, that potential is far less threatening today than it has been in the past. This is not, of course, to deny the obvious: First Amendment freedom-of-expression issues will continue to surface in a range of cases. But, comparatively, the Orwellian evil is not as likely to pose a clear and present danger to traditional First Amendment values. In China, Iran, and Bosnia, for example, the censorial hand of the oppressor mutes the dissenter; in America, the dissenter is effectively silenced by an oblivious commercial and entertainment culture.

Must we, can we, redefine the evil and the enemy of free speech in an effort to reconcile old-world Orwellian principles with new-world

Huxleyan predicaments? Pursuing this inquiry, we are likely to encounter in some readers an unfortunate and almost inevitable tendency toward ideological labeling. Much of what we offer is novel and perplexing, and some may be tempted to affix labels to our arguments and to make hasty conclusions. We urge you to avoid labels and to suspend judgment for several reasons. First, ideological labels mislead. The attempt to confront the Huxleyan dilemma may be stamped as a conservative agenda to salvage an elitist ideal in an otherwise egalitarian society. Yet certainly, "the stupefying effects of consumer capitalism and its mass media"[65] cannot be a thing of joy to either the reformist or the radical. Alternatively, any campaign for affirmative government involvement in the system of free expression may be branded as progressive or socialist or, in any case, as hostile to American free enterprise. But no conservative of integrity and public conscience can extol a culture that condones self-induced pleasure at the expense of thoughtful self-governance. The ideological labeling of these arguments serves only to confuse their substance. Second, hasty verdicts about the validity of such arguments may arrest any further inquiry beyond labels to determine whether Huxleyan dangers indeed threaten serious discourse. Finally, if you reach rashly for ideological categories, you may well be surprised by what follows.

Caution

Obviously, many have touched upon the application of First Amendment principles to the electronic media. Relatively few, however, offer proposals to mediate or eliminate differences in protection of speech based on the medium of communication. What is most striking about even these few studies is the failure to focus on the Orwellian-Huxleyan dichotomy. As Professor Simon Lee astutely maintained: "Whereas the media have changed dramatically over the last two centuries, the same old arguments over free speech seem to carry on regardless."[66] Metaphorically, the few who have looked at the First Amendment in an electronic age typically drive into the future with eyes focused on the rearview mirror.

Presently, we can identify three major First Amendment scenarios concerning differences between the old and new media. In shorthand, these schemas may conveniently be titled the classical (abolitionist) scenario, the modern (libertarian) scenario, and the reformist (regulatory) scenario. In various ways, each scenario is tied to an eighteenth-century mind-set that biases its vision of the First Amendment's role in our society. Ultimately, we find all three scenarios to be myopic—

though each contains fragments of great value, none fully gleans the paradox of the First Amendment in the age of paratroopers.

The CLASSICAL SCENARIO celebrates the Enlightenment philosophy of the eighteenth century—the century in which the First Amendment was born. Classicists hail an educated citizenry as the essential component of a free society and urge that serious learning requires emphasis on reading, writing, and face-to-face dialogue. The classical vision is collective, not egocentric. The traditional model of the American town meeting—citizens coming together, discussing, debating, and resolving issues—is the embodiment of this ideal. A classical regime champions moderation in all things: Self-restraint is the sine qua non of self-governance and interest in the public good.

Antithetical to this objective is the specter of self-indulgent and alienating consumption. Accordingly, the classicist views unchecked commercial entertainment as an ever present threat. The modern mass-amusement media imperil the very existence of the classical scheme. As the media evoke from the audience emotional responses to their stimuli, they tyrannize the public mind. Thus, at the center of the classical scenario, rationality, collective decisionmaking, and public discourse are united in the doctrine of the First Amendment. Any obstacle to or interference with this union is inimical to the principles of the First Amendment and may therefore be subject to prohibition.

Alexander Meiklejohn[k] is the leading American actor in the classical scenario. Many decades ago he warned of the exploitative nature of the electronic mass media. Rather than promoting important First Amendment values of collective decisionmaking, the electronic mass media corrupt and suffocate them:

> [T]he total effect [of commercial radio], as judged in terms of educational value, is one of terrible destruction. The radio...is not cultivating those qualities of taste, of reasoned judgment, of

k) The president of Amherst College circa 1912, Alexander Meiklejohn was a social philosopher best known in constitutional law circles for his classic *Free Speech and Its Relation to Self-Government* (1948). The work was later expanded under the title *Political Freedom: The Constitutional Powers of the People* (New York: Oxford University Press, 1965). We will return to Dr. Meiklejohn in Book III.

> integrity, of loyalty, of mutual understanding upon which the enterprise of self-government depends. On the contrary, it is a mighty force for breaking them down.

Consequently, this electronic medium must be denied First Amendment protection in the very name of the First Amendment:

> The radio as it now operates among us is not free. Nor is it entitled to the protection of the First Amendment. It is not engaged in the task of enlarging and enriching human communication. It is engaged in making money. And the First Amendment does not intend to guarantee men freedom to say what some private interest pays them to say for its own advantage.

Further developing his First Amendment thesis for the electronic media, Meiklejohn moved with even greater force against commercial television. In an incredible but seldom noted passage, he declared:

> On the whole, the "liberties" of what we call "Free Enterprise" are, I think, destructive of the "freedoms" of a self-governing society. The unregulated self-seeking of the profit-makers is much more dangerous in its effect upon the morality and intelligence of the citizen than that participation in regulatory action for the common good to which free enterprise has so often shown itself hostile.... [P]rivately sponsored television has proved to be even more deadly [than radio]. Those business controls of communication are, day by day, year by year, destroying and degrading our intelligence and our taste by the use of instruments which should be employed in educating and uplifting them.[67]

Václav Havel:
[Intellectuals should care about] whether a global dictatorship of advertisement, consumerism, and blood-and-thunder stories on TV will ultimately lead the human race to a state of complete idiocy.

"The Responsibility of Intellectuals," *New York Review of Books*, 22 June 1995, p. 36.

Moreover, arguing that Congress is empowered to "enlarge and enrich" freedom of the mind, Meiklejohn called for affirmative legislative measures to buttress the classical ideal of freedom of expression. Such measures seemed particularly necessary because our modern consumerist economy and electronic technology whet appetites for amusement contrary to the classical model of self-restraint.

More recently, Meiklejohn's thesis has been extended by one of his intellectual disciples, Professor George Anastaplo.[l] In a thought-provoking essay, Anastaplo criticized the effects of television on the viewing public, i.e., its addictive quality, its simplistic portrayal of reality, its threat to civic piety and associational values, its commercial drives for material consumption, and its detrimental impact on education. For Anastaplo, Meiklejohn's thesis led directly to a call for the *abolition* of commercial television:

> [T]he television industry should be abolished completely in this country. . . . [N]othing short of this can remove its crippling influence from American life. If this is indeed a society open to experimentation, then let us deliberately experiment for at least a decade with the remedy of complete suppression of television.

Predictably, Anastaplo advocated governmental regulation of television precisely to *further* First Amendment values:

> [T]here should be, in ordinary constitutional circumstances, both an absolute prohibition against previous legal restraints of the press and an absolute previous restraint (that is, total abolition) of the television industry. . . .
>
> I see in the abolition of television no serious First Amendment problem. Rather than abridge the "freedom of speech" guaranteed by the First Amendment, the abolition of television (and hence a radical reform of the mass media) would enlarge freedom of speech among us. . . . Thus abolition of television would probably contribute among us to the preservation of self-government and hence genuine freedom.[68]

Bold views. Yet such views may well be quite natural to those truly committed to the classical scenario of the First Amendment.

---

l) George Anastaplo was denied admission to the Illinois bar when he stood on his First Amendment rights against McCarthy-era oppression. Though he lost his 1961 Supreme Court case, Justice Hugo Black wrote a spirited dissent. Later Anastaplo authored *The Constitutionalist: Notes on the First Amendment* (Dallas: Southern Methodist University Press, 1971).

Directly opposed to the classical scenario, the MODERN SCENARIO rejects virtually any legal distinction based on the method of communication as contrary to First Amendment principles. Although it acknowledges that the operation of new electronic technology has implications for First Amendment doctrine, the modern scenario does not recognize any dissimilarities in the effect of different media types, or any evils that may be special to commercial television. Espousing utilitarian, libertarian, and laissez-faire notions, the modern program dictates a policy of government hands-off. The modern scenario fixates upon Orwellian fears to the exclusion of all others. Thus, it highlights the perils of any governmental control of the electronic media.

Perhaps the most highly regarded director of this scenario was the late MIT political science professor Ithiel de Sola Pool. As he warned in his *Technologies of Freedom*, the "degrading erosion of freedom that our system of communication faces today" is alarming:

> It would be dire if the laws we make today governing the dominant mode of information handling in . . . an information society were subversive of its freedom. The onus is on us to determine whether free societies in the twenty-first century will conduct electronic communication under the conditions of freedom established for the domain of print through centuries of struggle, or whether that great achievement will become lost in a confusion about new technologies.[69]

The modernist characteristically maintains that at least two phenomena require the extension of First Amendment protection to the electronic media:

- the increasing use of the same physical apparatuses (e.g., fiber-optic cable, airwaves, components of the new information highway) and technological formats (e.g., telephone, television) for electronic communication; and

- the growing cross-ownership in communications industries.

These two developments, among others, have fostered a "convergence" or a merger of technologies that undermines the long-honored rationales for special governmental control of electronic media. Moreover, the modernist argues that "[t]he extension of electronic means to do better and faster what the older modes of communication did with lead, ink, and paper" requires that the modern electronic format receive a "newer tradition" of protection from governmental control equal to that developed over the centuries for the press.[70]

George Gilder of the Discovery Institute, a modern-day ally of Pool, is convinced that the invention of a "teleputer" system,[m] a digitally switched fiber-optic computer network, heralds a communications revolution that should all but guarantee extensive First Amendment protection. So powerful are these new technologies that, in Gilder's view, "[t]he age of television, for all intents and purposes, [is] over." Unlike today's broadcasting system, he added, the new technology promises an untold number of personalized electronic possibilities, ranging from interactive audio-video communication to a plethora of program selections. These technological advances might "demassify" the television experience. With utopian expectations, Gilder believes that the teleputer "will reverse the effects of the television age.... Rather than exalting mass culture, the teleputer will enhance individualism. Rather than cultivating passivity, the teleputer will promote creativity."[71]

In a modernist society where technologies merge and teleputers abound, any First Amendment campaign to combat Huxleyan evils through governmental regulation paves the way of tyranny.

The REFORMIST SCENARIO is situated almost midpoint between the classical and modernist extremes, essentially advocating limited regulation of television rather than its abolition. Like its classical counterpart, the reformist heralds certain governmental actions as essential to the preservation of core First Amendment norms. Without affirmative government involvement, the reformist predicts that

m) The "teleputer" is "a personal computer adapted for video processing and connected by fiber-optic threads to other teleputers all around the world. Using a two-way system of signals like telephones do, rather than broadcasting one-way like TV, the teleputer will surpass the television in video communication." George Gilder, *Life After Television: The Coming Transformation of Media and American Life* (New York: W. W. Norton, 1994), p. 45.

corporate commercial interests will select programs based on advertising objectives alone, and that the unchecked laissez-faire market will produce a concentration of media ownership. The reformist rails against a powerful commercial broadcast industry that "continues to push for fewer obligations to the general public, while focusing programming efforts toward attracting an audience that maximizes its advertising revenue."[72] Although the reformists are concerned with the enlightenment and communal values of the First Amendment, they are more concerned with the amendment's potential to redistribute political and economic power in the media context.

The reformist scenario contains a subtle understanding of commercial television and the Huxleyan dilemma, but reformists are loath to admit the disquieting implications of that knowledge. Like their modernist counterparts, the reformists tolerate a realm of virtually deregulated commercial broadcasting, presumably to avoid charges of Orwellian government rule. Ultimately, this agenda places a guarded faith in the media's ability to save itself, in democracy's ability to patrol its self-indulgent behavior, in the public's ability to understand its best interest, and in the nation's ability to transform an altogether mass media into a more local one.

What this faith also presupposes is the active and knowing participation of the citizenry in a reformist enterprise. Reformists regard the right of public access to the airwaves as a necessity, "not simply from a need to improve the 'vast wasteland' of television programming" but also "to foster the development of a vast array of programming options from the maximum number of *different* sources.... The public—not government or corporate broadcasters or networks—should be given the opportunity to choose programs directly and to define what is in its own interest."[73]

An innovative contemporary expression of the reformist agenda is found in the thinking of public-interest lawyers Ralph Nader[n] and Claire Riley. The authors proposed the federal statutory adoption of Audience Network, a national, nonprofit membership organization funded by dues and voluntary private contributions. Audience Net-

n) Known colloquially as the Consumer Crusader, Ralph Nader played a key role in the passage of the Freedom of Information Act, established over two-dozen public-interest groups, and authored the influential *Unsafe at Any Speed* (1965), among other books.

work would be allowed free prime-time access on all television and radio channels for public interest broadcasting:

> Audience Network is a proposal designed to reestablish the First Amendment rights of the public. It would provide systematic public access to and programming experience over the airwaves, as well as better public representation in the regulation of over-the-air broadcasting.... It would use [prime time] to develop and air programs the membership wants on the airwaves and to educate the public about Audience Network's operation and broadcast regulation issues. Audience Network would also represent viewers' interests before the FCC, Congress and the courts.

The overarching objective of Audience Network is "to put daily, civic function behind the principle that information is the currency of democracy."[74]

These three approaches for reconciling the First Amendment with today's commercial television—what we label as classical, modern, and reformist scenarios—all fall victim to the rearview mirror problem in some way. That is, we cannot move into the future by freezing the First Amendment in its eighteenth-century enlightenment mindset. Neither can we progress to the future by applying the First Amendment as if the biases and dangers of commercialized media did not exist. Nor can we advance by interpreting the First Amendment as if the public craving for entertainment will not affect reform efforts. Moving into the future requires an appreciation of a paradox not played out in any of the scenarios. Against the scenery of the classical, modern, and reformist programs, we now grapple with the paradox of the First Amendment in an age of paratroopers.

Roderick Hart: ***Television can take us to the moon and back, but it cannot hand-deliver democracy to us.***

Seducing America: How Television Charms the Modern Voter (New York: Oxford University Press, 1994), p. 169.

Wrestling with the Paradox

A paradox: An apparently contradictory proposition that may nevertheless be true.
The paradox: The First Amendment cannot save itself without destroying itself.

Our Orwellian-Huxleyan dilemma is the crucible in which the paratroopers' paradox is formed. The eighteenth-century First Amendment, with its emphasis on serious public discourse and its adherence to an anticensorship maxim, can no longer easily coexist with the self-indulgent bent of a mass-entertainment culture. In order to protect this traditional vision, the First Amendment may need to be recast to distinguish between old and new forms of media. But once the government is empowered to regulate expression on commercial media, the old First Amendment specter of censorial oppression resurfaces. When this occurs, First Amendment protection collapses into First Amendment tyranny.

Eyebites: Reader Support Box

Classical Scenario =	Huxleyan fear supports affirmative governmental policy to promote serious discourse Defenders: Meiklejohn, Anastaplo
Modern Scenario =	Orwellian fear supports governmental hands-off policy re regulation of speech Defenders: de Sola Pool, Gilder
Reformist Scenario =	Huxleyan and Orwellian fears support public access to commercial airwaves Defenders: Nader, Riley

Yet to preserve the conditions for self-defined liberty and to promote the corollary anticensorship ideal, the modern First Amendment must be recast to protect *all* forms of media without distinction. The electronic First Amendment, however, unleashes the forces of self-amusement and commercial corporate gain. It thereby debases the values of meaningful public discourse, effective dissent, and informed collective decisionmaking, all in the service of a new mass culture. When this occurs, First Amendment liberty collapses into First Amendment triviality.

The natural desire is to avoid the paradox by navigating the First Amendment between the Orwellian Scylla and Huxleyan Charybdis. Such compromise seeks to preserve the ideals of the classical vision while averting censorship, and to concede the ideals of the modernist vision while stemming triviality. Yielding to two media masters may prove ineffective, however. Ironically, elevated public discourse must strive to flourish on a leveling commercial medium wed to pleasure. When this occurs, First Amendment compromise collapses into First Amendment ineffectiveness.

As the careful reader may have already gleaned, this summary of the paradox sets the stage for our critique of the three scenarios.

The classical scenario invites tyranny.

The modern scenario embraces triviality.

The reformist scenario endures ineffectiveness.

To understand this is to cross the Rubicon.[o] We have, then, only to jump?

Classicists cannot suffer the idea: The world of Faneuil Hall[p] is gone. The CLASSICAL SCENARIO longs for that world. The classicists'

o) Again, crossing the Rubicon means understanding the differences between the Orwellian and Huxleyan forms of tyranny and appreciating the difficulties of developing First Amendment principles to suit electronic entertainment media. Those who attempt this venture are the First Amendment paratroopers who cross the Rubicon—and then jump? (Recall that the question mark is McLuhan's.)

p) Popularly known as America's Cradle of Liberty, Faneuil Hall was constructed in

love for the past infuses in them a romanticism that wars with reality. They reach for the future by returning to the past. At this juncture, the classicists confront the paradox.

In focusing on the past, the classicists do not appreciate that the media culture they abhor is part and parcel of a larger mass commercial culture. The ideal of the "marketplace of ideas" now operates within a vast commercial marketplace of which television is only a part. However appealing their polemical call for the abolition of television, they cannot possibly provide an answer to the First Amendment paradox. To indict commercial television is to indict our culture —perhaps even the entire American democratic regime. (This smacks of the esoteric lesson in Allan Bloom's *The Closing of the American Mind.*) When removed from the particulars of the First Amendment and applied to the generalities of culture and government in America, the classicists' argument is hyperbolic. Their agenda, then, serves more for shock value than as a serious proposal for change. Of course, its shock value exposes its futility.

The classical crusade to return to the past invites government action so abhorrent to the average American as to appear nothing less than despotic. The total abolition of television or even regulation approximating this goal would be viewed as the segue to an aristocratic (and, therefore, un-American) displacement of egalitarian and mass tastes. As Professor Postman astutely observed in his critique of the polemical classicist:

> Americans will not shut down any part of their technological apparatus, and to suggest that they do so is to make no suggestion at all. It is almost equally unrealistic to expect that nontrivial modifications in the availability of media will ever be made. Many civilized nations limit by law the amount of hours television may operate and thereby mitigate the role television plays in public life. But I believe that this is not a possibility in America. Once having

1742 and served as a meeting place for debates in opposition to the Sugar Tax of 1764 and the Stamp Act of 1765. In the next century, Faneuil Hall provided a forum for speakers such as Frederick Douglass and Susan B. Anthony. Here too, Daniel Webster delivered his famous remembrance address (1826) at a double service for John Adams and Thomas Jefferson. Today, Faneuil Hall is the centerpiece of an urban shopping mall.

> opened the Happy Medium to full public view, we are not likely to countenance even its partial closing.[75]

With a nation of Americans unwilling to budge from their television sets, the classical vision is doomed. Tersely put, we cannot get to their world from ours.

For the classical scenario to achieve any real measure of success without resort to Orwellian tyranny, two concepts of traditional First Amendment law would have to be redefined: first, the character of the perceived threat to free expression, and second, the concept of censorship. The classicists must elevate the Huxleyan tyranny over Orwellian tyranny as the greater enemy of free speech. Furthermore, for government to have the power to oversee the commercial entertainment media, certain forms of censorship must fall outside of the First Amendment's protective reach. That, in turn, would require that the speech and press clauses be significantly narrowed to justify government's "suppression" of the amusement media.

The American Way: Television packages our ideas and then seals our fate in Pandora's Box.

Yet armed with a redefined First Amendment, the paratroopers' paradox opens a Pandora's box. The classicists would raise the First Amendment as a sword against the private commercialism that assaults their free speech notions.[q] Among other things, once the classical agenda places an entire communications industry largely outside the First Amendment's protective reach, it must then allow for a hierarchy of protected speech. For example, it must then distinguish commercial from noncommercial expression, the serious from the trivial, and possibly print reporting from electronic programming. (What would the classicist do with television-like commercial print ventures such as *USA Today* or *People* magazine?)

q) From this perspective, the conservative classical agenda resembles that of its radical counterpart. Interestingly, both would empower government to contain the drives of corporate commercialism; of course, they would do so for distinct, perhaps contradictory, reasons. The combined forces of the ideological right and left may well threaten the viability of conventional constitutional doctrine in this area.

Curiously, the classicists' indictment of the status quo overlooks an important cyclical principle of the past. That principle pertains to the historically changing methods by which we communicate. The commercial television medium, which the classicists so abhor, largely replaced a commercial oral medium, the radio, which in turn largely replaced another commercial medium, print. Of course, today's classicists do not appear to abhor the effects of the print medium, which largely replaced the scribal medium that had earlier challenged the spoken word. (In antiquity, commercial oral speech was the province of the sophists, whom yesterday's classicists abhorred.) Yet each of these changes affected the social and psychological experience that had been represented by an earlier form of communication. To the critic of the print culture, for example, print artificially reduced and abstracted the living world of sight and sound to the dead confines of the typed page.[76] (Long ago, Socrates made a similar point in the *Phaedrus*.) In light of the cyclical principle at work here, the classicists' actual complaint is little more than a feeble attack on the very idea of *technology* linked to communication.

The MODERN SCENARIO is single-value based. Liberty is championed for liberty's sake and is largely divorced from other traditional First Amendment values. Essentially, the modernist understands the First Amendment as a vehicle for individualism rather than as an instrument for any public good. The modern scenario favorably portrays society as a collection of atomistic beings—a society in which the First Amendment preserves the conditions necessary for self-interested behavior. In Plato's words, it is "the city full of freedom and free speech" where there is "license" for all kinds of speech.[77] Laissez-faire in spirit, the modern scenario is ideally suited to the consumptive desires of a highly capitalistic and technologically driven society.

Modernists flatly reject the notion that the new pleasure principle of today's commercial media culture is problematic. If anything, they view it in a *positive* rather than a negative light. Modernists do not imagine the Huxleyan predicament as a threat to the system of free expression. To them, acting as if it were a threat is the real threat. (This will become more apparent in the "dialogue" at the end of Book I.)

The modernist campaign to extend First Amendment protections unsparingly to the commercial media reveals a hypersensitivity to the fears of Orwellian tyranny. Not surprisingly, the Orwellian threat makes the modernists acutely aware that the First Amendment cannot remain static in the face of dynamic changes in communication. Unfortunately, the modernists are unaware that the First Amendment likewise cannot remain static when triviality and amusement threaten to become accepted criteria for public expression.

Surely, the values of freedom of expression cannot be confined to an *unchecked* liberty interest. The modernists are so much on guard against censorship that they sacrifice all other traditional First Amendment values to governmental disinterest or to corporate design. Harvard professor Frederick Schauer, criticizing de Sola Pool's modernist theory, doubted "whether free speech interests are necessarily strengthened by the broadening of the First Amendment. We cannot ignore the extent to which an extension may be conducive to dilution."[78] His doubts are well founded, for the modernist First Amendment is basically indifferent to such dilution, a point duly registered by sociologist Todd Gitlin:

TV God

Larry King: *If we had booked God and O.J. was available, we'd move God.*

Howard Kurtz, "Should TV Talkers Give O.J. His Say?," *Washington Post*, 6 October 1995, sec. B, p. 1.

> [I]f we are serious about living in a democracy, the fundamental responsibility of the media should be to help people better pursue their rights and obligations as citizens, not to sell goods, . . . or sprinkle flakes of celebrity and blips of disconnected fact upon the daily life of a society otherwise dedicated to private gain. Democracy requires an active, engaged citizenry committed to determining and seeking the public good. As it is, the bulk of commercial television . . . reminds us to think of ourselves as consumers first and foremost.[79]

Once the modernists' liberty principle is unleashed, all other important First Amendment values are jeopardized. For example, effective dissent requires a social climate in which its message can be appreciated and acted upon. Worthwhile civic participation requires a citizenry that elects to do more than ingest television's soma tablets. An enlightened search for the common good requires more than atomistic desires for entertainment. Tracking Huxley's larger point, we see that the modernist concept of First Amendment freedoms equates "the lowest passions with the highest ideals."[80]

Finally, Pool speculated (and George Gilder now perceives) a growing merger among electronic technologies that promises to *demassify* communication and to enhance its intellectual potential more than commercial television ever could. The teleputer, Gilder assured us, will arrest television's "endless flow of minor titillations." Mindful of any criticism that we might not take the *new* communications revolution seriously, we doubt that television's electronic carnival will be leaving town any time soon. Why? In part because Gilder may himself be faulted for failing to take seriously the economic and sociopsychological forces that interact with the new technologies. Notwithstanding their obvious self-interest, CBS veterans Gene Jankowski and David Fuchs made a telling point when they argued:

> [T]here is a widely held belief that greater availability of information and improved presentation are going to trigger an increase in educational uses of the screen. A wave of autodidacticism will set in, with people studying lessons, doing homework, and getting individual responses at home. This scenario is often extended to the view that self-improvement will win out over ... *Murphy Brown* or *Oprah*. Our own belief is that this is not a question of technology, but of human nature.... We do not think that merging the screen or converging the world of information with the world of entertainment in a "telecomputer" will change the public's palate.[81]

W. Russell Neuman, director of communications research at MIT's Media Lab, conducted a five-year study to examine whether technological advancements like those trumpeted by Gilder will result in a fragmentation, or "demassification," of television's audiences. "The upshot? While the technology of mass communication will change dramatically," Neuman maintained, "the mass psychology and commercial economics of public communication will not." To elaborate, the viewers' "deeply ingrained habits of passive, half-attentive media use" and the industries' "[e]conomies of scale push[ing] in the direction of common-denominator, one-way mass communications" will determine the future direction of the mass audience.

"With some irony," Neuman concluded that "the most prominent result of an expanded communications capacity will be intensified competition for mass-audience tastes."[82] The same would hold true even if there were 500 or more cable channels or a nationwide fiber-optics network. Moreover, in an amusement culture where interactive electronics furnish *Nintendo* today and virtual reality tomorrow, the flow of minor titillations may rise to a flood level.

Granting Pool's and Gilder's projections on the merger of technologies, should such a merger necessarily require absolute First Amendment protection? Any answer must take into account that important consequences flow from ignoring the different technological attributes or commercial uses of the older and newer forms of communication. For example, the oral discourse that was the life force of eighteenth-century revolutionary and nineteenth-century

Simone Weil: ***There has been a lot of freedom of thought***

radical protests at Boston's Faneuil Hall is fundamentally altered when communicated via a staged and sound-bite medium. Merger of technologies notwithstanding, we should pause before equating the different forms of expression for First Amendment purposes. After all, Huxley's dystopia of today may make impossible Gilder's utopia of tomorrow.

The REFORMIST SCENARIO is, at heart, a laudable one. The reformists fight the good fight. Facing a mass culture obsessed with the entertainment fare fed to it by the captains of corporate media, the reformists pin their faith on the good sense of the citizenry and the media's ability to rise above themselves. The reformists neither resort to the censor's heavy hand nor insist on a governmental hands-off policy. They thereby reject the most odious aspects of the classical and modern scenarios. In this sense, reformists are of two minds and appear to grasp the paratroopers' paradox.

Yet their compromise position prompts us to reconsider the earnestness of their First Amendment objectives. Although espousing a platform for media education, the reformist agenda is more political than educational, more of Fourteenth Amendment equality than of First

Amendment rationality.[r] What animates the reformists is the desire to reallocate media power, to wrestle prime time from the commercial haves and to place it in the hands of the public have-nots. The power exchange, on closer examination, may achieve little else.[83]

The public appetite for self-amusement will inevitably corrupt or destroy the reformist educational agenda. For example, once the reformists have created their Audience Network to caution the public to the dangers of commercial broadcasting, who will want to watch it? On the one hand, if Audience Network's entertainment value cannot compete with the commercial media marketplace, it most likely will fail for lack of sustained interest. On the other hand, if its entertainment value is truly competitive, it will undermine its own endeavor to educate the public on media ecology. (PBS has long confronted the same quandary.)

ver the past few years, but no thought.

The Need for Roots, trans. Arthur Wills (Boston: Beacon Press, 1952), p. 33.

If Audience Network (the reformists' electronic town meeting) fails to educate, is there any *First Amendment* justification for grabbing a piece of the commercial television pie? Were they candid, the reformists would likely retort: "As long as we are on the screen, we are doing something." Ironically, this response dismisses all that ever mattered in the classical scenario — that is, the enlightenment rationality so essential to the reformist's high educational mission. Rather, this response blindly accepts the central principle of the modern scenario — media for media's sake. From this perspective, the acquisition of media power has no meaningful First Amendment purpose. If the power exchange alone is meaningful, it is only in an idle and rhetorical sense.

By grabbing power while forsaking core First Amendment values, the reformists cannot mediate between the classical and the modern scenarios. Once the reformists are stripped of their serious educational objectives, they come dangerously close to the triviality that plays so consistently in the modern scenario. The reformists may have grasped the paratroopers' paradox, but they have not escaped it.

---

r) In our discussion of pornography in Book III, we return to the question of the relationship between the principles of equality and free speech.

For now, the PARATROOPERS' PARADOX has survived the classical, modern, and reformist scenarios. Because the paradox remains, each scenario will continue to perplex its respective audience—and well it should. As long as each scenario fails to capture the larger play of forces among them all, its adherents will not understand the fullness of the dizzying paradox.

Understanding the paradox, we admit, creates a profound conflict in our First Amendment thinking. The fundamental tenets of the traditional First Amendment—its anticensorship command and its public-discourse rationale—suggest two different directions for governmental action. The First Amendment in the age of paratroopers tugs between hands-on and hands-off policies.

Quite remarkably, before commercial television was a staple in every household, Aldous Huxley well understood the magnitude of the paradox and its constitutional significance:

> The best of constitutions and preventive laws will be powerless against the steadily increasing pressures of... advancing technology. The constitutions will not be abrogated and the good laws will remain on the statute book; but these liberal forms will merely serve to mask and adorn a profoundly illiberal substance.[84]

Huxley and the paradox challenge us to consider: How do we empower the First Amendment? Must we—and can we—recast it to reconcile old-world Orwellian principles with new-world Huxleyan predicaments? Do we *really* wish to act upon the knowledge of the paradox?

Should we choose to act on our knowledge of the paradox and should we attempt to recast the First Amendment to wrestle with the paradox, there undoubtedly will be something lost and something gained. Whether the something lost or the something gained will render us better off or worse off cannot be resolved at this point. This uncertainty results in part because the Huxleyan predicament has not yet become a factor in First Amendment thinking. Hence, the terrain of the paradox remains virtually unexplored. "We're in unmapped territory," observed Bill Moyers, "where the image is the dominant grammar of our public conversation, and we're not even sure how to think about it."[85]

For now, our paratroopers are assailed by a cloud of paradoxical bullets as they cross the Rubicon and prepare to leap into the new First Amendment terrain. And this all points to the death of discourse? But that, of course, is another battle, another call for hope, and another Book. Meanwhile, there is still time to "talk" about life and death, liberty and law, and other things that matter.

The First Amendment in Bold Relief – A "Dialogue"

A special broadcast from the PBS affiliate in Chicago. Open with Jean-Joseph Mouret's Rondeau from the First Symphonic Suite. This music plays as background for spliced film scenes of Alistair Cooke, the Nixon-Kennedy debates, and occasional cutaways to the 1993 Jeffrey Masson v. Janet Malcolm *libel trial. In his own distinctive way, William F. Buckley introduces the program.*

What follows is a slightly orchestrated print "dialogue"[86] with the late syndicated columnist Max Lerner, University of Virginia political scientist David O'Brien, Northwestern University law professor Martin Redish, Vanderbilt University law dean Edward Rubin, former University of California at San Diego communications professor Herbert Schiller, and Georgetown University law professor Mark Tushnet. Except for the bracketed remarks, the words, though incomplete and rearranged, are theirs (circa 1990) and ours.

Collins or Skover: Mr. Buckley, we very much appreciate your extended and erudite introduction to this exchange.

William F. Buckley: [Gentlemen, I trust that you and your colleagues will live up to our expectations.

Professor Tushnet, how would you respond to the Collins and Skover characterization of today's commercial television?]

Mark Tushnet: I suppose that I have to admit it up front: I like television. And not the television that I'm supposed to like. I find *Masterpiece Theatre* pretty boring and ponderous most of the time. No, the television I like is MTV, some situation comedies, and some evening soaps; when, despite my workaholism, I've been stuck at home in the afternoon, I've been known to watch and enjoy daytime soaps.... I suspect [this] means that I would have to turn in my card for the intellectuals' guild, if I had a card (or if the guild existed).

Martin Redish: Admittedly, much of television's programming is not designed to appeal to the viewer's higher intellectual interests.

But for almost every *My Mother the Car* there has been a *Masterpiece Theatre*. Much of my own childhood interest in politics and history derived from viewing such shows as *You Are There*[s] and telecasts of the national political conventions. Even today, one can learn as much from *MacNeil-Lehrer*, *Nightline*, or *All Things Considered* as from anything available in the mass print media. None of the experts that [you] cite, I am certain, would suggest that the *National Enquirer* (or any newspaper published by Rupert Murdoch, for that matter) provides a more valuable contribution to public awareness than does a show such as *Nightline*.

Koppel & Kermit

Ted Koppel: Have we reached the level of the lowest common denominator? I would argue strenuously that we have not.

—Harvard University Speech, March 1994

Koppel: [T]he line between tabloid and mainstream journalism has become a lot less clear.

— *Nightline*, July 22, 1994

Kermit the Frog (anchor): Do you sort of feel any competitive stuff going on with [late-night entertainers like Jay Leno and David Letterman?]

. . .

Koppel: [W]e're kind of lucky because *Nightline* is the only program that's on at that time of night that is not . . . an entertainment program. . . . [W]e have an audience of people just like your audience . . . , [one] that is not necessarily looking for entertainment. And . . . that's probably a good thing.

Kermit: Sure.

—*Larry King Live*, April 1, 1994

---

s) The program to which Professor Redish referred was a television documentary drama hosted by the noted TV newsman Walter Cronkite. The show ran between 1953 and 1957. It included such programs as "The Salem Witchcraft Trials," "The Gettysburg Address," and "The Fall of Troy."

Collins or Skover: Martin, we generally agree that there is much in popular print that rivals television's triviality. Remember, we suggested as much when we noted that the jester's antics and the tabloid's sensationalism preexisted television's entertainment fare. But there is a larger point here, perhaps implicit in Mark's confession: Today, television is America's favorite form of soma, though by no means the only form. Even if there are as many *Masterpiece Theatre* programs as there are *My Mother the Car* shows, which is a rather outlandish proposition, the ratings tell the truth—amusing cars trump Alistair Cooke. For example, on the first night of the 1992 Democratic National Convention, more people were interested in Fox Broadcasting Network's *Revenge of the Nerds III* than coverage of the political event by all three of the major networks. As to your other point, we respond: In so far as other forms of soma contribute to our Huxleyan predicament, that only exacerbates the First Amendment dilemmas we identified.

Edward Rubin: Clearly, [Ron and David] are correct in judging Huxley's vision more prescient for our society.... [T]he unending flow of trivial, mindless entertainment is as American as apple pie. Television's role in American culture is evident in our popular characterization of television as the "boob tube," and its devotees as "couch potatoes."

Buckley: [What are we to make of the various First Amendment arguments advanced by our two constitutional paratroopers?]

Redish: With friends such as [Collins and Skover], the First Amendment right of free expression surely needs no enemies.

Skover to Collins: Does he mean that as a compliment?

Redish: To comprehend the dangers of excluding the electronic media from the scope of the First Amendment, one need only imagine the parade of free speech restrictions that would then become perfectly constitutional. The government could eradicate from the airwaves all shows urging a political position that it finds offensive. In addition, the government could ban all independent and uncensored news broadcasts and fill the airwaves with twenty-four hours of military music. Our electronic broadcasts would then resemble those heard and seen in Iran or Eastern Europe—or at least those broadcasts that used to be heard in Eastern Europe.... If our society sufficiently trusted those in power not to infringe on the freedom of speech and press, the First Amendment would not need to exist in its counter-majoritarian form.

Collins or Skover: Martin, we certainly have no quarrels with you about the evils of twenty-four-hour broadcasts of military music.

Redish: More importantly, fundamental principles of American democratic theory, of which the First Amendment is an outgrowth, rebel at the notion that an agent of the government—whether it be the judiciary, the legislature, or an administrative censorship board—may usurp the individual's right to decide what speech is valuable and what arguments are persuasive.

...[B]ecause a censorial approach to the First Amendment rejects the basic notion of individual intellectual integrity, any attempt by a governmental unit to gradate First Amendment protection on the basis of wholly subjective judgments concerning intellectual quality and merit runs directly counter to the essence of the First Amendment.

Rubin: [Ron and David's thesis] is provocative because it attacks the most sacred cow of liberalism; it recommends that we rethink our First Amendment doctrine, which entitles all forms of communication to full constitutional protection.

...The view that free speech is a basic value emerges from a belief in individual freedom, because free speech is an essential component of individual freedom as we understand it.

...The great insight of liberalism is that individual liberty itself can be used as a collective value; we as a society can design our mechanisms of collective action to maximize individual liberty. We thus declare that the goal of government is to have no self-generated goal—that government is an instrumentality designed to serve the people's needs. If that purpose is our political morality, we should not sacrifice free speech for participation. We should grant television, as speech, full First Amendment protection.

Collins or Skover: You two stake out a position that many of our readers—lawyers and nonlawyers steeped in the liberal tradition—are likely to hold initially. And like Martin, they may remain silent on the central question we posed—whether the Huxleyan lure of television's commercial entertainment culture collapses First Amendment liberty into First Amendment triviality.

Martin, yours is a somewhat elusive position. At the same time that you categorically refute our argument, you remain curiously mute about its central thesis. Your stance is predictable. The strength of your position, which we labeled modernist, depends upon a crucial move. Essentially, you confine the terms of the debate to a *single* concern—the Orwellian fear. Hence, you evaluate our argument by the very first premises we called into question. Specifically, we questioned whether the Orwellian threat of government tyranny is any longer the most serious threat to freedom of expression. We asked whether the commercial mass-communications culture fundamentally promotes any state of mind other than self-amusement. But by removing these questions from the debate, you dismiss de facto the Huxleyan dilemma.

Such counterattack and silence are entirely understandable. Why? Because any other response might concede that the self-realization principle is, or is becoming, one of self-gratification. You theorize that the First Amendment ultimately serves one high purpose—individual self-realization. Will you permit individual self-*realization* to be recast as individual self-*gratification*? Will you be willing to abase your elevated theory of First Amendment value to correspond with the realities of a commercial amusement culture? If so, there is no dispute among us that a once-respectable First Amendment theory may champion First Amendment triviality.

David O'Brien: The First Amendment's guaranties of free speech ... effectively relegated all political ... "truths" to matters of private opinion. The persistent problem for liberalism, as Professor Walter Berns observed [in his book *The First Amendment and the Future of American Democracy*], is simply:

> Liberalism knows nothing about happiness; [hence] there can be no official answer to the most important question: How shall I live? The role of the properly constituted government is therefore confined to guaranteeing the conditions that allow each man to pursue his privately defined happiness. Liberalism preserves the private sphere and fosters the self-defined private life.

What [Ron and David] ultimately invite us to consider is how the crisis of contemporary liberalism is no longer over the age-old concerns of *preserving* what liberalism cannot itself generate or command from the people. Liberalism must now *defend* the noble dream of the First Amendment and our capacity for public discourse and self-government against the new threats posed by the emergence of a "commercial and technological culture." Is the business of America really business? Are "We the People" really capable of deliberative choices and self-governance? Is liberal legalism capable of responding and reforming itself? Is there even an audience any longer interested in debates over the crisis of liberalism and public discourse — is anybody still really reading and thinking? These are some of the larger political questions provoked by the paratroopers' paradox.

"Holmes and Brandeis, dissenting."

A concept as dead as the two who made it famous.

Collins or Skover: David may be on to something here. For Martin and Ed's observations now put the modernist's First Amendment in bold relief. To give rhetorical currency to First Amendment theory, the modernist has long had to cloak the self-gratification principle in the garb of something more ennobling. There can never be a divide between self-realization and self-gratification for the simple reason that the modernist cannot tolerate any value judgments necessary to drive a wedge between the two.

Max Lerner:[t] Self-gratification involves the fulfillment of pleasures, whereas self-realization is a reaching for the fulfillment of total selfhood. I find fault with First Amendment doctrines if they indulge the immediate impulses to self-expression at the expense of values that are more integral to personhood and the culture as a whole. The problem, of course, is who is to decide. The answer must lie not only in the courts, but in the examined consciousness of a total culture out of which the courts derive their life view.

Tushnet: [I] take a somewhat skeptical view of the arguments presented by [Ron and David]. In part my skepticism arises from what seems to me their rather ahistorical understanding of the relation between popular media and political culture....

t) Sometime after this exchange, our lively friend Max Lerner crossed the Great Rubicon in June of 1992. One of his last published works is *Nine Scorpions in a Bottle* (New York: Arcade Publishing, 1994). Fight on, Max!

The historical point is simple. [You two], like many commentators uncomfortable with the present state of political discourse, appear to romanticize the past.... [T]o the extent that we examine political discourse in the decades after the expansion of the suffrage, we will find many of the same attributes that so disturb [you] about contemporary political discourse. Calling the Democrats the party of "Rum, Romanism, and Rebellion" is not that different from [the 1988 Bush campaign's] invocation of Willie Horton. And "Ma, Ma, where's my Pa? Gone to the White House, ha ha ha" is a bit less edifying as an expression of what we now call the character issue than recent expressions of that issue. Finally, the yellow press of the turn of the last century was surely the equivalent of the sound bite of thirty (or fifteen, or nine) seconds in today's technologically different society.

Rubin: [I have similar concerns. It] is inaccurate... to compare television programming to novels that could be read by only a literate minority, or to theatrical productions attended by the upper classes, to say nothing of comparing it to Locke's *Two Treatises on Government*. Of course, in a few extraordinary places, such as ancient Athens or Elizabethan London, the general population may have appreciated the very finest literature. But even these places were rather limited segments of their larger societies; the average Spartan or Boeotian was not attending Euripides's plays, nor were the great mass of rural peasants in Elizabethan England appreciating Shakespeare.

In fact, we really have very little information about the entertainment preferences of the average person in premodern society. The lower classes, as they were known then, certainly had less leisure time than their modern counterparts. Much of what they did with that time is lost to us because it was highly localized and generally unrecorded. We know that sometimes they sang and danced to charming music, told imaginative stories, or made beautiful handicrafts, but in admiring the results of these pursuits we are seeing the distillation of many centuries of activity. More often, probably, they stared into space or watched chickens bite each others' heads off. We really do not know, and most of our efforts to surmise are distorted by our pastoral nostalgia.

Collins or Skover: Of course, we generally agree with both of you that television did not invent the superficiality or triviality of America's political or other public expression. Here again, we emphasized that point several times. But we maintain that the commercial television culture has accentuated and amplified the superficiality and triviality of public discourse. Todd Gitlin summed it up well for us: "[T]here is precedent for a shriveled politics of slogans, deceit, and pageantry. But precedent is nothing to be complacent about when ignorance is the product."[87]

Tushnet: Romanticizing the past has a particularly troublesome effect on [your] argument for it leads [you] to overlook the possibility—which I would call an established proposition—that the forms of popular culture encode the culture as it exists.

... My own view is that people generally get what they want out of their culture, or, to put it differently, people make their culture as they want to make it.... What is more important, however, is the way in which people come to want what they want. There are some possibilities for manipulation, of course, but there are also some, and I believe substantial, limits on the ability of people to manipulate the deepest preferences of others. One such limit is that the manipulative aspects of cultural productions may give rise to audience resistance to the manipulation, leading to their reinterpretation of the productions.

... If, after all, political discourse has degenerated to the point at which citizens cannot understand the basic issues of contemporary politics, and if one of those issues is precisely the degeneration of political discourse, people will not *want* to adopt [regulatory reforms]. In short, if people have been successfully manipulated to have a certain set of desires, anything aimed at reforming the system that allows this manipulation is ruled out essentially from the start.

Collins or Skover: Basically, Mark, you point to the possibilities of political reform, albeit outside of established governmental channels. Resistance—the popular refusal to be manipulated in a particular choice of pleasures—is a potentially liberating force. This resistance, we believe, is what you hold out as the new First Amendment freedom. Aldous Huxley astutely perceived the predicament for political resistance within the modern popular culture: The crisis of modernity, he emphasized, is "the problem of happiness."[88] The central problem is one of people loving their servitude. Mindful of the Huxleyan perspective, we find your resistance thesis troubling for at least two reasons.

First, like Martin, you stand on an Orwellian platform and thereby discount the possibility of other tyrannies. Your idea of resistance is premised on the opposition of forces between the oppressed and their oppressors: The popular culture will evade domination by corporate tsars who attempt to dictate its tastes and co-opt its pleasure preferences. Your argument implies that the new totalitarianism resembles the old. This implication, of course, is what we deny first and foremost. The "problem of happiness" is that there is no *opposition* of forces, but a *marriage* of them. The bosses of the commercial amusement culture neither dictate nor co-opt the people's pleasures; they feed them indiscriminately and unceasingly. The new tyranny—which is self-imposed as much as it is other-imposed—extols such "freedoms." Any brand of soma is available. Consume as much as you want.

"Commercial television culture": A case of two "adjectives" devouring a noun.

Not surprisingly, commercial television pitches its product in ways to please the populace, in a grammar of diverse and amusing images. This is the democracy of the senses, the language of the commercial MTV generation. This is communication by music video, by powerful pictures rather than precise words, by short and disjointed visual messages. As MTV executives realize, any other communication talks "the [w]rong [l]anguage to 'TV [b]abies.'"[89] To appreciate the Huxleyan tyranny in the marriage of commerce and self-gratification one need only consider the classicist protests of Bill Moyers, the media critic: "If we continue to live in a never-never land of feeling good, ... if every message that comes to us has a hidden message of selling us something, if we try to govern ourselves by the pleasure principle, this 200-year-old experiment is finished."[90]

Our second objection to your resistance thesis is this: Who really is the romanticist here? When you invite popular resistance to commercial manipulation, you imagine a fight that is simply not fightable. As we have explained, the struggle against Huxleyan tyranny can be neither waged nor won on a syndicalist-versus-state-type battlefield. Mollie Steimer, Jacob Abrams, Hyman Lachowsky, and Samuel Lipman, the defendants in the celebrated 1919 *Abrams* case, would have nothing to resist in the Huxleyan state. Theirs was an Orwellian dissent, one out of character in the pleasure regime.

Here, once more, is the Huxleyan First Amendment in bold relief. The free speech principle is more rhetorical than real. With no iron-fist Orwellian danger, people no longer need James Madison's guaranty. Conversely, the 1791 constitutional defense mechanism cannot guard against the despotism of pleasure.

Mark, perhaps we "read" too much into your comments and you do not place full stock in the resistance thesis. If so, you may end up trading romanticism for powerlessness. You "say" that "political discourse has degenerated to the point at which citizens cannot understand the basic issues of contemporary politics, and if one of those issues is precisely the degeneration of political discourse, people will not want to adopt [regulatory reforms]." In sharp contrast to your reformist resistance thesis, here you appear willing to accept the Huxleyan dilemma.

Lerner: [Ron and David] present our legal culture, in its problems of First Amendment interpretation, with a threatened coup of dilemma thinking. In an age of electronic images, they comment, we face the choice either of being permissive toward a hedonic, self-gratification culture or of confining our culture with regulatory denials. The first choice would move us toward a Huxleyan pleasure-trap dystopia, the second toward an Orwellian thought-police dystopia.

Collins or Skover: Obviously, Max, we make our arguments at some necessary level of generality. We cannot say all of this is true for all Americans, at all times, and at all places. The question is, where are we *tending* and what should we guard against?

Lerner: We need some historical perspective here. The image itself has existed in people's minds from the time of Plato's cave. It is true that with the new communications technology, more people are caught up in a barrage of images. It is also true that too often the images are torn out of context, thus rendering sustained discourse more difficult. The impact of this technology on the marketplace of ideas, however, is more debatable than [the two of you] suggest. The image implanted on my retina by print, or by the screen, resounds in my mind with a whole set of other images that I have generated or picked up in my life. I mix them and take a leap of the imagination, setting the images within the frame of concrete experience, concepts, and ideas. Does this experience turn my mind into a clone of the economic marketplace? [As George and Ira Gershwin wrote in *Porgy* *and Bess*], "it ain't necessarily so." I find that the imaging in which I am soaked can goad and spur the vaulting of my own imagination. This phenomenon happens to everyone in the culture. Whatever the dominant academic culture may think of the "mass society," our culture probably represents the most creative civilization in modern history.

Collins or Skover: It is noteworthy that you mentioned the myth of the cave and the matter of creativity in the same breath. Recall, Max, that in Plato's famous cave reality is seen as "nothing other than the shadows of artificial things."[91] Indeed, there is much creativity in the cave, obviously too much! And is that not precisely the issue we need to address?

Lerner: [Yes, your argument] is a powerful piece of intellectual construction, and it could offer fruitful avenues of speculation in legal philosophy.

Collins to Skover: Does he mean that as a compliment?

Lerner: Yet, as often happens with dilemma thinking, however dramatic the horns of the dilemma, one questions the reality of the dilemma presented. The problem with dilemma thinking is the necessarily dichotomous nature of its either-or imperatives. The decision-making aspect of the judicial process veils the fact that if you get far enough into any problem you find fewer dichotomies than polarities. There are polar fields at the deep structure of human life that both oppose and intersect each other. It is always good advice to flee dichotomies and seek polarities.

...Is it hopeless then to steer a legal course between the Huxleyan pleasure trap and the Orwellian police state? I say no, at least not if we free ourselves of the two extremisms that I have noted—First Amendment absolutism and a totally permissive values relativism. Once free, we can address ourselves to the real problem—the spectrum of choices between indispensable freedoms, cherished personal preferences, business and financial interests, technological realities, and cultural and social desirabilities. These choices do not come neatly packaged in dichotomies or dilemmas, but in an ever-varying mix of elements that criss-cross each other and need disentangling. It will strain even the best of jurisprudential minds to draw a line of desirability when the spectrum doesn't come pre-demarcated for the line to be drawn. To paraphrase Holmes in his 1928 dissent in *Louisville Gas & Electric Co. v. Coleman*: Looked at by itself without regard to the necessity behind it the line seems arbitrary. But a line there must be.

Collins or Skover: Clearly, you're troubled by what you see as "dilemma thinking" in our work. Without addressing the full breadth of your concern, allow us now to respond by way of two points. First, whatever else its merits, dilemma thinking is salutary at *this* stage in First Amendment discourse. Emphasizing, as we do, a dichotomy between the Huxleyan and Orwellian evils goads those in and outside of the law to consider what is almost always ignored, namely, the Huxleyan dimension. If we are to have a "spectrum of choices" as you say, some real measure of dilemma thinking must be present. We cannot make a real choice, a real assessment of things, unless we are fully aware of the obstacles at play. And when it comes to the Huxleyan threat, we as a society are virtually oblivious to it. Second, we are at a loss why you are rather skeptical of our dilemma thinking and yet so freely embrace what you call polarity thinking. In this context, is there likely to be any significant difference between the two?

Lerner: Helplessness is not part of my vocabulary. I believe not just in the competition of ideas, but in the generation and creativity of ideas. The American people, once they are clear about purposes, have never lacked resourcefulness in ways and means to bring those purposes about. The intellectual elite, to a great extent, see us as a mass culture and a dying Roman empire. But we are Greece as well as Rome, and—however different the forum—the element of creativity exists in us, much as it did in Athens.

We once had the mystique of rational discourse—that of taking other people's ideas and our own seriously and using communication media to express them. What has happened to it? Why are so many intellectuals so obsessed with our commercial culture and its communication technologies that they no longer have an abiding faith in the possibility of widespread rational discourse? I suspect that the larger culture does not feel this pessimism. But a determinist, antibusiness culture is more likely to feel it; and along with it comes a mindset hostile to the new technology. . . .

I do not believe that these are insoluble problems for a creative civilization. One of the symptoms of decline and eventual death in the Roman empire was the feeling that it was surrounded by insoluble problems. I think that a dialectic of polar thrusts and choices exists, and that what we regard as an insoluble problem is simply a more complex dialectic or polarity of those thrusts and choices. In the end, this dialectic can tame and control our technology as it has done with technologies in the past. I don't say that it necessarily *will*; I say that it can....

In its remarkable trajectory thus far, America has transformed its technologies and has been transformed by them, always emerging as a more complex organism. It is a mistake to think of the current technology merely as a new toy for the senses, a new "thing" to be possessed and exploited, a new form of materialism.

Collins or Skover: We take hope, Max, from your ever-optimistic emphasis on the ascendant side of life and the mind. But we may all need the grace of Clare of Assisi, the patron saint of television, in order for your hopes to be realized.

As you defend American ingenuity, we cannot ignore that the key word in your credo is "complex." That an "organism" is "complex," as you put it, does not necessarily mean that it will be *better*. And as we suspect you know, when speaking of our culture it may be impossible to treat the two words as synonymous. After all, Max, you yourself have warned against "[u]nchecked capitalism in the marketplace of ideas" and likewise cautioned that "with the thrust of technology, the dangers [of the commercial culture] are very much present."

With a strong faith, you seem to dismiss the Huxleyan dilemma while grudgingly confessing its significance for the modern First Amendment. Well, maybe this is what you call polarity thinking. For us, it's still a dilemma by any other name.

Rubin: [Ron and David] have concentrated only on the effect of television, and not on its meaning for people in our society—its "essence," if one wants to use a fancy term.

...[Meaningful political participation] at either the national or regional level is not an opportunity available to everyone; the scale is too large, the issues are too complex, and the required resources are too extensive. Most people who participate in any meaningful sense either command considerable power or participate as a full-time occupation. The image of virtuous citizens coming home from work to engage in political caucuses over the weekend and then present their conclusions to the legislature is rather fanciful....

The participatory ideal of citizens who inform themselves, engage in lively debate, and make their views known to those in power is outmoded. It simply is not practical in a vast, bureaucratic state in which each national representative has a constituency of at least half a million people....

In this political context, the importance of television is its meaning and inherent nature rather than its influence. In essence, television is our link to national and regional government, the medium connecting us to institutions that otherwise would be impossibly remote....

Television provides a sense of immediacy and direct connection for members of a mass society. Through television, we see and hear our political leaders and watch major events as they unfold.

...With the exception of a few unusual places in a few unusual times, most people probably spent the vast bulk of their leisure time on entertainment rather than on political debate. What television does, however—and this effect is central to its meaning—is to nationalize entertainment.

Collins or Skover: That is an excellent point, Ed.

Rubin: Throughout the country, people are watching the same shows at the same time. They are listening to the same sports event or to regional events interconnected through nationally organized leagues. Entertainment programming thus provides a sense of direct involvement with national events, just as news does. While news is obviously more closely related to politics, the interconnection that televised entertainment provides is far from being politically irrelevant. Such diversions secure our sense of ourselves as a nation, as a single group with a stake in each member's welfare.

In short, television creates an electronic network that connects several hundred million people across a continent to a single source of entertainment and information. It provides us with a common set of direct experiences, a shared body of images, situations, and events. Its meaning for us lies in this interconnection; we perceive its programs not simply as news or entertainment, but as *national* news or entertainment. Thus, television is intimately linked to our concept of citizenship.

Collins or Skover: Are you about to "say" what we think you are?

Rubin: [Yes.] Being a citizen of our nation and participating in its collective life includes obtaining information and perhaps entertainment through television. Indeed, this activity may be the average person's most important political act.

Collins or Skover: Martin, did you "hear" that?

Rubin: Voting in elections and contributing financially to political causes are brief, infrequent activities; obtaining information, however, is continual. For the politician, perhaps, information is important only when it affects such "bottom line" activities as voting or contributing. But from the citizen's perspective, acquiring information is an activity with value independent of its ability to guide votes or channel contributions. It is the most basic act of participation in the nation's collective life.

Collins or Skover: What was only latent in Martin's modernist view of the First Amendment is perfectly manifest in your version, Ed. You *appear* untroubled by the collapse of self-realization into self-gratification. As we understand you, the essence of First Amendment political action in the commercial amusement culture is to elect to watch television together—as you put it, this "may be the average person's most important political act."

Surely, this admission must be disconcerting to modernists like Martin. Ultimately, you vindicate the liberal First Amendment, but on terms that the modernist typically does not countenance. You relinquish as any primary value of the First Amendment the heightened norms of reasoned self-governance or self-realization. Indeed, we all become individuals intent on self-amusement who exercise our freedom as political animals to choose what television program to watch. Understandably, then, your First Amendment paradigm cannot be Athens; it is Huxley's soma tablet dispensary.

Again, the modern First Amendment is cast into bold relief. To borrow from you, Ed, "[t]he participatory ideal of citizens who inform themselves, engage in lively debate, and make their views known to those in power is outmoded." In short, "participation is not really a basic value in our normative scheme," as you've noted elsewhere. If this characterization appears odd, it is only so in light of the Orwellian perspective of the First Amendment, and not in light of the Huxleyan perspective of the modern First Amendment.

Buckley: [As you undoubtedly know, Professor Schiller, conventional First Amendment wisdom holds that *government* is the central threat to free expression. Do you believe this still to be so in our advanced market economy?]

Herbert Schiller: Historically, people viewed the source of the danger as the state.

... The [First Amendment framers] could hardly have foreseen Time-Warner, the Gannett Newspaper chain, General Electric's National Broadcasting Company, and media predators like Rupert Murdoch, Robert Maxwell, and Silvio Berlusconi.

... [Ron and David] fully recognize the media conglomerates' dominion over television and the press in general. [You two] are thoroughly familiar with the mechanics by which the media service, and live off of, the marketing needs of the rest of the corporate economy....

[Your] focus and emphasis, however, are puzzling. Despite the overwhelming evidence of corporate control of the media, [you] give priority to a subjective factor as the active and primary agent of the current cultural condition. [You] consistently define the "public's insatiable appetite for amusement," "the modern obsession with self-amusement," "the human drive for pleasure," "self-gratification," "the self-indulgent bent of a mass entertainment culture," and the "public appetite for self-amusement" as the central source of the problem. Despite an uncommon knowledge of contemporary capitalism's elaborate and sophisticated message-making apparatus, [you] thus wind up perilously close to blaming the victim—the public—for the appalling state of what now passes for democratic discourse....

Collins or Skover: Where, then, does the blame lie?

Schiller: Instead of regarding the public as the source of the problem and the First Amendment as an obstacle, we should place the main responsibility for present conditions on the basic drives of an unbridled market economy, a responsibility shared with the market economy's supportive legal pillar. With this starting point, the current scene becomes the most advanced stage in capitalism's long history of advantaging property rights. Beginning with the ownership of land, the advantage has progressed to industrial capital, and now to information....

Who then threatens public expression in America in the 1990s? Is it the individual's weakness and self-indulgence? Or is it an insatiable systemic need to envelop audiences with marketing messages, machined to smooth out all critical thought? If it is the latter, how may the problem be addressed? Must government destroy the First Amendment to prohibit a commercially sponsored tidal flow of triviality? Perhaps the question can be redefined to mandate a review of the role of the corporation in national existence?

Included in such a redefinition would be the reconsideration of several questions. Should huge private aggregations of assets continue to be regarded as persons? Should these persons possess First Amendment rights? Would the revocation of these rights threaten the rights of individual citizens? Is it possible that there is no Orwellian ogre in our future after all, unless we create one?

Collins or Skover: No doubt, Herb, just raising these questions makes many Americans anxious. If you're going where we think you are, then with friends like you the First Amendment needs no enemies.

Schiller: [I]f the public appetite for self-amusement is so powerful, perhaps more is needed than a reformist agenda narrowly focused on television. [You two] acknowledge the corporate connection to the media system. Why not then go to the source of the problem?

Television, as a medium, is not responsible for the enfeeblement of national public discourse. Neither is the weakness of the human species. It is the corporate capture of the total social organism—its political, economic, and cultural elements (especially the informational component)—that constitutes the core and urgent contemporary political problem.

O'Brien: [Ron and David's] quarrel . . . is not with the technologies of mass communications per se, but instead with commercial television. It is the marriage of traditional entrepreneurial economic interests with the technologies of mass communication that particularly worries them, though they find no less disturbing the commercialization of the print media with "advertorials" and corporate-sponsored books and publications.

. . . The paratroopers' paradox and the twin nightmares of Orwell and Huxley, in other words, raise larger questions about the sources and ways of American life. These questions run to the Constitution's creation of a large commercial republic and to the problems of education and morality in a liberal democracy and self-governing society. The "new commercial and technological culture" is rooted in

William A. Galston:
The gateway to the mind of America did not have to be rammed open by alien philosophy, the Enemy Without, for it was swung open to the invader by our inchoate longing for the beyond, the Enemy Within.

"Socratic Reason and Lochean Rights," *Interpretation* 16 (1988):101.

liberal capitalism. The Constitution created a large commercial republic and secured private economic rights to unlimited acquisition, and thereby effectively substituted private material acquisition for a public morality.

Collins or Skover: You are puzzled, Herb, by the emphasis that we place on the subjective factor, the public's obsession with self-amusement. You contend that in doing so we level blame primarily on the victim, the public, for the trivialization of democratic discourse. Rather, as we have stressed, it is the *combination* of commercial exploitation and the age-old drive for self-gratification that most threatens freedom of speech in America in the 1990s. We address a complex phenomenon of mutually interactive forces: a public weaned on entertainment feeds an industry that, in turn, feeds the public entertainment culture. In the brave new world, the captains of power dispense soma tablets, which the public is hungry to devour.

Without focusing, as we do, on the psyche of the American people, your reformist proposal may prove ineffectual. Requiring corporations to take responsibility for the dreadful state of public discourse, you consider unplugging the First Amendment cord from the commercial amusement industry. But is it possible to eliminate the Supreme Court's corporation-as-person doctrine without accounting for the ideology of the private corporationist state that America was and continues to be? Even putting aside the need for judicial line-drawing among types of corporations, could this reformist view take hold in an ever-increasing corporationist and consumerist America? Max deftly captured the point, "[a] capitalist culture cannot exist without capitalist values." Hence, "[w]hen the ends are the bottom line, the means become a profit nexus and a money ethic."

Some reformists, such as Newton Minow and Craig LaMay, have searched for a middle ground. For example, in their book *Abandoned in the Wasteland* they call for a variety of federal statutory and constitutional reforms in addition to technological reforms (e.g., V-chips on TVs) in order to improve the informational and educational content of programming, especially children's programming. However noble such efforts, are they not destined to collide head-on with a commercial culture and a body of First Amendment doctrine largely hostile to such "paternalism"?

Much more than First Amendment doctrine must change—and change radically, we think—before your reformist solution to the paratroopers' paradox can become a realistic one. Such reform may be less a jurisprudential program for resolving our First Amendment dilemma than a political program for the fundamental redesign of American society. This jurisprudential program might become a more realistic possibility were fundamental shifts in the American political and socioeconomic culture to create an environment conducive to judicial reform of constitutional doctrine governing corporations.

Schiller: In fact, [you two] recognize that the technology of television does not float free, so to speak, of social relationships. [You] write that it functions alongside "the commercialization of television as a profit-oriented enterprise." *It is necessary to give this relationship more emphasis.*

Collins or Skover: All right, Herb. Turn the page, as we go to that very point now in the next Book.

Buckley: [Gentlemen, you're mixing media. Even so, we look forward to what you have to "say." Meanwhile, thank you all for your participation in this thought-provoking exchange. Ladies and gentlemen, good night from Chicago.]

Book II
Commerce & Communication

It is a matter of public interest that [private economic] decisions, in the aggregate, be intelligent and well informed. To this end, the free flow of commercial information is indispensable.

—Harry Blackmun[1]
(jurist)

Great advertising is a storyteller, a romantic voice, an emotional persuader.... It must persuade in a way that romances and lures the customer unsuspecting into the brand's sticky web.

—David N. Martin[2]
(adman)

When we use TV, we're not using it to support First Amendment rights or artistic freedoms, we're using it because it's a good business decision for our client.

—Betsy Frank[3]
(adwoman)

Commerce & Its Handmaiden: Then & Now

MTV video shot of Madonna singing "Material Girl" with a neo-blues-beat romp. ♫♩ ♫♩ *"We are living in a material world, and I am a material girl."* ♩ ♫♩ ♫ *An elegant and coquettish Madonna continues to praise the coin of capitalism. Then all join in the chorus: "Everybody is living in a material world."* ♫♩ ♫ *Cut to text.*

Communication is the handmaiden of commerce.

America's channels of public expression serve more and more as the purveyors of private profit. Daily, our nation's mass media cater to the desires of the marketplace as they deliver a feast of messages to consume. These messages remind us, as does Madonna's music, that "we are living in a material world."[4] Yet these messages are more than solicitations to buy—they are the codes of our culture. In this commercial domain, we stand to become the sum of what we buy.

"We live by symbols," said Oliver Wendell Holmes.[5] No symbol is more celebrated in our system of free speech than his icon of the marketplace of ideas.[a] In the *ideal* marketplace, there is a "free trade in ideas" that fosters rational decisions by the citizen. In the *actual* marketplace, however, there is a free trade in commercial images that encourages fantasized decisions by the consumer. Much discourse moves between these two poles, though America's commercial culture tends ever more away from the ideal and toward the actual marketplace. Ironically, this actual marketplace is often surreal: It is

a) Though the metaphor is typically attributed to Holmes's dissent in *Abrams v. U.S.* (1916), Holmes wrote only of a "free trade in ideas" and "the competition of the market." Reportedly, it was Justice William Brennan who coined the "marketplace of ideas" metaphor in *Lamont v. Postmaster General* (1965). See Haig Bosmajian, *Metaphor and Reason in Judicial Opinions* (Carbondale: Southern Illinois University Press, 1992), pp. 49–72.

a place where the consumer exchanges money for magic, where commercial communication promises fantasy more than utility. This, at least, characterizes much in the marketplace of ideas as it operates in our system of mass advertising. It is a system frequently premised on the substitution of imagery for idea. Thus, it transforms the marketplace of ideas into a marketplace of commercial images.

In our culture of advanced capitalism, there is a striking redundancy in the notion of "commercial speech."[b] More specifically, public expression cannot be significantly separated from the influences of commercialism. As Burt Neuborne, a First Amendment authority and a spokesman for the Association of National Advertisers, accurately observed: "As a means of expressing shared values and a common national ideology, advertising dwarfs any other genre of communication."[6] To ignore the influences of commerce is to misunderstand the nature of much speech in modern America. To overlook the relationship between commerce and communication is to place the First Amendment in a false light. To comprehend more fully the phenomenon of commercial speech, we must look beyond First Amendment cases and commentary to the *actual* ways in which our culture communicates about and through commodities. We must think less about the marketplace of ideas and more about the marketing of items. Today, we can learn more about the operations and values of social communication from Saatchi & Saatchi[c] than from Holmes and Brandeis.

Jerome Barron:
Our constitutional theory is in the grip of a romantic conception of free expression.

"Access to the Press," *Harvard Law Review* 80 (1967):1641.

To this end, we start from the beginning. In what follows, we open with an account of the commercial message-making industry and the culture of modern mass advertising. This account marks the move-

b) Unless the context indicates otherwise, when we use the expression "commercial speech" or its equivalents, we refer to forms of communication that (1) presume a seller-buyer relationship and/or enhance the ethos of consumption, (2) are mass-oriented, and (3) are primarily imagistic in character.

c) Saatchi & Saatchi became one of the world's largest advertising agency holding companies in 1986 by mergers and takeovers that created a company with $7.5 billion

ment from the product-information format that typified early mass advertising to the "lifestyle" format more in vogue today. We then examine the processes and consequences of modern mass advertising and contrast these to a model that we label "classified communication." Next we discuss two key free speech values—rationality and individuality—as they are reconfigured in the new ages of "reason" and "self."[d] Finally, we explore free speech options in our capitalistic system and suggest that, in much of our culture, image is all, truth is irrelevant, there is no right to know, we are as we consume, and there is no Absolut® right of dissent. Against this backdrop, if modern commercial expression is to be constitutionally protected in a more honest way, it is primarily because it is speech in the service of selling. What this portends for the individual and the culture, and for the defenders and critics of commercial speech, is the larger subject of all that follows.

How do we communicate with each other?

This is as much a question about commercialism as it is about discourse. Whether public or private, our communications are infused with the objects, the symbols, and the ideology of commercialism. We talk about commodities, we refer to ideas and feelings given symbolic form and meaning by commodities, and we express the cultural values embodied in our commodified social system. But how does that system work?

The HISTORY OF MODERN ADVERTISING is the story of the general movement from product-information to image and lifestyle advertising. Spanning the period from the advent of the Industrial Revolution to the present, modern advertising has shifted its primary direction and focus. Once largely a utilitarian vehicle for informing the consumer about the construction, operation, and benefits of goods or services, the advertisement has become more of a transformative vehicle. Mass advertising now typically encodes goods and ser-

worth of business. By 1995, co-founder Maurice Saatchi quit the firm amid controversy, while his brother Charles remained.

d) Rational decisionmaking and individual self-realization are not the only values that theoretically may be promoted by the First Amendment; they are nonetheless among the central values most frequently invoked by courts and legal commentators to justify the extension of constitutional protection to expressive activities.

vices with symbolic meanings independent of their functional values.

Of course, advertising has been a staple of commerce in economies since ancient times. In primarily oral cultures, street merchants "shouted out the advantages of their pottery, fabrics, cattle, and even their slaves."[7] One of the oldest known written advertisements is a 3,000-year-old Babylonian tablet requesting the return of a slave. Centuries later, Johannes Gutenberg's invention of movable type ushered in a new age of commercial communication. The first printed advertisement in English appeared in 1477, announcing the sale of Easter rule books published by William Caxton. Shop signs and broadsides nailed to public buildings were common advertising devices prior to newspapers. By the middle of the seventeenth century, British newspapers, known as "mercuries," spread a variety of notices ranging from merchant shipping tables to patent medicine advertisements. In the American colonies, as many as ten of sixteen newspaper columns were set aside for advertising in the first daily newspaper. Prior to the Civil War, most newspaper advertising consisted of merchants offering goods and services to customers in their own locales. The styles and objectives of early newspaper ads became the models for the first period of the modern era of advertising.

As America became more industrialized from the 1880s to the 1920s, mass-appeal advertising paralleled the mass production of goods. Nationwide advertising directed the public's attention to the increasing variety and quantity of products distributed on a nationwide basis. The primary focus of most advertising design and copy during this period was the product itself—its construction, its performance, its uses, its price, and its advantages. *Product-information* advertising aimed both to familiarize the newspaper reader with the national brand and to introduce new products and educate the consumer as to their purposes. When Daimler and Benz's automobiles first appeared in 1885, when Eastman Kodak's cameras were first produced in 1888, and when Marconi's radio was first heard in 1896, manufacturers turned to advertising to explain the products to prospective consumers and to rationalize their purchases.[8]

Ad copywriting took on a formulaic style, popularized as "reason-why" salesmanship by the celebrated admen Albert Lasker and Claude Hopkins.[9] The turn-of-the-century trade journal *Printers' Ink* described reason-why copy as "[l]ogic, plus persuasion, plus conviction, all woven into a certain simplicity of thought—pre-digested for the average mind, so that it is easier to *understand* than to *misunderstand* it."[10] A revealing example of this advertising style was the 1905 advertisement for Gillette razors in which "we find testimonials, scientific data from the University of Chicago, and an exploded drawing of the new instrument."[11]

In brief, the basic character of advertising in the early modern period was more information than image, more rational than emotive, more need-based than desire-based. Thus, prior to the 1920s, "the implied relationship between people and products [was] utility.... The question for the consumer [was], What does this product do?"[12]

The product-information advertising form declined significantly after the 1920s. Generally speaking, it was replaced by a model of competitive mass advertising that stressed product imagery and product personality. *Product-image* advertising placed commodities within natural or social settings (such as landscapes or households) in order to project the meanings and values associated with those settings onto the commodities. Similarly, *product-personality* advertising equated the personal attributes of individuals (product users or members of a particular social group) with the qualities of the commodity. In its most exaggerated form, this advertising culminated in the personification of the product itself, infusing commodities with human traits or animal characteristics. Thus, for example, a fragrance could be sexy or a vehicle tigerlike.[13]

As product-information advertising yielded to product-image and product-personality advertising, "the older factual, prosy notice which focused upon the specifications of the commodity... gave way to a more lyrical type of appeal which focused instead upon the desires of the consumer."[14] Charles Revson, the founder of Revlon, Inc., acknowledged as much when he claimed: "In the factory we make cosmetics, in the store we sell hope."[15] Revson's point prompted cultural critics such as Guy Debord to argue that the "real consumer thus becomes a consumer of illusion."[16] Influenced by the new forms of advertising, the meaning of the commercial exchange altered fundamentally. Transactions of money for product image and personality largely eclipsed the earlier transactions of money for product utility. This new economic exchange was predicted by an early twentieth-century adman, James Collins, who presciently labeled it an "economy of symbolism."[17] Later, in *The Mechanical Bride* (1951), an equally prescient Marshall McLuhan analyzed the nonrational advertising phenomenon as aiming "to generate heat not light."[18]

A combination of factors interacted to promote the emergence of product-image and product-personality advertising between the 1920s and the early 1950s. Among the most significant were the commercial use of photography and radio, the rise of parity products, and the nascent industry of audience demographics and market-segmentation strategies.

Information Advertising—an idea that's gone the way of the Remington typewriter.

Technological developments, primarily those in photography and radio, offered novel and dynamic opportunities for the presentation of products. Importantly, photography's representational realism conveyed images as old print illustrations never could, and radio's sound conquered distance and time in transmitting commercial messages. Marketers exploited the possibilities of photography by intensifying the symbolic association between goods and the consumer's self-image. The "new possibilities for the visual in advertising ... stimulated the development of emotional, affective, or 'mood' advertising."[19] Likewise, marketers exploited the potential of Marconi's medium by commercializing radio's content and revolutionizing advertising's form. For example, today's popular soap opera[e] is the progeny of radio's experiments in blending dramas with detergents. Under the influences of photography and radio, product facts yielded increasingly to product fictions, and utility deferred increasingly to fantasy.

Additionally, competitive mass production resulted in substantially similar consumer goods. Products, standing alone, were essentially indistinguishable by their ingredients and functions. Numerous beverages, breakfast foods, cosmetics, and detergents, for example, became "parity products," set apart only by their brand names. "If products [did] not differ materially, they [could] nonetheless differ or be made to differ in *attributed* qualities, or 'image.' If consumers

e) "The soap operas were written by the agencies and usually revolved around emotionally excruciating family dilemmas. The challenge was to develop product 'tie-ins.' The term 'soap opera' itself, of course, refers to the sponsorship of detergent manufacturers and testifies to the blending of advertising and programming." William Leiss, Stephen Kline, and Sut Jhally, *Social Communication in Advertising* (New York: Routledge, 1990), p. 141.

believe[d] a product to be distinctive, this belief in itself [could] become a product attribute."[20] Marketers began to differentiate goods less by factual product information and more by product image and personality. "When brand image represents the only distinctive feature the advertiser has to sell, he is more likely to use irrelevant and nonrational appeals."[21] Essentially, advertising parity products took much of the reason out of reason-why copy.[22] As adman Rosser Reeves explained anecdotally: "Our problem is—a client comes into my office and throws two newly minted half dollars onto my desk and says, 'Mine is the one on the left. You prove it's better.'"[23]

Audience demographics and market segmentation strategies were among the more significant responses of the advertising industry to the parity-product phenomenon. Armed with data about prospective consumers—age, profession, income, gender, geographic locale—the advertiser could target that segment of the population most susceptible to a particular commercial message. Earlier advertising agents had sold *products* for manufacturers; by contrast, demographic and segmentation strategists now sold *audiences* to manufacturers. For example, once advertising agents identified the special audiences of certain newspapers and magazines, they could better align those audiences with their clients' products. As advertising historians Charles Goodrum and Helen Dalrymple put it, "[agencies] designed ads that 'looked like' the identified audience, talked like it, [and] were shown doing the things that audience did."[24] In like fashion, "[p]ublishers began to regard their publications not so much as products to be sold to readers, but more as vehicles that organized audiences into clearly identifiable target groups that could be sold to advertisers; [thus,] the audiences themselves became the 'products.'"[25] From this vantage point, the early notion of "product placement" meant placing potential buyers in the laps of manufacturers and distributors.

In sum, commercial photography and radio broadcasting "caused the first cracks to appear in the strictly rational orientation of the product-information format."[26] And as goods became more indistinguishable, advertising pitches became more distinctly alluring. Similarly, whereas the focal point of reason-why advertising campaigns was "*What* does this product do?" the focal point for audience demographics and market segmentation was "*Who* will buy this product?"[27] Cumulatively, these factors increasingly distanced advertising from factual product information.

Notions of lifestyle preoccupied the American mind more and more in the late 1950s and throughout the 1960s. At one end of the cultural spectrum, the newly released Xerox copy machine became a corporate status symbol, while at the other end the beatnik movement captured the imagination of the young. Increased affluence and the widespread popularity of television, among other things, opened the door for advertisers to promote the lifestyle ethic. Once inside, the advertising industry told commercial stories that linked the individual to a social group or to an economic class and simultaneously associated products with the style of consumption of that group or class.

Lifestyle advertising typically portrayed work activities (the homemaker baking or the office executive negotiating) or leisure scenes (golfing or entertaining) and depicted products as essential elements within those contexts. This form of advertising thereby gave the impression of a connection between the lifestyle and the product. For example, life insurance could be sold not by explaining actuarial facts and premiums, but rather by picturing tender moments of a loving family around the hearth, a family whose security needed to be ensured. By way of another example, it was the "Pepsi generation"—surfing, dancing, racing—that lived life to the fullest. In regard to deciphering these messages, Professors Leiss, Kline, and Jhally explained: "[T]he unifying framework of interpretation is action or behavior appropriate to . . . a social group or situation, rather than use, satisfaction, or utility."[28] The lifestyle format predictably distanced advertising even further from utilitarian messages and their reason-why logic.

The commercial television format and more sophisticated demographic research strategies fostered the growth of lifestyle advertising. Time took on a new meaning when commercial television was the medium. Programming of all kinds—from news broadcasts to miniseries—was delivered in compact packages suitable for the sale of advertising time blocks. Ever-rising costs cut the advertising slot into increasingly narrower time frames. The original one-minute commercial was replaced by the thirty-second one, which was in turn reduced to a fifteen-second blip. Obviously, time constraints had their impact on the logic of advertising; when seconds were the measure, there was little time for reasoned argumentation, comparative analysis, or meaningful product information. Lifestyle advertising's seductive images could have greater impact within such crammed quarters.

With Freudian fervor, "psychographics" revealed what was latent in earlier research: Consumers could be divided into market segments characterized by particular personality makeups, and advertisers could use this knowledge to their profit. "The ultimate goal of this research approach is to develop a group's so-called psychographic portrait, consisting of generally applicable personal values, attitudes, and emotions."[29] Psychographics, so prevalent in the 1970s, was supplemented or replaced by "geodemographics," which differentiate markets along postal zones with special social characteristics.[30] Aided by these more refined profiles, advertisers could better identify and exploit the wish-fantasies of potential consumers. Like demographic research prior to the 1960s, psychographics and geodemographics sold "segmented" people to producers, who in turn sold products to the segmented marketplace. Accordingly, psychographics and geodemographics further marginalized the role of product facts in favor of lifestyle images.

Advertising today need not be one-dimensional. To a greater or lesser degree, it may tap into all of the historical marketing formats: information, image, personality, and lifestyle advertising. The choice or mix of advertising forms depends on the intended audience, the product or service type, the social context for use, and the advertising medium employed. Consumers are likely to look for more product information in advertisements of certain items (e.g., homes) than others (e.g., cosmetics).[31] Obviously, advertising does not speak in the same tongue to all people at all times for all things. Still, the appeal to the nonrational pervades much of contemporary advertising. That appeal may manifest itself in different fashions, but generally it remains dominant. Like a milder form of "ice-nine" in *Cat's Cradle*,[f] it permeates everything.

---

f) *Ice-nine* was the fictional substance imagined by Kurt Vonnegut Jr., the ribald American novelist and former General Electric employee who wrote *Cat's Cradle* (New York: Holt, Rinehart & Winston, 1963). A "tiny grain" of ice-nine caused atoms of water to "stack and lock, to crystallize, to freeze" in a "novel way," resulting in a chain reaction that could invade all objects and freeze the entire earth. True to fiction, years later Vonnegut commercially exploited his novel ideas by designing an ad for a popular brand of vodka. See Maureen O'Brien, "Absolut Vonnegut," *Publishers Weekly*, 22 May 1995, p. 11.

Facts and figures alone reveal the telling link between commerce and communication:

- Each day of our lives, 12 billion display ads, 2½ million radio commercials, and over 300,000 television commercials are dumped into the collective consciousness.

- Advertising consumes almost 60 percent of newspaper space, 23 percent of network television prime time, 18 percent of radio time, and over 50 percent of magazine space.

- The U.S. Postal Service annually processes 38 billion assorted ads and 14 billion slick mail-order catalogues.

- During a lifetime, most people will devote a full year and one-half to watching commercials.

On the eve of the twenty-first century, America's marketpla

- TV home-shopping stations already reach some 50 million homes, generating $3 billion in annual sales.

- Product and service messages are plastered on everything from the painted sides of cows to dyed hot dogs, placed strategically in everything from books to movies, situated on everything from billboards in space[g] to the bottoms of holes on putting greens, pumped into everything from doctors' reception rooms to grade school classrooms, zapped through everything from phones to fax machines, and launched into the far reaches of computer "cyber-space."

- The *Philip Morris Magazine*—a slick and upscale periodical—boasted a circulation of more than 12 million, making it one of the largest circulation magazines in America.

g) The Space Advertising Prohibition Act of 1993 was introduced in the 103rd Congress to keep the heavens free of commercial advertising. With the failure of the proposed act, its looming First Amendment litigation issues were temporarily suspended.

- Over half of all American journalism and communications students forsake the fourth estate for careers in advertising.

- All this and more are made possible by the some $149 billion dropped into advertising annually.

- And the electronic highways to the future are already being paved with untold commercial possibilities spanning from advertiser-produced interactive computer programming, to interactive home-shopping, to a new computerized generation of infomercials, to on-line advertising.[32] Inevitably, the once ad-free Internet will be overrun by commercialism.

But this is only the quantitative side of the story. Qualitatively, what can we say about commercial communication? Ideally, "advertising is simply the distribution of information about products . . . that

ideas has largely become a junkyard of commodity ideology.

enables consumers to make rational choices."[33] Ideally, it satisfies the high mission generally ascribed to commercial expression by economists. And ideally, its effects are confined to commercial transactions. Does the ideal, however, comport with reality?

Advertising mogul John O'Toole[h] did not think so: "In reality, advertising is not about products but about a person and his life."[34] Echoing O'Toole, advertising industry experts Al Ries and Jack Trout held that advertising "concentrate[s] on the perceptions of the prospect. Not the reality of the product." They continued: "One prime objective of all advertising is to heighten expectations. To create the illusion that the product or service will perform the miracles you expect. And presto, that's exactly what the advertising does."[35] Illusion, not reality, is the referent. It is the thing sought and the thing bought. Elaborating on this theme, advertising critic Linda Benn maintained: "Although advertisers ostensibly sell products, their true stock-in-trade is the image, which portrays ideals, values, and ways of

h) John O'Toole was chairman of the board of the Chicago-based Foote, Cone & Belding, one of the world's largest advertising agencies. He remained president-CEO of the American Association of Advertising Agencies through early 1994.

life in the service of one thing: to get the consumer to buy, usually with appeals that have little connection to the product's intrinsic value."[36]

What precisely characterizes the phenomenon to which these commentators refer? Generally, the mass-advertising process takes from the culture, transforms what it takes, and then tenders back what it took and transformed. More specifically, the advertiser appropriates the culture's images and ideas and then associates them with particular products and services. By this association, a subtle but significant metamorphosis occurs: The meanings of images and ideas are infused into products and services, just as the meanings of products and services are infused into images and ideas. Once this metamorphosis is complete, advertising releases the altered meanings back into a commercialized world ready to deliver products and services.

There is something of a parasitic quality about such advertising. It feeds on the organisms of noncommercial culture—the culture's past and present, ideology and myths, politics and customs, art and architecture, literature and music, and even its religions. Moreover, "[c]ertain values such as love, friendship, neighbourliness, pleasure, happiness and sexual attraction are the staple diet of advertisements."[37] In general, advertising indiscriminately and completely draws from these sources their essential symbols. But in another sense, advertising ceases to be parasitic: Having reworked the meaning of cultural symbols, it sends them back in commercial forms. Thus understood, advertising "does not reflect meaning but rather *constitutes* it."[38] A moment's deliberation will reveal an irony here, one best articulated by an advertising executive: "[W]hat we're doing is wrapping up your emotions and selling them back to you."[39]

Mortals yearn for meaning, for ways to structure existence. Ready to exploit this yearning, the advertising system provides us with structures of meaning in the name of consumption.[40] Gillian Dyer describes advertising's process for structuring meaning in the following way:

> [Advertisements] create structures of meaning which sell commodities not for themselves as useful objects but in terms of ourselves as social beings in our different social relationships. Products are given "exchange-value": ads translate statements about objects into statements about types of consumer and human relationships.... And once this initial connection has been made we almost automatically accept the object for the feeling. People

> and objects can become interchangeable as in, for example, the slogans "The Pepsi generation," "The Martini set."[41]

The "exchange-value" enables us to think of products in terms of power, beauty, success, and the like. In a more socially objectionable way, this exchange value may prompt us to think of and relate to people in terms of products. For example, women are commodified to sell everything from cars to colognes. Their bodies, their sexuality, and their mystique are traded in countless economic transactions. Advertising thus pimps its products.

Only select values are traded in advertising's exchanges, however. Life is pictured as a Land of Oz—but without the Wicked Witch. It is a land of perpetual bliss, abundance, and novelty. Whatever darkness there is can be lightened by advertising's magic. Such fantasy communication requires that certain kinds of information about products and services be suppressed, for example, "the conditions of work in factories[,] the level of wages and benefits of workers[,]... [and] the effect on the environment of producing goods through particular industrial processes."[42] These and other *real*-world facts are anathema to advertising's mission. Bleak truths and cynical attitudes must be kept at bay. Select information thus becomes the whole truth.

In sum, today's mass advertising often has less to do with products than lifestyles, less to do with facts than image, and less to do with reason than romance. It is more a total cultural system than an exclusively informational one; it is "a social discourse whose unifying theme is the meaning of consumption."[43] This system refactors the marketplace-of-ideas equation: The *ideas* component is de-emphasized in favor of the *marketplace* component. "Commercial culture assigns no value or meaning to communications apart from their market value."[44] Hence, in the commercial culture, truth is that which sells.[45]

The Truth of Power

William Leach: Whoever has the power to
project a vision of the good life and make it prevail
has the most decisive power of all.

Land of Desire: Merchants, Power, and the Rise of a New American Culture
(New York: Pantheon Books, 1993), p. xiii.

Commercial Communication & Its Consequences

What follows when the values of communication are fused to the market? That is, what are the cultural ramifications of the commodification of discourse? Consider the following:

- The logic of discourse changes as commercial communication moves further and further away from the informational format.

- By commercially recontextualizing images and ideas, mass advertising debases the core values once associated with them.

- Insofar as certain forms of advertising succeed, the identity of the consumer is continually reshaped by a relationship to goods and services; indeed, the identities of goods and services themselves are reshaped as they are invested with fetishistic powers far exceeding their normal utility.

- Because of mass media's heavy reliance on advertising revenues, advertisers may directly influence the content of communication and indirectly reshape the media in their own images.

- A primary constant in mass advertising is the message to change products and services constantly—communication in the service of waste.

- When messages are disseminated largely because of their market value, the ideals of citizen democracy succumb to those of consumer democracy.

- As politicians mimic the strategies of mass marketing, the line between important political discourse and advertising becomes increasingly opaque.

Having summarized these consequences, we now probe each in turn.

Distortion of Logic and Debasement of Values

The 1960s African-American political declaration "Black is Beautiful" became a promotional anthem for hair products. Marketers later capitalized on the "X" in Malcolm X to sell baseball caps that since have become fashion statements.[46] John Lennon's "Revolution" became a commercial cause célèbre for peddling sneakers, even as the songwriter warned listeners to "free your mind instead."[47] Women's equality became synonymous with the liberty to smoke: "You've come a long way, baby!" Meanwhile, gasoline and chemical companies polluted the communications environment with unspoiled views of snow-capped mountains and green fields. Other advertisers identified silverware with the timeless beauty of spruce trees. A shirt commercial showed only a daisy field as the voice-over assured us that "[t]his shirt makes you *feel* like a daisy."[48] And Betsy Ross's Old Glory is waved constantly in the hawking of everything from clothes to cakes.

Nothing is sacred in the mass advertising world, either logically or normatively. Logically, there is often no rational connection between the commercial image and what is being sold. For example, is Brand X silverware *truly* like a spruce tree? How? Why is it more like a spruce tree than nonbiodegradable plastic? Or does wearing Brand Y shirt *truly* make you feel like a daisy? Why? And what does it really mean to feel like a daisy? Such a misuse of language occurs when words are divorced from any logical referent, what the French sociologist Henri Lefebvre has called "the decline of the referentials."[49] The logic of mass advertising capitalizes on meaninglessness. If intelligible at all, it is a special brand of logic. Jules Henry, in *Culture Against Man*, labeled it "pecuniary logic: ... a proof that is not a proof but is intended to be so for commercial purposes." Henry explained:

> This kind of thinking—which accepts proof that is not proof—is an *essential* intellectual factor in our economy, for if people were careful thinkers it would be difficult to sell anything. From this it follows that in order for our economy to continue in its present form people must learn to be fuzzy-minded and impulsive, for if

> they were clear-headed and deliberate they would rarely put their hands in their pockets; or if they did, they would leave them there. If we were all logicians the economy could not survive.[50]

One need not be an Aristotle, a Bertrand Russell, or a Willard Quine to understand a troubling truth latent here: "[I]n order to exist economically as we are we must try by might and main to remain stupid."[51] If these assessments seem exaggerated, then consider the views of an advertising insider. In his book *Strategy in Advertising*, Leo Bogart, the former advertising executive and vice president and general manager of the Newspaper Advertising Bureau, put it this way: "[Advertising] has helped devalue the coin of communication by developing a massive, unthinking tolerance for nonsense.... We are forced to take for granted too much that is ridiculous."[52] Indifferent to such criticism, the advertiser exclaims: *Vive la bagatelle*![i]

Moving to the normative realm, when the mind makes a quantum leap from a culture's values to the commercial objects with which they are juxtaposed, it does so at a cost to the traditional meaning of those values. For example, why should the ideal of nonviolent social reform as heralded in the song "Revolution" be equated with Brand X sneakers? Can this be done without perverting the songwriter's hope to "change the world"? T. J. Jackson Lears offered this response: "Think, for example, of the beating that words like... 'revolutionary' have taken in the consumer culture. One does not need to assume a precapitalist unity between word and thing to concede... [that, u]nder capitalism, visual and verbal signs become detached from all traditional associations and meaning in general is eroded."[53] Additionally, why should the ideal of the flag (raised at Iwo Jima) be the stock-in-trade of jeans and pastry ads? Do we not risk debasing the symbol of American sacrifice by these associations?

These examples demonstrate that the energizing of the commercial culture occurs, in part, by enervating the noncommercial culture; the meanings of commodities develop as the standard meanings of symbols collapse. Advertising, thus understood, "waters down values, wears them out by slow attrition, makes them banal and, in the long run, helps Americans become indifferent to them and even cynical."[54] This can be seen by way of two striking illustrations. In the summer

i) "Long live triviality!"

of 1991, National Public Radio aired the following interview concerning the advertising strategies of a major clothing manufacturer:

> **National Public Radio interviewer Linda Wertheimer:** [T]hree controversial [double-page clothing] ads depict a very young nun kissing a priest, a newborn baby only seconds old and a little blonde white girl next to a little black boy whose hair is fashioned in something that looks a little bit like horns. . . . What about these ads? What do nuns and priests, and newborns and little toddlers, blonde and black, have to do with selling T-shirts?
>
> **Bob Garfield, advertising critic for Advertising Age:** An important element of this whole campaign is to create controversy and generate publicity, which not only has a media value all of its own, it also enhances every consumer's exposure to [the clothing manufacturer's] ads. . . . So that when you're paging through some magazine and run across a picture of this newborn baby covered with the blood and the vernix and with the umbilicus still attached, instead of casually passing it, being aware of the controversy, . . . you're apt to look at it more seriously and to react one way or another.

Commenting on what he called "distraction marketing," Mr. Garfield continued:

> These ads were created for the express purpose of ticking people off, for creating controversy, for inflaming consumer outrage and so forth and so on. . . . It's really very cunning advertising . . . for a lot of reasons.
>
> Not only is there the publicity benefit, they also are a great example of what I call distraction marketing, and it's distracting because rather than focus on trying to . . . come up with some sort of rational benefit for buying a $49 cotton T-shirt, which [the clothes manufacturer] knows is not a rational kind of consumer behavior, they're kind of supplying a little three-card monte in creating a distraction over here so you won't pay attention to . . . the facts of the matter being that a $119 cardigan sweater is not a particularly good buy.[55]

Thereafter, the same national clothing company mounted a $60 million advertising campaign aimed at shocking the consumer and presumably at enhancing the products' name recognition. In the service of selling jeans and sweaters, the magazine ads depicted real-life tragedies: an anguished family at the bedside of a dying AIDS victim; three women mourning over a shrouded corpse, apparently shot and left to die in a pool of blood in the street; hundreds of refugees frantically swarming aboard a ship at dock; and an armed soldier clenching a human bone.[56] In these and similar ads, the explicit commercial message was limited to a colorful company logo strategically situated in the scenes. These advertisements were an extraordinary way to provoke public attention, draw media publicity, and apparently engender future profits.

Advertisers even plug into religion to preach their commercial gospel. For example, a radio station's billboard depicted Pope John Paul II listening to a stereo headset and read: "Father Knows Best."[j] Another billboard ad displayed a Catholic sister singing along to the tunes on her radio with the caption, "Nun Better." And "Simple Gifts," the nineteenth-century Shaker hymn that once was "a paean to a purified, moral life," has been used to hype everything from Oldsmobiles to TV miniseries.[57] Still other ads are similarly brash but are not always perceived as such. For example, an advertisement for extravagant jewelry in the form of a cross ran in a Florida newspaper[58] on Good Friday in 1991; it urged readers, "Share Our Passion." What is even more amazing than the advertiser's boldness is that the ad drew little or no public complaint. (We suspect that Bernardino of Siena, the patron saint of advertisers,[59] would deny his blessings to such missions.)

Don't Look Back

Bob Dylan: It's easy to see without lookin' too far that not much is really sacred.

"It's Alright, Ma (I'm Only Bleeding)," Columbia Records (1965)

News Item: Dylan's 1963 ballad, "The Times They Are A-Changing," is now a jingle in a commercial TV ad.

Steve Jamison, "Bob Dylan, King of the Jingle," *San Francisco Examiner*, 14 February 1994.

j) It is a sign of our commercial times that Madonna dedicated her 1990 album *The Immaculate Collection* to "The Pope, my divine inspiration." The dissident Sinéad O'Connor's *Saturday Night Live* insult to the pope prompted sharp public criticism; Madonna's comment drew virtually none.

Such advertising is as much, if not more, a commentary on the transformation of basic values in the commercial culture as it is a description of the products for sale. In fact, the creative director who designed the startling clothes campaign professed only to be illustrating socially significant events: "[E]verybody uses emotion to sell a product. The difference here is we are not selling a product. We want to show... human realities that we are aware of."[60] Admittedly, such advertising, whatever its purpose, may sometimes have collateral positive effects, as perhaps in directing the public's attention to social issues. The point, however, is that the commercial culture is ultimately enhanced even when the advertiser identifies a socially significant issue as its own on which to pronounce. From this vantage point, the American culture is no longer commercial simply because it values materialism and furnishes an abundance of consumer goods. Ours has become a commercial culture in a much more intrinsic and pervasive sense. The beliefs, ideas, and behaviors that mold or reflect our national character are now re-created in a product's image. Once this occurs, the old norms take on a new meaning inseparable from the commercial ethic.

Conversion of Consumer and Commodity Identities

"I think, therefore I am," said René Descartes. Were he alive today, Descartes more appropriately might say "I buy, therefore I am." In effect, the founder of modern philosophy would be confirming that, in our consumer culture, to be is to buy, and what is bought identifies who we are.

Mass advertising does more than sell goods and services; it is a discourse of symbols that *characterizes* consumers. Insofar as certain forms of advertising succeed, the identity of the consumer is continually reshaped by a relationship to goods and services. Advertising critic Judith Williamson captured this point: "We differentiate ourselves from other people by what we buy.... In this process we become identified with the product that differentiates us."[61] Differentiation and consumer self-identification are, of course, the objectives and the modus operandi of modern marketing strategies: Many advertisements portray reality with personality attributes and lifestyle images. Advertising displays the kinds of cars we should own, the kinds of clothes we should wear, the kinds of alcohol and soda we should drink, the kinds of perfumes and colognes we should use—in short, the kinds of people we should be.

The lesson of advertising is that we learn who we are by how, and by how much, we perceive existence through a commercial lens. Our discourse and visions of life are colored by advertising's fictions. "[W]hether or not it sells cars or chocolate, [advertising] surrounds us and enters into us, so that when we speak we may speak in . . . the language of advertising and when we see we may see through schemata that advertising has made salient for us."[62] By this process, we are invited to invade the bodies of commercial fantasy figures and become them—making us "body snatchers" in the marketplace.

Beyond reshaping our identities, advertising reshapes the identities of goods and services as it invests them with fetishistic powers far exceeding their normal utility. In primitive magic, a fetish was an amulet or talisman that carried a spirit's powers. In current usage, a fetish is any object infused with an emotional charge. With the decline of reason-why advertising, it did not take marketing experts long to appreciate the fetishistic potential of advertisements. A 1912 trade journal suggested as much: "[It is] possible through advertising to create mental attitudes toward anything and invest it with a value over and above its intrinsic worth." Only a decade later, advertising agent James Wallen proclaimed that "you do not sell a man the tea, but the magic spell which is brewed nowhere else but in a teapot."[63]

A consumer culture that savors a particular liquor because it helps on "the rocky road to love," that splashes on a particular cologne because "everyone needs a hero," or that writes with a particular pen to create literature as great as "The Case Book of Sherlock Holmes" is a culture that injects products with powers.[64] It is a culture in which "[i]deas, feelings, time past and time future, worlds and people can all be miraculously contained in objects. . . . Life and meaning are attached to objects that might seem worthless in themselves. In all societies but our own we call this fetishism."[65]

Redefining the Medium and Its Messages

What is the connection between advertising revenues and the forms and functions of media? It has long been assumed that media managers have regarded the public as their principal customers, that publications and programs were themselves the primary products that the media delivered, and that commercial messages should be independent from noncommercial messages. These assumptions implied a hierarchy of communication that elevated content over commerce.

Generally, these assumptions are less and less valid. The new assumptions are the exact opposites of their predecessors. Media managers now regard advertisers, not the public, as their principal customers. The media now deliver readers and audiences as "products" to the advertisers.[66] And the wall between commercial and noncommercial editorial content is breached regularly. Today, content is not consistently elevated over commerce. In fact, the two are often made indistinguishable.

Examples are legion. Saturday-morning cartoons frequently are guises for extended toy and cereal commercials. More recently, advertisers have become bolder, airing full-length children's programs that star animated commercial characters; these characters are drawn from corporate logos that are typically identified with snack-food ads. Even family-hour programming is now integrally blended with commercialism. For example, a well-known fast-food clown, decked in the company colors, reads to children "from a book emblazoned with the company's golden arches symbol." Similarly, "commercials" directed to adults masquerade as regular programming. A syndicated half-hour fashion program, underwritten by marketers, invites TV viewers into department stores to admire the sponsors' products. More daring still, prime-time network TV "commercials" have surfaced as full-hour entertainment specials.[67]

Ad-vice / Ad-infinitum

Infomercials = a sort of mental date rape.

Product placement = a practice so pervasive that it's hard to find "the real thing" any more.

Advertorial = the Trojan Horse advertisers bring into our collective consciousness.

Where commerce and communication mingle so indiscriminately, television becomes "a deregulated fleamarket, an international garage sale," warns CBS *60 Minutes* correspondent Morley Safer. The fleamarket of "infomercials"—programming vaguely identified as commercials—attracts as many as 83 million American viewers a month to a single huckster. The "king of infomercials," Mike Levy, appeared on television "more often than any single person in America, maybe the universe." However cynically media purists might dismiss this phenomenon, Syracuse University communications scholar Robert Thompson countered: "These infomercials . . . are every bit as indicative of our society as *Moby Dick*, *Leaves of Grass*, [and] *The Scarlet Letter*."[68] The truth may be that they are *more* indicative of our society, our commercial culture.

Additionally, media increasingly cater to advertisers by mixing commercial and noncommercial messages in a wide variety of other formats: Documercials, commercial video news releases, product placements, and advertorials are imaginative ways to pitch products.[69] As the commercial line is pushed further into traditionally noncommercial quarters, even media "reports" and "editorials" are too often prepared to satisfy advertisers[70] or produced by the advertisers themselves.[71] In all of this, product-friendly "reporting" appears to honor objective journalistic standards while it advances the special financial interests of advertisers. These practices tend to camouflage the true commercial bent of such reporting and thereby capitalize on the public's trust of noncommercial journalistic integrity. Commenting on such practices, *Washington Post* reporter Paul Farhi has observed that "even the most reputable broadcasters and publishers are knocking new holes in the wall that traditionally has separated news and entertainment from their advertising departments."[72] When this occurs, of course, "hard news" can all too easily collapse into "soft sell," with the result that critical reporting becomes unlikely or even impossible.

Advertising pressure does more than influence content; it sometimes dictates it. Indeed, when advertisers wield their financial clout, they may enforce private economic censorship with a hand as heavy as the government's. Such private censorship may be either direct or indirect. One telling example of direct censorship was the ultimatum of one of America's leading advertisers, Procter & Gamble, that its products could not appear in any print medium that included "*any* material on gun control, abortion, the occult, cults, or the disparagement of religion."[73] An equally telling example of indirect or self-censorship is revealed in the editorial policy of the *Arkansas Democrat* (now the *Democrat-Gazette*): Editorial content must not be critical of advertisers. In a blunt and unusually candid explanation of the paper's policy, managing editor John Robert Starr said: "Our policy is no different from every other paper I know about: People hired as columnists by the paper do not trash the advertisers."[74] Other examples of direct and indirect economic censorship[75] involve reporters' failed attempts to cover topics ranging from prescription drugs to tobacco and alcohol, from car dealers to real-estate agencies, and from cosmetics to fast foods. Even nonlibelous political dissent, when critical of advertisers, is subject to outright suppression.[76]

Commercial speech represents commercial power. That is, advertisers can influence and dictate the content of communication because mass media rely heavily upon advertising revenues. Competition for the marketing dollar is rife. With the multitude of media options and the occasional tightening of recessionary advertising budgets, media managers elect increasingly to please advertisers at almost any cost. This coddling of advertisers' interests is turning the fourth estate into the corporate estate.

Communication in the Service of Waste

The dictionary definition of "consumer" discloses much about the nature of commercial communication. The consumer is the one who destroys or expends by use, the one who devours all. In a highly advanced capitalist world, with seemingly endless supplies of goods and services and a communication network to promote them, this definition takes on an uncommon meaning. Whatever earlier connotation there may have been, today's idea of consumption refers more to gratifying countless impulses than to meeting central needs. "[L]uxury is a necessity of life," reads a full-page department-store ad.[77] This idea is sustained by an advertising system that feeds the voracious mass appetite with the promise of delights in "new and improved" ways of life.

"New and improved" and "distinction with a difference" have become the maxims for an economic regime that relies upon the replacement of products to stimulate its markets. Since World War II, America often has practiced a "dynamic obsolescence" that goads consumers to reject today what was satisfactory yesterday.[78] That goods are often substituted today for yesterday's functional equivalents is of little concern to a commercial system governed by disposability. The primary concern is that the consumer not seriously doubt "the live-for-the-moment ideology that primes the market and avoids the question of the future, except insofar as that future is defined by new, improved items for purchase."[79] Advertising's live-for-the-moment mind-set may temporarily be confined and subdued during periods of economic, political, ecological, or natural disasters. Yet even in hard times, the marketing message remains largely unchanged. Retail consultant Carol Farmer explained, "[t]he marketing challenge of the 90's will be to sell more in an era of less."[80] Visions of yachts, penthouses, and high fashion that once graced the settings for advertising products may yield to more commonplace pictures of public transit, the family home, and rugged outdoor wear; the stress on value may replace the earlier message of luxury; and advertisers may wrap themselves more in the environmental "green" flag than in overt images of waste.[81] Still, in the end, the rule is not conservation but continuous consumption.

Mass advertising both reflects and fuels the process of dynamic obsolescence as it prods consumers to define and redefine their desires. The only constant in mass advertising is the message to change products and services constantly. "Beyond encouraging us to dispose of that which we have and replace it with that which they are selling, 'the commercial message' itself... embodies the ideal of conspicuous consumption."[82] This is not the discourse of conservation; rather, it is discourse in the service of waste.

Citizen Democracy Versus Consumer Democracy

In the dawn of the twenty-first century, much of America's public expression is commodity-fixated—communication about and through commodities. "[A] significant portion of our daily public 'talk' and action is about objects (consumer goods), and about what they can do or should mean for us."[83] The commercialization of communication not only affects our self-identity but also our identity in the American polity. That is, talking about and consuming commodities are now among our most significant "political" acts.

One of the pillars of our ideal of a republican form of government is an informed and active citizenry. Essential to this paragon of democracy is vigorous participation in the processes of representative government, reasoned decisionmaking, equal responsibility to the community, competent exercise of the franchise, and, when needed, meaningful dissent. Candidly, this eighteenth-century revolutionary notion of democracy ultimately cannot exist with a self-indulgent polity and a highly commercialized political state. Broadly speaking:

- the General Will has become the will to buy;
- the Common Good has become common goods;
- liberty from monarchical tyranny has become liberty for market choices; and
- the public forum has become the shopping mall.

Civic republican notions of equality anchored in the bonds of mutual obligation run adrift in a sea of commercialism that equates equality with "keeping up with the Joneses" or, for the fortunate, "keeping up with the Gateses." In short, our citizen democracy has become, in Stuart Ewen's words, a "consumer democracy."[84]

In a consumer democracy, consumption is the *raison d'être*. It is the "premise for 'human liberation,' to be attained in lieu of, and despite the failures of, social and political liberation." Indeed, the ethic of consumption now acts as the intermediary between the state and the individual. Consumption is "institutionalized, not as a right or enjoyment, but as the citizen's *duty*."[85] Whatever is made of this insight, it animates the daily workings of much of our advertising. When one of the citizen's highest duties is consumption, the traditional values of political discourse can plummet to their lowest level.

Commercialization of Politics

The concept of the voter as consumer necessarily leads to the concept of the politician as seller. "The fact that election campaigns are indistinguishable in form (and often in content) from product marketing campaigns is the single most dramatic instance of the triumph of the advertising model of persuasive communication in modern society."[86] As early as the Eisenhower-Stevenson presidential contest of 1956, *Nation's Business* magazine predicted that Democrats and Republicans alike would market candidates using the same techniques that advertisers employ to market products. Over thirty years later, for example, the 1988 Bush-Dukakis election fulfilled the prediction. Convict turnstiles and tanks were among the integral images in the candidates' political plugs.[87]

Advertising-agency professionals serve as "media consultants" to the candidates and orchestrate elections as if they were mass-marketing campaigns. All three of the major candidates in the 1992 presidential election race turned to Madison Avenue gurus. George Bush, Bill Clinton, and even Ross Perot[88] came to realize that "[t]he second most visible part of a campaign, after the candidate, is the advertising."[89] Voter attitudes are studied and the electorate segmented by the same research strategies employed for selling pretzels and beer. By the grace of audience demographics and psychographics, the candidate becomes a "package put together by pollsters, image-makers, pulsetakers, and speech writers."[90]

All throughout, candidate *image* governs, and reason-why information is too easily disregarded. That is, a candidate is contextualized in some peculiar but sympathetic environment while concrete and detailed discussion of important issues of the day is largely forsaken. Both advertisers and politicians appreciate the force of repetitive and concise slogans. In the 1992 presidential election campaigns, for example, Bill Clinton rarely spoke without invoking the pitch "courage to change"; meanwhile, the incumbent George Bush asked again and again, "Who do you trust?" As politicians master the strategies of advertising, the line between important political discourse and mass marketing becomes increasingly faint. Citizen consumers "buy an argument" with the same pecuniary logic by which they buy products and services. Indeed, presidential aspirant Walter Mondale counseled voters in 1984 to approach politics in the same way they buy burgers[91] — "Where's the beef?"[k]

All of these consequences of commercial communication might prompt us to reconsider the structure of traditional First Amendment analysis. Is the central question, as typically thought, whether commercial expression should receive constitutional protection? Or is it whether the government should act affirmatively to fortify the First Amendment wall against the battering ram of mass commercial advertising? Historically, it was thought that the sole or primary enemy of free expression was the state. Today, the consequences of commercial communication reveal that the private captains of the advertising empire may prove to be an enemy of equal stature. In this light, Justice

k) "Where's the beef?" was a popular advertising slogan for a major fast-food hamburger chain.

Hugo Black's 1945 commentary on First Amendment press freedoms takes on a bolder and broader meaning:

> It would be strange indeed... if the grave concern for freedom of the press which prompted adoption of the First Amendment should be read as a command that the government was without power to protect that freedom.... Surely a command that the government itself shall not impede the free flow of ideas does not afford non-governmental combinations a refuge if they impose restraints upon that constitutionally guaranteed freedom.
>
> ... Freedom of the press from governmental interference under the First Amendment does not sanction repression of that freedom by private interests.[92]

To restructure the First Amendment so as to permit some governmental regulation of corporate advertising messages is to set the legal guaranty against the commercial culture. This point, however, ought not be discussed without first considering what category of commercial communication might buttress, rather than damage, the *traditional* edifice of the First Amendment.

The *ideal* of commercial speech is most fully realized on the daily pages of the CLASSIFIED ADVERTISEMENTS—call it classified communication. Justice Harry Blackmun's assurance that commercial expression will serve the high purpose of intelligent and well-informed decision-making is best exemplified by the following kind of advertisements:

FORD–'76 1/2 ton. 390 w/CJ heads. New exhaust C6, new S. Swampers. $2300/OBO. 703 (123-4567)

Similar informational advertising often appears in the Yellow Pages, in commercial flyers, and on storefront signs. To say that such forms of advertising typify the First Amendment ideal strikes us as comic, as well it should. These holdovers from the era of mercuries, broadsides, and leaflets do not represent the overpowering side of commercial communication as we experience it daily. What, then, are the differences between the classifieds and modern imagistic mass advertising? How do these differences explain the special affinity between the classifieds and Justice Blackmun's First Amendment?

There is an old-fashioned and romanticized quality about classified communication. We expect the seller and the advertiser to be the same person. We assume that the classified ad is directed to individuals searching to buy a particular good. We envision a simple message inviting one-on-one dealing to sell a single item. We look for text that explains the product and identifies the price. Above all, the classifieds represent the world of individualized exchange of commercial facts.

Today's advertising industry stands in stark contrast to the romanticized world of classified communication. Advertising and marketing agencies broker the commercial relationship by coming between seller and buyer. Rather than soliciting ready customers, modern advertising cultivates an overall spirit of buying among the ready and unready.[93] Mass advertising by definition depersonalizes commercial communication. Simple text about product and price is easily overshadowed by metaphorical images and lifestyle messages. Above all, much of today's mass advertising can be classified as fantasy more than fact.

Thus, individual consumers communicate with each other through the classifieds quite differently than marketers communicate with consumers through mass media. (Who of sound mind would respond to a classified for our '76 Ford ½ ton if the ad said only: "This truck will make you feel like an urban cowboy"?) Thus, classified communication resonates more with Justice Blackmun's First Amendment ideal than modern mass advertising can. The ideal derives its staying power from two key values: the worth of the individual and the worth of informed decisionmaking. In principle, if the traditional First Amendment were ever to embrace commercial speech, it would find classified communication the most deserving of constitutional protection.

Commerce, Communication & the Constitution

Two centuries after Patrick Henry of Virginia uttered the celebrated words "but as for me, give me liberty, or give me death!" the keepers of the American Constitution extended that liberty to classified advertising. In *Bigelow v. Virginia* (1975),[94] Justice Blackmun's First Amendment was recruited in the service of an advertisement in the *Virginia Weekly*, which read:

> **UNWANTED PREGNANCY**
> **LET US HELP YOU**
>
> Abortions are now legal in New York.
> There are no residency requirements.
> **FOR IMMEDIATE PLACEMENT IN ACCREDITED HOSPITALS AND CLINICS AT LOW COST**
>
> Contact
> **WOMEN'S PAVILION**
> 515 Madison Avenue
> New York, N.Y. 10022
> or call any time
> (212) 371-6670 or (212) 371-6650
> **AVAILABLE 7 DAYS A WEEK**
> **STRICTLY CONFIDENTIAL.**
> We will make all arrangements for you and help you with information and counseling.

That the First Amendment should be enlisted to protect such communication is not surprising. Conventional wisdom holds that the link between this advertisement and a woman's right to an abortion best explains the Court's ruling. But the conventional wisdom falls short. At stake here was nothing less than the First Amendment ideal embodied in classified communication. This same ideal lies buried in the jumble of the Court's commercial speech opinions and in the clutter of those who defend or criticize those opinions.

A New Age of "Reason"

Western civilization marked the eighteenth century as its "age of reason." The Enlightenment was a period of faith in human reason, of a confidence in the supreme power of rationality to govern all aspects of life. It was the time of François Voltaire, Denis Diderot, Immanuel Kant, and Sir Isaac Newton—all champions of the mind's capacity to ferret truth out of a universe of information. A similar faith permeates the modern writings on commerce and communication. This faith borrows the rhetoric of its eighteenth-century predecessor but applies it to a radically new context—modern mass advertising. From this context emerges a new age of "reason."

Michael Gartner, former president of NBC News, echoed the Enlightenment's call for truth through reason in championing the cause of modern advertising.[l] "Commercial speech is protected," he argued, "because it fosters informed decisionmaking among consumers. It maximizes the flow of truthful information to consumers so that they can make realistic choices as to their needs."[95] Beyond the borders of commercial television, a more sophisticated but comparable explanation comes from the legal academy via Professor Martin Redish (one of our "dialogue" participants in Book I):

> When the individual is presented with rational grounds for preferring one product or brand over another, he is encouraged to consider the competing information, weigh it mentally in the light of the goals of personal satisfaction he has set for himself, counterbalance his conclusions with possible price differentials, and in so doing exercise his abilities to reason and think; this aids him towards the intangible goal of rational self-fulfillment.[96]

l) In the wake of the NBC scandal concerning an allegedly rigged GM truck crash test, Michael Gartner resigned as president of the network's news division in March 1993. See Elizabeth Kolbert, "New President Resigns as Budget and Morale Drop," *New York Times*, 7 March 1993, sec. 4, p. 2.

And of course, in Justice Blackmun's Court "the free flow of commercial speech" certainly "serves individual and societal interests in assuring informed and reliable decisionmaking."[97] More recently, Justice Anthony Kennedy struck a similar note on the tenor of commercial expression: "The commercial marketplace, like other spheres of our social and cultural life, provides a forum where ideas and information flourish."[98]

This "informational function"[99] seems central to the Court's approval of commercial expression as a form of protected speech. Indeed, of the major commercial speech cases in which governmental regulation has been invalidated, nearly all "involved restrictions on either purely or predominantly informational speech, such as the bans on price advertising." By comparison, governmental regulations were sustained in cases not involving "predominantly informational advertising."[100] The Court's rulings affirming the constitutional importance of commercial expression concerned advertisements akin to the classified communication model as we have described it.[101] (Tellingly, some European laws explicitly draw distinctions between "informational and promotional advertising" with differing standards of legal protection.[102])

Although the Court may be perceived as confining its holdings only to classified communication, Justice Blackmun and his colleagues never expressly acknowledged this point. Not surprisingly, avid defenders of commercial speech rights interpret this silence as a license to apply the Court's principles to the full spectrum of modern mass advertising. "We trust individuals to evolve [commercial] preferences in a rational manner," argued Burt Neuborne.[103] Having hoisted the Enlightenment banner, Neuborne and others exhort us to treat all forms of legal advertising as if they were created equal. For First Amendment purposes, a Spuds McKenzie beer ad presumably would deliver as much information necessary to a commercial exchange as did our '76 Ford truck classified ad. If Neuborne and other commercial speech advocates were to deny this, then their routine justification of "informed" decisionmaking would be no more than rhetorical flourish.

Even those who laud constitutional protection for commercial speech freely admit that government may regulate or even ban such expression if it is clearly false or deceptive. This exception derives a good measure of its force from the firm commitment to reason in the marketplace: If commercial communication were patently to subvert informed and rational economic decisionmaking, it would frustrate the underlying constitutional objective. Hence, the glorified mission of agencies such as the Federal Trade Commission is to serve as the watchdog of truth in the marketplace, to preserve some quantum of the old reason in the new age of mass advertising.

By associating itself with the defenders of the old reason, modern mass advertising claims a high level of constitutional protection. But it does so talismanically. Merely by invoking the norm of informed and rational decisionmaking, imagistic advertising professes to promote it. Exploiting the weighty importance of reason for its own ends, such advertising does precisely what it does best: It appropriates the symbols of informational advertising, re-creates them in its

Commercial speech is one of the best

own image, and returns them to the legal community in the form of constitutional defenses. What is returned, of course, is not the old reason but the "new and improved" version.

Distancing themselves from the defenders of the old reason, federal appellate judge Alex Kozinski and attorney Stuart Banner (both of whom will join us shortly in the "dialogue" that follows) feel no compunction to draw on Enlightenment rhetoric in making their constitutional case for lifestyle advertising. At the outset, unlike others, they recognize that the Court's pronouncements on commercial speech say little about how mass advertising actually works. Far from promoting a *rational* transaction, imagistic communication typically "is not commercial speech at all because it does not even meet the threshold requirement of *proposing* a commercial transaction."[104] For them, our Spuds McKenzie beer ad apparently invites the consumer to do nothing more than enjoy the dog's antics. Why, then, protect such expression? In large part, Kozinski and Banner believe that commercial expression cannot meaningfully be distinguished from other forms of protected communication; since much advertising appropriates our culture's political, religious, and social symbols, it falls under their constitutional umbrella. Extend this reasoning, and the Spuds McKenzie beer ad may be re/cognized as an art form.

If we follow the Kozinski and Banner line, mass advertising need not don the garb of rationality. It might claim a high level of constitutional protection because it is part and parcel of most expression, rational or not. Reason-why criteria are no more required in the sphere of commercial communication than they are in that of political communication. Thus, by merging the two spheres, the new reason argues that our commercial culture is beyond enlightenment.

The New Age of "Self"

The Enlightenment was not only the age of reason but also the era of the self. Faith in the individual, the autonomous self, was essential to the eighteenth-century credo. The political and moral philosophies of David Hume, Charles-Louis Montesquieu, and John Locke portrayed the person as a free, rational, and self-governing agent who was both

uys in today's marketplace of images.

the source of political authority and the ultimate justification for its exercise. These philosophers established the intellectual foundations that support much of the current liberal theory of free speech. Grounded in the eighteenth-century concept of the self, First Amendment theory holds that the preservation of conditions for individual self-realization is a central objective of, if not the primary purpose for, free speech rights. At its core, the First Amendment exalts the liberty of individual action through self-expression.

In 1886—the same year in which the Statue of Liberty was dedicated in New York Harbor—American liberty was given a new face. Almost a century after the close of the Enlightenment, the liberty that was once accorded only to individuals was handed over to corporations as well. A unanimous Supreme Court declared that corporations were "persons" under the Fourteenth Amendment and were entitled to the blessings of liberty.[105] "Thus, the Court converted an amendment primarily designed to protect the rights of African-Americans into an amendment whose major effect, for the next seventy years, was to protect the rights of corporations."[106] Remarkably, as historian Howard Zinn reported: "Of the Fourteenth Amendment cases brought before the Supreme Court between 1890 and 1910, nineteen dealt with the Negro, 288 dealt with corporations."[107] Once the self had thus been transformed, it was entirely predictable that corporations would eventually seize First Amendment liberties for their own expression as well.

This constitutional transformation of the individual self to the corporate self has drawn sharp dissent from traditionalists and progressives alike, most recently in the commercial speech context. The defenders of the old self cannot tolerate the idea that the free speech values associated with individual autonomy and self-realization should now be affiliated with corporate communication for profit. One such defender, law professor C. Edwin Baker, argued that, unlike other forms of protected communication, corporate speech for profit does not "create or affect the world in a way that has any logical or intrinsic connection to anyone's substantive values or personal wishes. . . . It lacks the crucial connections with individual liberty and self-realization that are central to justifications for the constitutional protection of speech."[108] So viewed, since corporate expression does not and cannot further the inherent values of individual selfhood, it cannot lay equal claim to First Amendment security.

In the new age of self, not only the corporation but also the individual is given a different identity. Modern commercialism has played a significant role in converting the individual self and the citizen self into the consumer self. The ideology of consumption consists of a value system that equates acquisition with self-realization: "We are living the period of the objects: that is, we live by their rhythm, according to their incessant cycles."[109] Image, personality, and lifestyle advertising nourish the consumer self as they invite us to "recreate ourselves every day, in accordance with an ideology based on property—where we are defined by our relationship to things, possessions, rather than to each other."[110] In all of this, consumerist ideology insists upon the premise of freedom so critical to the traditional notions of citizenship: that we exercise "free choice" in realizing the consumer self that we want to be. Hence, WE THE PEOPLE become a consumer sovereignty.

The defenders of the old self find the development of the consumer self as objectionable as the development of the corporate self. These defenders maintain that mass advertising in a capitalistic order actively "attempts to *create* and *manipulate* values"[111] in ways compatible with profit-maximization. When people and their values are dictated in terms of profit, our system of expression moves away from commercial-free self-determination toward commercial-dependent self-determination. As Jean Baudrillard powerfully put it: "The entire discourse on consumption aims to transform the consumer into the

Universal Being, the general, ideal, and final incarnation of the human species."[112] That is why the defenders of the old self view commercial speech as "directly at odds with the aim of the [F]irst [A]mendment. It denigrates rather than affirms human liberty."[113]

This condemnation of commercial speech could be leveled evenhandedly against all forms of advertising, whether informational or otherwise, as long as classified ads are placed by profit-seeking corporations. In this respect, both proponents and opponents of commercial communication may see no need to distinguish between informational and imagistic advertising, although they arrive at different conclusions. The defenders of the old self, however, would be sympathetic to the model of classified communication to the extent that it fosters expression that is more personalized and less mass oriented, more "reason-why" and less imagistic, and more economical and less extravagant—in short, discourse that is more individualized.

But is there really a place in the age of the new self for individualism divorced from commercialism?

Communication & the Capitalist Culture

One need not master *The Wealth of Nations* or *Das Kapital* to discern that the character of communication in America is largely determined by its capitalistic economic system. The question relevant for an Adam Smith or a Karl Marx—whether the impact of commerce upon communication produces a better or worse society—need not be addressed now. What is more immediately relevant to our inquiry is the question of how the commercial culture of mass advertising affects the key free speech values identified by the Court and commentators.

One thing is absent from most of the learned legal treatments of commercial speech—reality. Few in the law see the need to understand the advertisers' world as the advertisers do. And fewer see the implications of the *actual* workings of advertising on their visions of free speech. Once seen, the connection of commerce to communication radically alters the views of both the defenders and critics of commercial speech.

Eyebites: Reader Support Box

Old Age of Reason =	Notion of commercial speech premised on rational decisionmaking
New Age of Reason =	Notion of commercial speech premised largely on imagistic appeal, though often justified on grounds of rational decisionmaking
Old Age of Self =	Notion of commercial speech premised on the importance of the individual self as a rational decisionmaker
New Age of Self =	Notion of commercial speech that equates the rights of corporations with those of individual speakers, and that equates the citizen-self with the consumer-self

Those who champion the role of reason in the marketplace either do not understand the functioning of today's marketplace or do not understand the function of yesterday's reason. The reality of the mass-advertising marketplace is simply

IMAGE IS ALL

Image, not information, is the touchstone of much of our commercial communication. The next time you think of reason-why advertising, look at any popular magazine:

- Liqueur ad with suggestive beach scene: "All over the country, people are enjoying Sex on the Beach."

- Women's blue-jeans ad with Matisse-influenced drawings and Picassoesque sketches of women: "Woman Combing Hair" and "Woman With Gold Hoops."

- Four-page clothing ad with scenes of a couple hugging and kissing with an American flag waving in the background: "A kiss is still a kiss/The Spirit of Today's Generation."[114]

The flood of such examples from the print and electronic media alike suggests that "the information model has never had much relevance for national consumer product advertising. The explicit function of spectacular image-based . . . advertising is not so much to inform as it is to persuade."[115] Adman David Martin told the neophytes in his profession how important it is to capitalize on imagistic and emotional persuasion: "You will . . . have a hard time finding a truly gifted creative [advertising] person who thinks that straightforward, rational persuasion will be noticed in today's media clutter."[116] And when students of government, law, and journalism consider the famous marketplace-of-ideas metaphor in connection with commercial speech, they should take special note of what advertising expert John O'Toole had to say on the matter: "It is not in the nature of advertising to be journalistic, to present both sides, to include information that shows the product negatively in comparison with other entries in the category."[117] Even if it mattered, who in the marketplace would or could challenge, for example, the suggestions that people are enjoying sex on the beach or that women comb hair and wear gold hoops?

Entire categories of commercial communication are essentially bereft of any real informational content. For cosmetics, fragrances, alcohol, tobacco, clothes, and other products, billions of advertising dollars say much about image and little about information. The mass advertiser all too often strives to create a lifestyle environment with "minimal 'logical' connection with the product."[118] These efforts give new meaning to the Latin root for advertisement: *advertere*—to direct one's mind toward.[119] Indeed, studies indicate that "the depiction of consumers as rational, problem-solving beings is actually a highly limited description of buyer behaviour."[120]

Mass advertisers and their mass consumers have embraced the reality of commercial communication: There is no place for the mind in the marketplace.

Those who rely on the criteria of false and deceptive speech to confine the constitutional boundaries of commercial communication either do not understand the appeal of mass advertising or do not understand its relationship to truth. The reality of the mass-advertising marketplace is simply

TRUTH IS IRRELEVANT

Trained to scrutinize advertisements for accurate informational claims, the public watchdogs (such as the Federal Trade Commission) and their industry counterparts (such as the National Advertising Review Council) have less and less to do in today's imagistic ad world. For example, how would such oversight groups determine the truth or falsity of the following commercial messages?

- Soft-drink commercial depicting a rock singer performing in front of, and mingling with, a teenage audience at a drive-in movie theater: "Don't care about movie stars who live in Hollywood. Don't like their attitude; don't think I ever could. Don't want the good taste, I know what tastes good. Why is the best thing always misunderstood? Just give me what the doctor ordered. Just what the doctor ordered. Hey, give me a [brand named soda]."

- Cigarette ad with a man and two women frolicking in a swimming pool: "Alive with pleasure!"
- Designer-jeans ad with a woman unzipping a man's trousers; opposite page photograph of man raising middle finger of right hand in obscene gesture: [Brand name of product].
- Cologne ad supposedly picturing a father holding his young son: "[Brand name] for Men."[121]

For this and much advertising that is not deliberately and explicitly informational, the dichotomies of truth versus falsity and deceptive versus accurate are purposeless. The hyperbole created by image, personality, and lifestyle advertising cannot be evaluated along the same matrix as empirical claims generally found in product-information advertising. This is what Jules Henry labeled "pecuniary truth," a philosophy contained in three postulates: "Truth is what sells. Truth is what you want people to believe. Truth is that which is not legally false."[122]

In the regime of pecuniary truth, successful advertising techniques use words and images to push expectations beyond their reasonable orbit so that the consumer may yield uncritically to an ad's persuasive force. For example, does anyone really believe that smoking a particular brand of cigarettes will make him or her alive with pleasure? Does anyone really believe that splashing on a specific cologne will more endear a father to his son? Of course we do not literally believe these messages but only act as if they could be true. Developing Henry's argument, Judith Williamson drove home the pointlessness of legal regulation of pecuniary truth: Advertisements are "so uncontrollable, because whatever restrictions are made in terms of their verbal content or 'false claims', there is no way of getting at their use of images and symbols.... [I]t is images and not words which ultimately provide the currency in ads."[123]

The honorable Justice Holmes notwithstanding, mass advertisers and their mass consumers are well aware of yet another reality of commercial communication: There is no test of truth in the marketplace.

Those who laud the public's "right" to know either do not understand what it would really mean for the public to *know* or what it would really mean to impose such a right on America's commercial media. The reality of the mass-advertising marketplace is simply

THERE IS NO RIGHT TO KNOW

The right to know is a notion of the public's constitutional guaranty to a full and unfettered measure of information—quantitatively and qualitatively sufficient to promote rational decisionmaking in all matters political, economic, and otherwise. This right is inextricably tied to both the rationality model of the marketplace of ideas and the political model of participatory governance. In fact, such a right was collaterally touted as a justification for First Amendment freedom in the *Virginia Pharmacy* case,[124] which championed the informational function of commercial expression. For these reasons, the right cannot be honored in a highly commercial culture where image is all, where truth is irrelevant, and where citizen democracy is eclipsed by consumer democracy. This is but another way of saying that the right to know cannot coexist easily with commercial mass advertising.

Moreover, to impose a public's right to know on the media would challenge the freedoms from governmental interference that the American commercial press has long enjoyed. Charting a direction never followed by the Supreme Court, Justice William O. Douglas perceived a necessary connection between the public's right to know and any First Amendment protection of press liberties: "The press has a preferred position in our constitutional scheme, not to enable it to make money, not to set newsmen apart as a favored class, but to bring fulfillment to the public's right to know."[125]

Indeed, if the Douglas perspective were given full force, the First Amendment would place a sword in the hands of the public to be used against any commercial media that did not vindicate its right to know. Such a scenario is particularly problematic in the context of America's economic realities. The commercial media, as we know them, would be hard pressed to survive in our capitalistic society if they could not be heavily subsidized by the message-making machine of mass advertising.[126]

It is no surprise, then, that the Douglas dissent stands as a romantic aberration in a culture captured by commerce. The public's right to know could never be more than what it has become—an idle slogan. Even as a slogan, it is at war ideologically with a system that permits advertisers to influence and dictate editorial content and that allows uninhibited consumer reporting to succumb to advertiser-friendly copy. In such a system, the public hears everything that advertisers want it to hear and relatively little that they don't.

Ultimately, mass advertisers celebrate and their mass consumers tolerate the reality of commercial communication: The right to know has no currency in the marketplace.

Those who defend the traditional First Amendment faith in individual autonomy and who therefore oppose the rise of the corporate self and the consumer self either do not understand the relationship between commerce and communication or do not understand the futility of attempts to divorce the two in our capitalistic system. The reality of the mass-advertising marketplace is simply

WE ARE AS WE CONSUME

"The business of America is business," said "Silent Cal" Coolidge.[m] This axiom holds as true in our culture generally as it does in our economy. That is, America's highly advanced capitalism thrives on the union of the economic marketplace with the marketplace of ideas. Our identity as Americans is a combination of *citizen self* and *consumer self*. This identity is molded by communication filled with the symbols of commerce. In today's America, it is ever more difficult to detect any form of public expression, including religious speech, that can remain altogether free of commercial taint.[n] Even "noncommercial" public television and radio are becoming increasingly sponsor-dependent.[127] Ultimately, it is impossible to disentangle commerce from communication and preserve America as we know it.

Remember that the defenders of the old self (progressives and conservatives alike) insist that there can be no individual liberty where

m) In his January 17, 1925 speech to the Society of American Newspaper Editors, President Coolidge's actual words were "After all, the chief business of the American people is business."

n) Reportedly, the late magician Doug Henning and spiritual adviser Maharishi Mahesh Yogi once planned to create a $1 billion Maharishi-Veda Land theme park on 1,400 acres near Niagara Falls, Ontario, to combine recreation with spiritual activities.

mass-advertising creates and manipulates core personal values. But a harder look at the mass advertising process reveals that any corruption of the old self is not a one-way phenomenon. It is not simply "them against us," but also "us against us." Our commercial system feeds the massive appetites of a people charmed by consumption. Advertising spokesman Burt Neuborne put it squarely: "[N]o evidence at all exists to support the paternalistic notion that commercial speech manipulates hearers into involuntary choices. Quite the contrary, *no form of communication is more sensitive to the wishes and whims of hearers*."[128]

Ironically, in our consumer culture, it is precisely the defenders of the old self who are likely to be seen as manipulative, elitist, and undemocratic. For most Americans, individual autonomy is synonymous with consumer autonomy. Our most cherished freedom is the freedom of choice, the liberty to choose our lifestyle. It is an arresting fact that the modern preoccupation with freedom of choice was popularized in a wartime advertisement for vacuum cleaners. Tracking FDR's "Four Freedoms," a 1944 *Saturday Evening Post* advertisement proposed another: "The Fifth Freedom is Freedom of Choice."[129] Predictably, those who champion commercial speech have seized on the notion of freedom of choice to buttress their constitutional case. "In short," Judge Jacob Fuchsberg instructed us, "political freedom may be so dependent on economic freedom that the pursuit of one cannot be readily divorced from the other, certainly not without drastically circumscribing the freedom of people to exercise a choice among basic competing values."[130]

TRUTH + ADVERTISING = INSANITY

That, at least, is the formula of the comedy film *Crazy People*. It is the story of an advertising copy man who works at a respectable New York firm run by a CEO who insists: "You have to drill, drill, drill that target audience until they are consuming your product, not because they love it, but because they can't escape it."

Skeptical of this philosophy, our leading man one day decides to mend his ways and tell the truth. "Let's not fool the public anymore.... Let's level with America," he implores a co-worker. The response is predictable: "We can't level, you crazy bastard. We're in advertising!"

Ignoring this sane advice, our truth-in-advertising crusader writes ads such as these:

- "Buy [Car X]. They're boxy. But they're good. We know they're not sexy. This is not a smart time to be sexy anyway with so many new diseases around. Be safe instead of sexy."
- "[Ad for national phone company]. We're tired of taking your crap. If we fold, you'll have no damn phones."

Not surprisingly, our noble friend is chauffeured off to a sanitarium.

Crazy People (Paramount Pictures, 1990)

Considering the character of commercial expression, it is readily apparent why America's self-identity is bound up with commercialism. As we explained earlier, modern mass advertising in our culture seems to be other than what it is—it appears to be individualistic, familial, communal, political, patriotic, egalitarian, artistic, or scientific. Long ago, the advertising industry moved from an easily identifiable commercial posture, represented in the product-information or reason-why format, to a cultural posture most commonly exhibited in the lifestyle format so prevalent today.

From a First Amendment definitional standpoint, it is increasingly difficult to demarcate the realms of the commercial from those of the political and cultural, to distinguish commercial expression from the most preferred forms of democratic speech. For example, is a cigarette company's campaign to celebrate the Bill of Rights a commercial or political venture?[131] Is an alcohol company's campaign to publicize the dangers of drinking and driving a commercial or humanistic measure? Is a shopping mall association's campaign to "honor" our soldiers in the Gulf War a commercial or a patriotic gesture? Is a clothing company's campaign to "end racism and the killing of people in the streets" a commercial or a social message? Is such advertising a mercenary form of the "fighting faith" of the First Amendment?

Assume workable definitions could be found to patrol the boundaries between commercial messages and important cultural discourse. What then would be the result of placing mass advertising beyond the lines of constitutionally protected expression? Probably little. Given the enormous political and economic power of corporate advertising interests, commercial communication would persist largely unencumbered by governmental regulation. On the whole, American consumers have not seen fit to bite the mass-advertising hand that feeds them, although they have allowed some advertising restrictions for products clearly dangerous to health and safety.[132]

Realistically, many of the broadsides against commercial speech (often made by progressives, not liberals) may prove to be politically meaningless, mere shadowboxing. Indeed, the success of any radical agenda depends on more than simply withdrawing constitutional protection from commercial speech. A bolder move is required. Recall that the defenders of the old self argue that commercial speech "*is directly at odds with the aim of the first amendment*" and that it "*denigrates rather than affirms human liberty.*"[133] With commercial speech cast as a clear and present danger to free speech values, the withdrawal of First Amendment protection must be accompanied by political action. Some affirmative steps in the form of regulatory controls must also be taken before the old self can be recaptured in our new culture.

In reality, the radical attack on commercial speech launched by the defenders of the old self is an attack on our advanced capitalistic and mass popular culture.[o] With romantic spirit, they may hope to overthrow the culture by undermining commercial communication. And indeed, given the omnipotence of mass advertising in America, there is some logic in undoing capitalism by assaulting one of its mainstays. Logic notwithstanding, the defenders of the old self must confront a perplexing political problem. How can a free speech theory with either strong neo-Marxist (progressive) or aristocratic (conservative) overtones be adopted by a capitalistic culture? Part of being the American capitalistic culture is having the American mass-advertising system. Advertising has become an essential thread in the American cloth. Ultimately, the defenders of the old self are likely to fail because consumerist America would inevitably recognize that one cannot remove the thread without unraveling the cloth.

Money talks every time an advertiser coins a new phrase. No wonder the currency of public expression is devalued.

Those who equate commercial speech with political dissent either underestimate or overestimate the subversive force of dissent. The reality of the mass-advertising marketplace is simply

THERE IS NO ABSOLUT® RIGHT TO DISSENT[p]

In our consumerist popular culture, virtually no form of dissent is forbidden. In fact, dissent is typically encouraged. Young and old

o) Book III advances the same general point in connection with pornography.

p) Absolut Vodka spends some $30 million annually on witty advertising that plays on its name, such as "Absolut Perfection," etc. See Barry Brown, "Magazine's Parody Makes Marketer Absolut-ely Mad," *Advertising Age*, 27 July 1992, p. 3; Kalle Lasn and Bill Schmalz, "Absolut Debacle," *Adbusters Quarterly*, Summer–Fall 1992, p. 2.

alike are invited to reveal their rebel stripes by donning a James Dean, John Wesley Harding, or Axl Rose T-shirt. For the more radical, Malcolm X baseball caps are commercially available. Rappers, punks, and Mapplethorpe types all may, to paraphrase Shakespeare, strut and fret their hour upon the stage of pop life and then be seen and heard no more. Skinheads and Manson-family members, too, are in demand on the tabloid and TV talk-show circuit. And the big tent certainly has room enough for the opposite—the likes of the National Federation of Decency, Morality in Media, and the American Family Association. All messages are created equal, since almost all can be adapted to suit the commercial culture, where truth and untruth, morality and immorality, tumble together.

What cannot be tolerated by the gatekeepers of commerce, however, is dissent that poses a clear and present danger to the capitalist culture and its economy. Of course, far-reaching expression on the fringe—for example, Andres Serrano's *Piss Christ*—may temporarily be sacrificed in order to appease lawmakers. CULTURE-JAMMING, by contrast, is one form of dissent that the captains of commerce are not likely to countenance. But what kind of dissent is this?

- An advertising photo of a riderless horse grazing in a snow-covered graveyard, with the caption "Marlboro Country."

- An advertising photo of a bedraggled, middle-aged woman sitting at the breakfast table, holding a cigarette and a glass of vodka, with the caption "Every morning's a Smirnoff morning."

- A television commercial showing an innocent-looking youngster with a fixed stare, as the voice-over announces: "Kathy is eight, and she's addicted... it changes the way she talks... the way she acts... the way she thinks. She is addicted... to television."[134]

Culture-jamming, the method common to these examples, is a subversive practice designed to expropriate and sabotage the meaning of commercial messages. Typically, culture-jamming aims for auto-cannibalization: Commercials or advertisements devour themselves. Just as the entertainment-consumption complex filched America's most cherished images, language, and values, so the culture-jammers now use the same tactics to obstruct that complex. These pop-culture dissidents "draw upon the given facts of our society, this cacophony of fragmentary media images, to describe things as they are."[135] Professor Stuart Ewen notes that at the heart of culture-jamming is "the hope that there could be another kind of world, a world where rather than incoherence there could be coherence, rather than a devaluation of the human in favor of the commodity there could be an understanding of the commodity in the service of the human."[136]

Predictably, the corporate captains may move to squelch such treachery. They are likely to recruit the law of business libel, trademark infringements, and copyright violations to suppress this dissent. Similarly, the caretakers of mass expression—the major commercial television stations—may refuse to air the culture-jammers' paid public-interest spots.[137] Ironically, Nike's TV messages of racial harmony, directed by filmmaker Spike Lee, are viewed as a form of social criticism; but it is a criticism largely neutralized by commercial television's co-optation. Real radicals, our culture-jammers, would take a different tack. Their "commercial" might depict a group of young, racially mixed basketball players wearing expensive sneakers. As this group shoots hoops, a different group of young, racially mixed kids shoots bullets at them. The "commercial" closes with the murderers stealing the footwear from the bloody bodies. The caption: "Nike. Shoot your best shot."[q]

Ironically, the same mass advertisers who hoist the banner of commercial speech alongside political speech are all too ready to censor culture-jamming dissent. In the conflict between the marketplace and ideas, the right of dissent is minimalized unless it can be marginalized.

The same Justice Holmes who laid the foundation for the marketplace-of-ideas metaphor in the era of the syndicalists was also the one who warned laissez-faire capitalists that "a constitution is not intended to embody a particular economic theory."[138] Holmes did not foresee, however, a world where the metaphor would override the warning. He did not imagine a nation where the symbol of the mar-

q) Alternatively, the Nike caption might read: "Just do it!"

ketplace of ideas would itself become the handmaiden of commerce. Just as "[l]ate nineteenth- and twentieth-century financial and industrial moguls went to sleep at night secure in the knowledge that their world turned on the principles of economic laissez-faire,"[139] so early twenty-first century advertisers sleep soundly believing that commercial communication is generally safe in the free speech marketplace.

If commercial communication is safe, it is not because it *actually* furthers the First Amendment's traditional values of rational decision-making and self-realization. Rather, it is because it has effectively co-opted the marketplace metaphor. Meanwhile, the defenders of commercial speech both on and off the Court have ignored the difference between today's commercial expression and the noble purposes of the First Amendment. If they were to be frank, they would concede that the real reason for constitutional protection of modern mass advertising is less ennobling: It is speech in the service of selling.

Constitutionally speaking, if the new moguls of commerce are to rest easily, they must perpetuate the lie of the marketplace-of-ideas metaphor. If they cannot, they must convince the Court to embrace explicitly their laissez-faire theories in the law of free speech. Then the constitutional law of communication might, for the first time, be aligned with the realities of commerce. Constitutional candor might also give rise to the conditions necessary for a more realistic form of resistance. No longer would the critics of advanced capitalism and mass consumerism be required to confine their opposition to cramped quarters, namely the terms of traditional free speech theory. If the Court were to place the real rationale for commercial speech in bold relief, resisters might then attack the resulting constitutional law for what they see it to be — capitalism devouring communication.

Of course, that the resistance can be made more real does not mean that it will be any more potent. For this is a peculiar type of resistance. Unlike the popular defiance of the *Conseil National de la Résistance*[r] in wartime France, the resisters against commercialism may themselves be met by popular defiance as they fight against the business of America. The majority is not likely to sympathize with the resister's cry — the ideas and imagination of the populace register far too closely with the codes of commerce. In America, as in Henrik

r) The *Conseil* was a resistance group that fought the Gestapo during the French occupation.

Ibsen's famous 1882 play, the social doctor will be seen as "an enemy of the people."

For now, an ignoble lie endures.[s] And the lie reflects the perplexities of our commercial culture. In this culture, the law of free speech necessarily bows to the demands of commerce. Madisonian ideals slouch toward Madison Avenue. If the First Amendment can no longer promote its traditional values, it is because the commercial marketplace no longer especially values them.

s) We turn to this larger topic in the Epilogue.

Absolut® Protection? –A "Dialogue"

Scene: Studio 2A at WNET on Manhattan's West Side. Open with Italian opera singer Cecilia Bartoli's rendition of Antonio Vivaldi's eighteenth-century "Sposa son disprezzata." After her performance, the camera shifts immediately to a round-table scene with Bartoli and PBS interviewer Charlie Rose. As his conversation with Bartoli closes, the host breaks to a corporate underwriter—"enhanced" identification for a soft-drink company. The program resumes and the camera centers on Rose seated with "dialogue" participants around his celebrated oak table situated in front of a black backdrop. Rose introduces the topic, identifies the participants, and then (contrary to his practice) announces that the discussion will proceed largely unmediated.

What follows is a slightly orchestrated print "dialogue"[140] with attorney Stuart Banner, marketing expert Leo Bogart, communications professor and advertising expert Sut Jhally, federal appellate judge Alex Kozinski, and University of Richmond law dean Rodney Smolla. Except for the bracketed remarks, the words, though incomplete and rearranged, are theirs (circa 1993) and ours. This fictional TV program has yet to air.

Collins or Skover: Thank you, Mr. Rose, for this forum and for your introductory remarks.

Charlie Rose: [Professor Jhally, would you mind opening the discussion on the Collins and Skover thesis? You are, after all, an expert on advertising as social communication.]

Sut Jhally: Collins and Skover have done us a great service in summarizing and condensing the immense amount of literature that informs their own original discussion of the First Amendment, commercial culture, and constitutional protection. They have provided an excellent overview of the history of advertising, its colonization of the horizons of public expression, and the deceptive rhetoric of "the marketplace of ideas" that acts to legitimate the existing status quo in which powerful corporate interests dominate.

Alex Kozinski or Stuart Banner: [Yes.] They've convincingly demonstrated that the practice of advertising out there in the world looks quite a bit different from the descriptions of advertising in the opinions of appellate courts. Regardless of whether this divergence has any implications for the First Amendment, it is an important point in itself. If courts are going to apply the First Amendment to commercial speech with any coherence, they should have a grasp of what commercial speech actually is.

And [these two] are on to something even bigger. Read ["Commerce & Communication"] in conjunction with ["The Paratroopers' Paradox"] and you're left with the unsettling feeling that developments in communications may have outpaced developments in the law. Many of our legal concepts—freedom of the press, appellate review, copyright—were born when non-face-to-face communication was almost entirely in writing. The legal landscape has remained largely unchanged, despite obvious technological transformation. None of this may make the slightest bit of difference, but whether change is necessary, and if so what kind, are questions that deserve serious thought. [Their] line of inquiry . . . should provoke a great deal of commentary on this subject. One need not agree with them to appreciate the value of the debate they open.

Collins or Skover: We are grateful for these kind words and for everyone's willingness to join in this "dialogue" tonight.

We had hoped that our thoughts might prompt some new discussion and debate about certain First Amendment issues. As the evening wears on, even if it happens that there is more disagreement than agreement among us, that may be for the best. After all, in the scheme of things, who's to complain about "fighting words" and friendly knocks where the First Amendment is concerned?

To borrow from Machiavelli, Fortuna being what it always is, one may see an author praised one moment and damned the next.[141] True to fate, we suspect that your kind words may soon run out.

Rodney Smolla: There is, concededly, a haunting verisimilitude to [Ron and David's] claim that mass advertising does, in a diffused and collective sense, transform the culture, degrading the quality of all our ambient public discourse. [You two] are most persuasive when pointing out that the commercial exploitation of the symbols and images of noncommercial culture is parasitic and tends to trivialize, dilute, and debase those symbols. [You] are on far weaker ground, however, when [you] intimate that regulation is the answer to this problem.

Collins to Skover: I think I hear Fortuna's footsteps.

Smolla: Regulating the marketplace on these grounds clearly cannot be squared with the assumptions underlying modern First Amendment theory. But even if [you] choose not to accept those First Amendment assumptions—and [you] are of course free to urge that those assumptions be discarded—presuming to regulate mass advertising in order to defend high culture or to elevate public discourse is misguided social policy.

[You] use the American flag as a primary example of the debasement of cultural symbols through commercial exploitation. . . . I accept that any use of the flag is likely to have symbolic significance, and that in the eyes of many, to use it to sell jeans or burn it to express exasperation with the Republican Party is to debase it. But the flag is not Betsy Ross's, nor the government's, nor the culture's, to shelter. The short answer . . . is that the First Amendment protects this type of symbolic debasement. The long answer is that it should.

Kozinski or Banner: [Ron and David] have (1) stated what they understand to be the values explaining the existence of the First Amendment; (2) analyzed a given type of speech to demonstrate that it does not advance those values (and may even advance their opposite); and (3) concluded that the First Amendment should therefore not protect the type of speech being analyzed. . . .

. . . The First Amendment, one might think, prevents the people's representatives in legislatures from prohibiting speech the majority doesn't like. That's the whole point. People might quibble about *why* that should be so, or about the *values* served by freedom of speech, but there seems to be no debate that the First Amendment bars the majority from suppressing the speech of some simply because others find it to have little value.

Given that premise, it strikes us as odd to argue that a particular form of speech shouldn't receive First Amendment protection solely because that speech has little value. This is exactly the type of argument the First Amendment should foreclose. People value speech differently, and all sorts of different people think that all sorts of different speech are valueless or downright pernicious. . . . If all it takes to remove First Amendment protection from a given kind of speech is that a sufficiently large number of people finds the speech less valuable than other kinds, we may as well not have a First Amendment at all. Such an understanding of the First Amendment—according to which speech not valued by a majority receives no protection—throws all speech regulation questions back into the political arena.

Collins or Skover: We think that it is important to raise two key questions. First, as to Alex and Stuart's last comment, do we understand you to be saying that, at bottom, the First Amendment supports *no* value other than speech for speech's sake? If that is so, you must agree with us that the ennobling theories of the First Amendment—the ones courts and commentators invoke—have no place in today's commercial culture. Second, do you two and Rodney really understand us to be saying or suggesting that the First Amendment should not protect commercial communication?

Friedrich Nietzsche:

Leo Bogart: [May I jump in here? Ron and David] take us right up to the brink of the conclusion that advertising should not enjoy the protection of the First Amendment, but they never make it over the edge. While they set up a vigorously phrased brief against advertising, they distance themselves from it in the concluding section of their [work]—referring to it as the "progressive critique," almost as though it were one they declined to share.

Collins or Skover: Thank you, Leo, for bailing us out. Mindful of what we actually stated, perhaps it is best to let the folks in our audience judge for themselves:

- Nowhere did we state what Rodney implies or what Alex and Stuart claim we say. In fact, we offered much to the contrary. We dedicated much argument to critiquing the progressive (and conservative) broadsides against commercial speech in the American culture.

- In this regard, we asked: "How can a free speech theory with either strong neo-Marxist (progressive) or aristocratic (conservative) overtones be adopted by a capitalistic culture? Part of being the American capitalistic culture is having the American mass-advertising system."

- To reiterate, we concluded: "Advertising has become an essential thread in the American cloth. Ultimately, the radical critique is likely to fail because consumerist America would inevitably recognize that one cannot remove the thread without unraveling the cloth."

- But we said even more. In discussing the futility of true-false distinctions in much commercial speech, we noted "the pointlessness of legal regulation of pecuniary truth."

It is terrible to die of thirst in the ocean.

Beyond Good and Evil, trans. Walter Kaufmann (New York: Vintage, 1966), p. 81.

- Finally, we took some issue with Justice Hugo Black's implication that the First Amendment endorses affirmative governmental regulation of private commercial communication. We stated: "To restructure the First Amendment so as to permit some governmental regulation of corporate advertising messages is to set the legal guaranty against the commercial culture."

Certainly, you gentlemen should understand that we are not hell-bent on slaughtering the sacred cow of commercial speech protection. As long as you all openly admit the apparent conflict between traditional First Amendment theory and today's commercial practices, the cow might be milked for all it's worth.

Kozinski or Banner: [Ron and David's] work is *anti*historical, in that it doesn't depend on what the First Amendment says or how it has ever been understood. The First Amendment poses a difficult practical problem: It is quite short and does not explain what counts as "speech," what counts as "freedom," or what counts as "abridging." To fill the chasm between the broad rule and its application to specific cases, a great deal of thinking has to be done. There are, in broad outline, two ways of going about it—the history-based approach and the theory-based approach.

Under the history-based approach, which has tended to be the specialty of judges (and hence lawyers trying to persuade judges), one looks to past practice to figure out what the First Amendment means. . . . [This approach] rests on the notion that at least some aspect of the meaning of the words used in the First Amendment remains consistent over time. It implies that the views of people who may no longer be living exert at least some influence on today's understanding of the First Amendment.

The theory-based approach has largely been the province of academics. Under this technique, before one looks at how the First Amendment has been understood in the past, one constructs a theory of communication capable of demonstrating that a particular type of speech should or should not receive constitutional protection. Armed with the theory, one can then examine the past cases to determine which ones were correctly decided.

. . .

"Commerce & Communication" provides a perfect opportunity to think about theory-based approaches because it is as close to a pure theory-based [argument] as one is ever likely to find. [Your analysis contains]... no discussion of any cases interpreting the First Amendment (except a brief mention of the descriptions of advertising contained in some of the Supreme Court's commercial speech cases), and no attempt to discern what the real-life First Amendment might mean.... Lurking unstated in the background is the assumption that the First Amendment is a vessel empty enough to receive whatever content [your] theory suggests should be poured in.

Collins or Skover: We plead no contest to your charge that we have not added to the voluminous and often hackneyed debate droning on the subject of historical intent and its relationship to constitutional interpretation. It is enough for our limited purposes to remind folks that James Madison, the father of the First Amendment, was not mad about this method.[t] And we leave it to others to engage in the more esoteric debate as to whether even mechanical historicism is not in some way theory-based. After all, if history is the sole or primary guide to interpreting the First Amendment, that choice itself is based on some theory of value. But since we ultimately take no stand on whether commercial speech should or should not be constitutionally protected, we trust that history and decisional law will support us in some respect.

t) "As a guide in expounding and applying the provisions of the Constitution, the debates and incidental decisions of the Convention can have no authoritative character." Letter from James Madison to Thomas Ritchie (September 15, 1821), in *Letters and Other Writings of James Madison*, vol. 3, ed. W. C. Rives and P. R. Fendall (New York: Worthington, 1884), p. 228.

Alex and Stuart, if you must divide the universe of First Amendment thinking, why must it be restricted to history-based or theory-based approaches alone? Why can't the "*real*-life First Amendment" (your words, our emphasis) be understood from the vantage point of the real-life experience of commercial communication? To do that would require yet an additional approach—what we label a "cultural approach" to the First Amendment. Later, we will develop this approach more fully. For now, it is enough to say that this approach asks several significant questions: If we look at American commercial speech as it is, rather than as it should be, what would we find? Having made such a discovery, what then would our notions of the First Amendment be were they premised on that experience? Nothing here should be unfamiliar to the careful reader of "Commerce & Communication," who is invited to consider an approach to the First Amendment consistent with the realities of the marketplace of commercial advertising.

Kozinski or Banner: [Your] work is [also] *a*historical, in the sense that [it suffers] from a romanticized vision of the past. Contemporary popular culture may, depending on one's standards, be junk, but the same has been said about popular culture in every era. We have no reason to believe (and [you two] provide none) that reasoned discourse represented any greater fraction of total communication 200 or 100 years ago than it does now. Our predecessors were up to more than attending town meetings and writing *The Federalist*: They were also singing bawdy drinking songs, reading racy French novels, publishing nasty false attacks on members of the opposing political party, and touting the virtues of all kinds of quack medical treatments. [The] we're-going-to-hell-in-a-handbasket tone [of your argument] relies on a view of the past that we doubt could be supported with facts.

Collins or Skover: You two should have been in our first "dialogue." Precisely such charges—though unfounded there as here—were leveled by Ed Rubin and Mark Tushnet. We have much the same response to you as we had to them.

That discourse may have been more enlightened a century or two ago is a claim that we neither do nor need make. What we do surmise, however, is that functionalist "reason-why" advertising represented a greater proportion of mass commercial expression a century ago. And more importantly, even if you two can show otherwise, the task of reconciling the traditional First Amendment to today's commercial expression is thereby made no easier.

Romanticizing the past is one thing; romanticizing the present is yet another. Who among us are the out-of-touch-with-reality romanticists? Is it we who reveal the gulf between modern mass advertising and the First Amendment's touted norms of rationality and individuality? Or is it rather you who continue to justify First Amendment protection for commercial speech along those traditional lines? Certainly, you both exhibit a sophisticated understanding of the workings of mass commercial advertising. Why, then, do you appear to toe the old First Amendment line that romanticizes the present? Gentlemen, if you hold otherwise, just speak the words and the truth will set you free.

Finally, you two depict us as prominent members of the "we're-going-to-hell-in-a-handbasket" crowd. We cannot allow this charge to go unanswered. Succinctly, we appreciate this depiction nearly as much as the Devil loves holy water. Remember, the commercial culture appears low only from the lofty place of traditional First Amendment values. In one important sense, low or lofty is of no moment to us. Unless free speech law is squared with modern commercial communication, we need not sit in judgment over this matter. Till then, we are content to give the Devil his due and are willing to echo the words of the pimp in the musical theater production of *Miss Saigon.*

Charlie, do you mind if the sound crew plays a few videotaped bars from *Miss Saigon*'s "The American Dream"?

Strains of the Miss Saigon *score as performed by Jonathan Pryce fill the studio.*

What's that I smell in the air,
the American dream.
Sweet as a new millionaire

. . .

Luck by the tail.
How can you fail?
And best of all it's for sale.[142]

Smolla: The baggage carried by commercial speech is the bias of the intelligentsia. That segment of American culture that lives for a life of the mind, and indeed makes a living by living for the life of the mind, will naturally harbor some disdain for the coarser entries in the marketplace of ideas—those ideas that sell only goods and services.

To the intellectual or the academic, speech that is rational, analytic, and contemplative will usually receive higher marks than speech that appeals to passion and prejudice.... [W]hen the passion is attached only to a product, when an effort is made to short-circuit the brain, discard *Consumer Reports*, and get people to buy something by engaging them in fantasies about their own personas and lifestyles, the academic is likely to be intolerant....

This judgment, however, itself reflects a bias that is undemocratic and intellectually elitist. It is not so much an upper-class bias or leisure-class bias as it is a vocational bias, a bias likely to be found in many academics and others who live by and for words and ideas. I am part of that vocational class and I share the bias, a bias that often looks with disdain upon much of mass culture—mass commercial culture, mass political culture, mass entertainment culture, mass journalistic culture.

But what follows from this bias? In an open democracy, can it be that intellectuals have a mandate to push government to regulate mass culture in the service of elevating it? Or should we who pride ourselves on living in the "real" marketplace of ideas demonstrate the democratic liberality that the marketplace metaphor really stands for, and understand that mass culture will always be with us?

Bogart: It is true that much of today's mass advertising can be classified as fantasy more than fact. The trouble is that one man's fact is another's fantasy.

Collins or Skover: We find it puzzling, Rodney, that you brand us as elitists. Ironically, we are the very ones who pointed out that the defenders of the old self (progressives and conservatives alike) are likely to be seen as manipulative, elitist, and undemocratic. (Similarly, in "The Paratroopers' Paradox," we contended that intrusive governmental regulation of commercial television would be viewed as the segue to an aristocratic and un-American displacement of egalitarian and mass tastes.) Furthermore, we baldly asserted that America's self-identity is bound up with commercialism and that it is impossible to disentangle commerce from communication and preserve America as we know it. Such contentions, of course, ought not to imply that we go to the other extreme and embrace the excesses of contemporary commercial communication. Our express purpose, it must be remembered, is more descriptive than normative.

After all, we bring the First Amendment *down* from the cloistered chambers of Justice Blackmun and his black-robed colleagues to the open air of the people's marketplace. Let us repeat our sentiments noted in the Prologue: "[W]hat the elite few say about the First Amendment does not mirror what the many do with it. Hence, the truer reference point of the free speech guaranty is the unremarkable talk of popular culture rather than the remarkable discourse envisioned by constitutional doctrine and theory." Make of that what you will.

Bogart: Our identity as Americans rests on far more than the combination of our citizen selves and consumer selves. Our lives entail a constant shifting and adaptation, as we play child, parent, spouse, friend, neighbor, worker, boss, birdwatcher, baseball fan, and a multitude of other roles. That does not disprove the point that these relationships influence our consumption habits, and that consumption influences them in turn. But we lose our grasp on the subject if we minimize its complexity.

Collins or Skover: Leo, your warning is well taken. But the investigation that you would have us now embark upon raises far-reaching issues more suitable for another dialogue. For now, what is telling in your observation is that it is difficult, if not impossible, to separate out the complex interactive forces that affect our lives. Whatever other forces may be at work, clearly commerce is in our veins, befriending red corpuscles and warring with the white ones.

Jhally: [Absolutely.] "[D]iscourse through and about objects"[143] ... permeates the spaces of our public and private domains. This commercial discourse is *the ground on* which we live, *the space in* which we learn to think, and *the lens through* which we come to understand the world that surrounds us. This development, so well described by [Ron and David], should not come as a surprise. It is what happens when production, and the necessary distribution and consumption of commodities, comes to be the defining rationale for the organization of social life.

Indeed, this discourse occurs when economic growth becomes not simply an economic goal but a *value* from which happiness and satisfaction derive for individuals. Moreover, economic growth is a value that is expressed in the most compelling and powerful forms by an advertising industry that spends more energy and resources on creating messages than any other creative force in society (perhaps even in human history). . . .

The economy in such a vision is not merely a mechanism that provides employment through increased production, but is the fountain from which flow the sources of real happiness—commodities. This powerful vision, spread by an unbridled advertising industry on a world scale, has conquered not merely the Western industrialized world but Eastern Europe and much of the Third World. It is at the present time the motivating force of social change on a global scale. Personal welfare, satisfaction, and happiness—indeed political freedom itself—are directly linked with the presence of an "immense collection of commodities."[144]

Smolla: I cannot accept that we are largely the sum of what we buy. Concededly, we may, in a limited and figurative sense, be the sum of what we *buy into*, including our "investments" in fantasy. But the mere fact that the commercial marketplace is filled with images calculated to aggrandize our fantasies does not mean we *are ourselves transformed* into fantastical beings.

. . .

All of us, all the time, are invited by modern advertising to imagine that we are something we are not. We are cajoled to imagine ourselves as more sexy or chic or athletic or smart or rich than we really are, and to consume accordingly. The menu of potential fantasies is almost limitless. Products thus become fantasy-facilitators. But does this marketing of fantasy actually alter self-identity?

. . .

. . . Sixty percent of the newspaper space may be filled with advertising, but that advertising does not command 60 percent of the average reader's attention. We are inured to most of these advertisements and commercials; they wash over us without even dampening the skin. We often do not stop to even read or watch the ads at all, and when we do, they rarely penetrate or connect with our consciousness, let alone transform our identity. True, we are all persuaded and seduced from time to time by these ads, encouraged to make irrational or impulsive consumer choices. But that kind of persuasion and seduction is endemic to social life; we run across it constantly and develop mechanisms to filter it out and fend it off.

Collins or Skover: Rodney, our overall portrayal of the commercial culture does not turn on assessments of the seductive power of particular advertisements to dictate particular buyer behaviors. In his book, *Strategy in Advertising*, Leo emphasized that "[advertising's] importance lies not in having elicited a specific purchase response to a specific ad. The real significance of advertising is its total cumulative weight as part of the culture—in the way in which it contributes to the popular lore of ideas and attitudes toward consumer products."[145] Bob Garfield, the advertising critic for *Advertising Age*, concurred with Leo when he claimed that "Ads R Us." "What better archive is there, for the social and cultural history of our age," Garfield asked, "than the aggregation of a half-century's commercials?"[146] It is the essential role of advertising in developing the consumer culture's pervasive ideology—that we regularly identify ourselves by our habits, patterns, and communities of consumption—that is the focal point of a perspective more complex and dynamic than you indicate. In part, this perspective tracks Sut's account of consumption as "an inherently *social* activity, not an individual one."[147]

Roger Waters (of Pink Floyd): [When the audience is mass], the whole thing becomes more about commerce and less about communication, music, human feelings and values.

Washington Post, 28 April 1993.

Smolla: Commercial speech, as speech, should presumptively enter the debate with full First Amendment protection. The theoretical question should not be what qualifies commercial speech for First Amendment coverage, but what, if anything, *disqualifies* it. In my view, there are no convincing arguments for disqualifying most modern mass advertising from constitutional protection....

Collins or Skover: However *doctrinally* true this presumption may or may not be, the larger *theoretical* question is really quite different than the one you raise. The more significant question is: What does such a presumption of absolute protection imply? Among other things, it might imply that all speech is created equal, that all speech either serves the same value or no value, or that all speech (from grunts to hate speech) is valued for speech's sake alone. You know, Rodney, if this is the point to which we have come—and we may well have—you may be surprised where this takes us in talking about the relationship between discourse and the First Amendment.

We gather you have more to say about the problems of disqualifying mass advertising from First Amendment protection. So, we'll reserve our full theoretical argument for a little later.

Smolla: In classic First Amendment terms, . . . the one thing the government may not do is regulate speech because it "sells" a lifestyle, fantasy, ethos, identity, or attitude that happens to be regarded by most as socially corrosive.

. . .

The very "excesses" of modern advertising that might at first make it seem a likely candidate for heavy legal regulation are actually the attributes that most qualify such speech for the heightened constitutional protection we routinely grant other categories of speech. Indeed, the distinction that is central to [your] argument, a distinction that seeks to drive a wedge between the rational and irrational components of advertising, is one that has been repudiated in virtually all other areas of current First Amendment doctrine. The refusal of current First Amendment jurisprudence to accept a schism between the rational and irrational elements of speech (or, to use slightly different terms, between the intellectual and emotional content of speech) is sound—indeed, I would say vital to the American conception of freedom of speech. Commercial speech should be no exception.

Bogart: What makes the possibility of restricting advertising so unappealing, even terrifying, is that it is impossible to extricate its messages from their surroundings, just as it is impossible to separate the information functions of which [Ron and David] approve from the image-building aspects they detest.

Collins or Skover: This blurring of the lines between the commercial and the noncommercial is, remember, an issue on which we dwelt. Once your claims are conceded, Rodney and Leo, what flows from them? One consequence seems sure. Justice Harry Blackmun's rationality defense of commercial speech collapses at the knees as quickly as the Colossus of Rhodes tumbled to ruins.

Rose: [Since this is late-night public television, I'll let you guys get away with such high-brow references. Even so, we're running out of time, and I want Professor Jhally to have his say as well. So forgive me, gentlemen, for interrupting.]

Jhally: [Thank you, Charlie.] A commercially dominated media system is unable to pose hard questions . . . for fear of turning off audiences who are much more used to experiencing pleasant feelings than having to think about hard issues.

In this sense the advertising system systematically relegates discussion of key issues to the peripheries of the culture. Instead, it talks in powerful ways of desire and fantasy, pleasure and comfort....

Collins or Skover: Precisely, Sut. This brings us back to the theoretical argument that we started to make earlier in response to Rodney.

Unless we misunderstand you, Rodney, you seem a bit uneasy about "the commercial exploitation of the symbols and images of noncommercial culture." You seem troubled about this "parasitic" phenomenon that "tends to trivialize, dilute, and debase those symbols." Yet you argue that it is futile to attempt to elevate public expression through regulation. Apart from regulation, are you inferring that there is a *need* to elevate communication in the marketplace? You, after all, concede "a haunting verisimilitude" to our "claim that mass advertising does, in a diffused and collective sense, transform the culture, degrading the quality of all our ambient public discourse."

True?

C. Wright Mills: *[F]reedom cannot exist without an enlarged role of human reason in human affairs.*

The Sociological Imagination (New York: Oxford University Press, 1959), p. 174.

Is this degradation of discourse not an inevitable consequence of your absolutist First Amendment position? In fact, your constitutional posture does more than protect such trivialization—it perpetuates it. By elevating mass advertising's pap to the level of fundamental discourse, you invite the citizen self to become the consumer self; you invite the distortion of logic and the debasement of values; and you invite the commercialization of politics. Essentially, you unite the marketplace of ideas with the marketplace of items.

If we cannot stem the trivialization of discourse, it is in part because the absolutist First Amendment makes it impossible. If we attempt to regulate the commercial exploitation of discourse, we may violate the First Amendment's restraints on censorship. Once again, we confront the paratroopers' paradox, but now in the context of commercial communication. Where does all of this leave us? Are we flirting with the death of discourse?

Smolla: [I'd like to make a final point.] Rather than require speech to have redeeming social value to qualify for First Amendment protection, our society protects a great deal that has little or no plausible social value in the eyes of many. Indeed, the things that most bother [Ron and David] about mass advertising are also things that characterize much of the speech in American mass culture. Whether Americans are talking about sex or politics (or both together), for example, our discourse is often not discourse at all, but rather fantasy and sound bite.

Vast quantities of the speech in the modern American marketplace consist of symbol, image, and fantasy. For example, the billion-dollar marketplace for pornographic speech . . . is largely a trade in sexual fantasy. . . .

Collins or Skover: Wait a moment. You're getting ahead of us, Rodney. In fact, the link between discourse and intercourse is the very next thing on our agenda.

Rose: [Well, gentlemen. This was certainly an unprecedented moment in the history of television. Thank you all for participating. Tomorrow night our guests will be Henry Kissinger and Henry Winkler.]

Book III

Discourse & Intercourse

[During the French Revolutionary era, the] standard tales of buggery, adultery, incest and promiscuity . . . became a kind of metaphor for a diseased constitution.

—Simon Schama[1]

We cannot rely on rigid rules and regulations to structure everything in our lives. . . . We are sexual beings, and . . . eroticism pervades every aspect of our consciousness.

—Camille Paglia[2]

Each society gets the pornography it deserves.

—Elizabeth Fox-Genovese[3]

The Rise of the Pornographic State

*Scene: Wichita, Kansas, college library, late evening. Anthony meanders along tall rows of books, stacking works on French revolutionary history while listening to Sade's "No Ordinary Love" on his Walkman headset. An illustrated classic—*The Vaginal Fury of Marie-Antoinette, Wife of Louis XVI (1791)*—catches his eye. Ignoring the scholarly text, Anthony eagerly flips to the photographed engravings that depict the engorged genitals of the queen and her orgies with court nobles. Stealing away with his discovery to the men's room, Anthony joins in the ecstasies of the ancien régime. Fast fade-out.*

America forever flirts with the pornographic.

This tendency toward the graphic—the harlot-graphic[a]—is a state of mind and a cultural state. Yet it is an uneasy state of affairs, for America both celebrates and condemns its love of the carnal. This Janus-like view of erotic life animates our conceptions of free speech. Ultimately, America's ambivalent love affair with pornography gives rise to a new image of the state—a republic of images. And pornography is the lodestar in this republic.

Imagine a place in which there is little or no discord about pornography because there is little or no meaningful *discourse* about it. Imagine a place in which people gladly trade the reality of human beings for *images* of that reality, a "virtual reality." Imagine a place in

a) The term "pornography" derives from a combination of the Greek words *pornē*, meaning harlot, and *graphos*, meaning writing. In recorded history, the most ancient use of the term is a lone reference in Athenaeus's *Deipnosophists (The Sophists at Dinner)*, a second-century collection of culinary and related anecdotes. See Athenaeus, *The Deipnosophists*, vol. 6, trans. Charles B. Gulick (Cambridge: Harvard University Press, 1937), p. 63 (567b). Among other places, the word resurfaced in nineteenth-century art history literature to label the erotic artifacts unearthed from the ruins of Pompeii.

which there is erotic *self*-expression but little or no communal expression. Imagine a place in which sexual *war* and sexual *pleasure* are synonymous and unending. Imagine a place in which carnal expression is an article of *faith*. Imagine, again, a place in which rubber speaks and we *know* it. Imagine a place in which deliberative democracy and sexual harm are no more than *respectable stories*. Imagine, if you can, the death of discourse. As you will see, you have just imagined the pornographic state.

The state that we invite you to imagine is called "pornutopia."[4] As the Greek derivation of the term implies, it is a peculiar place, a no-man's-land of sensual indulgence. It is a hormone-happy state. Pornutopia is *not quite* America as we now experience it. Yet in significant ways, it is the state that liberal America aspires to be. Pornutopia emerges as the forces of self-gratification, mass consumerism, and advanced technology merge. The greater this synergy, the greater is the tendency toward a culture in which self-gratification defines self-realization, in which the irrational decreases the rational, and in which images dominate discourse.

If the old utopian First Amendment were ever to become the new pornutopian First Amendment, James Madison's reasoned discourse would bend to pornutopia's raw intercourse. Indeed, the commercial entertainment culture has left much of the old First Amendment utopia far behind but has yet to cross the boundless frontiers of the new First Amendment pornutopia. In today's culture, America faces a conundrum. On the one hand, government regulation to keep pornutopia at bay is likely to become increasingly futile. If the current synergy of forces either remains constant or accelerates, constitutional attempts to constrain pornographic expression will collide with and eventually succumb to the popular culture. On the other hand, government indifference to the lure of pornutopia will reinscribe the First Amendment beyond all recognition. Boldly stated, deliberative discourse dies and is reincarnated as image-driven onanism.[b] In what follows, consider how America's quest for pornutopia has altered and continues to alter our culture and our traditional understanding of the First Amendment.

---

b) Onanism, a medical term for masturbation and a term popularized in the nineteenth century, derives from the Bible. (Genesis 38:8–10)

At the outset, we offer a few words about the word "pornography." Our use of the term is not confined to current legal definitions, including definitions of "obscenity." Nor is our use of the term limited to that of any of the current ideological camps on the legality of pornography. For us, what is important about pornography is that

- it trades in depictions of sexual acts, primarily through highly eroticized images;
- it is publicly available, typically through commercial distribution;
- it is not a static phenomenon: its appearance alters as it pollinates the commercial entertainment culture; and
- if pornography is communication—a questionable claim—it is communication of a different order than the deliberative discourse said to be at the core of the First Amendment.

Admittedly, our use of the word "pornography" might be seen as too narrow or too broad. Both penal law and Supreme Court decisions reveal, of course, that there can be pornography without mass production, commercial distribution, or pictures. Yet for over two decades pure print erotica,[c] even if mass-produced and commercially distributed, has been functionally immune from criminal censorship.[5] Today, prosecutors simply have little or no interest in the likes of the Marquis de Sade's *The 120 Days of Sodom*, D. H. Lawrence's *Lady Chatterley's Lover*, Henry Miller's *Tropic of Cancer*,[d] or even the infamous *Sweet 69*.[6] Furthermore, we have no squabble with those who may charge that our

Ours is the era of the image: The naked printed word provides comparatively little erotic rush.

c) With the advent of digital typographic erotica on the Internet and other computer bulletin boards, lawmakers and prosecutors will take a renewed interest in regulating these communications. Such enforcement attempts are likely to be quite difficult, if not futile, given the worldwide and substantial engagement in "net.sex," the decentralized character of computer technology, and the extraordinary commercial profits at stake.

d) Interestingly, Charles Rembar, the lawyer who defended *Lady Chatterley's Lover*

notion of pornography is so broad that it might encompass the artistic. In fact, the pornographic enterprise aims to blur lines and to pose as a disseminator of material with serious artistic value.

Sexualized expression is certainly not foreign to Western civilization. Even the Greeks embellished their drinking cups with group sex scenes and the Romans adorned the villas of Pompeii with bas-reliefs of bestiality. Still, it is a long way from the theater of Dionysus to the X-rated video boutiques of New York's Eighth Avenue. Indeed, the rise of the pornographic state (as we know it) is a relatively recent historical development.

The pornography of the past is not the pornography of the present. In the past, it was often political; today, it is largely apolitical. In the past, it was typically blasphemous or seditious; today, it is typically erotic or perverse. In the past, it was generally produced for the elite few; today, it is generally mass-produced. In the past, its methods of communication often left much to the imagination; today, its electronic technology often leaves little to the imagination. The pornographic state traces back to antiquity, though its boldest tracks are found in modernity.

In the West,[e] pornography's recorded past is marked by such notable events and figures as • the theatrical performances of Aristophanes's ribald *Lysistrata* (411 B.C.) and his *Assembly of Women* (392 B.C.) • the Roman poet Ovid's *Ars Amatoria*, a manual for adulterers (circa first century B.C.) • the lustful Roman "novel" *Satyricon* by Petronius (circa first century A.D.) • and the witty accounts of Greek prostitution and homosexuality in Lucian's *Dialogues* and Athenaeus's *Deipnosophists* (circa second century).[7] Paging swiftly through history, we come next to • pornography's early traces in England,

and *Tropic of Cancer* in state and federal courts, declared after his 1966 U.S. Supreme Court victory in the Fanny Hill case that this precedent meant that "[l]iterary censorship was gone." "Reading a book," he added, "is a private affair. We are not talking about billboards or skywriting, or that ubiquitous, intrusive medium, television." Harry Clor, ed., *Censorship and Freedom of Expression* (Chicago: Rand McNally, 1971), pp. 28, 29.

e) Vatsayana's *Kama-Sutra* (circa first century A.D.), a mystical tract on the art of lovemaking, is the most renowned ancient Eastern erotic work.

The Exeter Book, a monastic collection of earthy poems and riddles (circa eleventh century) • Boccaccio's *Decameron*, the printed Italian tales of clerical seductions (1358) • the notorious Italian sonnets of Pietro Aretino accompanying twenty detailed erotic engravings in a compilation known as *Arentino's Postures* (1524) • François Rabelais's five-part *Gargantua and Pantagruel*, an "unusually vigorous blend of scatology and satire" (1532–1552) • and the Inquisition's infamous list of banned books, the *Index Librorum Prohibitorum*, prepared by Pope Paul IV and issued by the Council of Trent (1559–1564).[8]

Moving along, we arrive at the seventeenth and eighteenth centuries to bear witness to • the British Licensing Act of 1662, censoring "heretical, seditious, schismatical or offensive books or pamphlets" • the racy divorce-trial accounts of adultery as reported in the English newspapers during and after the reign of Charles II (circa mid-seventeenth century) • the two-score bookselling career of Edmund Curll, the "father of English pornographic publishing," who was convicted for printing obscene works (1725) • the greatest collection of French erotic works from the *ancien régime*, gathered from 1836–1844 and stored until 1980 in the famous *Enfer* (Hell) section of Paris's Bibliothèque Nationale • the best-sellers in eighteenth-century French pornography, like *Thérèse philosophe* (1748) and *Correspondance d'Eulalie* (1784), that employed eroticism to advance the causes of the Enlightenment and the Revolution • John Cleland's *Memoirs of a Woman of Pleasure (Fanny Hill)*, the crown jewel of the English pornographic novel (1750) • George III's stirring proclamation against "licentious prints" (1787) and the first British anti-vice societies created to enforce the king's edict (circa 1800) • and finally, the Jesuit-educated Marquis de Sade's bizarrely pornographic writings (1784–1800), which "fervently advocated" the "inversion of all values, sexual and other, that govern civilized behavior."[9] These and other unmentionable events tell much of the story of the pornography of the past.

In this sweep of some 2,200 years, we may discern several important attributes of the old pornography. From ancient Greece to the Enlightenment, Western culture's pornographic traditions were steeped in political satire, religious blasphemy, and social critique. Classical Greek comedy often resorted to sexual and even scatological antics to satirize public figures, to criticize the philosophers, and to demean the deities. For example, Aristophanes's *Lysistrata* mocked the male military establishment by sexual humor and obscene innuendo: As the Athenian commissioner of public safety threw open the cloak of a Spartan herald, he exclaimed: "You clown, you've got an erection!" Shortly thereafter, the herald was asked how things were in Sparta, to which he replied: "Thangs is up in the air. The whole Alliance is purt-near 'bout to explode." And when the good commissioner inquired, "What was the cause of this outburst?" he was told that the strapping Spartan woman Lampito was to blame.[10] By such pornographic devices, *Lysistrata* was playfully indecent for a most serious and decent purpose—to undermine war efforts.

Lysistrata—The Modern Eroticized View:

As late as 1955, lawyers in the U.S. Postal Service deemed Aristophanes's antiwar classic to be "plainly obscene" and "calculated to deprave the morals of persons reading [it] and almost equally certain to arouse libidinous thoughts." What was political satire in Athens became perverted sex in America. Today, *Lysistrata* no longer offends: Its subversive message is not fully appreciated, and its print form provides relatively little erotic charge.[11]

Centuries later, the Roman Church wielded immense censorial power over pornographic works issuing from Renaissance printing presses. What typically provoked ecclesiastical outrage was not so much carnality as its union with heresy. Giovanni Boccaccio's *Decameron* was one of the first printed books to arouse the attention of an omnipresent papal eye. As historian H. Montgomery Hyde stressed, amidst the wanton tales of adulterous seductions, "the Church remains the greatest foil for Boccaccio's fun." Pope Paul IV turned this insult into Boccaccio's injury by placing the novel on the *Index Librorum Prohibitorum*. Again, "this was not because of indecency, but because of the author's blasphemous attribution of sundry crimes such as greed and mendacity to the clergy."[12]

The Decameron—The Modern Eroticized View:

"All editions of Boccaccio's *Decameron* coming before this office have been declared nonmailable," reported the solicitor to the U.S. chief postal inspector in 1928. Meanwhile, the president of Oklahoma University complained that his copies of *The Decameron* were "destroyed by Customs officials." Predictably, the modern obsession with prurient interests replaces the earlier objection to heretical influences.

From 1500 to 1800 sexual organs and encounters were depicted explicitly by word and image in books, newspapers, and flyers; the main purpose of such depictions was to denounce the governing elites of church and state in England, France, Italy, and other European nations.[13] A familiar prototype of early print pornography, successfully employed in the French classics *L'Ecole des Filles* (1655) and *Les Liaisons Dangereuses* (1782),[f] used conversations between prostitutes and exchanges of letters between aristocrats.[14] These print "dialogues" exposed the hypocrisy of conventional morality and mocked the nobility and the clerics who flagrantly violated their own sexual regulations. In the decades around the French Revolution, a flurry of political pornography condemned the corruption of the court, much of it targeting Queen Marie-Antoinette, the king's ministers, and the aristocratic deputies of the National Assembly. One such example, captioned *Ma Constitution*, portrayed the renowned Lafayette on bended knee fondling the exposed "res publica" of Marie-Antoinette. Another example from the same period caricatured a monk with a full erection carrying a model of the French royal palace and saying: "I'm coming.... I am the good Constitution."[15]

Ma Constitution—The Modern Eroticized View:

For the revolutionary French, the pornographic was mainly political because the political had become pornographic. In many senses, then, pornographers fought fire with fire. By contrast, in contemporary America, the pornographic is seldom elevated to the political. Pornography revels in what it is—expression that typically generates more erotic heat than political light. In this sense, today's pornographers do not fight fire with fire, but in(ex)cite us to fuck with fire.[g]

Not only ideology but limited production and relatively restricted readership characterized the pornography of the past. As anthropologist Bernard Arcand explained, "[P]ornography was at first an

f) *L'Ecole des Filles*, a work of unknown origin, is widely acknowledged to be the first pornographic text published in French. Choderlos de Laclos's *Les Liaisons Dangereuses* is one of the most celebrated examples of the rhetorical device of an exchange of explicit pornographic letters.

g) Although one of us has reservations about the use of the "f-word," both of us feel constitutionally relieved by U.S. Supreme Court precedent. See *Cohen v. California*, 403 U.S. 15 (per Justice Harlan, 1971) (the "f*** the draft" case).

extremely limited field. Until very recently, erotic works of art, engravings, illustrations, and performances were rare and very costly."[16] Prior to the age of print, only the elite who could afford handwritten manuscripts might have enjoyed the likes of Lucian's *Dialogues*. And even after the great Gutenberg invention, only the literate could comprehend the likes of Boccaccio's *Decameron* or de Sade's *Justine*. The growth of commerce, the spread of literacy, and the appearance of technologies of imagery all converted the past into the present. At long last, modern pornography could make its debut.

"Modern Times"

The past two centuries have marked the precipitous rise of the pornographic state. Significant nineteenth-century events and figures include • the 1815 Pennsylvania state court conviction of Jesse Sharpless and his five cohorts on a specific charge of obscenity, the first of its kind in America, for exhibiting a painting that explicitly depicted intercourse • the New York publishing enterprise of William Haynes (the father of American print erotica) that was responsible for issuing *Fanny Hill* and some 320 other pornographic books from 1846 through 1870 or so • the first appearance in English (1850) of a form of the word "pornography" in an art history manual cataloguing obscene Pompeiian artifacts housed in the Italian "Secret Museum" • the first and long-lived test of illegal obscenity, declared by Chief Justice Cockburn of the Queen's Bench in *Regina v. Hincklin* (1868) • the obscene photographs of Henry Hayler's family members, 130,248 prints of which were destined for European black markets but unexpectedly seized by London bobbies (1874) • and the bluenose Anthony Comstock, who boasted that his four-decade campaign to enforce the 1873 federal Comstock Act had "destroyed 160 tons of 'obscene literature' and convicted 'persons enough to fill a passenger train of sixty-one coaches.'"[17]

Rushing headlong into the twentieth century, we ought to take note of such signposts as • the 1906 publication of attorney Theodore A. Schroeder's *Freedom of the Press and "Obscene" Literature*, one of the first American constitutional tracts on the topic • the 1907 French flick, *Le Voyeur*, an early stag film • the obscene mail trials of 1930 to 1956 • the first U.S. Supreme Court reference to "'hard core' pornography," found in Justice Harlan's dissent in *Roth v. United States* (1957) • the seminal (and ovarian) studies of the Kinsey Institute and of Masters & Johnson, promulgating "all the sexology and 'orgasm' research begun in the late sixties and popularized in dozens of sex manuals" • the 1972 opening of the sixty-two-minute box-office smash, *Deep Throat*, initially attended by hundreds of thousands and ultimately grossing over $50 million • the much-ballyhooed 1970 and 1986 reports by federal commissions on the American pornography industry, reaching diametrically opposed conclusions on its evils • the technological wizardry ranging from libidinal home videos and sex gadgets to computer "cybersex" services such as SEXTEL and COMPUSEX and beyond to "virtual" sexuality • and finally, the quarter-century explosion of pornography's gross profits, from an estimated $500 million in the late 1960s to more than $10 billion in the 1990s.[18]

When pornography moved through modernity to postmodernity, the outlines of the pornographic state became ever sharper. Notably, SEX and its IMAGE took on lives of their own largely divorced from church and state. Entire scientific and social "disciplines" — medicine, psychiatry, criminal justice, civil regulation, and community controls, etc. — responded in important part to the rise of the pornographic state. These disciplines, in turn, developed new discourses on sex that contributed to the sex-obsessed mind-set.[19] As pornography scholar Walter Kendrick incisively observed: "[O]ne could now conceive of 'sex' in its own right, sorting it out from the moral, legal, and religious contexts in which it had hitherto been embedded." Kendrick confirmed that "[n]ot until very late in the nineteenth century would the sifting be completed, leaving us today with a notion of sex as something like advanced calisthenics. 'Pornography' as the twentieth century has known it requires this understanding of sex for its very existence."[20]

Technology played a definitive role, as well, in portraying sex as an object of more commonplace, yet frenzied, perception. The mechanical and electronic reproduction of photos and the inventions of cinematic and audio-video imagery made possible the mass production and distribution of inexpensive erotica to blue-collar and illiterate consumers. In a culture otherwise inured to the technological power of commercial images,[h] the many and varied tides of pornography flowed with an almost inexorable force, repeatedly frustrating any governmental or social campaigns to dam them. Indeed, "no government wants to admit that it no longer has the means to control pornography. The good old days when it was possible to burn books

h) Recall our arguments in "Communication & the Capitalist Culture" in Book II.

and destroy printers' plates are gone."[i] The most effective restraints on pornography, if any, are to be found today in a marketplace that maximizes profits. Hence, a few frames (but only a few) from Madonna's steamy *Body of Evidence* (1992) landed on the cutting room floor because the film was "intended for mass marketing, not an art film crowd, [and] the producer considered it 'crucial that it be acceptable to exhibitors throughout the country.'"[21] In effect, nothing is commercially obscene unless the captains of commerce fear that it manifestly repulses mass tastes or offends mass values. Money matters more than morals.

Yet the very idea of commercial restraint is ironic since the marketplace is forever appealing to the erotic within us. How can we be restrained by the very commerce that lures us, by what a *New York Times* editorial once labeled the "utter degradation of taste in pursuit of the dollar"? Admittedly, the market may cater to the common core, but it does so by tempting us with forbidden apples, which we find increasingly hard to refuse. "Modern pornography tries to outdo itself, to be ever more excessive, which is perfectly in keeping with all our other enterprises," Professor Bernard Arcand observed. "[A]bove all, the modern citizen is drawn to the pleasures of excess, the excitement of exploring the limits of experience, where one feels the borders fading away and savours the enervating sweetness of losing control, of ecstasy."[22] Consummate commerce!

With the rise of the pornographic state of mind and culture, the Erotic intensifies—"immune to argument, invincibly self-righteous, engorged with indignant passion."[23] It is almost a life unto itself, a life with its own logic.

Toward a New Logic

In full flower, pornography's logic exposes its viewers to themselves—to the contradictions within. Thus viewed, it is a form of exhibitionistic communication with a logic of its own.

i) For example, according to the U.S. Department of Justice (circa 1986), only 2 of 12,000 police in Chicago, 8 out of 6,700 police in Los Angeles, and 2 of 1,500 police in Miami were assigned to combat pornography. Moreover, national and local efforts to police "cybersex" and "virtual sex" are considerably less availing.

The Logic of the Erotic

The Erotic speaks passionately even when it is silent.

Whatever else may be said of this proposition and its implications —and we will "say" more about both later—it is not likely to be held up as a central public value by any worthy system of freedom of expression. In fact, the author of *A Worthy Tradition*,[24] the late Harry Kalven Jr., spoke to this point when he argued that constitutional protection of speech critical of government is indispensable to a free society although protection of erotic expression is not.[25] Essentially, Kalven's assertion reflects the age-old commitment of Western democratic societies to politics by public reason rather than by private passion.

As long as the First Amendment is rooted in Madisonian soil, the ideal of a democratic state inevitably entails reasoned political discourse. Though there are other free speech values, the traditional concept of the First Amendment would be unrecognizable without some meaningful dedication to the political function of public reason. A well-informed and active citizenry might best maintain a stable and just society through an open exchange of ideas rationally related to the public good. This, at bottom, is the premise typically invoked by jurists and scholars to legitimate American constitutional government.

Witness the testimony of University of Chicago law professor Cass Sunstein concerning "a well-functioning system of free expression.... Following the Madisonian conception, I suggest that such a system is closely connected to the central constitutional goal of creating a deliberative democracy." The system promotes "government by discussion," aiming "to ensure broad communication about matters of public concern among the citizenry at large and between citizens and representatives." Above all, "the system of deliberative democracy is not supposed simply to implement existing desires."[26] Rising above narrow self-interests, the deliberative citizenry is to define and foster broad-based public interests. Building upon this cornerstone of public reason, Harvard philosopher John Rawls declared: "[T]he aim of political liberalism is to uncover . . . a reasonable public basis of justification on fundamental political questions."[27]

In light of this, why should the free speech system of any deliberative democracy protect pornography? Sunstein's answer is quite simple: "Sexually explicit works can be highly relevant to the development of individual capacities. For many, it is an important vehicle for self-discovery and self-definition." This admittedly low-value speech, lying at the periphery of the noble Madisonian First Amendment,[28] is nevertheless included within the zone of constitutional protection, presumably because individual self-realization *might* contribute ultimately to reasoned democratic discourse.[29] In this sense, the pornographic experience enriches political expression.

However pornography is understood, there are troubling consequences for the Madisonian ideal when the pornographic experience is coupled with public expression. In this regime, is it any longer possible to differentiate Madisonian self-realization from pornutopian self-gratification? Is it any longer possible for rational logic to trump erotic logic? Is it any longer possible to distance public good from private self-indulgence? And finally, will this regime tend to collapse the First Amendment theory of reasoned discourse into a principle of pleasure?

Implicit in these questions is an important point rarely made explicit in most current theories of free speech. That point is the potentially corrupting influence of certain forms of private expression on public discourse. The noble Madisonian First Amendment stands to lose its staying power when it is trivialized, marginalized, and eroticized by a mass commercial entertainment culture wed to self-gratification, particularly pornographic gratification. In such a world, the Madisonian ideal is subverted because key prerequisites for that system are perverted. Plainly put, the traditional system of free expression *mis*functions in our contemporary popular culture. It misfunctions to the extent that we equate gratification with realization. It misfunctions to the extent that pornographic images masquerade as political ideas. It misfunctions to the extent that a public photo of one person urinating into another's mouth is said to call for "fierce protection of speech"[30] that purports to further deliberative democracy. In all of this, the First Amendment is re-created so that personal pleasure is the ultimate political purpose.

The modern creed: Liberty is License. And America saw that it was good–very good.

The regimes of profit and pleasure point to pornutopia. The pornographic state depends on interactions among advanced capitalism, mass commercialism, electronic technology, and unbridled entertainment. Clearly, sex appeals and sex sells. Pornography, whether the "vanilla" erotica of cable TV or the seedy hard-core video, commodifies sex. Whereas our society prohibits the sale of sex, we are much more tolerant about the sale of the image of sex. We forbid the sale of men and women but often allow the sale of their sex divorced from their persons. Basically, pornography tracks the modern mass-advertising process: Pornography takes an individual's sex, imagistically transforms and packages it, and sends it out for commercial sale in a mass market. Like commodification generally, pornography trades the essence of the person for a money-making image. The pornographic state is a republic erupting with images—images that promise to make the unattainable attainable. It is a domain where "uninhibited, robust and wide-open" fantasies dominate.

Within this fantasy realm, private passion overrides *public reason* as the key rationale for constitutional protection of expression. The pornutopian within us must disregard or disbelieve Justice Felix Frankfurter's admonition: "It must never be forgotten . . . that the Bill of Rights was the child of the Enlightenment [and that behind] the guarantee of free speech lay faith in the power of reason."[31] Frankfurter's plea for reasoned discourse will fall on deaf ears. Madison's Enlightenment logic, which elevates the linear rationality of the printed word, will give way to pornutopia's erotic logic, which exalts the chaos of the electronic image.

Indeed, the erotic logic of the pornographic state becomes an "antilogic," a system of contradictions. The power of pornography derives, in part, from its phantasmagoria: Its shifting series of images are both there and not there, both real and unreal. As law professor Susan Etta Keller suggested, "[i]t may be the combination of feeling real and not being real that makes the pornographic representation 'work'... by successfully imitating and not being at the same time."[32] This phantom-like quality of pornography begets yet other contradictions. Viewers of pornography engage in voyeuristic and exhibitionistic acts that both include and exclude them, and that never disappoint but often frustrate them. Media theorist Annette Kuhn summarized well these oppositions: "While luring the spectator with the promise of visual pleasure, pornography in the final instance excludes him from the action. Frustrating though this may be..., a lack of closure opens up a space... where he is free to complete the action as he pleases, in his own imagination."[33] At its extreme, pornography legitimates logical contradictions in the viewer's conscious desires. For example, the "fantasy of rape" (in which the victim resists seduction, is forcibly overpowered, but nevertheless finds sexual satisfaction) "may involve wishes and positions which, logically, cancel each other out—the wish to have something and not to have it."[34] In all of its modes—reality but unreality, inclusion but exclusion, fulfillment but frustration, anxiety but pleasure—pornography's erotic logic stimulates the old mind of the First Amendment in new ways. Thus stimulated, concentration is constitutionally protected to guarantee masturbation; and the old First Amendment rationality is reconfigured beyond recognition.

Not only rationality but the concept of free speech in the service of the *public good* is redefined in the pornographic state. For the ideal of Madisonian deliberative democracy, speech is not simply expression for its own sake, but discourse to promote reason in public affairs. Ideally, the First Amendment's negative command of "no law" keeps government at a distance; this permits a well-informed and active citizenry to realize significant social objectives, whether political or otherwise. Pornutopia, by contrast, values the negative command to further its own conceptions of the First Amendment as a way of life. Government is kept at bay to guarantee a free-feeling culture—one in which the high may crumble into the low, civic virtue may yield to self-indulgence, and public good may succumb to private pleasure.

What if, however, America's mass pornography were linked to political protest of the fifteenth-to-eighteenth-century Western European variety? If it were, pornographic lampooning could merge passion with political speech. Pornographic works could take on political significance precisely because they were *de*eroticized. Then, the First Amendment might not view pornography as antagonistic to its public-good rationale. From the Madisonian perspective, such pornography might legitimate the erotic by rendering it satirical or seditious. If this form of political pornography could be heralded as expression in the service of the common good, it is a far cry from pornutopia's common fare. Whereas political pornography once generated public controversy for public discourse and action, the pornographic state now offers its erotica to generate individual pleasure in private consumption. More important, whereas political pornography was deeroticized, the pornographic state reeroticizes its messages without regard to civic virtue or the public good.

Characteristically, the pornographic state ignores the norms of self-restraint and social responsibility essential to the high ideal of Madisonian deliberative democracy. That is, pornutopia continually pushes the boundaries of social conventions. It entices us to transgress taboos in an unceasing search for novel ways to self-gratify. "In pornographic sexuality, taboos become mechanical, fixed, and easily crossed. There is taboo on one side, and 'free' pleasure on the other, in a tabooless zone.... [T]his generates the endless appeal of the 'everything is permitted.'"[35] On the First Amendment altar, pornutopia sacrifices the very notion of the public good to the interests of private pleasure.

With this sacrifice, the pornographic state redefines the fundamental character of democratic regulation of expression. First Amendment law traditionally equates the public interest with lawmaking by representative government. In pornutopia, however, the public interest may no longer be linked solely to representative majoritarianism; it may well be related to the majoritarianism of popular appetites expressed in the mass commercial entertainment culture. A jurist in the pornographic state, for example, clearly would reject any Federal Communication Commission limits on indecent broadcasting. This freedom-loving jurist would likewise lend First Amendment cover to tabletop dancers clad in pasties and G-strings, or allow "skin theaters" to project their pornographic messages in public school and church zones.

It may seem puzzling that a judge in pornutopia would invoke the First Amendment to intervene between the popular culture and representative majority rule. If laws mirrored such a culture, there would be no need for First Amendment intervention, since no expression would be suppressed. Why, after all, wouldn't laws always reflect the eroticized culture of the pornographic state? The answer can be put simply: The "anarchistic" quality of erotic self-expression in pornutopia is fundamentally at war with the notion of a government of laws. To repeat, the very mission of the pornographic culture is to push all boundaries, including the fixed lines of the law. To the extent that law is oriented to the old ways, it will be out of sync with the new ways of the pornographic culture. Pornutopia is forever young. The judges of this state should likewise be prepared to keep the pornographic First Amendment forever young.

As erotic logic overtakes the traditional First Amendment, a key liberal justification for constitutional protection is transformed. That justification—the promotion of self-realization—becomes increasingly indistinguishable from pornutopia's promotion of self-gratification. Our colleagues, law professors Jerome Barron and C. Thomas Dienes, intimate as much when they observe: "If one accepts the liberty model of speech, it can be argued that even obscene material can aid in self-awareness and self-development."[36] Indeed, becoming more self-aware of pornographic desires impels one to develop them further.

The Delphic injunction of the Madisonian free speech guaranty is "know thyself."
The Dionysian maxim of the pornutopian First Amendment is "feel thyself."

The primary appeal of self-realization in deliberative democracy is to master oneself; the "primal appeal" of self-gratification in the pornographic state is "to lose oneself, lose it utterly."[37]

Pornutopia's self-gratification radically transforms the First Amendment concept of self-expression. Pornography entices people to lust after sexualized images while readily abandoning the experience of real people. It concocts a pseudoworld in which all too frequently decent talk among men and women succumbs to indecent views of men and women, togetherness surrenders to selfness, and contact and communication between the sexes yield to autoeroticization. When pornography leaves the commercial quarters of its producers and enters the private sanctuaries of its consumers, "communication" between producers and consumers might be called discourse in only the loosest sense of the term. Alternatively, in a much more revealing sense, pornography might be seen as a "one-way process," in which "[t]he image is not forged for purposes of communication, but for the joy which is the [viewer's]. The [viewer] and the medium are self-sufficient."[38] Notably, this idea gives new meaning to the popular First Amendment phrase *self*-expression. As reconstructed in the pornographic state, self-expression is not communication about the self to others. It is rather the self silently "talking" back to itself through an image. At the core of this revised notion of self-expression is a revised right to be *let alone*, a right to self-expression free of the entanglement of communication with living beings.

Are not objections to vulgarity undemocratic?

Electronic technology (along with profit and pleasure) plays a crucial role in the evolution of the pornographic state. Much of today's pornography is the product of the cinematic revolution that accustomed the American psyche to the human body in motion. Film-studies expert Linda Williams insightfully observed: "With the invention of cinema, . . . fetishism and voyeurism gained new importance and normality. . . . Cinema implanted these perversions more firmly, normalizing them in technological and social 'ways of seeing.'"[39] Tomorrow's pornography may well be the product of a computer revolution that habituates the American psyche to "net.sex" and virtual reality.

The much-praised electronic information highway is paved with erotic intentions and runs through many a digital red-light district. Nancy Tamosaitis, coauthor of the best-selling *The Joy of Cybersex*, observed: "What is not so widely acknowledged by on-line enthusiasts such as Vice-President Al 'Information Highway' Gore . . . [and presumably House Speaker Newt Gingrich?] is that an impressive amount of traffic on the Internet is sexual in nature."[40] With cursors flashing and fingers flying, "net.voyeurs" cruise adult-oriented newsgroups such as the all-popular alt.sex on Usenet. They pick up tantalizing morsels of information on such specialized subgroups as alt.sex.first-time, alt.sex.fetish.fashion, alt.sex.bondage, and for the more violent of heart, alt.sex.guns. Anything is possible on the net, even forays into the unusual worlds of alt.dead.porn.stars and alt.sex.necrophilia. The pictorially dependent are drawn to Usenet photo and simulated picture files such as alt.binaries.pictures.erotica, alt.binaries.pictures.bestiality, and (as if it might be differentiated from the others) alt.binaries.pictures.tasteless.[41] With no centralized ownership and little meaningful governmental oversight, whatever "net.censorship" exists is self-imposed by commercial on-line services. Even on this front, several forces inveigh against effective censorship: the massive traffic in net.sex; the competitive drive to offer more robust services; and pornography's digital civil liberties defender, the Electronic Frontier Foundation.[j] For now and the foreseeable future, it may be green lights ahead for sex on the electronic highway.

The erotic may extend well beyond net.sex. Only "listen" (as you read) to "sexpert" Susie Bright and others muse on the delights of virtual reality: It is "an instant invitation to bring my most forbidden taboos to life.... The line between fantasy and reality would shift very quickly." Moral and constitutional qualms aside, "you could even have sodomy in Georgia."[42] As envisioned by computer's high tekkies, virtual reality would be a future regime of "interactive tactile telepresence,"[43] in which technology would offer a dizzying surfeit of sexual opportunities in a marketplace now called "cyberspace." Without fear of venereal diseases or emotional commitments, and with frenzied visual, aural, and tactile sensations, real people could share erotic

alt.sex.logic

Erotic Logic: Why settle for the real when the unreal is so exciting?

j) The Electronic Frontier Foundation, created in 1990 by Mitchell Kapor and others, is an association committed to shaping and protecting the nation's electronic communications infrastructure. "EFF has been working to make sure that common carrier principles are upheld in the information age. [Such] principles require that network providers carry *all* speech, regardless of its controversial content." Electronic Frontier Foundation e-mail "General Information" letter to authors, 15 March 1995 (emphasis added).

moments with imagistic "people." In cyberspace, pornography's wild polygamy would triumph over today's monogamy. Thus liberated, the once adulterous spouse need no longer steal away to motorcars or motels for tantalizing trysts.

Whatever today's technology may be, it is more important to ponder tomorrow's technology and its consequences. And what may those consequences hold in store for the pornographic state? Imagine a society of advanced technology in which pornographic virtual reality could be privately produced and privately experienced without any fear of law's intervention. In other words, imagine a culture in which consumers themselves are producers of pornography created with entirely generic and legal home technologies. *Practically speaking*, this would place pornography beyond virtually all legal restraints. Feminists, moralists, civic republicans, and other pornography critics would take their place in history alongside the likes of Prohibition's Anti-Saloon League. In pornutopia, people are intoxicated with their First Amendment rights.[k]

Anthony lies in his cyberspace bed, caressing his seductively postured and scantily clad electronic friend. He fantasizes access, feels access, and climaxes. He revels in his erotic logic. In this state, he is totally expressed.

k) As understood today, the potential of virtual reality may be meaningful or meaningless. Even if its promises prove to be hyped, what is important for us is the ever greater public *yearning* for a simulated reality. Indeed, this yearning for cyberlife may be so strong that real people ascribe technological powers to virtual reality that may be unattainable. In this way, virtual reality may be a double fantasy. See Benjamin Woolley, *Virtual Worlds: A Journal in Hype and Hyperreality* (New York: Penguin Books, 1992).

Body Politics & the Ambivalent Citizenry

Ambivalence: "The coexistence in one person . . . of contradictory emotions or attitudes toward the same object or situation."[44] The dictionary defines us and our contemporary attitudes toward pornography. Elaborating on this point, political scientist Richard S. Randall contended: "If the human capacity for pornography is universal, the human interest in censoring it is no less so. This is the paradox of eroticism: we cannot be *characteristically* human without both the pornographic and the impulse to control it."[45] Whatever else holds true for pornutopia, the character of modern America divides the self between the erotic and the antierotic. Pornography is deplored because it dehumanizes; yet it delights because it is all too human. Likewise, pornography is condemned because it enslaves the soul; yet it is celebrated because it releases the body.

On the one hand, WE THE PEOPLE love our pornography:

- Today, Americans spend upward of $10 *billion* annually to peruse ribald magazines, ogle at hard-core films, ring sex-talk phone numbers, and cozy up with steamy cable TV, seamy videocassettes, and sultry DVDs.

- "[F]rom 1965 to 1985, all the major forms of pornographic communication became available in the United States through mainstream channels of commerce."

- A 1986 survey in *Adult Video News* revealed that over 1,500 new X-rated videos were marketed annually. Subsequently, the Adult Video Association reported that adult-video sales and rentals soared 75 percent between 1991 and 1993. By some estimates, Americans rented almost 800 million pornographic videos in 1994 alone.

- Notably, it is claimed that women now rent 40 percent of all hard-core videos; and according to a *Redbook* magazine survey, almost half of the women polled view pornographic films regularly.

- According to a 1994 study, picture erotica ranked first in traffic volume among all newsgroups on Usenet, the world's largest electronic bulletin board; and 4 of the top 10 newsgroups featured assorted sexualized visuals.[46]

Moreover, America's captains of commerce feed the public's sexual appetites by tendering ever more daring depictions of the erotic life to sell alcohol, cars, fragrances, jeans, and magazines (from *Sports Illustrated* to *Vanity Fair*).[47] On the entertainment front, Americans revel in TV talk-show tales of bizarre sex escapades, delight in TV series' libidinal titillations, and take pleasure in a wide variety of risqué magazine advertisements. In one wild week in 1992, Americans splurged on more than a half-million copies of Madonna's *Sex*, a pricey collection of photo erotica running the kinky gamut from anal sex to naked men bound in dog collars.[48] Sex clubs, sex boutiques, sex classifieds, sex electronic billboards, sex computer technology, sex garb, sex toys, sex aids, sex aphrodisiacs, sex greeting cards . . . Sex, SEx, SEX!

Whereas America passionately celebrates the carnal life, it occasionally strives to patrol the gates of pornutopia. Our culture's strong tendency toward the pornographic is tempered by a weaker, though significant, opposition to it:

- Conservative religious groups, radical feminist organizations, and moderate civic leagues protest most vociferously the excesses of the sex magazine, video, DVD, and net.sex industries.

- Obscenity commissions, task forces, law centers, and enforcement units study and crack down on erotic trafficking.

- All fifty states and the federal government have penal codes restricting materials of prurient interest.

Antiracketeering laws, FCC laws, prostitution laws, kiddie porn laws, dial-a-porn laws, civil rights laws, nuisance laws, zoning laws, antidisplay laws, electronic highway laws . . . Laws, LAws, LAWS!

This ambivalence toward the pornographic state affects the ways Americans do and do not communicate about pornography. In one respect, the topic of pornography is so personally and politically charged in our times that we the people can never leave the subject. Americans must talk about pornography and the politics of pornography and must talk about both intensely. In another respect, the diverse and divisive quality of the debate has made it virtually impossible to establish even a starting point for meaningful discourse. Ideological camps—e.g., conservative moralists[49] and radical feminists,[50] liberals and libertarians,[51] the exotic neo-Freudians[52] and Foucaultians[53] —may gather along pro-censorship or pro-pornography lines. These pro-and-con divisions, however, disguise the fact that conformity in result has little to do with conformity in reason. The camps disagree fundamentally on their respective understandings of key concepts for the First Amendment treatment of pornography. "[S]hould pornography be viewed as obscenity? as sexual exploitation? as gender-specific sexual exploitation? as tyranny or domination? as self-expression? as an indication of sexual liberation? as speech? . . . as 'defamation'? or perhaps even as 'harm'?"[54] Without any rational meeting or near meeting of the minds at even basic definitional levels (i.e., the meanings of sex and pornography), productive discourse is unlikely.

Consider in this regard journalist Leon Wieseltier's general observation: "[W]here once there were rational deliberations that led to an end, there are now emotional conversations that lead everywhere, and never end." For that reason, "[t]here is no point in looking for consensus where there is no consensus, or where consensus is available only at a level of such generality that it is morally and politically banal." Ironically, though our society prides itself on promoting the free *exchange* of ideas, in the battle over pornography few, if any, ideas are ever exchanged. The battle represents, as author Salle Tisdale said, a "paralyzed" discourse.[55] Too often, there is controversy but no communication; there is monologue after monologue but no dialogue; and there is clamor but no reflective silence.

Looking solely at the ideological whirlwinds, one would believe that the law of obscenity was likewise in a state of hopeless turbulence. Yet there is relative calm in the eye of the storm, in the case law

Caution: Legalese Ahead

of the Supreme Court. Once the Court moved through the troublesome dicta of *Chaplinsky v. New Hampshire*[56] and the amorphous tests of *Roth v. United States*[57] and its progeny, it settled (for better or worse) on the *Miller v. California*[58] approach. For over twenty years now, the components of Chief Justice Warren Burger's handiwork have survived the commotion that has swept away many other constitutional precedents. Unlike, for example, abortion law, search and seizure law, and sovereign immunity law, the constitutional standards for obscenity are comparatively stable.

One obvious reason for this doctrinal stability is that the *Miller* standards defer considerably to the fact-based determinations of local juries.[59] Put another way, questions of obscenity are left, by and large, to twelve tried-and-true jury members rather than to black-robed judges. In the *Miller* world, free speech liberties are pitted against community standards. Hence, the national First Amendment must bow to the local First Amendment, and federalism trumps freedom. All of this, of course, squares with the antipornographic side of the American mind. But there is another side to which even the *Miller* Court appealed in its own subtle fashion.

One unorthodox explanation for this doctrinal stability is that the Court has made possible governmental toleration of erotica short of the extreme in pure pornography.[60] Notwithstanding much of the conventional wisdom, the Court's rulings may have allowed a *wide*, but not unlimited, measure of commerce in the highly lucrative business of pornography.[l] If so, why? Is it because of erotica's artistic value? Is it because it does not appeal to prurient interests? Is it because it is not patently offensive to a reasonable person? Then again, is it because pornography cannot be separated from other forms of protected speech? These are the standard questions posed about pornography's claim to First Amendment value. As America leans toward pornutopia, we question whether the inquiry should be so confined.

Can it be that the Supreme Court's decisions mean to authorize Americans to flirt with much pornography? Despite the Court's moral posturings, its grudging sanction of erotica may have more to

l) Recently, Judge Bork observed: "*Miller* has done little to help communities that have been searching for some way to control the torrent of pornography." Robert H. Bork, "What to Do About the First Amendment," *Commentary*, February 1995, pp. 23, 27.

do with our national culture's obsession with pleasure and profit than with any genuine concern for *Miller* morality. What little the justices may take from the markets of kiddie porn and the seedy peep-show booths on Hollywood Boulevard, they more than make up for by licensing the captains of commerce to flood the interstate markets annually with $10 billion worth of erotica. What little the justices may deny to lovers of bestiality flicks, they compensate for by indulging countless others with slightly less unusual sexual appetites.

They may well recognize that the balance of ambivalence in America's popular culture is regularly tipped in favor of pornography. Indeed, they may also understand that the prevalence of pornography is an index of the free speech much valued in today's commercial entertainment society. Mindful of this possibility, feminist historian Elizabeth Fox-Genovese insightfully declared: "The deregulation of the pornographic commodity has as much to do with the freedom to buy and sell as with the freedom to speak or to act. Yet most of the participants in the debate over pornography fall silent on the question of market regulation."[61] Ultimately, the silent justices may be censors, but they may be seen as well to be defenders of American commerce.[62]

War & Pleasure in Pornutopia

[The] Common-wealth [is] the mother of Peace.
—Thomas Hobbes[63]

[T]he domain of eroticism is the domain of violence, of violation.
—Georges Bataille[64]

The state of pornutopia is like no other. Sex is pleasure. Sex is war. War is pleasure. Politics is paradox.

Thomas Hobbes, the father of the modern state, imagined a political order in which pleasure might coexist with civic peace. Hedonism, properly understood, is the foundation upon which civil society can be erected. Life-sustaining pleasure is a common good, and politics should preserve the conditions for its pursuit. Indeed, mortal passions and appetites spawn the very notion of individual rights. The greatest of these passions—self-preservation and comfort—might be harnessed by the sovereign state to overpower the monstrous forces of uncivilized men in the state of nature. Taking them out of that hostile state, speech assists in both the formation and the peaceful perpetuation of the commonwealth. Hobbes's momentous contribution to political discourse is that he "instil[led] the spirit of political idealism into the hedonistic tradition." As the first modern political theorist, he "liberated hedonism [from] its previously hidden, private or apolitical character, and transformed it into a political doctrine."[65]

A bastardized Hobbes is the father of the pornographic state. The new Leviathan, like its 1651 predecessor, still celebrates lively hedonism as the foundation of society—but it is an eroticized selfishness.

The new Leviathan still secures the greatest of human passions—but they are sexual passions too often untempered by the specter of death.

The new Leviathan still promotes individual rights—but they are rights at civil war with the old commonweal.

The new Leviathan still cherishes speech—but it no longer concedes a difference between use and abuse where erotic expression is at stake.

In the pornographic state, the animating principle is the pursuit of pleasure over and above all else, including the fear of death.

In the comfort of his Noe Valley condo, Anthony slips out of his clothes and onto his couch. He turns off the lights and zaps on the adult entertainment cable channel. Lysistrata, *a 1968 porno film, fills the darkness. Positioned for excitement, Anthony fixes on the man-hating heroine as she gently seduces her female friends. Ultimately, Lysistrata is sexually betrayed; she stabs her female lovers and herself to death; and Anthony is spent.*

The link between political power, war, and sex is as old as politics itself. Indeed, it was precisely this connection that the Greek poet Aristophanes played upon in the classic *Lysistrata*. When the women of Athens and Sparta went on a sex strike in order to end a twenty-one year war, their gender power did more than obtain the peace—it changed the nature of the regime. The well-being of the state had to be left to women lest men destroy it; and the welfare of the state depended on women's governing men's eros. In this sense, body politics transformed the body politic. If, as this lesson teaches, the political can be sexual, then control over sex brought control over politics and vice-versa. The feminist Lysistrata seized this control for women. One problem for the Lysistratan agenda, of course, was that Aristophanes's classic work was anything but a morality play; it was a comedy. A gynecocracy based on female rule of body politics was seen as farcical because it was seen as futile, even unnatural.

In ancient Greece, men portrayed Lysistrata as comic. In a modern pornocracy, men portray her as tragic, but only after she acts out her pornographic role. Where once she saved men, now she serves them. Where once she brought peace to men, now she is scripted to bring death to women. The pornographic *Lysistrata* is a discourse of death. But what are we to make of it? Is it basically pornographic violence against women? Or is it essentially an opinion about the desirability of violence? Or is it ultimately the violation of another that is inherent in sex?

Responses to these questions largely depend on those to whom they are posed. "Listen" (as you read) to the stirring protests of Catharine MacKinnon: "[W]hat do men want? Pornography provides an answer.... It is their 'truth about sex.'... [W]hat men want is: women bound, women battered, women tortured, women humiliated, women degraded..., women killed. Or, to be fair to the soft core, women sexually accessible... wanting to be taken and used." Accordingly, the radical feminists see in *pornographic violence against women* a complex link between political power and sex. For them, the welfare of the political state depends on women's govern-

---

JAMES MADISON —
THE FATHER OF THE FIRST AMENDMENT

Mari Matsuda (law professor): We need to get away from male-centered notions of free speech.

Kathleen Barry (activist): [Pornography is] the graphic depiction of patriarchy's view of women.

Marilyn French (author): The entire discourse about sex has been created by men. There's nothing we can do about it.

Andrea Dworkin (author and activist): It's not the speech of women that's being protected [by the Constitution. Pornography] is a way of making women into chattel. Who do they belong to? The pimps and the consumers of the magazines and the movies.

"Symposium: Where Do We Stand on Pornography?" *Ms.*, January–February 1994, pp. 32–45.

Question: Does the First Amendment have a mother?

---

ing men's *rea*—the male sexual disposition. They seek to transform the body politic by directing certain aspects of male "discourse" about the sexual. Essential to women's political power, then, is control both over their bodies and over eroticized images of their bodies. Consequently, the radical feminists aim to seize regulatory control over pornography. And strangely enough, in this respect the modern view of the radical feminists harkens back to the traditional view of

Thomas Hobbes—that all citizens are entitled to the full protection of the state. The state cannot ensure the security of all women and at the same time tolerate pornography, "a form of forced sex, a practice of sexual politics, an institution of gender inequality."[66]

Some defenders of the modern liberal state may concede, *arguendo* or otherwise, that pornography represents male violence toward and subjugation of women.[67] For them, however, even that concession is not sufficient to trump the right of erotic expression in the service of pleasure. Why? Because some Americans deplore pornography's violence and subjugation, and others celebrate pornography's representations. Hence, representations of sexual violence and subjugation, even those that *arguendo* cause severe physical or psychological harms, are reduced to *opinions about the desirability of such harms*. Government, then, may not endorse one opinion or desire over another.

Following this logic, Judge Frank Easterbrook warned the radical feminists that in the eyes of his liberal state there is no one correct view about the value of representations of sexual violence and subjugation: "This is thought control. It establishes an 'approved' view of women, of how they may react to sexual encounters, of how the sexes may relate to each other. Those who espouse the approved view may use sexual images; those who do not, may not."[68] Such arguments border on the absurd for the radical feminists: "Behind [Easterbrook's] First Amendment facade, women were being transformed into ideas, [into] sexual traffic... protected as if it were a discussion, the men uninhibited and robust, the women wide-open." Sympathetic to this critique, Professor Frank Michelman noted that Easterbrook's First Amendment strategem "seems to reflect a remarkably devil-may-care stance towards privately wrought subversions of liberty and equality."[69] Indeed, even Thomas Hobbes did not conceive of a hedonism so great as to question the desirability of physical security. As modern liberalism approaches the pornographic state, however, little but this hedonism is understandable.

Once unchecked hedonism is legitimated in the pornographic state, the *violation of another inherent in sex* and in its pornographic images becomes more understandable. Pornutopia knows no limits. In this state, Eros (the god of love) and Thanatos (the god of death) embrace each other. Eros yearns for life's ultimate passions even in the face of death. In modernity, Thomas Mann vividly portrayed these passions in his famous novella *Death in Venice*. His self-disciplined hero, Gustav von Aschenbach, gradually loses himself as he pursues the beautiful lad Tadzio in an "immensity full of promise"[70] culminating in death. The champions of the pornographic state accept fully that erotic desire is a psychological quest to lose one's individuality in an uncivilized fusion with another. Georges Bataille, the philosopher of pornutopia, made the point forcefully: "The whole business of eroticism is to destroy the self-contained character of the participators as they are in their normal lives." Pornography, as it frames reality, re/presents "the elemental violence [that] kindles every manifestation of eroticism." The heightened erotic within us is a transgressor of taboos, particularly moral and legal edicts against violating the lover. Social scientist Mary Caputi described the pornographic as "that dimension of culture that allows us to cross boundaries, exceed limits, apprehend the irrational, and experience the dialectic between life and death." Pornography is essential to our culture, Caputi added, because it puts us face-to-face with Thanatos, the death drive.[71] Hence, pornography represents the syllogism of primordial sex: Sex is pleasure. Sex is war. War is pleasure. As pornography violates Thomas Hobbes's rule of peace, pornutopia constitutes the new Leviathan.

Disputes about free speech are almost always high constitutional moments.... They signal that something is wrong somewhere, either with the body politic or with ourselves. That something may have little to do with free speech.

—Simon Lee[72]

In *Letters from a War Zone*, radical feminist Andrea Dworkin threw down a gauntlet against pornography: "The war is men against women; the country is the United States."[73] Professor Camille Paglia, the nemesis of the radical feminists, picked up the mail glove: "[S]ex is basically combat.... [T]he sexes are at war."[74] What is the war and who are the combatants? For Dworkin, the battle against pornography is part of the war against the subordination and violation of women. For Paglia, by contrast, the battle for pornography is part of the war for the liberation and fulfillment of women and men. In the struggle between these camps, those who demand protection clash against those who pursue unbridled pleasure, the sexually dominated clash against the sexually dominant, and the sexually objectified clash against their sexual objectifiers.

Interestingly, this war is producing a state of constitutional affairs in which free speech is no longer the exclusive domain of the First Amendment. For the radical feminists, the First Amendment must now share the battleground with the equality principle: "[T]o defend pornography as consistent with the equality of the sexes is to defend the subordination of women to men as sexual equality."[75] Constitutionally speaking, "if true equality between male and female persons is to be achieved, . . . the threat to equality resulting from exposure to audiences of certain types of violent and degrading material [cannot be ignored]."[76]

Sex is best when we would kill (others? ourselves?) for it.

Thus understood, the equality principle can be used as a cannonade against the pornographic state. Were concerns of gender equality to triumph over free speech liberties, pornutopia would be unimaginable. Yet pornutopia's protectors are not without their own forceful strategic moves. Free speech liberties in the pornographic state would happily promote an egalitarianism for sexualized tastes that do not conform to community appetites. Hence, pornography's one-way sexual degradation (women demeaned by men) could be remedied by pornographic depictions equally degrading to both men and women of all sexual tastes. In pornutopia, women porn men, men porn women, women porn women, and men porn men with equal vengeance. In essence, the pornographic state is constituted to ensure equality of eroticized exploitation.

Thomas Hobbes would be mortified at the prospect that his theory of political peace might one day lead to a sexual war of all against all. Such monstrous hedonism would devour the dictates of Right Reason. That much seems plain. By Job, we are asked, "Who can confront [the new Leviathan] and be safe?"[77] Perhaps no one. And that is just how life is "lived" in pornutopia.

Rubber, Reason & Religion in Pornutopia

[O]bscene... utterances are no essential part of any exposition of ideas.

—Justice Francis Murphy[78]

[W]e do not accede to [the] suggestion that the constitutional protection for a free press applies only to the exposition of ideas.

—Justice Stanley Reed[79]

Years ago, the justices gathered in the basement of the Supreme Court on "movie day" to watch such films as *I Am Curious—Yellow*. During one of those showings, Justice John Marshall Harlan was heard to say, "By Jove. Extraordinary." Borrowing Justice Potter Stewart's line, some law clerks chimed in jocularly: "That's it, that's it, I know it when I see it."[80] Stewart's famous quip is commonly invoked to emphasize *seeing* as grounds for denying First Amendment protection to pornography. What is overlooked, however, is the *knowing* acknowledged in the "I know it when I see it" maxim. From that perspective, the meaning of Justice Stewart's playful quip turns 180 degrees: Seeing pornography conveys a message that can be known.

Anthony enters a sex shop on New Orleans's Bourbon Street, walks directly to the erotic clothes rack, and gawks at shiny black rubber skirts and stockings. The rubber speaks to him and he knows it.[m]

Is rubber speech? Absurd as this may seem, in the pornographic republic of images this question must be answered, and answered seriously.

m) Perhaps rubber also "spoke" to the nineteenth-century American antipornography crusader Anthony Comstock, who once boasted of using the federal law that was his namesake to confiscate and destroy 60,300 rubber articles.

At its core—its hard-core—the pornographic state holds that it is impossible to define the meaning of *speech* in the text of the First Amendment. The pornographic man, though he may talk 'til the end of time, will never define or even concede the possibility of defining speech. For him, speech is many things; in fact, it is all things. At the very least, it is *expression*, and most assuredly it includes self-expression. It may be symbolic or just conduct. It may be ideational or simply emotional. It may be musical or pictorial. It may be intentional or unintentional, communicative or noncommunicative, public or private, or it may be no more than an image of an image of something once thought real. Speech may even be rubber speaking to Anthony.

In the pornographic state, the very notion of a fundamental right to free speech is an occasion for unabashed dancing in the streets or bottomless dancing on bar tables. It is a cause for celebration, for waving flags or even burning them. It is a right to turn ideas into images, silence into sound, and even a right to turn nouns into verbs. It is, above all else, a constitutional license to porn the world and everything in it.

Thomas Hobbes, the philosopher of pleasure, reminds us that a refusal to define something reduces talk about it to mere opinion or belief.[81] That is precisely the point in pornutopia. There is no fact (even death?) that cannot be equated with fantasy, and truth resides only in the subjective eye. This refusal to define pornography might lead some to believe that First Amendment freedoms are indistinguishable from other constitutionally claimed liberties having nothing to do with expression. Quite the contrary. The defenders of pornutopia must label free speech as seminal, indeed as essential to the good life. They may not be able to define speech, but they know it when they see it. Since such seeing is believing, for them the First Amendment guaranty of freedom of speech is an article of faith.

If the modern mind is in the eye of the beholder, then we are all pupils.

James Madison, the creator of the First Amendment, could envision a nation where the constitutional divide between church and state was demarcated. The language of the First Amendment suggests as much. Its first sixteen words, granting protections for the American religious experience, were separated from the protections of speech, press, and assembly set forth in its last twenty-nine words. Thus conceived, the text of the Amendment distinguished the religious from the political, the pious from the profane.

In contrast, the cultural boundaries between the spiritual and the secular in pornutopia are anything but clear. In the pornographic state, those who oversee the symbols assigned to our notions of truth and value are not our parish priests, ministers, or rabbis, but rather the producers and distributors of erotica. Madonna's immensely successful *Immaculate Collection* album (dedicated to "*The Pope*, my divine inspiration")[82] and Andres Serrano's *Piss Christ* photo[83] bear witness to this claim. Indeed, the blending of faith and fantasy is essential to the ideology of pornutopia. Not only may "spirituality" be played out in a variety of peep shows but a profound and unquestioning belief in erotica itself is rapidly becoming our creed, and communion with its spectacles our daily bread. The faithful are those who believe in the Pornographic Gospel, perhaps with a bit of agnostic hope thrown in for security's sake.

With this, the Madisonian mandate takes on new meaning. Broadly speaking, the First Amendment's initial sixteen words once could be viewed as safeguarding a nonrational faith in God, whereas the last twenty-nine could be seen as securing rational self-government. Now, as nonrationality commingles with rationality, and as erotic expression assumes religious import, we witness the unification of the First Amendment's two major components. The free speech clause merges with its free exercise analogue. Theoretically, the ultimately "preferred position" in constitutional values could be reserved for porn talk. And as the protectorate of pornutopia, the First Amendment itself could become a religious symbol, the new Sacred Writ. No wonder, then, that Americans adore their First Amendment freedoms.

Incredibly, no less noble a figure than Alexander Meiklejohn played a role in moving American constitutional law away from the old Madisonian utopia and toward the new pornutopia. Recall from Book I that it was the classicist Meiklejohn who championed free speech in the name of rational self-government. When in 1961 the social philosopher extended his self-governance rationale beyond the political debates of the town meeting to literary and artistic expression, Meiklejohn opened the gates of free speech in such a way that they might never be closed to pornography. Addressing the governmental regulation of print erotica, Meiklejohn asked: "Shall the government establish a censorship to distinguish between 'good' novels and 'bad' ones? And, more specifically, shall it forbid the publication of novels which portray sexual experiences with a frankness that, to the prevailing conventions of our society, seems 'obscene'?" He answered with an "unequivocal 'no.'... [T]he authority of citizens to decide what... they shall read and see, has not been delegated to any of the subordinate branches of government. It is 'reserved to the people,' each deciding... whom he will read, what portrayal of the human scene he finds worthy."[84] This self-authority, of course, glides all too readily from speech to art and music, and then to erotica and beyond in the American commercial entertainment culture. In principle (and especially in a democratic pleasure state), Plato well understood the consequences of mingling the political with the artistic; that is why, in the *Republic*, Plato sent the poets packing. Even the less philosophical Robert Bork balked at the pornographic implications of Meiklejohn's admission: "Constitutionally, art and pornography are on a par with industry and smoke pollution."[85]

Mindful of this dilemma, the enemies of pornutopia seek to drive a wedge between the artistic and the pornographic, between the likes of the late Federico Fellini and the lively Larry Flynt.[n] The foes of the pornographic state hold firmly to Justice Potter Stewart's belief that hard-core pornography "cannot conceivably be characterized as embodying communication of ideas or artistic values inviolate under the First Amendment."[86] The opponents of pornutopia seek to make explicit what is implicit in this argument: Speech *can* and *must* be defined to exclude erotic excesses. For them, the sine qua non of First Amendment protection is that expression be a *communication*—the transmission of a "mental stimulus" that is "designed to appeal to the intellectual process" rather than "to produce a purely physical effect."[87] Expression is speech "precisely to the extent that it derives from and appeals to the intellectual end of the intellect-emotion continuum."[88]

Preeminent among the guardians of the old First Amendment

n) Federico Fellini's cinematic erotica were enthusiastically applauded in high-art circles; Larry Flynt's ultra-lewd magazine *Hustler* is passionately appreciated in less lofty quarters.

gates are legal philosophers John Finnis, Frederick Schauer,[o] and Joel Feinberg. They concluded that hard-core pornography is not protected by the First Amendment because it does not satisfy even the threshold requirement of "speech." Pornography is not "communication" because its intended and actual effect—sexual arousal—is "perceived as a primarily *physical* reaction."[89] And it is perceived as such by both the purveyor and the user of pornography. "The panderer is participating in the marketplace of prurient interest," we are reminded, "not in the marketplace of ideas." As for the pornographic consumer, "[t]he fundamental question is simple: does the reader look for 'titillation' or for '*intellectual* content'?"[90] Essentially, hard-core pornography is no more than a "masturbatory aid."[91] "So-called 'filthy pictures' and hard-core pornographic 'tales' are simply devices meant to titillate the sex organs *via* the mediation of symbols. They are designed exclusively to perform that function and are valued by their users only insofar as they succeed in that limited aim."[92] Hence, rubber can never be speech, for "much of what this material involves is not so much portrayal of sex, or discussion of sex, but simply sex itself."[93] Accordingly, "[t]he basis of the exclusion of hard core pornography from the coverage of the Free Speech Principle is not that it has a physical effect, *but that it has nothing else.*"[94]

If Finnis, Schauer, and Feinberg are genuine about their mission (and we believe they are), they must trespass upon more First Amendment ground than they might be willing to admit. After all, how does one distinguish hard-core pornography from art in a culture that knows no definition of art? Controversial photographer Robert Mapplethorpe answered playfully: "Pornography is fine with me. If it's good it transcends what it is." Evidently, Frederick Schauer agreed: An "artist" is entitled to depict arms stretching into anuses or to represent one person urinating into another's mouth. Can that "speech" be abridged? "Absolutely not. It's not even close," Professor Schauer was heard to say. Apparently, Mapplethorpe's art/porn transcended what it is because of who he was and where it was. "The very fact that it's by Mapplethorpe and it's in a museum would . . . lead me to say it's not even close," Schauer confirmed.[95]

o) Among his First Amendment endeavors, Professor Schauer served as one of the members of the Attorney General's Commission on Pornography and significantly influenced the contents of its final report (1986).

Implicit in Schauer's observation is a perplexing premise: When a curator mounts a pornographic picture on a museum wall, he turns porn into art. But it might just as well be the opposite. Hasn't the curator turned the museum into a porn palace? One need not take sides in this debate over aesthetics in order to appreciate that pornography is what it becomes and remains what it was.

"CONGRESS SHALL MAKE NO LAW . . ."
ART & NON-ART IN REPUBLICAN EYES

(Excerpts from Senate Debates on Funding of the Arts)

Jesse Helms (R.–N.C.): [T]his pornography is sick. But Mapplethorpe's sick art does not seem to be an isolated incident. . . . [Furthermore,] I cannot go into detail about the crudeness and depravity of [Andres Serrano's] art. . . . I will not even acknowledge that it is art. I do not even acknowledge that [Serrano] was an artist. I think he was a jerk.

James Jeffords (R.–Vt.): We have to create [art] for ourselves. What we create should be a reflection of ourselves.

Congressional Record, 26 July 1989 (101st Congress)

John Danforth (R.–Mo.): The issue is: How good are we at defining whether something is suitable art or non-suitable art and how do we draw those definitions?

Congressional Record, 29 September 1989 (101st Congress)

Quoted in *Culture Wars*, ed. Richard Bolton (New York: New Press, 1992), pp. 73, 75, 78, 82, 104, 106.

Moreover, how does one fight hard-core pornography without likewise fighting the all-too-human mind-set in our increasingly pornographic culture? Sexual release needs the mind's eye. May not as much mental energy be expended on hard-core pornography as on a dime novel? If so, is pornography nonspeech more because of where it takes us than how it takes us there? In other words, it appears that the likes of Finnis, Schauer, and Feinberg may be more concerned with orgasm than with cognition. On this score, they are destined to be outcasts in a culture that prefers retinas in the service of pleasure to retinas in the service of reason. As Camille Paglia, the queen of pornutopia, reminded us: "The sexual revolution is not just about what you do with your body—it's about what you do with your mind."[96] This lesson is at least as old as classical mythology. The Greeks recognized that Pleasure was born from the union of Eros and Psyche.

If these adversaries of the pornographic state cannot ultimately win the war, they can at least take honor in the knowledge that they have launched a powerful broadside against pornutopia. For indeed, there are troubling consequences from forsaking the search for a definition of speech that distinguishes art from pornography. Those consequences, Schauer reminded us, have to do with things like rubber—and plastic and leather.[97] Unless the concept of speech is somehow delimited, the prophylactic of the First Amendment will protect any erotic act or eroticized object that might stimulate orgasm. And some call this the ultimate freedom. But even the progressive left must appreciate that "a society unwilling or unable to trust to its own instinct in laying down a standard of decency does not deserve to survive and probably will not survive."[98]

As he receives his "last rights" in pornutopia, Anthony is in heaven with his rubber.

Respectable Stories for an Unrespectable State

The modern state lives through stories; and it lives for stories. Respectable stories help to construct a worthy identity and character for the state. Most important, to serve their function, these respectable stories must be presumed to be true. This presumption is critical precisely because these stories may be untrue. If such stories do not ring true, they stand to lose any supposed power to preserve and ennoble the state. First and foremost, this is what the respectable storytellers fear.

Storyline: Reasoned democracy animates the modern First Amendment culture.

This respectable story is a tall tale insofar as our society tends ever more toward the pornographic state. As that state is dedicated primarily to self-gratification, virtually everything in it wars against the First Amendment norm of reason in the service of the common good. It is a state moved more by the Bacchanalian than the Apollonian, more by private intercourse than public discourse. The pornographic state turns the Madisonian deliberative utopia into a debauched dystopia.

Why, then, should any respectable notion of the First Amendment cling so fiercely to the protection of pornography? There are at least two possible answers. First, the liberal state (unlike its radical and conservative counterparts) will not withdraw constitutional protection from any but the most blatantly harmful forms of pornography. Consequently, the liberal state can hope to redeem its respectable story only by endorsing the proposition that pornography somehow fosters self-realization, which in turn may foster reasoned democracy. But insofar as pornography is allowed to flourish, is not the currency of reasoned democracy devalued proportionately? Labeling pornography as a force for self-realization does not change pornography, but it may well change democracy.

Lurking below the first answer is a second and more cynical answer. Is it possible that the larger hidden agenda here is to perpetuate the story of reasoned democracy simply to promote pornutopia? Phrased differently, are the proponents of reasoned democracy using a respectable story to lend credence to an unrespectable state? We raise these questions because we suspect that the defenders of the liberal state realize the wide gulf between their First Amendment theory and the culture's free speech practices. Moreover, we suspect that the defenders of the liberal state realize that they cannot endorse virtually unbridled and indiscriminate pleasure as a principle of the First Amendment without embracing hedonism. Ironically, the liberal state appears to invoke reason in order to realize passion.

What if the arguments—think of them as stories—advanced by Louis Brandeis and Josephine Goldmark[p] in the famous *Muller v. Oregon*[99] brief were mistaken? Is it important whether the brief's claims of harmful effects to women from overwork were scientifically true? Perhaps as a commitment of turn-of-the-century progressive reform, it was of no moment whether there were actual harms necessitating legal protection of women workers. After all, the harm principle was the best argument to tender in an America then ruled by a laissez-faire constitutional philosophy. But can a similar harm principle prevail in today's debate over pornography and the First Amendment? Here again, is there a need for a respectable story?

What kind of argument against pornography can be made in a culture that trades in images of sexual pleasure, traffics in the commerce of endless amusement, and trumpets individualism as the governing ideology? Stated differently, what kind of Brandeis-Goldmark brief might prevail in the approaching pornographic state? Ever since the sexual revolution of the 1960s, America's libidinal appetites have been unleashed and largely unaffected by regimes calling for civic decency. Accordingly, the moral argument against patently offensive erotica has been unable to carry the day even under the conservative Burger and Rehnquist Courts and the more conservative Reagan and

p) At the turn of the twentieth century, these two progressives advocated widespread worker reforms ranging from maximum hours for women employed in laundries and factories to minimum wages for all.

Bush administrations. Meanwhile, one wing of the feminist movement has often scrutinized male-dominated pornography with a critical eye while distancing itself from conservative moralism. What antipornography feminists needed was a striking argument for self-restraint and societal regulation, one that might win approval in a pleasure-bent commercial culture. Heed their rising voices!

For the Prosecution:

Robin Morgan:
"Pornography is the theory, and rape the practice."[100]

Wendy Kaminer:
"Pornography is speech that legitimizes and fosters the physical abuse and sexual repression of women."[101]

Gloria Steinem:
"[P]ornography is about power and sex-as-weapon."[102]

Susan Griffin:
"[A]bove all pornography is in itself a sadistic act."[103]

Model Antipornography Civil-Rights Ordinance:
"The harm of pornography includes dehumanization, psychic assault, sexual exploitation, forced sex, forced prostitution, physical injury, and social and sexual terrorism and inferiority presented as entertainment."[104]

Collectively, these and scores of other like charges present an argument that may be compelling even in today's culture: Pornography must be prohibited to the extent that it is the embodiment and the cause of personal harms.[105] There are, however, counterarguments that may be equally or more compelling.

For the Defense:

Ronald Dworkin:
"If [the harm] claim could be shown to be even probable through reliable research, it would provide a very strong though not necessarily decisive argument for censorship. . . . [N]o reputable study has concluded that pornography is a significant cause of sexual crime."[106]

Nadine Strossen:

"[T]hat exposure to sexist, violent imagery leads to sexist, violent behavior [is a claim for which] there is no credible evidence."[107]

Richard Posner:

"It is especially reckless to conclude that pornography in the United States today is a major cause of harm to women."[108]

Elizabeth Fox-Genovese:

"The proponents of curtailment would have an easier time if it could be demonstrated that pornography actually causes, or even substantially contributes to, the perpetration of... violent crimes against women.... Sadly, such proof is lacking."[109]

Edward Donnerstein and Daniel Linz:

"The issue of pornography and its relationship to violence will continue for years, perhaps without any definitive answers. We may never know if there is any real causal influence."[110]

Essentially, these counterarguments challenge the validity of the antipornography harm principle, a principle ardently contested by Nadine Strossen in her *Defending Pornography.* Inferentially, Strossen and other critics invite us to ask: Can it be that the radical feminists are consciously or unconsciously perpetuating their own tall tales? Is it possible that their harm principle is necessarily more rhetorical than analytical? And if so, is resort to their respectable story a critical diversionary tactic in a culture otherwise charmed by erotica's excesses?

Pornography is but another commodity in a capitalist culture that exploits sexual fantasies to feed consumerist desires. If some pornography is sexist and misogynist, it reflects the larger culture of such mass messages. Simply observe the day-to-day fare on commercial television and radio, in magazines and on billboards, and in our ordinary conversations and social dealings. Like the commercial culture generally, pornography holds sex out as a disposable commodity – "a commodity to be turned in for next year's new, brand new model."[111] Pornography is to the mass commercial state what blood is to the body; efforts to withdraw it "would be futile because pornography is not some wart on the surface of capitalist culture"[112] but is at the heart of that culture. Mindful of the culture's life flow, feminist author Wendy Kaminer was blunt: "If society is as sexist as Andrea Dworkin and Catharine MacKinnon claim, it is not about to adopt a feminist agenda when it sets out to censor pornography."[113] What are we to make of this?

If the antipornography feminists realize the futility of censoring pornography while tolerating rampant commercialism, then lurking below the harm principle is a more grandiose tale. Is it possible that the larger hidden agenda is to perpetuate the story of pornography's harms simply to subvert the male-driven capitalist state? Could it be that for antipornography feminists "the dirty secret at the heart of our culture is not sex, but money?"[114] Obviously, a great deal more than pornography is put into issue by the harm principle; it ultimately challenges the socioeconomic structures at the base of our republic of eroticized commercial images. A move toward a (radical) feminist theory of the state inevitably hacks at the very roots of our mass commercial entertainment society. "The alternative to pornography, then, stands or falls with the alternative to capitalist and patriarchal society as a whole."[115] Little wonder that even a full-blooded conservative such as George F. Will could label the radical feminist agenda "the *most* radical assault on free speech in American history."[116] Antipornography is the practice, anticapitalism is the theory.

Egg on our Face?

Simon Lee: *"We are all familiar with Voltaire's dramatic declaration in support of free speech: 'I disapprove of what you say but I will defend to the death your right to say it.' But, disappointingly, Voltaire said no such thing. His comment was, in fact, 'What a fuss over an omelette.'"*

The Cost of Free Speech (London: Faber & Faber, 1990), p. 3.

As the old Madisonian discourse dies, it is remade in pornutopia's images of intercourse. Enlightenment logic gives way to erotic logic. Ambivalence toward pornography surrenders to love of body politics. The common good lapses into a common sexual death wish. The old reason and religion perish and are reunited in a pornographic faith. Reasoned democracy becomes a democracy of desires, and sexual harms become sexualized. America is not yet pornutopia. Ambivalence remains. The old discourse is not yet dead. Still, as the vital signs of Madison's First Amendment weaken, they make way for "life" in the pornographic state.

Clad in a long trenchcoat, Anthony enters the Venus Envy cinema, sits down in an empty row, and watches Caligula[q] *as the Roman emperor collapses in a bacchanalian revelry of sex and violence.*[117] *Anthony is too preoccupied to realize, however, that in the theater of pornutopia the climactic moment is the death of discourse.*

q) *Penthouse International*'s Bob Guccione, one of the film's producers, characterized it thus: "Comparing an X-rated film to *Caligula* is like comparing the shootout at the O.K. Corral to the Second World War."

How Worthy a Tradition? – A "Dialogue"

Scene: An enchanted June evening in the Beverly Hills area of Los Angeles, near the University of California campus. Traveling along Charing Cross Road, guests pass through electronic gates to enter the grounds of a magnificent estate dominated by a majestic two-story mansion. As they arrive at the door, they are greeted by handsome young men who escort them into the grand salon. Later, at the appointed hour, the host appears to preside over a culinary feast. Dinner completed, they retire to the library, where the evening's affairs begin.

What follows is an orchestrated print "dialogue"[118] with rabbi and former public broadcasting producer Suzanne Singer, political scientist David O'Brien, feminist historian Elizabeth Fox-Genovese, law professor and political scientist Cass Sunstein, and law professor and American Civil Liberties Union national president Nadine Strossen. Except for the bracketed remarks, the words, though incomplete and rearranged, are theirs (circa 1993–1995) and ours. The banquet itself, quite unfortunately, is merely the stuff of which fantasies are made.

Collins or Skover: Let us begin by thanking our remarkable host for his generosity and for bringing us all here this evening to exchange ideas about "Discourse & Intercourse." We hope this to be a memorable and stimulating discussion, one that will be captured in a special First Amendment documentary. To enable this, our conversation will be recorded on videotape. Suzanne Singer graciously has agreed to act as the moderator for tonight's dialogue. Suzanne.

Suzanne Singer: [Thank you, Ron and David, for inviting me. True to my role as moderator, I will limit my comments to an occasional question for the rest of you to discuss. Is that all right?]

Collins or Skover: Yes, Suzanne. That is just fine. Given the topic, we all may benefit from your moderating influence. So, ask away.

Singer: Is control of Eros essential to the well-being of the state?

Collins or Skover: Well, Suzanne, there's nothing like taking the cerebral elevator straight to the top floor of the Empire State Building. This is, after all, the ultimate question, is it not?

It is safe to say that most of the great Western political philosophers believed that Eros must be checked in order that civic virtue might survive and flourish. And as we emphasized in Book I, the whole point of the Huxleyan warning is that unbridled pleasure is synonymous with tyranny. Of course, if the state is pornutopia, control of Eros is itself tyrannical.

Nadine Strossen: [Ron and David, you sound so un-American.]

Collins or Skover: Does that mean that we may be called before some modern-day House Un-American Activities Committee? If so, can we count on you to defend us?

Strossen: [Certainly, that's my business. Now, if I can get back to my point. The] celebration of individuality [is] an idea of central importance in [any] society that respects (at least in theory) the inherent dignity, worth, autonomy, and equality of every human being. In other words, the *individual* freedom at stake is also a leading *community* value. So, while you seem to denigrate the "principle of pleasure" that assertedly underlies pornutopia, I would describe it instead as the principle of *choice* or self-determination, equally important from personal and societal perspectives.... Precisely because it preserves and promotes individual autonomy, sexual expression is at the core of human rights.

Collins or Skover: Nadine, it appears as though you are suggesting that the pursuit of unrestrained Eros—which is the animating principle of pornutopia—poses no danger to values such as dignity, worth, autonomy, and equality. Even if individual freedom, however understood, is a leading community value, it is certainly not the only such value. In fact, at some point, it may make other *community* values unattainable. In the context of sexual expression, the Madisonian opponents of pornutopia realize the need to drive a wedge between the principle of pleasure and the preservation of the polity. How far are you willing to push your point? For example, is John Stuart Mill's *On Liberty* the political manifesto for pornutopia? Can you countenance, indeed would you choose, pornutopia as your *ideal* regime?

Anthony enters the room and sits off to the side. Titillated by the talk, he waits to see where it will lead. With his ears sometimes attuned to the dialogue, he picks up a copy of Wired magazine and peruses it.

Skover to Collins: (Whispering) Don't look now, but guess who just appeared? It's that virtual character, sleazy Anthony!

David O'Brien: [May I interrupt? You two are going a bit far afield here.] I quarrel with your contention that modern American liberalism is approaching the pornographic state. You are provocative but seem wrong, or wrong-headed. At least, you mislead in suggesting that the United States is approaching pornutopia. [You would have us believe that] the United States is in some kind of free-fall into a new sorry, sordid state of affairs.

Collins or Skover: David, if you mean to say that Americans do not now copulate everywhere, every minute, and with everyone, you have no dispute with us. As the 1995 sex surveys revealed, perhaps we are not approaching that state of affairs.[119] When it comes to real sexploits, America often shows its puritanical side. Remember, David, we argue that our nation remains ambivalent about sex. But recall also the astonishing figures on domestic commerce in erotica. They are a telling indicator of the other side of the American psyche, the one driving us toward pornutopia. Critical to our analysis is that Americans are increasingly charmed by the *images* of sex, that Americans increasingly turn sexually *inward* rather than sexually outward, and that Americans increasingly choose the *virtual* over the real when it comes to sex and life. This is what we label the new *self*-expression.

Bored by the guests and their dialogue, Anthony inquires of one of the servants about the mansion's private video bedrooms, their location, and their erotic stock. Asked to wait until he is given a key, Anthony proceeds to the corner, takes Michel Foucault's The History of Sexuality *off one of the shelves, and begins to examine it.*

Elizabeth Fox-Genovese: [Ron and David's] arresting—and all too convincing—evocation of pornutopia ... mirrors the world in which we are what we buy, with the small difference that what we are buying is sex. This is the logical conclusion of Marx's vision of commodification with a vengeance. And they perceptively argue that the First Amendment defense of pornography as expression amounts to little more than the defense of commerce. In effect, they are advancing a troubling syllogism in which (1) pornography is self-expression, (2) self-expression is commerce, hence (3) pornography is commerce. To label pornography a force for self-expression, they suggest, does not change pornography, but it may well change democracy. And they suspect that the defenders of the liberal state may well understand that they cannot endorse virtually unbridled and indiscriminate pleasure as a principle of the First Amendment without embracing hedonism. Thus, however ironically, the liberal defenders of the First Amendment appear to invoke reason in order to realize unrestrained passion. If, however, we return to our syllogism, we may be permitted to ask what passion is this that turns the commingling of human bodies into a commerce? Surely not the passion of love in the traditional sense with its religious overtones of self-abnegation, communion, and perhaps transcendence. Yet it is hard to call to mind a culture in which sheer avarice has been celebrated as a guiding passion.

Singer: Why is "a public photo of one person urinating into another's mouth" not a valid political statement?

Cass Sunstein: I think that Mapplethorpe's work is part of democratic deliberation.

Collins or Skover: One person urinating into another's mouth has out-and-out deliberative democratic meaning?

Sunstein: Okay. All I want to say is that Mapplethorpe, in my view, is a sexually explicit [artist] whose work has self-conscious democratic implications. . . . Now, I might be wrong on Mapplethorpe. I'm perfectly prepared to judge that.

Collins or Skover: *Self-conscious* democratic implications? By this, do you mean *subjective* artistic intent in the service of some purportedly democratic cause? If so, consider what follows from positing that free speech principles protect an expressive act merely because a speaker, a writer, or an artist subjectively believes that this act furthers deliberative democracy. First, any meaningful difference between deliberative and nondeliberative communications completely disappears. Second, any realistic definitional difference between the political and the nonpolitical likewise vanishes.

Strossen: [There is something implicit in this exchange that concerns me.] I am troubled by the seeming certainty that there is a "pornography" that can be defined, identified, and relegated to second-class First Amendment status because it is somehow less central to self-fulfillment and self-government than other expression. Even assuming *arguendo* that each of us can "know it when we see it" in terms of which materials serve that (allegedly) less elevated role in our lives and psyches, no societywide definition would be possible.

Just consider the historic and contemporary examples of material that clearly can promote both self-fulfillment and self-government but that nevertheless has been attacked—in some instances successfully—as "pornographic" and "obscene." My book [*Defending Pornography*] is filled with such examples: information about birth control and abortion; sex education materials; safer sex information; art and literature; information about and protests against sexual harassment and sexual abuses; family photographs; materials about lesbian and gay sexuality.

Since our government has always regulated—or sought to regulate—in the realm of sexuality, key questions about government policy, as well as individual identity, are intimately bound up with sex. The sexual *is* political. How, then, can we purport to protect political expression, but not sexual? And . . . it is precisely the sexual expression by, about, or on behalf of individuals whose ideas are relatively unpopular, or who belong to groups that are relatively disempowered or disliked, that will always be most at risk. Unfortunately, those individuals include women, feminists, reproductive-freedom advocates, lesbians and gay men, and lesbian-gay rights advocates.

Collins or Skover: If the sexual is political, then by the same logic is the political sexual? That rather sounds like the sexualized politics of pornutopia, no?

Cass, correct us if we are wrong, but didn't your *New Republic* review of Nadine's book take her to task on precisely the "sexual is political" point? In order to be duly accurate, here as elsewhere, let us read aloud an excerpt from your review, which we happen to have with us:

> Nor is it helpful for Strossen to claim that pornography is "political," a term that she does not define. Maybe pornography is political in the sense that it appeals to political outsiders and dissidents; maybe it is political in the sense that it is (sometimes? often?) sexist. But if speech that is political in these ways is protected by the First Amendment, then a lot of speech apparently counts as political—including, for example, . . . misleading commercial speech, and child pornography, and threats to assassinate the president.[120]

Whatever the merits of your argument, Cass, it sounds curious coming from you. After all, isn't Nadine's maxim that "the sexual *is* political" another way of saying that sexually explicit expression has "self-conscious democratic implications," assuming that we understood you correctly?

Sunstein: But, I'm saying that the self-realization theme is not really about democratic deliberation. That's another First Amendment theme.

Collins or Skover: Fair enough. Then, would you please explain this?

Sunstein: I do know some people... who think that pornography is not very well connected with deliberative democracy though it is connected with self-realization, and so that means it's not outside of

If the Madisonian critique is taken to heart and acted upor

the First Amendment altogether.... [Pornography] is a frequent vehicle by which people figure out what their sexuality is.... I mean, it's self-gratification, yes. But there is something to it also that deserves the name of self-realization. That isn't really about deliberative democracy, but it is a First Amendment value. Then the question would be, at least for the deliberative democrat: If it serves the interest in self-realization, but not the interest in deliberative democracy, what sort of burden must the state surmount in order to allow regulation? And that's a question.

Collins or Skover: You've put quite a bit on the table. Let's see if we can digest it. Returning to Suzanne's question, Mapplethorpe's urination photograph might be placed on (or over?) the First Amendment mantel, as we now understand you, not so much because it furthers democratic deliberation but rather because it furthers self-realization, which is something different. The link between self-realization and deliberative democracy may, nonetheless, be much stronger than you indicate here. If we think of self-realization in a more traditional, philosophic sense (say, an Aristotelian sense), then surely self-knowledge is fundamentally linked to the telos of deliberative democracy. We are, each and every one of us, political creatures. That, at least, is a revered maxim of many schools of political philosophy and should indeed be central to anyone who espouses deliberative democracy. Of course, such philosophers would be unlikely to concede that

Mapplethorpe's yellow art has anything to do with self-realization, properly understood.

Moreover, you suggest that some pornography may be protected in the name of self-realization. And you appear to recognize a difference between self-realization and self-gratification. Presumably, the more pornography promotes self-realization, the more likely it is to receive First Amendment protection; conversely, the more pornography promotes self-gratification, the less likely it is to receive constitutional protection. But what the difference is in your mind between the two forms of pornography remains unclear to us. As you undoubtedly appreciate, pornutopia does not distinguish between self-realization and self-gratification. For you to distance deliberative democracy from pornutopia, there must be some criteria by which to

: could be the most subversive ideology of our times.

differentiate realization from gratification. Given our culture, we realize what a formidable undertaking that is.

One last question. Would it make any difference in your mind if Mapplethorpe's photographs had never been mounted in a museum but debuted instead in a XXX video entitled *Hard to Swallow*?

O'Brien: [You two] are giving First Amendment scholars such as Cass Sunstein a good whacking here, though not entirely their just measure. They are dreaming of "deliberative democracy" and other romantic notions while lying to themselves, perpetuating what you dignify by calling "respectable stories."

Collins or Skover: Whoa, David! Things may be getting a little *too* uninhibited, robust, and wide open.

Strossen: [Gentlemen!] I flinch at your distinction between "self-realization" and "self-gratification." It reminds me of Robert Bork's dismissive treatment of what I (and virtually all modern Supreme Court justices) consider to be fundamental human rights by cavalierly labeling them as "gratifications." It is no coincidence that authoritarian governments have always tried to maintain strict controls on sexual matters—including sexual expression—and that newly democratized governments, which initiate protections of human rights, witness a flourishing of sexual expression.

[T]hroughout history, pornographic writings and drawings have consistently been used to express ideas that challenge the status quo, the prevailing political and religious orthodoxies. Just as, on a personal level, pornography breaks down sexual taboos, so too, on a communal level, it breaks down political, social, religious, and economic taboos.

Collins or Skover: Nadine, you're really flying the ACLU banner here, which is fine in theory even if it is not fine in free speech jurisprudence. Whatever our position may be—and, God knows, it is not Borkean!—it is from the perspective of the traditional First Amendment that a distinction between self-realization and self-gratification is critical. Simply put, our question is: Is not the integrity of any First Amendment value of self-realization jeopardized if it becomes synonymous with self-gratification? Conversely, is it not disingenuous to protect self-gratification in the name of enlightened self-realization?

Singer: May I play the devil's advocate for a moment? Can't the physical lead to the intellectual? Can't the release people get from experiencing pornography give them the space to become clear, rational thinkers? This is a way in which one could argue that pornography serves the Madisonian ideal.

Strossen: [Certainly!] I reject the notion that the paradigmatic *style* of protectible expression is "rational logic." I consider Justice Harlan's opinion in *Cohen v. California*,[121] recognizing the importance of the emotive value of expression, to be one of the most significant contributions to our First Amendment jurisprudence. Central to our self-expression and to our communal discourse are not just rational logic, but also emotional appeals—in matters of politics, religion, art, and all other areas of personal and communal concern.

Collins or Skover: Although there are connections between your claims, you two ultimately appear to come from different conceptual quarters.

Nadine, your point is so complex that we can do little more than approach it gingerly and answer it only partially this evening. We appreciate the force of your argument that protected expression may have both rational and emotive dimensions. But that argument begs the essential question. Is expression that has emotive appeal protected solely for that reason? Even James Madison, despite any distaste for vulgarity, might have conceded the political significance of Paul Cohen's infamous antidraft jacket. But what if Cohen's jacket had no *obvious* political referent? What if he wore a jacket in public bearing a *Hustler* magazine centerfold? Presumably, this is emotive expression, but can we as readily conclude that it is entitled to constitutional protection? It is the pornutopian First Amendment, not the Madisonian one, that allows the emotive to stand alone.

As an aside, Nadine, we are intrigued by your use of the term "emotive" to describe pornography, which is typically viewed as libidinal. So likewise with the term "sexpression" as used in your book. But these are topics for another evening's dialogue.

By comparison, Suzanne, you posit that pornography might be a sort of release valve for rational reflection. We climax so that we may contemplate. We porn, therefore we think. Beyond jest, there is some degree of truth here. Insofar as we sate the libidinal within us, we are more likely to pursue the cerebral. In other words, the sensible life may require balance in all things—rational and erotic. But let's play out the logic of this argument a bit. If porn takes on auxiliary First Amendment value because it creates a space for Madisonian deliberation, then what about things like cold showers, taking a nap, and working out at health clubs? All of these may also be release valves for pent-up passions. Are they, therefore, entitled to auxiliary First Amendment protection? In the more sexually intensified state of pornutopia, by contrast, the release-valve theory is seminal to First Amendment thinking. That is why rubber, plastic, leather, and lace are all protected expressions in pornutopia.

Still posed in the corner of the library, a frustrated Anthony strives unsuccessfully to read Foucault. He yearns for self-realization but yields once again to self-gratification. With key now in hand, Anthony quietly slips away to a private video bedroom on the second floor of the mansion, where he satisfies his appetite for a taste of "Hard to Swallow." *His valve released, his mind is clear for a second try at Foucault.*

Sunstein: Do you [two] think that the Madisonian critique of pornutopia is persuasive? [O]ne could say it's persuasive on its own theory, but then the question would be, is that a theory you endorse?

Collins or Skover: Good question, Cass. Empirically speaking, in today's mass commercial entertainment culture, the Madisonian critique seems ever less persuasive. Of course, the critique would never be influential in the exaggerated state of pornutopia.

Whether it could be compelling in modern America depends on what our culture's free speech values really are. Normatively speaking, the critique should be of paramount importance to anyone concerned about deliberative democracy or self-realization. Abandoning the Madisonian perspective would reinscribe a First Amendment largely foreign to many of the central tenets of our long-standing free speech jurisprudence.

At base, if one is unconcerned about enlightenment succumbing to entertainment, about serious political and social ideas surrendering to commercial images, and about self-realization collapsing into self-gratification, one will either ignore the Madisonian critique entirely or view it merely as an irritating gadfly.

O'Brien: There is no denying that, like some exploding star, the discourse of sexuality is expanding with *The Joy of Cybersex* and all it promises. Yet the road down commercial sexual exploitation and increasing specialization in a multitude of erotica was laid long ago. It runs back to the dawn of modern western liberalism.

Collins or Skover: If we didn't know you better, we'd say such comments are inspired by the teachings of the late Leo Strauss, particularly as articulated in his book *Liberalism: Ancient and Modern.*

O'Brien: [I'm glad you know me better.] Sex in the West was and remains sinful, at least for all but the knowing or unknowing hedonistic followers of modern western liberalism's anti-Christ. With a slow but sure hand, modern western liberalism beat back and all but conquered Christianity. At least, Christianity was dislodged and gradually a multiplicity of discourses on sex was liberated.

. . .

[P]ornography is an expression — the banality, if you will — of modern western liberalism. It was present at the creation of modern western liberalism and will be around as long as the latter survives. Or to play with genealogy a bit, the pornographic was both parent and offspring of modern western liberalism's assault on Christianity's long repetitive monologue and regime of power. The pornographic enjoys an incestuous heritage and continuing relationship with the other children of modern western liberalism: reason and the rejection of faith, faith in not merely Christianity but in any public truth; materialism's twins, specialization and the commercialization of free-market capitalism; and, finally, the passions of possessive individualism.

Collins or Skover: Of course, there are contemporary liberal thinkers such as William and Miriam Galston, Michael Ormond, Will Kymlicka, Elizabeth Wolgast, and Amitai Etzioni who see things differently and who are trying to steer liberalism down a different path, one consonant with more ennobling values.

O'Brien: The pornographic was tied to the politically and religiously subversive in the sixteenth century, and in some form remains so. . . . [T]he first pornographic works were almost indistinguishable from political subversion and rationalistic Enlightenment philosophy that defined modern western liberalism. At stake in that self-defining moment was the rejection of clerics, the Church, and ultimately faith —the teachings of faith in sin, teachings that had aimed to ease the burdens of fears about, and the inescapable fact of, death.

By the beginning of the nineteenth century, pornographic works were largely democratized, more widely available. That, of course, is due to pornography's ties to western liberalism's materialism in more ways than one, but not the least of which was satisfying the passions of possessive individualism.

. . .

Pornography is a banal expression of the excess of possessive individualism and the demands for instant gratification. Pornography offers the possibility of prolonged, repeated possession of pleasure by individuals who have been disabused of faith in a public truth. They merely want to deny, put off, or delude themselves about the inevitability of death. Pornography thus has a certain attraction in appealing to, in celebrating, and holding out the hope of mastering pleasure. But, it does so only by further isolating the individual, captivating him or her into specializing in a kind of material gratification that western free-market capitalism and commercialism stand all too willing to exploit, and must exploit.

In sum, pornutopia arose with modern western liberalism. . . . To call pornography banal, distracting, and disgustingly trivial, is by no means to dismiss the so-called problem of pornography or, if you insist, "the pornographic state." For, again, pornography is the expression of modern western liberalism. Moreover, the problem with pornography and with western liberalism is all but certain to grow for two reasons: (1) the fear of death has become even more pressing and absorbing with the spread of AIDS, and (2) as you note, the new technologies of commercial capitalism, including Internet's "information highway," lead to erotica.

E-Deconstruction

Virtual reality and net.sex will eventually deconstruct today's law of pornography.

Collins or Skover: David, we appreciate this scintillating historical synthesis, however judged by others. Whether you find modern western liberalism's excesses objectionable is unclear to us. Still, in the context of the First Amendment, your observations lead us to believe that you find Madisonian principles irreconcilable with modern liberalism. Hence, if Madisonian discourse is to be preserved, it must be saved by others of more conservative or radical persuasions. We suspect that this would come as a rude surprise to liberals such as Cass.

Singer: [Ron and David suggest that the antipornography feminists may have a larger agenda in mind, one to which they refer by way of an aphorism:] "Antipornography is the practice, anticapitalism is the theory." Do you think this is really what the feminists have in mind?

Sunstein: [No.] Let me start with [Catharine] MacKinnon. It might be that she's wrong on the facts; it might be that [Ronald] Dworkin and [Richard] Posner are wrong on the facts. But, I don't think it would be right to say she's lying and her real target is the capitalist state.... I think MacKinnon is against a form of sexual hierarchy. And she thinks pornography is a causal ingredient in that, and she has empirical claims. I'm sure she's not lying in the sense of stating an intentional falsehood. It might be that she's got the facts wrong, but there's that.

Strossen: [Cass, the] most comprehensive recent review of the social science data is contained in Marcia Pally's 1994 book *Sex and Sensibility.* It exhaustively canvasses laboratory studies that have evaluated the impact of exposing experimental subjects to sexually explicit expression of many varieties, and concludes that no credible evidence substantiates a clear causal connection between any type of sexually explicit material and any sexist or violent behavior.

Collins or Skover: Beyond the empirical debate, we wonder, Cass, how much sense it makes to divorce existing forms of sexual hierarchy from the capitalistic context in which they arise. In other words, to oppose one may well be to oppose the other. We believe that the antipornography feminists would own that pornography is but another commodity in a capitalist culture that exploits sex to feed consumerist desires; that if pornography is sexist and misogynous, it is because our commercial culture is sexist and misogynous. To echo sociologist Todd Gitlin, "[t]he alternative to pornography, then, stands or falls with the alternative to capitalist and patriarchal society as a whole."[122]

On another point you made, a second look at our words on this matter will reveal the tentative character of our thought. We are more inclined to raise questions than to level charges. Even so, Professor MacKinnon's "storytelling," as we label it, need not be seen in a negative light. In fact, we analogized it to the noble work of Louis Brandeis and Josephine Goldmark in their famous *Muller v. Oregon* (1908) Supreme Court brief. Moreover, we raise such questions because of the rather cool reception that the antipornography feminists' empirical claims have had in many quarters of the scientific community. Jonathan Rauch, though flip, captured something of this disposition when he argued that "people who are not radical feminists can no more see the harm of pornography than a fish can see water."[123]

Strossen: I think that [the Collins and Skover] theory, that at least some antipornography crusaders are motivated by anticapitalism, is insightful. Certainly, in my debates with both "radical feminists" and "religious right" antiporn activists, they often emphasize that the production and distribution of pornography is a multibillion dollar industry, and contend that the profit motive should strip the expression of constitutional protection. But why? If the profit motive were enough to deny constitutional protection, then we would have no free speech for anything from the *New York Times* to works of literature and scholarship,... to the *Federalist Papers*, to religious tracts, to antipornography jeremiads.

Collins or Skover: That may be precisely why the radical feminists have to couch their arguments the way they do, with the predominant focus on sexualized harms and patriarchy rather than on commercial exploitation and profit. Again, given the force of our capitalistic culture, we certainly understand what would motivate them to proceed in this way.

Fox-Genovese: [Ron and David] mercilessly push their compelling and troubling argument to its logical conclusion. Pornography is no wart on the surface of capitalist culture, but rather the essence of its implacable development—the transformation of sex into a disposable commodity. Under these conditions, what can it avail us to attempt to censure pornographic expression, which, like the proverbial repressed, will inevitably return? Nothing. But then, if we assume that the antipornography feminists are not stupid or naive—and Catharine MacKinnon assuredly is neither—perhaps the campaign against pornographic expression is but an intentionally misleading tactic in a larger war. For if we take pornography to constitute the essence of the late capitalist state, why should we not assume that those who war against pornography . . . really intend the destruction of the "male" capitalist state itself?

. . .

Again, consider [Ron and David's] logic. Does it not suggest that the best way to attack capitalism is to attack free speech? Buried in this suggestion lies the unarticulated assumption that speech is indeed a form of commerce—that the metaphor of the marketplace of ideas has become a reality. If so, postmodernism has triumphed with a vengeance. Ideas have become nothing but commodities and should, accordingly, be subject to the regulations appropriate for commercial speech. And note the irony, postmodern theory trumpets itself, first and foremost, as a revolt against the commercialization of culture that it attributes to a capitalism it ostensibly opposes.

. . .

[A]lthough I believe [Ron and David] to be precisely on target in suggesting that the radicals intend a transformation of our state, I do not share their confidence that the real target is capitalism, if for no other reason than that since the collapse of the socialist countries, radicals no longer even pretend to have an alternate socio-economic system to recommend. If I am right, we are confronting radicals who claim a progressive mission to destroy our democratic polity in the name of equality, while tacitly defending the dissolvent effects of the global capitalist economy, also in the name of equality. Whatever the intellectual merits of this position—and I do not hold them in high esteem—its policy implications spell disaster.

Singer: [Y]our book provides lots of titillation intellectually, but does not necessarily lead to useful conclusions.... Do you have suggestions of ways to redefine the First Amendment? Or are there other protections we need to invent?

Collins or Skover: At first, you took us to elevated realms. Now you want us to descend and touch the earth. As you know, it's a long way between the two. Still, your question is fair, one no doubt shared by others.

Fine, we will be business-like. First, we see ourselves as hard-nosed and therefore refuse to ignore the incredible gap between what is preached on Sunday about the high values of the First Amendment and what is practiced every day in our mass commercial entertainment culture. Remember, as we noted in the Prologue, our approach starts from the bottom up. Second, we offer at least one option for bridging this gap, a cultural approach to the First Amendment. This approach dispenses with pretense; *it speaks the unspoken*; indeed, it gives unprecedented new meaning to our understanding of the First Amendment. Admittedly, we also caution against what we take to be the consequences of adopting such an approach. True to democratic principles, we leave the choice to you and our readers. Now it seems that *you* are the one hesitant to make a choice. And so you fault us for being unrealistic!

Forgive us, maybe we are being unfair, or at least appear so, which brings us to our third reason. Unless and until the Huxleyan, the commercial, and the pornutopian become part of our First Amendment thinking, there can be no real solutions—if only because no one perceives any real problems. You see, Suzanne, if there is nothing broken, there is nothing to fix. But one cannot have it both ways, as we indicated to Professor Smolla in our exchange at the close of Book II. That is, we cannot lament the passing of the Madisonian First Amendment and at the same time embrace the brave new world of the modern First Amendment. Perhaps that is what you were getting at when you asked whether we need to *redefine* the First Amendment, whether we need to *invent* other protections.

Redefining the First Amendment, inventing new protections, these are tall tasks. Such undertakings demand extraordinary thought—philosophical, political, and practical. This is no Mr. or Ms. Fix-It task. No mere tinkering with current decisional doctrine can do what you are asking. In essence, this was our message to Herbert Schiller in the dialogue at the end of Book I.

All of this makes us wonder whether you want us to be Janus-like, to look in two directions at once in order to guard two doorways, one of the past, the other of the present. By Zeus, are you asking us to be gods? Tempting as that is, we must decline the invitation, for we know how that story ends.

Playfulness aside, here is where we are left, practically speaking. On the one hand, grant us that Huxleyan harms are really harmful and we can then begin to redefine the First Amendment and invent new protections. On the other hand, if you deny this, we need do no more. This means, however, that hypocrisy will continue in our First Amendment jurisprudence as high Madisonian values are assigned to low modern practices. Since that is the topic of our Epilogue, we shouldn't get ahead of ourselves.

Singer: [Though I would love to go on, there comes a time when it is best to leave well enough alone. We have arrived at that hour, late in the day.]

Collins or Skover: Thank you all for coming, and thanks to our host for this unbelievable forum. Good night.

Epilogue

Requiem aeternam dona eis, Domine;
*et lux perpetua luceat eis.**

Scene: Montpelier burial ground. June 29, 1836. The strains of the first movement of Wolfgang Amadeus Mozart's Requiem intensify as the corpse of James Madison is lowered into the ground. An outpouring of grief from the bereaved accompanies the preacher's haunting declaration—"dust unto dust." No monument marks his greatness. Sudden darkness.

Same burial site twenty years later. Dusk nears as preparations are made to raise a towering granite obelisk over the grave. Meanwhile, old comrades succumb to a morbid temptation: "The coffin [is] opened, and, except that one cheek [is] a little sunken, his appearance [is] the same as in life."[1] *Shift to text.*

The face of Madisonian discourse remains. Contemporary America thrives on expression. People incessantly talk, listen, write, read, type, and watch. Televisions, radios, telephones, computers, faxes, books, newspapers, magazines, billboards, and interactive technologies endlessly carry our messages. Billions upon billions of dollars are steadily invested to promote the enterprise of free speech. Yet despite outward appearances, this is not quite the vibrant face of Madisonian discourse. Insofar as that high-minded ideal is synonymous with enlightened reason, deliberative method, and public purpose, mass expression in America threatens to make that ideal unrecognizable.

The difference between noble Madisonian principles and modern practices is far too striking to ignore. As applied in this book, the *cultural approach* to the First Amendment aims to identify the magnitude of this difference and its meaning for the future of discourse in America. By way of a fleeting glance, consider again:

* "Eternal rest grant them, O Lord; and let perpetual light shine upon them." The first words of the Introit from the Requiem Mass for the Dead.

Book I

Eyebite Recap

- the difference between the old principles of political speech (rational decisionmaking, civic participation, and meaningful dissent) and the new practices of an electronic entertainment culture (trivialization, passivity, and pleasure);

Book II

- the difference between the informational principles of commercial speech (marketplace of economic ideas) and the imagistic practices of a mass commercial advertising culture (marketing of items); and

Book III

- the difference between the lofty principles of artistic expression (self-realization) and the low practices of a pornographic culture (self-gratification).

These differences, of course, characterize the often dominant entertainment, commercial, and sexualized trends in today's popular culture. Such differences between old First Amendment principles and new free speech practices dramatically re/form traditional notions of discourse in America. By way of rapid recollection, consider the following:

Book I

- Paradox: In the modern mass entertainment world, the traditional First Amendment may have to destroy itself to save itself. With governmental regulation of the amusement culture, First Amendment protection is likely to collapse into First Amendment tyranny. Without such control, First Amendment liberty is likely to collapse into First Amendment triviality.

Book II

- Dilemma: In the commercial marketplace, communication in the service of sober economic reason is overwhelmed by communication in the service of compulsive pecuniary logic. To preserve reason in the marketplace, the First Amendment must steadfastly deny much protection for modern mass advertising. To preserve freedom in the marketplace, the First Amendment must zealously affirm laissez-faire values.

BOOK III

- Conundrum: In pornutopia, deliberative discourse dies and is reincarnated as image-driven eroticism. On the one hand, governmental regulation to keep pornutopia at bay is likely to become increasingly futile. On the other hand, governmental indifference to the lure of pornutopia is likely to recast the First Amendment in wanton ways.

These puzzles invite an all-too-human temptation to depict the world of communication other than as it is: to equate amusement with enlightenment, fantasy with fact, and the base with the elevated —in short, to lie. We now turn to the what and why of that lie.

Deliberate Lies & Deliberative Democracy

There is an innocence in lying which is the sign of good faith in a cause.
—Friedrich Nietzsche[2]

Does it matter whether the Shroud of Turin is fake? Perhaps as an article of faith—a First Amendment Free Exercise matter—it is of no moment whether the Cloth of Christ is real. After all, here we are in the realm of religious belief. But should we yield to the same temptation when we cross the divide to the free speech guaranty of the First Amendment? Is there room in that realm for a deliberate lie?

Strange as it may seem, this issue lies at the center of many free speech theories—theories that cannot easily be reconciled with today's popular culture. In fact, the need for a deliberate lie may well be key to any notion of a First Amendment premised on deliberative democracy. THE DELIBERATE LIE: THEY ARE WHAT WE SAY. We[a] say we protect speech primarily to promote reasoned decision-making, public participation, and self-realization. Yet we know that much expression in the popular culture undermines these First Amendment values. And, in the face of this, we imagine that Madisonian discourse will prevail—that they will become what we say. But how can it prevail?

Perhaps the answer lies in the "*civilizing force of hypocrisy*," as law professor and political scientist Cass Sunstein emphasized. In other words, Madisonian discourse might be preserved insofar as a noble veneer can camouflage ignoble expression. Implicitly, Sunstein justified the deliberate lie by claiming that "at least we can say that in

a) In this paragraph, "we" refers to one side of the "we/they" dualism: "We" are the enlightened few, whereas "they" are the irrational many; "we" are the politically active, whereas "they" are the politically passive; "we" are the self-realizers, whereas "they" are the self-gratifiers. In any case, "we" are the conservators of the traditional First Amendment and "they" are the champions of the modern First Amendment.

a system of public deliberation, everyone must speak as if he were virtuous even if he is not in fact."[3] Such hypocrisy, we are assured, "'is the tribute that vice pays to virtue.'"[4] The animating hope is that such First Amendment hypocrisy "might even bring about a transformation in preferences and values, simply by making venal or self-regarding justifications seem off-limits."[5] Incredibly, such claims have received little attention in the community of contemporary First Amendment scholars. Indeed, even Professor Sunstein does not probe these contentions and their consequences. In the spirit of full disclosure, it is critical to make more explicit what is implicit in Sunstein's argument.

The Prince of Lies

> ***Niccolò Machiavelli:*** *[F]or a long time I have not said what I believed, nor do I ever believe what I say, and if indeed sometimes I do happen to tell the truth, I hide it among so many lies that it is hard to find.*
>
> *The Letters of Machiavelli*, trans. Allan Gilbert (Chicago: University of Chicago Press, 1961), p. 200.

To foster any positive transformation, the deliberate lie operates in two critical ways. The first is *aspirational*—to preserve to the greatest extent possible the principles of Madisonian discourse. The aspirational liar is prepared to defend the popular cultures of mass entertainment, commercial communication, and pornography as largely consistent with the elevated aims of the traditional First Amendment. This tale-teller dwells on an island of respectable discourse in an ocean of unrespectable expression. Within the Madisonian domain of *protected* speech, the well-intentioned liar grants a public easement to the likes of TV tabloid talk shows, information-free advertising, and video and computer sexploits. By the liar's efforts, the many might develop an appetite and aptitude for deliberative democracy. That, at least, is the hope. Essentially, the aspirational liar (silently) agrees with the Renaissance Dutch philosopher Erasmus: "Thus for the crass multitude there is need of temporary promises, figures, allegories, parables . . . so that little by little they might advance to loftier things."[6]

The reverse side of the deliberate lie is *regulatory*—to prevent to the greatest extent practicable the complete takeover of the Madisonian estate by unbridled popular expression. Significantly, this must be done seldom and without appearing too elitist, too antidemocratic, too un-American. When the excesses of the carnival culture reach high tide, the regulatory liar is prepared to *deny* First Amendment protection on constitutional grounds. This is made possible by familiar constitutional doctrines such as First Amendment exclusions for categories of speech, intermediate standards of judicial review, and restrictions on the time, place, and manner of expression. Hence, intermittent FCC cleansing of the public airwaves, judicial classification of commercial advertising as "low-tier" speech, and community zoning of adult entertainment businesses are several of the many devices used "neutrally" by the regulatory liar. Through the liar's efforts, the many might be kept from casting off all the restraints of civic-minded Madisonian democracy. That, at bottom, is the ploy. Fundamentally, the regulatory liar understands that the traditional First Amendment might increase its "longevity if [it] can manage to keep the hedonic motivator aligned with [its] visions of the good life."[7]

Deliberate hypocrisy as a tribute to democratic virtues? A deliberate lie in defense of the First Amendment? Facially, these notions appear oxymoronic, if not constitutionally sacriligeous. They may, however, prove less perplexing if the reader considers (albeit only in a preliminary way) the First Amendment as *political philosophy*. Thinking this way, the reader may better appreciate the relationship of the deliberate lie to any idealized system of deliberative democracy. That relationship concerns the overarching "political problem" of any democracy—"how to get consent to wise decisions or wise leadership."[8]

The political genius of the deliberate lie hearkens back to Book III of Plato's *Republic*. There Plato assumed that any "good city is not possible . . . without a fundamental falsehood; it cannot exist in the element of truth."[9] This is so because "the character of men's desires would make it impossible" for the truth about discourse and political power to be told. By virtue of the lie, "the citizens can in all good faith and conscience take pride in the justice of their regime, and malcontents have no justification for rebellion."[10] If even some of the same pertains to modern America, then the old First Amendment is guarded by lies. Accordingly, the artful way to fortify Madisonian discourse is to fabricate its vitality.

However artfully the deliberate lie may be fabricated, today there is ample reason to question its realistic potential, its capacity to function effectively. Even if one believes in the civilizing aspirations of the lie, is lying the best way to achieve them? The medicine of the deliberate lie may be too weak to cure the First Amendment ills of the modern body politic. It's rather like prescribing aspirin to relieve madness. A people increasingly charmed by electronic amusement, commercial consumption, and erotic fantasy is increasingly immune to the sobering influences of high Madisonian responsibilities. What civilizing force, then, could the deliberate lie remotely hope to have in an incredibly unrestrained culture of self-gratification? Self-indulgence is likely to force our modern civilization away from any salutary faith in Madisonian principles. In fact, the most likely consequence is that the civilizing aspirations of the deliberate lie will be entirely trivialized. Watching "junk" television becomes important political participation, buying into the images of lifestyle advertising becomes sound economic decisionmaking, and frolicking with pornography becomes artistic self-expression.

Even if the deliberate lie could be effective, it may well backfire. What if the tale-teller believes in lying but not in the tale told? What if the liar does not share the honorable aspirations of the well-intentioned? In this case, the same lie used for worthy purposes by some may be recruited for unworthy purposes by others. And there is no sure escape from this possibility for abuse. In this realm, there are no foolproof lie detectors. It is well to remember that "a benevolent self-righteousness disguises the many motives for political lying which could *not* serve as moral excuses.... These self-serving ends provide the impetus for countless lies that are rationalized as 'necessary' for the public good."[11] Among other such ends, the *non*aspirational liar may be determined to solidify the status quo distribution of real-world power among the haves and have-nots. To maintain the political and socioeconomic power of the governing elite and to diminish that of its opponents, this liar is willing to manipulate aspirational platitudes for regulatory purposes. To illustrate: The marketplace-of-ideas metaphor has been invoked disingenuously, both in public and legal forums, to defend the vested interests of those who clutter the commercial marketplace with nonrational communication in order to sell items. And our highest free speech values are likewise exploited by the mass media to equate entertainment with enlightenment and pecuniary interest with the public interest.

Such exploitation is latent in *Turner Broadcasting System v. Federal Communications Commission* (1994). Both Congress and the *Turner* Court rubberstamped the arguments of commercial broadcasters that a significant portion of their programming must be carried by cable systems in part because such fare is critical to an informed

Formula for a Lie

Logical Premises:	The more deliberative the discourse, the more elitist the culture. The less deliberative the discourse, the more democratic the culture.
Logical Conclusion:	Deliberation descends as democracy ascends.
Liar's Conclusion:	Deliberation and democracy ascend together.

electorate. Surprisingly, the broadcasters prevailed in the face of a key First Amendment principle—that government ought not interfere with the editorial discretion of communicators. Even more incredibly, a majority of the *Turner* Court tolerated such regulatory interference in order to ensure public "access to free [broadcast] television programming—*whatever its content*." At bottom, *Turner* safeguarded the right of the people to free entertainment. Any other explanation of the Court's technical handiwork smacks of a deliberate lie.[12]

Beyond its maze and mechanics, moreover, the deliberate lie betrays much of the very cause it purports to serve. There is little that is democratic in the deliberate lie. Indeed, the more the lie furthers deliberative discourse, the more likely it is to appear undemocratic. Entirely mindful of this tension, philosopher Sissela Bok cautioned: "Deception of this kind strikes at the very essence of democratic government.... Deceiving the people for the sake of the people is a self-contradictory notion in a democracy." Moreover, is the lie not astonishingly hypocritical? Is there not something intrinsically hypocritical about the civilizing force of hypocrisy? While claiming to champion the democratic ideal, the deliberate lie forsakes one of the essential tenets of that ideal. As classicist Carl Page explained, "Being misled in this way appears to rob adult human beings of sovereignty in determining their own good. Lying treats those ruled as means and not ends, thereby trespassing on their freedom as individuals."[13]

Democracy professes disdain for public lying. This is entirely in keeping with the general skepticism of our times about all public teachings, whether political, religious, or aesthetic. Modern democracy cannot rest easily with the specter of lies lurking about it. Thus, "[i]t would not be excessive to claim that in the Western tradition deception has commanded as much aversion as death itself."[14]

The Discourse of Death

Death plucks my ear and says, "Live—I am coming."

—Oliver Wendell Holmes, Jr.[15]

(on the occasion of his 90th birthday)

If the deliberate lie cannot save deliberative discourse in modern democracy, what then? A guileless answer: We can avoid First Amendment paradoxes and lies by trading in idealized Madisonian principles for modern cultural practices. This is a far more genuine jurisprudence—what we have called a *cultural approach* to the First Amendment. This approach is open to abandoning the pretenses of the Enlightenment: absolute truths, reasoned inquiry, civilized public discourse, informed decisionmaking, and restrained self-realization. In contrast, this approach stands ready to embrace openly the conventions of the popular culture: contingent truths, entertainment ideology, imagistic talk, compulsive consumption, and libidinous self-gratification.[16] Finally, this approach retracts the deliberate lie and returns "discourse" to democracy: WE THE PEOPLE will say what we are.

But can We the People survive an approaching composite of a brave new world, a fetishized marketplace, and a frenzied pornutopia? Can the human psyche endure a cultural approach to the First Amendment that abandons all cultural hypocrisy? Dr. Sigmund Freud, among others, wondered about these kinds of questions: "[It is] a debatable point whether a certain degree of cultural hypocrisy is not indispensable for the maintenance of civilization."[17] The eminent doctor's diagnosis suggests that, in the modern free speech context, certain public lying may save us more than damn us. Such lying could well be required more for its *survival* force than for its civilizing force; more for the preservation of some modicum of First Amendment order than for the attainment of elevated Madisonian discourse; and more for discouraging self-destructive nihilism than for reinforcing exalted foundationalism.[b]

To argue that Madisonian discourse can survive without a deliberate lie may prove to be disingenuous or self-deceptive. After all, as David Nyberg and other philosophers have argued, deception might well be "an essential component of our ability to organize and shape the world, to resolve problems of coordination among individuals who differ, to cope with uncertainty and pain, to be civil and to achieve privacy as needed, to survive as a species, and to flourish as persons." Even more forcefully, Professor Nyberg surmised: "We deceive . . . so that we might not perish of the truth." If the defenders of deliberative democracy appreciate these social and survival functions of deception, what prompts them to lie? At base, they fear that much in the modern communications culture poses real and lasting threats to traditional free speech values. Moreover, they understand that they cannot publicly acknowledge these fears as justifications for governmental constraints on democratic excesses. Hypocrisy can be civilizing only to the extent that the public does not know the *full* truth about the First Amendment. Put differently, the polity cannot claim a basic right to know. It is at this juncture that free speech ideals confront political philosophy. The spectrum of choice is between the Socratic principle that the unexamined life is not worth living and the Oedipal lesson that "the well-examined life may prove unlivable."[18]

George Steiner:

[T]he human capacity to utter falsehood, to lie, to negate what is the case, stands at the heart of speech... and culture.

After Babel: Aspects of Language and Translation (New York: World Publishing, 1971), p. 214.

If America's free speech system needs lies to *live*, a cultural approach to the First Amendment may well be a discourse of *death*. To forsake any conserving lie could eventually expose our free speech order to the unsettling influences of nihilism. The constitutional law

b) For our limited purposes, "foundationalism" refers to an objectively knowable and value-laden world in which truths are neither historically contingent nor culturally contextual, and in which rational discourse can lead to the enlightenment and betterment of humankind. Conceptually, "nihilism" is its opposite.

governing discourse could then tend toward a First Amendment without limits—an Absolute First Amendment far beyond the Madisonian imagination of the late Justice Hugo Black.[c] And discourse could then be driven more and more by a runaway engine of amusement, consumption, and passion. Echoing this idea, philosopher Loyal Rue asserted more generally: "The single most important regulating force within a social ecology is [its governing lie].... Without this [lie] a culture would lose its unity of purpose to an onslaught of diffuse meanings and thus begin its descent into social chaos."[19] Such arguments appear to condemn the cultural approach to the First Amendment as an instrument of culture death: A democracy may be unable to pursue naked truth if it must nurture an ennobling lie to preserve some *semblance* of social purpose and destiny.

Whatever the past, Madisonian free speech ideals may no longer be viable. Whether or not these ideals ever provided a semblance of social purpose and destiny, today they are increasingly ill suited to perform their aspirational and moderating functions. If nothing else, the cultural approach to the First Amendment reveals the often maladaptive character of eighteenth-century ideals in a twenty-first-century environment. Succinctly, high Madisonian notions of free speech seem practically irrelevant. When we feed on TV and video soma for an average of some forty-seven hours weekly, consume the fruits of a yearly advertising budget of $149 billion, splurge some $10 billion annually to gorge our insatiable sexual appetites, and more, we are unlikely to tolerate a First Amendment regime that is intolerant of such pleasurable practices.

Collins to Skover: Before we end, David, I think we should return to a question we discussed the other evening in Seattle. Do you

c) Justice Hugo Lafayette Black (1886–1971) held to a literalist and absolutist interpretation of the First Amendment's dictates that "Congress shall make no law" abridging the freedoms of speech. Accordingly, he called for full constitutional protection of politically subversive dissent, libel, and obscenity, among other forms of speech. See Edmund Cahn, "Justice Black and First Amendment 'Absolutes': A Public Interview," *New York University Law Review* 37 (1962):549–563. In a 1961 First Amendment case, Black ended a forceful dissenting opinion with the admonition: "We must not be afraid to be free" (366 U.S. 82, 116).

recall our conversation about the differences between our cultural approach and the modern scenario of the First Amendment described in Book I?

Skover to Collins: Yes, Ron, I remember how much we struggled with that question. You're right, we should return to it now. So, what *are* the major differences between the modernist view and our cultural approach?

Collins to Skover: First, there are no Huxleyan evils in the modern scenario, only Orwellian fears. In the name of libertarian values, modernists assign virtually absolute First Amendment protection to most forms of expression. By maximizing the speech rights of the popular culture, modernists feed the consumptive desires of a highly capitalistic and technologically driven society. Ultimately, modernists are willing to engage in deliberate lying when necessary. They will champion electronic visual entertainment, mass advertising, and pornography as indispensable to self-rule or self-realization, rather than defend them as essential to self-gratification.

Skover to Collins: Unlike the modern scenario, the cultural approach takes account of the Huxleyan dilemma. Yet this approach is inherently less concerned with results than with reasons. Whether free speech rights are maximized or minimized is of no great moment, so long as what is said about the First Amendment resonates with what is done in its name. Deliberate lying—even to promote deliberative democracy—is the worst of all evils. High ideals of Madisonian discourse ought not be invoked to protect the low practices of mass communication. Rather, it is necessary to compare and contrast the actual workings of a speech culture with the First Amendment principles offered to legitimate that culture. Truth-telling is imperative, whatever its consequences.

Collins to Skover: Does this mean that our cultural approach is essentially a call for candor?

Skover to Collins: Surely it is that, but it is much more. The cultural approach recognizes that First Amendment values are to be determined as much by what We the People practice as by what they, the elite, preach. These values may not be our most ennobling; indeed, they may be downright embarrassing to admit. But they are the free speech codes by which our culture elects to live.

Collins to Skover: You know, David, in a very important sense our cultural approach *may* be a meaningful way to pursue high First

Amendment ideals. Ironically, it may be far more meaningful in this regard than the deliberate lie.

Skover to Collins: I gather this is ironic because the deliberate lie, which purports to further high values, may be less successful in that pursuit than the cultural approach, which countenances the corruption of such values.

Collins to Skover: Exactly. Charmed by the deliberate lie, the culture may be restrained by civilizing forces, but it is unlikely to *internalize* civilizing values. After all, lying is a form of social control, not political education. There can be no deliberative democracy without deliberation, no Madisonian rewards without Madisonian integrity. If we never confront the reality of our hypocrisy, we can never really escape it.

The animating spirit of the cultural approach is that, once we confront the reality of First Amendment hypocrisy, we will no longer wish to perpetuate it. On the one hand, we may restructure life, law, and discourse in order to actualize Madisonian ideals. On the other hand, we may give up all Madisonian pretenses and romp in a debauched dystopia. That possibility is what makes the cultural approach so very risky.

Skover to Collins: Yes, but there are also risks in shunning the cultural approach. Madisonian ideals could vanish without our ever knowing it.

The Madisonian First Amendment is going the way of agrarian America. Like the harmonious, wholesome, and romantic images of the farmer's life, traditional free speech values are overshadowed by modern technology and materialism. Yearn as we may for those worlds, they belong to the past. If James Madison's dreams for the First Amendment are to have any future meaning, we must forswear the fantasies in which we now revel. Bluntly, We the People must toil to become what we are not.

But why should we become other than what we are? Expecting modern Americans to embrace serious meaning and sober moderation is, after all, undemocratically paternalistic. As the noted historian Daniel J. Boorstin cautioned: "It is true that [America's popular culture] has opened the floodgates of trivia . . . and pseudo-events. But why must there be equilibrium? To talk somehow of balancing these things is what totalitarian societies try to do in their efforts to limit [freedom of] choice."[20] Frankly, We the People detest utopian tyrants and delight in remaining what we are.

In the First Amendment odyssey between what We the People are and are not, there looms the harrowing task of maneuvering between the Modern and the Madisonian. The character of that venture generally has not been appreciated by either the defenders or critics of American free speech law. Treating the popular culture of expression as Madisonian, they understand neither the odyssey nor its risks. Recalling Marshall McLuhan, we no longer can equivocate: "We have either to assume a large new role or to abdicate entirely. It is the age of paratroopers."[21]

The end is near.[d] Discourse is dying. Paratroopers are falling. As they descend, our heroes are inspired by Albert Camus's poignant affirmation: "I do not give the human race more than one chance in a thousand. But I should not be a man if I did not operate on that one chance."[22]

THE END

d) If you just opened to this page for a final answer, you will be disappointed—this is not that kind of book. Or if you came this far and expected a neat and categorical solution, well, you have yet to grasp our stated purpose. Remember, *you* are the judge. *You* are to decide. Otherwise, if you think our First Amendment case unconvincing, argue your own; and if you think any single "answer" airtight, you would be well served to reread this book.

Afterword

New "Truths" and the Old First Amendment—The Last "Dialogue"

Scene: A state-of-the-art conference room at The Freedom Forum in Washington, DC. Conversations among the press and audience members are interrupted occasionally as one or another glances in an easterly direction through floor-to-ceiling windows. There, looming in their vision, is the nation's Capitol building, now nestled within a palette of intensely colored foliage that glows brilliantly on a fall afternoon. The hum of voices ebbs as the panelists file to the front, and seat themselves behind a long rectangular table. Once a signal is given that the Internet-live broadcast connection has been made, the symposium sponsored by The First Amendment Center begins.

What follows is a slightly orchestrated print "dialogue"[1] with political scientist Shadia Drury, communications theorist Robert Hariman, philosopher David Nyberg, philosophy and religion scholar Loyal Rue, and sociologist Richard Stivers. Except for the bracketed remarks, the words, though incomplete and rearranged, are theirs (circa 1996) and ours.

Collins or Skover: We begin with Bickel. In 1973, Professor Alexander Bickel spoke the following words at Yale Law School: "If [our values] are lies, they are . . . true lies; if illusions, then indispensable ones. To abandon them is to commit moral suicide."[2] Bickel had free speech theory in mind. The renowned constitutional scholar posed a paradox: lies may be vital to the life of the First Amendment.

To some, perhaps most, this complex passage may sound odd, especially coming from the lips of the counselor recruited by the New York Times in the *Pentagon Papers* case.[3] For it was in that controversy between government and press that the foreign-born Bickel vindicated a basic tenet of American democracy—deception is antithetical to the First Amendment.

As far as we can say, Bickel never resolved the tension between lies and First Amendment values that he so poignantly identified. Regrettably, his reflections on free speech theory ended with his untimely death one year after his Yale lecture. He never told us how lies could be true, or exactly why illusions are indispensable. No, he left those questions unanswered and slipped gently into the night.

This afternoon's symposium invites us to pick up where Professor Bickel left off. It presents an opportunity to return to the "*sketch*" of the topic explored in the Epilogue of *The Death of Discourse*. That sketch introduced perplexing connections among lying, free speech theory, and political philosophy. We had hoped that others might engage us in drawing more detailed portraits. Happily, our colleagues are willing to do that with us today.

If for no other reason, today's exchange is important because it will feature the ideas of scholars, outside the law, on values within the law of the First Amendment. As we emphasize in our book, discourse on free speech stands to benefit considerably from the contributions of those who think beyond the letter of the law. This is entirely consistent with the notion in *The Death of Discourse* that the First Amendment is more than law—it is a way of life.

So, let the proverbial (or, more fittingly, *verbal*) games begin!

Collins or Skover: Professor Drury, since you've written about those who veil their truths, perhaps we should begin with you?

Shadia Drury: [You two] suggest that [Americans] should be brave enough to face up to the reality of our debauched pornutopia. Only then can we hope to have one chance in a thousand for saving ourselves and our discourse. However, [you] are disturbed by [your] conclusions and are led to ask Nietzschean questions: Is it possible to live in the face of the deadly truth and forego the life-saving illusion?

[You] abhor the lie as much as death itself and bid us to face the truth about ourselves and our dystopia without flinching. But there are some confusions in [your] valiant devotion to truth.

. . .

To my mind, the question [for First Amendment law] is not whether we indulge ourselves in fictions; the question is, do our fictions contain hard truths and noble ideals or are they simply forms of self-deception intended to excuse self-indulgence and indolence?

Collins or Skover: Forgive us if this seems like a Nietzschean question, but what do you mean by *fictions* that "contain hard truths"?

Your use of opposites—fiction and truth—is offered to our audience as if the two are easily reconciled. We are reminded of Woody Allen's quip: the lion and lamb may lie down together, but the lamb won't get much sleep. Then again, perhaps you see us as sticklers in our demand for consistency.

Drury: [Yes.] It sometimes seems as if [your] devotion to truth is so grandiose that it leaves no room for ideals or for the inevitable discrepancy between the ideal and the actual.

David Nyberg: [I agree.] It is here that [you two] separate [yourselves] from the modernists [in your book] who are willing to engage in deliberate lying when necessary, because [you] insist on truthtelling no matter what the consequences. *Fiat veritas, et pereat mundas* (or "Let there be truth, though the world may perish"). [Your] ethic begins to sound potentially lethal.

Robert Hariman: Heroic truth is the truth of Socrates in the *Apology*: the great individual who will speak truth to power, who will refute our collective denial and insist we face our participation in evil. . . . I can't help but wonder whether *The Death of Discourse* carries a yearning for a heroic world [replete with heroic truths]. In such a world, one could again speak with such individual courage and moral power that the leviathan of modern culture would be stopped in its tracks. David would slay Goliath and St. George skewer the dragon while a single, honest orator delivered a simple speech under a gray sky and the audience of citizens felt the better angels of their nature soar, free at last.

Collins or Skover: Robert, we are overwhelmed by your rhetorical flair; it rivals that of the great orators of antiquity such as Gorgias and Protagoras.

The way all three of you characterize our passion for truth recalls to mind a fetching pun: "Tell your boss what you think of him, and the truth will set you free." Not only may we be unable to afford the truth, but the very pursuit of truth appears troublesome to you, at least as a First Amendment enterprise. Why is this so? Are you suggesting that Alexander Meiklejohn's truth-based approach to the First Amendment was frivolous or ill-informed? If so, what are you inviting the defenders of free speech to do instead?

Nyberg: My own belief is that [your] overenthusiastic use of "lie" and "truthtelling" eventually will blunt both as analytic tools, and that a strict morality about lying and truthtelling precludes a sagacious understanding of these important forms of human conduct as well as their most important cognates, namely, deception and narrative truth.

Collins or Skover: Do you mean that a logically rigorous approach to our understanding of lying and truthtelling is a useless analytical tool? Or how much play must be in the joints before these concepts are useful to us? More importantly, are we talking about a matter of degree or a difference in kind?

Nyberg: Proceeding on the assumption that the First Amendment is a cultural symbol that embodies a variety of competing values, ... I want to elucidate what it means to tell a lie ... and to tell a narrative truth. My purpose here is to show that Madisonian First Amendment conservatorship can be better described in many if not most instances as based upon narrative truth (granted its fictional and deceptive qualities) rather than upon deliberate lies.

...

Clearly, lying is one way of misrepresenting reality as you take it to be, but what makes lying special, and different, from other forms of deception? The formal properties of a lie are these: 1) a statement, something spoken or written; 2) a belief in the mind of the statement-maker; 3) an intention in the mind of the statement-maker; and 4) the character and rights of the person addressed.... [W]e can say that lying means making a statement (not too vague) that you want somebody to believe, even though you don't (completely) believe it yourself, when the other person has a right to expect that you mean what you say.... What matters most is what the "liar" believes and intends to achieve as a result of making the statement in question.

[In contrast,] a coherent narrative, any coherent narrative, has persuasive power. Fit and meaning are sought to trump disorder and chaotic experience. Narrative truth can be defined as "the criterion we use to decide when a certain experience has been captured to our satisfaction; it depends on continuity and closure and the extent to which the fit of the pieces takes on an aesthetic finality. Narrative truth is what we have in mind when we say that such and such is a good story, that a given explanation carries conviction, that one solution to a mystery must be true. Once a given construction has acquired narrative truth, it becomes just as real as any other kind of truth."[4]

...

The discourse that is law can be seen as a disciplined method of collective self-education. It is a discourse that repeats the familiar in the novel circumstances of new cases to remind us how important are the practices and principles we have brought with us from the past.... But it is also a discourse that relies upon the introduction of new narratives rendered in pragmatic language—language meant to bring about changes in the way that we should think and talk about what seems familiar but may be different in some significant aspects. When lawyers or judges make a legally formal interpretation of a case, they are finding a narrative home for the anomalous new event. When narrative coherence gives satisfaction, we call this truth. Such narrative truth is in its very nature provisional, as is historical truth, or scientific truth. This is no cause for despair. Provisional narrative truth, arrived at through principle-driven legal discourse, provides guidance and modulation, focused on the future, as times change. From this point of view, it makes no sense to search for historical validation of modern interpretations of the First Amendment, nor does it satisfy the mind to revert to the more rudimentary concept of "lie."

...

Thus, when the First Amendment conservator argues that this particular instance of mindless television programming, devious advertising, or degrading pornography deserves First Amendment protection because it will be better for us in the long run if we act in that way now, we cannot say the argument is based in truth. The conservator could not possibly know such a truth, but the argument can, and should be made in order to bring about its truth.

The very nature of legal argument is to contrast one way of talking, one narrative, with another. It is not merely, or often, to pit liars against truth-tellers.

Hariman: Perhaps the greatest liability [in Ron and David's concept of First Amendment] "lying" is that it activates a wholly representational hermeneutic: words are more or less accurate depictions of that to which they refer, which in turn allow more or less accurate assessments of the subjective conditions (intentions, sincerity) of their formation. Despite the ubiquitous use of speech to represent the world, that is only one of its functions. Also of considerable importance is the ability to constitute a sense of individual and collective identity. Political intelligibility and action requires more than saying

"Thucydides, an Athenian" or "We the People" or "Liberty, Equality, Fraternity," but it cannot occur without such statements. From this analytical perspective, the inevitable gap between ideal statement and real practice is of interest, but is hardly an inherent source of concern. Political activity may be seen as either falling away from an ideal or as tending toward it. Each perception may be right or wrong in the particular case, but it is more important to see how the act of labeling constitutive discourse as either "ideal" or "real" invariably will mislead one about its function. Likewise, the test of the First Amendment is not so much that it provides an accurate representation of American discursive habits, but that it can provide the rhetorical norms for renewing specific discursive practices.

Drury: The problem with our modern world is that politics is no longer seen as the domain of judicious lying. Lying has become synonymous with politics, and politics has infiltrated every domain of life. Lying has therefore become a way of life. But this state of affairs could not have come to be unless lying was rehabilitated and transfigured into the supreme virtue of the postmodern world. Taking its cue from Nietzsche, the postmodern world has dispensed with truth; and in a world devoid of truth, what else can there be but lies? But in the absence of truth, can we call the fabrication of reality a lie? Nay, that is impossible when the lie is all the truth there is.

In the postmodern world, there are interpretations without texts, inventions without reality, and conventions without nature. In a world where reality and truth are a void, the creative art rules supreme. In such a world, what could be more creative than lying? After all, a great lie, one that is believed, gives form to the void, imposes order on chaos, and creates the world *ex nihilo*. In such a world, one must dispense with lies and ideologies because they contain a hint of moral contempt, a certain self-righteousness, and a smug belief that there is a truth beneath the lie and a justice that transcends ideologies. The electronic media and its capacity for instant mass communication lend itself to this state of affairs.

Collins or Skover: There seems to be a common thread connecting your various perspectives on the modern use of "truth" for First Amendment purposes. To all appearances, David, you appeal to narrative truths as epistemological criteria for the First Amendment. You argue that "Madisonian First Amendment conservatorship can be better described in many if not most instances as based upon narrative truth (granted its fictional and deceptive qualities)." Doesn't something of this mindset also inform your notion, Robert, of the "test of the First Amendment" as providing "rhetorical norms for renewing discursive practices?" And it is precisely *this* philosophical position that prompts Shadia to protest that "the postmodern world has dispensed with truth. . . . In a world where reality and truth are a void, the creative art rules supreme."

John Donne:

The sun is lost, and th'earth, and no mans wit
Can well direct him, where to looke for it.

"An Anatomy of the World," *The Complete Poetry of John Donne* (New York: New York University Press, 1968)

The Enlightenment and narrative concepts of truth, however similar they may appear, are as different as Aristotle and James Madison on the one hand, and Richard Rorty[5] and Stanley Fish[6] on the other. Essentially, the move from Enlightenment truth to narrative truth parallels the transition from the modern to the postmodern. This transition substitutes aesthetics for foundationalism; "that art is worth more than truth is the dominant principle of our time."[7]

Furthermore, where there are narrative truths, there must also be narrative lies. Understandably, neither David nor Robert wishes to call attention to this point. What is interesting, however, is the confusing tumble of truthtelling and lying brought about by their narrative enterprises. Too much talk of narrative can be dizzying. In order better to target the discussion, we offer the following defining points in rapid-fire:

- Madisonian ideals are anchored in Enlightenment truths. By contrast, narrative truths afford no really safe harbor for Enlightenment truths.
- In principle and practice, traditional Madisonian values war with pluralistic narrative truths and varying aesthetic judgments.
- One defender of Madisonian ideals (whom we call the classicist) is intolerant of those corruptive influences of the popular commercial culture that invite Huxleyan tyranny. By contrast, the defender of narrative truths (somewhat like the free speech advocate we call the modernist) tolerates a great measure of the popular commercial culture in order to avoid Orwellian tyranny.
- Another defender of Madisonian ideals (whom we call the reformist) compromises Enlightenment values as a pragmatic measure while firmly believing in them. By contrast, the defender of narrative truths does not ultimately believe in the Enlightenment,

but is willing to advance "salutary" Madisonian myths.

- The defender of Madisonian ideals withholds constitutional protection from the excesses of "junk" and pornographic speech. By contrast, when narrative truths are elevated, their defender protects such speech, but in the name of moderating values.
- For the defender of Madisonian ideals, there can be "noble lies" in furtherance of discernible truths. By contrast, for the defender of narrative truths, it is far more difficult to call the fabrication of reality a lie, because there are no hard truths.

These points indicate that the old First Amendment is radically different from the new "truths" told about it. To defend the former is to attack the latter, and vice-versa. Therefore, it is critical to remain clear-minded about the ramifications of moving from the Madisonian to the postmodern. Let us now examine together some of those ramifications.

Drury: In my view, [you two] fail to distinguish between deliberate lies and ideals. Every culture needs ideals to inspire and guide it, to give it character and form. But there is always a discrepancy between the ideal and the actual because no society can live up to its own ideals. If ideals are confused with lies and made to fit reality, then society would have no ideals. A devotion to the truth about ourselves need not exclude an account of our ideals because our ideals are themselves part of the truth about us.

Collins or Skover: Shadia, we agree. But an ideal must still represent a normative baseline. Unless you grant this, your argument invites the very Nietzschean nightmare that you seem to disdain. To that extent, we question whether today's free speech practices have fallen so far away from First Amendment principles as to challenge their integrity as ideals.

Hariman: [But, there is a] mythic underpinning [to] any human society. Narratives, such as those of eternal return or unending progress or liberating reason or popular will, provide the symbolic material with which a society forges its destiny. . . . For our purposes, the lesson to be learned is that any society depends on systematic (although not absolute) inattention to its contradictions, an inattention that is directed mythically and for which realism can be a corrective but not a substitute. The First Amendment surely has a mythic register that neutralizes some of the contradictions between theory and practice. I doubt, however, that there is a point at which, if either myth or the law of contradiction has to give way, the rest has to go with it. Myth is everywhere and nowhere, and so has no need of strategic deceit and little fear of enlightenment.

Drury: [I may not go so far as that.] Problems arise when the discrepancy between the ideal and the actual becomes so great that it is intolerable. At this point, the world ceases to be a place with lofty ideals that are not fully actualized. We begin to feel that we are living a lie—a lie in the soul as Plato understood it.

Nyberg: We need protection from assault—physical, psychological, spiritual, economic—by free speakers with imperfect motives, but we need protection, too, from the imperfect wisdom, temper, and prudence of government regulators. Free speakers' assaults may overwhelm us temporarily such that we resent and may want to deny their right to speak in that manner ever again. However, overwhelmed as we are, we should not let that experience extinguish our obligation to preserve and protect the greatest provisions of the Constitution, first among them, perhaps, the First Amendment.

It helps in meeting that obligation to recount the "Madisonian narrative truth" (not lie!), what Loyal Rue might call a cultural myth: "[C]ultural myths are powerful means of cooperation because they function to integrate the domains of human interest into a comprehensible narrative unity and to safeguard the culture against an influx of meanings that might otherwise disrupt social coherence.... By integrating the domains of human interest into a narrative unity, myth offers [us] a paradigm for harmonizing [our] needs for intelligibility, pleasure, and self-esteem."[8]

Agreement on moral beliefs is perhaps the single most effective factor making for a unified society. Where moral agreement is lacking, so also is social cohesion. In America, where a liberal, humanistic morality rooted in pluralism is a fact of life, as well as a defining characteristic of the means for governing democratic social institutions, we may not reasonably hope for agreement on moral beliefs insofar as these are at the core of competing conceptions of the good life. What we may hope for, and with good reason expect to be the case, is legal protection for these competing conceptions and differing moral beliefs against encroachment by indignant people who are offended to their own core by some expression-difference. Like wise parents, government should say "No" only when necessary, then stick to it—trying not to confuse the merely urgent with the really important.

The Madisonian rationale for First Amendment protection of speech is not a "deliberate lie." It is a coherent, satisfying narrative that should be told over and over in order to bring about its truth pragmatically.

Collins or Skover: *The Death of Discourse*, as originally presented and now revised, does recognize a phenomenon somewhat akin to the free speech narratives that you posit. The book points to this phenomenon, not so much as a philosophical matter, but more so as a socio-economic cultural matter. Hence, in the mass commercial entertainment culture, "truth is irrelevant," "truth is what sells," "there is no test of truth," and "truth is what you want people to believe." In fact, commercial narratives draw much of their blood-flow from postmodern attitudes toward truth and lying. Men wear shirts and feel like daisies; liberation comes to women who puff cigarettes; chemical and gas companies console us with promotional visions of snow-capped mountains and green fields. These are the narratives of We the People, not those heroic narratives told by the elitist conservators of the First Amendment.

None of you has explicitly championed these narratives of the capitalist marketplace. Do you agree with us, *sub silentio*, that there is an immense gap between Madisonian First Amendment "ideals" and many modern free speech practices? In any case, such a gap is obfuscated when you begin to engage in motivational analysis for "lying." That is, you seem less concerned with the dissonance between First Amendment "ideals" and cultural practices than you are with the intentions of those who rationalize that dissonance. For us, the focus turns 180 degrees—this notwithstanding our bold claims about "deliberate lies" and our tentative speculations about those who advance such "lies." However informative a discussion of the spectrum of volitional untruths, is it not more fruitful to examine the high against the low, rather than to fix on perplexities akin to criminal culpability under the Model Penal Code?

Albert Borgmann: An epoch approaches its end when its fundamental conviction begins to weaken and no longer inspires enthusiasm among its advocates.

Crossing the Postmodern Divide (Chicago: University of Chicago Press, 1992), p. 48.

Let us offer one preliminary answer to the question we've posed. The greater the divide between Madisonian ideals and commercial entertainment realities, the more muted is the voice of those ideals. Though ideals by definition presuppose some discrepancy between the aspirational and the actual, no First Amendment narrative can tolerate a span so wide as to erode belief in its ideals. A culture's noble free speech theory loses its staying power if it is no longer likely to be believed. Ultimately, to remain functional, a Madisonian myth (or any ennobling narrative) must be a likely object of trust.

Richard Stivers: [As I see it, you two] desire to shock people into seeing that the guiding principles of the First Amendment are contradicted by the practices of popular culture. [You] admit that a great risk accompanies [your] approach because, rather than returning to Madisonian principles, we may openly embrace hedonistic norms.

Collins or Skover: That's correct, Richard. The viability of any Madisonian myth is fundamentally what we question in the Epilogue of *The Death of Discourse*. We ask whether the First Amendment ideals espoused by courts and commentators—the stuff of which "noble lies" or "cultural myths and narratives" are made—are or could really be shared societal values. To that end, our "cultural approach" abandons (though at no little cost) the old ideals in the name of new realities. But why? Our reply has everything to do with what Professor Nyberg appropriately calls "pragmatic language." That is, what real chances do Madisonian principles or elevated narratives stand in a carnival culture? In the end, however, Professor Nyberg's own "pragmatic" argument proves unresponsive. It is one that sounds "too ideal," and extends little beyond Echoing narratives "over and over" . . . and over and over and over.

Collins or Skover: Putting lies aside (if only for a moment), let us consider instead the role of hypocrisy in First Amendment thinking. That is, what are we to make of a liberal democracy that encourages base practices to masquerade as noble principles? Does modern constitutional liberalism depend on hypocrisy to survive? And just how candid can any free speech narrative be?

Eminent philosophers and social scientists have argued that hypocrisy is endemic to life and law. Much in the character of the modern democratic state, they contend, not only allows hypocrisy in governance, but demands it. Correlatively, stringent insistence on truth-telling imperils the health of liberal democracy. The late Professor Judith Shklar, for example, maintained that "hypocrisy is one of the few vices that bolsters liberal democracy."[9] Such hypocrisy stems from the disparity between a polity's creed and its conduct. "This disparity often develops over time as an institution comes to serve purposes other than those for which it was established."[10] As we've suggested, the move from Madisonian truths to narrative ones carries with it the baggage of hypocrisy.

Drury: [I am glad for the turn in the discussion here.] The idea that First Amendment discourse involves a deliberate lie seems rather far-fetched. There is no doubt a certain hypocrisy on the part of those who use First Amendment arguments in order to defend speech that serves no purpose other than their own pecuniary advantage. But this hypocrisy is plain for all to see. There is no reason to think that those who use First Amendment arguments are deliberate liars of a regulatory or aspirational variety. Nor are they blind to the fact that their First Amendment arguments serve to protect pornography and unbridled commercialism.

. . .

Instead of focusing on First Amendment discourse as a deliberate lie, it is more reasonable to argue that freedom has given way to license, and that this fact itself threatens freedom because freedom cannot be sustained without a modicum of self-restraint. Moreover, it is illegitimate for the First Amendment to be used to protect pornography and blatant commercialism. Restrictions on advertising and pornography are quite compatible with the intentions of Madisonian discourse and its ideals. When cigarette companies complain that the restrictions imposed on their advertising rob them of their freedom of speech, no one takes their argument seriously; their lie is so blatant that it fools no one.

Collins or Skover: Well, this would surely be news to Justices Kennedy, O'Connor, Scalia, Souter, and Thomas, who often extend free speech protections for "blatant commercialism," including the First Amendment claims of tobacco companies.[11] To us, of course, this is not astounding; indeed, the opposite result might be more surprising. For, conceptually, to withhold First Amendment protection from advertising and pornography in today's mass commercial entertainment culture is not as simple as you would have us believe, Shadia.

Advertising and pornography are no longer, if they ever were, insular categories that can be surgically removed from the body of our culture. The commingling of the commercial and non-commercial is so extensive that what was once "blatant" is now "blatant" and "mainstream" at the same time. This blending is so significant that Americans now define their very lifestyles and identities in terms of commodities. To discount these points is to allow a form of censorship in modern America tantamount to tyranny. Of course, the specter of censorship prompts some "Enlightenment" liberals to tolerate hypocrisy.

What do such free speech cases tell us, then, about the relevance of a *hypocritical* First Amendment? Granting, *arguendo*, the importance of credible First Amendment narratives, must one also grant the necessity of a hypocritical narrative or myth? Hypocrisy typically enters into such narratives whenever elevated free speech values are heralded. By contrast, narratives that reflect the popular commercial culture do not depend on such hypocrisy, if only because they more closely align low realism with low idealism. When the ceiling crashes through the floor, hypocrisy is no longer foundational. Liberal democracy of the postmodern variety must suffer a significant degree of narrative hypocrisy because it is unable to free itself altogether of traditional Madisonian values. Sociologist Todd Gitlin—an astute defender of Madisonian liberalism—puts it forcefully: "The immense gravitational field of the Enlightenment is not so casually escaped, even by its critics."[12]

Those of you who have embraced postmodern First Amendment narratives without entirely shrugging off the Enlightenment's values have chosen an uneasy position—one of owning mythic hypocrisy that cannot be revealed, at least not too often or too openly. Political pragmatism would appear to dictate that free speech narrators hide behind a curtain as opaque as the one that concealed the pitiful wizard in the Land of Oz. (Somewhat puzzled, we ask you: Was the wizard a wonderful story teller? An imaginative myth maker? A confused narrator? A profound philosopher? A deliberate liar? Or all of the above?) In more familiar free speech territory, exactly how candid can our narrative conservators of the First Amendment be when it comes to the tales they tell?

Consider, for example, an imaginary opinion of the United States Supreme Court, a portion of which follows:

> Justice ANONYMOUS announced the judgment of the Court, and delivered an opinion with respects to Parts II, III-A, IV-D, and V-C(1), which is for the Court:
>
> I
>
> We are called upon to determine the constitutionality of a Kansas law that restricts specified kinds of imagistic cigarette advertising on World-Wide Web sites and other computer on-line services located within the state. Among other arguments, Petitioners maintain that such commercial expression is protected under the Free Speech Clause of the First Amendment as made applicable to the states by the Fourteenth Amendment. For the reasons set forth below, we agree and reverse the judgment of the state supreme court.
>
> This case comes to us against the backdrop of our profound national commitment to the narrative of truth, however understood or defined, as one of the central purposes behind the First Amendment. Moreover, this narrative serves other important First Amendment values, such as the myth of the marketplace of ideas and the respectable tales of deliberative discourse, broad and fluid as those narratives must necessarily be. Those who won our independence were not openly nihilistic; they realized the importance, nay the necessity, of high-minded stories to rationalize the protection of almost any form of expression, communicative or otherwise. The civilizing force of such myths may serve to make us what we say we aspire to be. These narratives, then, inform the "analysis" that follows....

We suspect that any proponent of narrative truths would hesitate to sign onto this opinion. Perhaps we are wrong. If not, what does this sample opinion suggest about the character of hypocritical myth-making? Duly mindful of motivational analysis, we wonder at what point a narrative of hypocrisy unravels into something less grandiose: a deliberate lie, perhaps? One revealing point of demarcation, it seems, would be the unwillingness of a narrator to be forthright with his or her audience. The greater this unwillingness, the greater the likelihood that hypocrisy deconstructs into lying.

Nyberg: I am not quite comfortable acquiescing to [Ron and David's depiction of the modern American free speech culture. Your] argument that First Amendment protection of the trivial in public expression will lead to a collapse into First Amendment triviality is based on a fallacy, the fallacy of composition. In other words, what is true of some of its parts is not necessarily true of the whole. (A man may be wearing awful, ugly shoes, but that does not mean he is an awful, ugly whole person.) Although the First Amendment may well be used to protect the trivial, it continues (primarily?) to protect the profound as well. The fact that there may be trivial First Amendment performances does not in itself imply that the First Amendment work is trivial or will collapse into triviality.

Ponder this: "Man has to choose between peace of mind deriving from a pleasing delusion and peace of mind deriving from the unpleasing truth."

Leo Strauss, *Liberalism: Ancient and Modern* (New York: Basic Books, 1968), p. 85

Hariman: [Exactly. Ron and David's] basic problem is one of tunnel vision. Those who are so worried about the consumer culture and particularly about the influence of the advertising and entertainment industry through the mass media need to be reminded that other modes of communication still exist and, indeed, are thriving as well. Overproduction is not limited to any one sector of the capitalist economy (as this discussion demonstrates, perhaps). One basic limitation in [your] cultural analysis . . . is that it looks only at the popular culture instead of the mix of cultural texts. The influence of advertising will stem from its immediate and accumulative influence on viewer consciousness, but it also has to operate in conjunction with a plethora of other forms of communication.

. . .

Like too many culture critics, [you two] look only at what [you] don't like.

Instead of examining high quality deliberative discourse and observing what happens to it, [you] focus on what might threaten it. . . . Instead of seeing how citizens might get a composite picture of an event or issue from a variety of media such as the *New York Times*, the nightly news, the morning call-in show, the weekly newsmagazine, the prime-time docudrama, the *Reader's Digest* story, and the B-movie video, [you] point to the most egregious examples of low culture that supposedly are displacing all of these other productions. Instead of considering how "We the People" might be segmenting or otherwise dividing into groups—some more and some less connected to political affairs ... —[you] look only for indices of general decline.

...

Currently, commentators from right, center, and left are lambasting TV talk shows for being everything [Ron and David] decry. These shows, we are told, traffic in sleaze, encourage unrestrained emotionality, and generally have no redeeming social value. The implication is that the American public is being coached to be fascinated with deviance, distracted from the issues and methods of public affairs, addicted to titillation, and stupid. The critic's analysis usually consists of no more than *ipse dixit* references to supposedly egregious subjects, slapping a label on the whole genre, and lamenting the cultural decline. What we don't see is what actually happens on the show, which often (not always) is a reasoned examination of a moral subject drawing on many points of view. What we don't consider is how the show is an exercise in the development of rational criteria for judgment (and often the reassertion of community standards). If reason has to elbow its way into the room, so much the better for reason. What we don't ask is whether the general subject of the shows—which is the sociology of contemporary private life and the question of how to live within a pluralistic, open society—is being served much better (at least for some groups) than by supposedly more valuable programming. And we certainly don't consider that the polity might be better served by honest sleaze than by self-righteous posturing.

Stivers: I have to admit ... that I agree in the main with [Ron and David's] analysis, especially in regard to their depiction of television and advertising [and the impacts of those industries on the character of American public discourse.]

...

Television appears to be describing reality, particularly in news programs, documentaries, talk-shows, and game shows. In effect, it is reconstructing reality by taking reality out of its temporal and cultural context. Reality as we live it still retains, no matter how small, some meaning (order of truth); but television expunges this meaning and recomposes reality as a logical sequence of image fragments.

...

We have now reached the turning point: not only is television about reality, but reality is on television.... When television momentarily focuses on an issue, it becomes a "real" issue; when television leaves it behind for a new issue, the old issue is eliminated from our immediate experiences and thus becomes a non-issue. A society of the spectacle turns life into a visual drama, a show; and the most real show, the most "objective" show, is that on television. Television has become the most important authority of dramatized information among the various mass media. We are fascinated with the possibility of being on television or meeting someone who is on television (a celebrity), because it is only here—television—that our subjective experiences (which are experienced emotionally as real) can be objectified.

...

The decline of discourse is marked by [television's] proliferation of symbols that are ephemeral. Advertising turns every product into a symbol. Cologne symbolizes sexual prowess, the sports car success, and so forth. But these symbols have no staying power, for advertising must constantly experiment with pseudo-meaning. The products come and go, and so do their symbolic meanings. These symbols are "sterilized symbols," for they (not the products, but the symbolic meanings) no longer have a practical purpose... as an integral part of culture; rather, they serve as a means of propaganda. Political symbols suffer the same fate as advertising symbols. Politicians are sold like products.

...

This helps to explain why discourse has become so manipulative. Public relations is fast becoming the universal discourse. Propaganda, advertising, and public relations are psychological techniques (nonmaterial technology) whose sole function is to bring humans into conformity with the demands of a technological civilization, including greater efficiency in production and consumption. Today, one can speak and write that which is only possible, not necessarily factual, as long as it allows one to succeed. Politicians, athletes, entertainers, and celebrities tell the media that which will enhance or protect their image. College graduates tell interviewers that which will help them obtain a job. Increasingly, we are selling an image of ourselves to others, one that will allow us to manipulate them.

Collins or Skover: What impresses us in this exchange, first, is the starkly different portraits of the current state of American discourse that the three of you present. Robert and David suggest that the gap between high First Amendment principles and low free speech practices is far narrower than we describe it. In contrast, Richard generally accords with our depiction of a wider gap, and elaborates upon it methodically and colorfully. Whereas Robert finds socially valuable morality plays in the highjinks of a sit com or the bathos of a talk show, Richard sees psychologically manipulative power plays. These are not mere differences of degree, but distinctions of kind. Given such widely disparate perspectives, is it any surprise that you three are polarized over our portrayal of contemporary American television and advertising?

Second, David and Robert's arguments presume that there are pockets of private and public expression that remain largely immune from the ubiquitous influences of our mass commercial entertainment culture. Such cultural immunity is a phenomenon that Richard's position explicitly denies. Of course, we are sensitive to the likelihood that the ascendancy of that culture may not affect everyone the same way. But ours is a postmodern reality in which essentialist distinctions between public and private domains or political and commercial speech categories increasingly blur. In such a world, we question whether any sectors of expression can be so easily cabined off from the dominant trends in today's popular culture of amusement, consumption and self-gratification.

Thus, in Book I, we argue that billion-dollar commercial efforts to institutionalize the pleasure principle through the all-pervasive medium of television will have some telling effect on the structures of both individual and social communication. Along the same lines, in Book II, we analogize commercial advertising to "ice-nine" in *Cat's Cradle*, as it permeates everything in our culture. And, in Book III, we observe that the political pornography of old has given way to the apolitical pornography of today that

Goethe:

There is a curious custom in the British Navy: all the cordage of the Royal Fleet, whether heavy or light, is twisted so that a red thread runs through whole ropes, by which even the smallest piece can be recognized as Crown property.

Johann Wolfgang von Goethe, *The Sufferings of Young Werther & Elective Affinities*, ed. Victor Lange and trans. Elizabeth Mayer & Louise Bogan (New York: Continuum, 1990), p. 238.

promises individual arousal in private quarters. In all of this, we ask whether Goethe's image of the British navy's cordage—"twisted so that a red thread runs through whole ropes"—is not an apt metaphor for the omnipresent and potent effects of our commercial entertainment culture in every arena of expression?

Hariman: I submit that if we do recognize how each of us negotiates multiple roles, discourses, technologies, and texts within a society based on the overproduction of signs, we see not a clear case of the death of discourse but rather processes of appropriation, reconstruction, willed inattention, and the like that suggest much thicker cognition and more civic virtue than one might suspect by looking at advertising, entertainment, or pornography alone.

Once again, the problem of assessment comes from using the wrong standard. If we begin with the Madisonian model, then it is difficult to see its imitation today. In place of the classical modes of invention on standard topics of public debate, today the production of public address is characterized by continual recombination of a wide range of essentially incoherent templates. One reason we can "feel" the irrelevance of the model of Madisonian speech is that the culture of modernity is being driven by its own technologies of exchange to a point of radical, discursive plurality. So it is that the same communicators can mix modern studio production with Biblical morality, or biological explanations with assertions of free speech, or bureaucratic diction with calls for radical social critique, or advertisements for sheer pantyhose with images of feminist self-assertion. Stated differently, there is indeed a radical relativism within modern society, although only at the level of discourse production. Once brought into the realm of representation, everything becomes capable of being re-appropriated into wildly discrepant contexts.

This discursive condition becomes particularly evident the more one drops down into vernacular rhetorics. The high cultural, official, institutional forms of public address remain the most conventional, that is to say, the most unmixed discourses.... For obvious reasons, the higher level civic discourses are the more constrained, institutionally and generically. Yet most of us most of the time are in the opposite situation: while speaking at the PTA meeting or the departmental meeting or wherever, we can and do draw on whatever verbal resources we have consumed through all our media of consumption. As we are fitting words to highly specific situations, in respect to immediate experiences, we still draw on typical forms of appeal but with a relatively weak sense of compositional restraint. Ordinary public address is largely a process of *bricolage*, the individuated, artistic, provisional adaptation and organization of diverse materials from other texts designed for other contexts. Although it is true that the mass media are appropriating all forms of culture, it also is the case that the people return the favor, taking those commodified signs and reinstilling use value as they put them to work in their own persuasive practices.

Collins or Skover: It is revealing to "hear" Robert admit that he "feel[s] the irrelevance of the model of Madisonian speech"—an irrelevancy that we would have him fully realize, rather than just feel. You reject the Madisonian model as a standard for measuring the constitutional merits of modern discourse, Robert. We wonder, then, how far you would have First Amendment protection extend to further your own model of *bricolage*. What "diverse materials from . . . texts designed for other contexts" will count in today's marketplace of ideas? Will the postmodern idea of "texts"—a notion that deconstructs the division between fixed text and fluid context—now govern the realm of free expression? Then, might any verbal or non-verbal act be constitutionally equivalent, insofar as it is a "commodified sign" to be "put to work in [our] own persuasive practices"? If not, why not? If so, where does all of this lead?

Our puzzling barrage of questions reminds us of our provocative conversation with Suzanne Singer at the end of "Discourse & Intercourse." As our audience may recall, Suzanne had proposed that "the release people get from experiencing pornography [might] give them the space to become clear, rational thinkers," much in the service of traditional Madisonian ideals. We responded quite similarly to her then as we do to you now. When all release valves for pent-up passions become entitled to auxiliary free speech protection, we argued, America will have moved far down the road toward pornutopia. Do you, Robert, really offer any greater safeguards against our Huxleyan predicament? Or will *bricolage* bring on the brave new world of trivialized, commercialized, and sexualized public expression, fostered under a post-Madisonian First Amendment?

Loyal Rue: Collins and Skover have made a very strong case that the commercialization of American culture has gone too far and that the phenomenon may indeed be irreversible. But they have not told the whole story. The whole story is likely to be bleak enough, but it just might leave room for a slightly happier ending.

. . .

What about the schools? . . . [W]e should not underestimate the possibility that the tastes of American consumers of culture might be elevated by means of education. The educational establishment is still largely independent of the media culture, and increasingly hostile toward it. I am unsure of what happens in the grade schools and high schools, but I do know that many college-level courses in the social sciences and humanities take a rather dim view of the media culture, providing their students with some pretty effective prophylactics to make them more critical consumers. Enough of this, and the entertainment-advertising complex would have to correct for a more sophisticated audience.

Hariman: [Precisely.] The key to any measures taken in the spirit of civic-republican reform ought to be developing rhetorical competencies rather than restricting competing forms of expression. . . . Because we want to have rational public debate, we ought to develop those procedures that will ensure it.

. . .

I would rather live in a community where the common response to hateful graffiti is not for the institution to post guards and paint over the wall, but for other citizens to write a counter-statement beside or over the offending words; a community where pornography is legal, but citizens are quick to publicly ridicule its users; a community where advertising would not be banned, but the government and interest groups would buy newspaper space to reprint speeches by public figures. This idea of using or working around the First Amendment to maintain the rhetorical competency necessary for democratic government is not a liberal balancing of discourses so much as a civic-republican belief that the civic virtues of courage, self-control, civility, a capacity for consensus, and the like are not given but developed, and developed in important part through the practice of public debate.

Nyberg: The institutional failure that deserves more attention here, to my way of thinking, is an educational one; it is the failure to instill in [the American youth] a sense of self-discipline, a disposition to seek and appreciate excellence, and a belief in the long-term benefits of moderation, or balance in the ways that we live. We need better-educated consumers, not more government regulation of "speech."

. . .

In my opinion, the best manner in which to moderate, remedy, or prevent offensive forms of "free speech" from turning us all into Gadarene swine is not more laws or more repressive interpretations of existing laws. Rather, the best manner is education. Centralized regulation is never as effective as internalized regulation; standardization is never as good a policy as voluntary acceptance of, or self-generated high standards used for guiding judgments about, what is a good life to live. The will and the ability to filter mass media expression could be proposed as a goal of education; indeed, effective media filtration could be seen as a criterion of successful education in learning how to act freely.

Collins or Skover: You three attempt to duck our free speech critiques of the popular culture by relying on education, by raising public consciousness, and by refining the tastes of Americans. With the fighting spirit of the late Robert Maynard Hutchins (the great American educational theorist and past president of the University of Chicago), you tie the fate of discourse in America to a faith in education. Your appeal on behalf of education is valiant; for us, it even resonates—to use Professor Hariman's term—with narrative heroicism. But is yours a battle that can be won?

We wonder whether the education that you envision does not war with a culture ever increasingly steeped in the excesses of the marketplace. To what extent is it likely that the mission of education can stand significantly free of the commercial entertainment culture? Even as Professors Nyberg and Rue endorse the educational campaign, they are sober enough to admit that the odds of victory are slim. David concedes, despite his aspirations, that we are starting from the point of "institutional failure." And Loyal's optimism is heavily qualified, as he notes: "The whole story is likely to be bleak enough, but it just might leave room for a slightly happier ending."

Skepticism is amply warranted. If education is to combat rampant commercialism and the like, educators must be mindful of how commercialism pervades education on various fronts. On the *operational* front, public elementary and secondary school districts are trading more and more with marketers to overcome the constraints of tightening instructional budgets:

- Millions of our nation's public school students are tuned in daily to Channel One—the station that pumps ads into classrooms—this despite protests by the National Education Association and the National PTA. About one-fourth of American middle schools and high schools are a captive audience for that channel.[13] A demographic study of Channel One schools revealed that "schools with the greatest concentration of low-income students are more than twice as likely as the schools with the wealthiest students to have Channel One."[14]
- American corporations by the thousands supply curricular and extracurricular materials, from teacher's forestry guides prepared by Weyerhaeuser with self-serving "instructional" questions, to ad-laden book covers, to corporate logos on athletic uniforms and in athletic facilities.[15]
- A company called YouthStream mounts advertisement boards in 7,200 high school locker rooms, and boasts in its promotional materials that it reaches 70 percent or more of American high school students with corporate advertising.[16]
- Anecdotal evidence tells the story even more strikingly. Palmer High School in Colorado Springs, for example, supplements its revenue by leasing school property to corporate advertisers. Hanging a six-foot long banner inside the school costs a marketer $700 or more per year; for $2,500 or more, corporate logos can be painted on the side of a yellow school bus. With "plenty of blank wall space left to fill," Superintendent of Schools Kenneth Burnley boasted, the district is "just scratching the surface of potential revenue."[17] Banners and buses today, walls, lockers, bulletin boards, desks, chalk boards, book pages, and computer screens tomorrow.

Lest we be misunderstood, our larger point is that commerce's many threads are interwoven more and more into the fabric of American education. While our classrooms are not yet overtaken by commercialism, there are discernible trends in that direction. Such trends are antithetical to instilling the ethical values of republican simplicity, those of Adams, Jefferson, Emerson, Thoreau, and the like. Hence, on the *ideological* front, the commercialization of our schools is likely to redefine the aspirational goals of the "good life." When students are educated less about civics and more about commerce, less about self-restraint and more about unbridled liberty, and less about public virtue and more about private gain, the lessons of the marketplace become the lessons of the schoolhouse. Whatever else, this is not education in *sophrosyne* (sobriety, moderation).

Hariman: [Even in the face of such trends,] instead of imagining the death of deliberative rhetoric, we should consider how it is or can be reformulated within postmodern culture. Our text here can be Walter Benjamin's insight about the relationship between photography and art. The important question, he noted, was not whether photography was an art but what art could be within a world dominated by photography.[18] Likewise, the question should not focus on whether popular culture is high quality discourse (or the death of high quality discourse) but rather on what high quality discourse will have to be to exist within popular culture.

. . .

[T]he focal point for reorienting the First Amendment should be protecting and nurturing particular communities that allow the development of the rhetorical competencies required for achieving deliberative judgment in an open society. These communities will range from high schools to electronic networks to worker video cooperatives to talk shows and beyond. Less likely to be valued from this perspective are corporate public relations campaigns, monopolistic programming of the mass media, and institutional support for celebration of any one lifestyle (whether marginal or mainstream). The

Consider this: Can we untangle hypocrisy fr

distinctions at work here have less to do with high or low quality speech, commercial or noncommercial speech, artistic or non-artistic status, prurient or public orientation, or even majority or minority interest; they primarily are distinctions regarding the openness of the forum, the level of participation allowed, the recourse to the means of persuasion, the purpose of the communicative exchange, and the opportunity for those who participate to exercise and develop the attributes of deliberative discourse.

Collins or Skover: But, Robert, if education and other such open fora are to "reorient" us, to what direction or end? Is it, first and foremost, *paideia*—the shaping of character to develop well-informed and socially responsible citizens? Or is it rather job training in the service of economic self-interest and pleasure? In this regard, psychology professor Barry Schwartz reminds us that "the moral character of a culture is bound up with our judgment of the set of practices that the culture encourages and supports." In a society that teaches its future citizens to be entrepreneurs and consumers, "the good person becomes the good pursuer of wealth."[19] It is nearly tautological: a culture that highly values commerce will teach, above all, the values of commerce.

Hypothetically, even if education were to be essentially purged of all of commercialism's contaminations, it is puzzling to imagine what that education would be like. To reinvigorate Madisonian values, would education return civic republicanism to the public mind? But then what? Would we defend the fundamental right of all to all forms of expression, and teach the need to tolerate the base? Seemingly, this education would never move the commercial entertainment culture beyond the point where it is now, or ward off the Huxleyan dilemma to which it is tending. Or would we emphasize the need to combat the base, and thus withhold constitutional protection from expression inimical to our high ideals? (This, at least, is what one renowned liberal educator, Dr. Alexander Meiklejohn, urged. For it was this past president of Amherst College, later chairman of the Experimental College at Wisconsin, who declared adamantly that the First Amendment ought not safeguard commercial speech.[20]) Seemingly, this education flirts with the censorship associated with Orwellian

disonian values by educating ourselves?

regimes. In the end, has this conundrum not reintroduced, in the guise of educational reform, a similar version of what we labeled in Book I as the "Paratroopers' Paradox"?

Stivers: I think that Ron and David have provided a serious and accurate critique of advertising, television, and pornography. I am not convinced, however, that you two fully understand how unprecedented [the fate of significant public discourse] is in a technological civilization.

. . .

The Constitution was authored at a time when the United States was still in the milieu of society with a traditional sense of truth. The intent of the First Amendment was to protect serious discourse from the tyranny of government. Law would not insure the free search for truth, but rather, prevent its abridgment. Today, there is little evidence of a widespread concern for serious discourse, let alone the freedom to engage in such. The Constitution is completely at odds with the main thrust of a technological civilization and with the real sentiments of people (not always expressed in public opinion polls).

The institution of law [arose] in the milieu of society, along with literacy, an agricultural economy, and the city. It supplant[ed] ritual and, under the aegis of justice, provide[d] for a greater measure of individual freedom. Like all other social institutions in the milieu of technology, law is transformed from a moral institution to a technical one.... As French legal historian Jacques Ellul observed: "Law is totally losing its validity and significance. It is becoming a technical device for administration and organization. In other words, law no longer has the objective of bringing justice. Today it is an instrument in the hands of administrators, in the hands of the state—an abstract instrument for administering and organizing the society."[21]

. . .

[As these and my former arguments demonstrate,] law has become technical, discourse has become manipulative, and truth has become equated with power (success). Is your cultural approach to the First Amendment sufficient to meet this challenge?

. . .

If the "low practices of mass communication" are the embodiment of [our] new dominant cultural norms, then the return to Madisonian ideals is only a remote possibility.... If, as [you two] assert, there is no place in democracy for a lie (in the traditional sense), then genuine democracy is dead; for public relations and its ideal of truth as power has become the universal discourse.

. . .

In my view, the probability of a return to Madisonian ideals is small indeed and will take more than a shocking discourse, even if this is the necessary first step.... Nothing short of a nonviolent cultural revolution, no matter how unlikely it may be, will allow us to escape the modern tyranny of technology. Ultimately, the Orwellian danger and the Huxleyan danger are one. For, just as technology in the form of the mass communication media controls us through the positive reinforcement of consumer pleasure, technology in the form of the totally administered political state controls us through a relentless proliferation of rules and regulations.

Rue: [Like Richard, I find that Ron and David provide] a soaring and insightful tour of the First Amendment landscape. . . . More than a constitutional treatise, *The Death of Discourse* offers a penetrating critique of the American mind and its lack of restraint in pursuit of liberty, prosperity, and pleasure.

. . .

Although there is much to commend and admire in this important work—especially the care with which it observes traditional values of discourse—[I believe, again like Richard, that you] do not bring it in for a safe landing. After a brief and brilliant flight, the whole enterprise stalls, as [you] parachute to safety.

Those of us remaining on board are left wondering whether [you] cherish traditional standards of discourse or not. [You] do raise a hopeful question about the future meaning of James Madison's dreams for the First Amendment. But do [you] have a postmodern version of this dream? [You] think we need to rechart our course, admonishing us to "toil to become what we are not." But what is *that*? And by *what means*? And *why*?

. . .

I will begin by modifying the approach taken to First Amendment issues, or, for that matter, to *any* issues of human existence. [You] commend to us [your] *cultural* approach, which is primarily a descriptive account of how we behave rather than a normative program for how we ought to behave. [Your] cultural approach may be enough to get the issues aloft, but it gives us no bearings for constructive thought about the future of the First Amendment. I believe a better approach, for both descriptive and prescriptive purposes, is a *bio-cultural* approach. A bio-cultural approach has the virtue of reminding us that the primary function of human culture (including all cultural conventions, such as speech and law) is to assist homo sapiens in meeting the challenges of adapting to the physical environment.

. . .

[You] have raised questions about the viability of First Amendment rationality in the context of popular culture. [You] produce an analysis showing that the rationality of First Amendment practice flatly contradicts the rationality of First Amendment doctrine. From the point of view of [your] cultural approach, there is folly in our reason. But from the altitude of a bio-cultural perspective, there is much more to dwell upon than First Amendment issues. The scope of our folly includes far more than a bit of sophistry in jurisprudence. It includes profound irrationality in our economic system, our political system, our technological values, our morality, and our religion. The Edict of Nature is this: bring forth all of your charter documents and let them stand before the bar.

Let us begin with a relatively minor document, say, the First Amendment. How viable is the First Amendment as a biological adaptation? . . . [T]his question can be asked more precisely: to what extent does the practice of guaranteeing freedom of speech contribute to the achievement of personal wholeness and/or social coherence? The answer must certainly be that there is no way to tell without looking at the details of those individual persons and distinctive groups who are impacted by particular speech acts. This is precisely what makes First Amendment issues so thorny for policy makers—that is, the particulars are so complicated that they defy all confidence in policy decisions.

Take, for example, the pornography debate. Is it the case that exposure to sexually-explicit material is conducive to the achievement of personal wholeness? This sounds very much like a straightforward empirical question, and we would dearly love to have it answered by some decisive psychological study. But this is certainly too much to ask. A very small measure of common sense and experience tells us that it depends entirely on the persons involved. For some persons exposure to sexually graphic material at a certain stage in their life may be personally constructive and therapeutic, but for others it may result in emotional trauma. It is nearly impossible to tell. There are many ways to become a whole person, just as there are many ways to prevent the achievement of wholeness. Pornography, I suspect, earns marks on both sides.

Another steamy issue surrounding the porn debate is whether exposure to sexually explicit material and violent imagery has any causal influence with respect to violent crimes against women. Here again, we find two answers. Certainly yes and certainly no. Everything depends on who is involved. There are some men in the world for whom naughty pictures are hair triggers to violent behavior, and others upon whom pornography has no effect whatever, or perhaps even a positive, sympathetic effect. There is virtually no way to tell in advance. The human being is a mind-bogglingly complicated biochemical machine.

The point of all of this is simply to say that very little, if anything, can be said with confidence at the policy level about the consequences of speech acts. The dynamics of causality are far too complex and fine-grained to be captured effectively by the kind of probabilistic arguments that might support policy. To suppose that legislation can settle these matters one way or another is like supposing one can play a penny whistle while wearing boxing gloves. . . . Wisdom here would suggest that where there is doubt — and here there is little else — let the issues be determined locally. All of which implies, of course, a withholding of constitutional protection.

At this point, it might be observed that a bio-cultural approach takes the point away from [Ron and David's] argument that traditional First Amendment principles contradict contemporary First Amendment practice with respect to pornography. I have argued that protection for speech acts should be considered relative to the conditions for personal wholeness and social coherence, and not relative to the ideals James Madison had in mind. In other words, when Madisonian principles are ignored, the troublesome contradiction vanishes. And if there is no contradiction, then there is no call for theories to justify hypocrisy with a noble lie. There may well be a need for noble lies in the affairs of human life, but not, it seems, at the level of proximate values.

Stanley Rosen: **[F]earless thinking has fearless consequences.**

Hermeneutics as Politics (New York: Oxford University Press, 1987), p. 138.

Collins or Skover: Clearly now, we have left the valleys of narrative truths, hypocrisy, and deliberate lies, and taken flight toward the heights where Professors Stivers and Rue would have us soar. For this mission no Piper Cubs will do; bring out the F-14A Tomcats. We are, after all, entering the realm of fearless thinking.

Richard and Loyal maneuver around the topic of First Amendment deliberate lies for two basic reasons. First, [you two] believe that Madisonian principles are virtually irrelevant in our highly technological and entertainment-driven society. Second, you understand *The Death of Discourse* to be about more, far more, than America's free speech system. Ultimately, you admonish us: we must never forget that it is a *civilization* we are examining.

Essentially, Richard, your technological critique moves us from talk about First Amendment reforms to talk about the transformation of America as a civilization. And you, Loyal, call on us to think beyond that "relatively minor document" known as the First Amendment, so that we dwell on the profound irrationality in our economic system, our political system, and our technological values (among others) from "the altitude of a bio-cultural perspective."

Rue: [Yes, indeed. And why not?] What is responsible for the frenzied binge of consumerism characteristic of the past fifty years? A combination of factors, for sure, but not the least of these is the development of a media culture that goads and glorifies the lifestyle of consumption. [Ron and David, you] have given us a useful ontogeny of the entertainment-advertising complex, and [you] have—rightly, I believe—linked the growth of this monster in part to an erosion of First Amendment nerve.... But the real question is the one that bears upon our prospects: what would it make sense to do under the present circumstances?

...

We often hear it said that we get the culture we deserve, but it would be more accurate to say that we get the culture we have allowed to be highly profitable. So let the high priests of low culture produce whatever trash they wish, and allow them to hawk it with whatever manipulative ads they can devise, but tax the bejeebers out of them in the bargain. When trumpery is viewed by the investment community as a high-risk venture, then it will surprise no one to find less of it on offer in television ads. Here we have a good old-fashioned Darwinian strategy for selecting against undesirable cultural traits. Tax the trivia out of the market, and the advertisers left on the scene may have something informative to say about something worth buying. And if, as we are told, television programming is merely a way of delivering audiences to advertisers, then we might expect the post-tax adjustment to bring positive results.

...

[Ron and David] have attempted to convince us that we have all but lost the battle to maintain the conventions of articulate culture against the constant barrage of "mediacracy." We are, finally, captives to the media culture, destined to live by its machinations and defenseless against its momentum. We cannot legislate against the media culture because it has co-opted the First Amendment—it is thereby free to use its wiles to create and maintain an absolute public aversion to its regulation. The proposal I have offered above (in other words, local regulation of pornography and federal luxury taxes) are well beyond the realm of possibility, for how could such proposals gather support in a culture where the target of legislation gets to ration the bullets and determine who shoots?

Thus, we begin to see that *The Death of Discourse* is about more than the death of discourse; it is ultimately about the loss of liberty to govern ourselves. We have, it appears, one small and pathetic freedom left: the freedom to deceive ourselves into believing that we remain free. But to exercise this freedom would do no more than add comedy to impotence—like the weakling who claims he could silence the schoolyard bully, but, as it happens, he just doesn't want to.

So at last we are brought to the heart of the matter: is it too late to save the American experiment of self-governance? . . . Here is my two-part answer: no, perhaps it is not too late, but even if it is, what's all the fuss about?

Collins or Skover: Loyal, do you really mean to "say" what we think you are "saying"? With your last question, we are reminded of Friederich Nietzsche's aphorism: "[D]isdain of that which belongs to the present moment is an integral part of philosophical contemplation."[22] Are you engaging us here in a Nietzschean moment?

Rue: [Take it as you will. For it is the two of you who] have made a very strong case that the commercialization of American culture has gone too far and that the phenomenon may indeed be irreversible. . . . What if [you] are prescient in fearing that it is too late to save the American experiment in self-governance? So what? What is the worst that could happen? The Republic might fall into ruin, and the sovereignty of the nation would be lost. The patch of land between Mexico and Canada might become the former United States of America. Okay, so what's all the fuss about? It's bound to happen sooner or later, so why not sooner? No one with an ounce of historical sophistication could seriously believe that the American experiment will still be humming along, say, five thousand years from now. Surely the experiment will have been transcended by then. Even a thousand years is a challenge to the imagination. Or five hundred.

Maybe it's not too soon to begin thinking about what comes next. If the trajectory of the experiment is destined to continue on its present course, then in a hundred years or less the excesses of radical individualism will have brought us to the point where we might say "good riddance" to the American Dream. Perhaps we're already at that point. A bio-cultural perspective on social organization suggests that the values of personal wholeness and social coherence should be held in balance, that individual rights and social responsibilities should matter equally. But certainly no honest assessment would find such a balance in our present circumstances. We are even now to the point where mild sanctions in the name of the common good are deeply resented as infringements upon personal liberty. There is no exaggeration in the account that we are a nation in terminal imbalance—where every frustration of a neural itch is seen to violate an entitlement, where every instance of personal inconvenience is quickly and conveniently parlayed into litigation. The trajectory continues with ratchet-like precision, goaded by the advertising imperatives to "go for it" and "just do it" (where "it" is whatever you like), and guarded by a legal profession having no greater sense of civic virtue than did the Athenian Sophists. Who, indeed, could be blamed for declaring good-riddance to a social experiment so miserably failed?

Collins or Skover: Bold statements, Loyal. Hyperbolic or prescient, your reflections—and those of Professor Stivers—engage *The Death of Discourse* in two important dialogic ways. First, you both begin (explicitly or otherwise) to play out the consequences of our "cultural approach" to the First Amendment. The cultural approach, as we sketch it, may extend to Richard's sociological claims about technology and to your own ecological claims about civilization. Our approach need not validate these claims in order to recognize the value in seriously considering them. Such thinking is made possible, of course, precisely because your discourse about the First Amendment covers the terrain from Orwellian tyranny to Huxleyan tyranny, and beyond.

Second, you two escape the paradox of the traditional First Amendment as formulated in *The Death of Discourse*. You do so, however, by denying the relevancy of Madisonian ideals and challenging the viability of Madisonian government. Fundamentally, you appreciate our hypothesis that the traditional First Amendment cannot save itself without destroying itself. In the spirit of Albert Camus, you courageously engage us in a "discourse of death."

It remains with you, our audience members, to decide whether our fearless friends have brought their terrifying Tomcats in for a safe landing, or whether they, too, have parachuted. You be the judge.

Our time is at an end. We now take our leave, grateful to our colleagues for engaging us in this last dialogue. If we meet again, may our discourse be as lively. Good evening, and may we all fare well.

Credits

Scene as credits roll: Summer night. An Orlando road. In an old beat-up convertible, Collins and Skover drive by the surreal aura of Disney World. The sounds of Paul Simon's "You Can Call Me Al" fill the AM radio air: ♫♩♫"A man walks down the street. He says: 'Don't want to end up a cartoon in a cartoon graveyard... I don't find this stuff amusing anymore ... What if I die here?'" ♫♫♩ Singing along, the two speed down the long highway. Then sudden blackout.

There are many to thank for much. Years of work have been enriched by the valuable help of family, friends, and colleagues. This is their special page.

Heartfelt applause as the credits roll for:

• Janet Ainsworth • George Anastaplo • Daniel Barbiero • David Barron • Jerome Barron • David Boerner • Melinda Branscomb • Robert Chang • Jeanne Clark • Sidney DeLong • Antonia Fondaras • Joe Goffman • James Hemphill • Linda Hirshman • L. De-Wayne Layfield • Hans Linde • Kenneth Masters • John Mitchell • Larry Mitchell • Dennis Patterson • Neil Postman • H. Jefferson Powell • Steven Pressman • Jill Ramsfield • Charles Reich • Chris Rideout • John Scanlan • Pierre Schlag • Suzanne Singer • Kellye Testy • Wende Vyborney Hawkins.

The Lorenzos de Medici of this project:
• Deans James Bond, Rudy Hasl, and Kellye Testy of Seattle University School of Law for their "magnificent" sponsorship
• Dean Jack Friedenthal of George Washington University National Law Center
• Dean Robert Reinstein of Temple University School of Law.

The editors of the
• *Harvard Law Review* • *Stanford Law Review*
• *University of Cincinnati Law Review*
and especially our early and thoughtful supporters at the
• *Texas Law Review*. Some of the now
largely reworked and expanded mise-en-scènes in this book
originally previewed in these periodicals.

The dramatis personae who engaged us in dialogue
— oral or written.

Our friends at Carolina Academic Press:
• Keith Sipe, Linda Lacy, and Scott Sipe.
Our patient and persistent editor:
• Gordon Massman of Westview Press.
Our artful producers: • Bruce Mau of Toronto with Chris Rowat
• Alex Lubertozzi of Top Five Books.
And our talented production assistant:
• Nancy Ammons of Seattle University School of Law.

The organizers and conferees at the symposia where the early
sketches of this work were first presented:
• New York University Communications Conference (1990)
• National Rhetoric Society's Biannual Conference, Texas (1990)
• Central State Regional Communications Conference, Chicago (1991)
• Harvard Law School Symposium, Cambridge (1993)
• American Political Science Association Annual Conference,
New York (1994)
• University of Florida Communications Conference on
Milton's *Areopagitica*, Tampa (1994)
• Catalunya Department of Justice Conference on Free Speech,
Barcelona, Spain (1994).

Our dedicated and understanding partners and families
— those supportive souls behind the scenes:
• Susan A. Cohen • Seán P. O'Reilly • and our Parents
— *vivamus atque amemus.*

Gratitude is the Memory of the Heart.
— Jean Baptiste Massieu

Endnotes

The reader who is content with the bare bones of the argument will find the text self-sufficient; the [end]notes have occasionally been used to put a little flesh on the bones.

—Grant Gilmore
The Death of Contract
(Columbus: Ohio State University Press, 1995 ed.)

Endnotes for Foreword

1. Proverbs 17: 9 NEB. Decontextualized and rephrased, this proverb is given suggestive meaning for writers who are audacious enough to issue third editions of their works.

2. The characterization of print-based closure informing this paragraph is developed more fully in Ronald K.L. Collins & David M. Skover, "Paratexts," *Stanford Law Review* 44 (1992): 509—552.

3. Dylan Thomas, "A Refusal to Mourn the Death, by Fire, of a Child in London," in Dylan Thomas, *Collected Poems 1934–1952*, ed. Vernon Watkins (New York: New Directions, 1971), p. 112.

4. Alfred Lord Tennyson, "Ulysses," in Alfred Lord Tennyson, *Selected Poems*, ed. Aidan Day (New York: Penguin, 1992), p. 94.

5. Roy Porter, *Studies in European History: The Enlightenment* (New York: Palgrave Macmillan, 1996), p. 1.

6. A more detailed account of the current state of civil liberties incident to the American "war on terrorism" is beyond the scope and purpose of the Foreword. This paragraph was informed, however, by several works that are recommended for fuller exploration of the subject: The Reporters Committee for Freedom of the Press, *Homefront Confidential: How the War on Terrorism Affects Access to Information and the Public's Right to Know*, RCFP White Paper, no. 3 (Arlington, VA: The Reporters Committee for Freedom of the Press, 2003); Richard C. Leone and Greg Anrig, Jr., eds., *The War on Our Freedoms: Civil Liberties in an Age of Terrorism* (New York: PublicAffairs, 2003); Nancy Chang, *Silencing Political Dissent: How Post-September 11 Anti-Terrorism Measures Threaten Our Civil Liberties* (New York: Seven Stories Press, 2002); Danny Goldberg, Victor Goldberg, and Robert Greenwald, eds., *It's a Free Country: Personal Freedom in America After September 11* (New York: RDV Books, 2002); Lawyers Committee for Human Rights, *A Year of Loss: Reexamining Civil Liberties Since September 11* (New York: Lawyers Committee for Human Rights, 2002); Noam Chomsky, *9-11* (New York: Seven Stories Press, 2001).

7. Infra p. 25.

8. Quoted in Eve Pell, "The Knock at the Door," in Danny Goldberg, Victor Goldberg, and Robert Greenwald, eds., *It's a Free Country: Personal Freedoms in America After September 11* (New York: RDV Books, 2002), p. 180.

9. Sandra Silberstein, *War of Words: Language, Politics and 9/11* (New York: Routledge, 2002), pp. 121–123 (quoting Jeff Milchen's Web-based article, "The Greatest Danger Comes from Within").

10. Jane Kirtley, "There They Go Again," *American Journalism Review*, http://www.ajr.org/Article.asp?id=2756, January/February 2003. We are grateful to Sean Gillespie, a member of the 2003 Seattle University Law School seminar on Mass Media Theory & First Amendment Jurisprudence, who pointed us to this source and elaborated on its argument.

11. Ben Berkowitz, "TV's War News Coverage Outdrawn by Comedy Repeats," *WashingtonPost.com*, http://www.washingtonpost.com/wp-dyn/articles/A6782-2003Mar21.html, 21 March 2003.

12. Bob Herbert, "The Art of the False Impression," *NewYorkTimes.com*, http://www.nytimes.com/2003/08/11/opinion/11HERB.html, 11 August 2003.

13. Jim Rutenberg, "Suffering News Burnout? Rest of America Is, Too," *New York Times*, 11 August 2003, sec. C, p. 1.

14. Danny Schecter, "How the Media Threatens Civil Liberties," in Goldberg, Goldberg, and Greenwald, eds., *It's a Free Country*, pp. 171, 173.

15. Dan Rathers and Cokie Roberts quoted in John F. Stacks, "Watchdogs on a Leash: Closing Doors on the Media," in Leone and Anrig, Jr., eds., *The War on Our Freedoms*, pp. 237, 251.

16. Michael Tomasky, "'Patriochialism': September 11 and the Death of Debate," in Goldberg, Goldberg, and Greenwald, eds., *It's a Free Country*, pp. 164, 167.

17. See, e.g., Lizabeth Cohen, *A Consumers' Republic: The Politics of Mass Consumption in Postwar America* (New York: Knopf, 2003), p. 401; Silberstein, *War of Words*, pp. 124–125.

18. See, e.g., Karen Hosler, "Approve Tax Cuts Quickly, Treasury Chief Urges House Action," *Baltimore Sun*, 14 February 2001, sec. A, p. 1; Gary Martin, "Divided House OK's Core of Bush Tax Cut," *San Antonio Express-News*, 9 March 2001, sec. A, p. 1 ("[The $1.6 trillion tax cut gives] an average $400 tax refund to families to spend on consumer goods and services. The President portrayed the tax cuts as a tonic for impending recession.").

19. Allan Sloan, "Consumption, Conspicuous or Not," *New York Times*, 2 February 2003, sec. B, p. 12 (review of Cohen, *A Consumers' Republic*).

20. Jeff Rundles, "Paying for Patriotism," *Colorado Biz*, http://www.cobizmag.com/ column.cfm?columnist_ID=3, January 2002.

21. Infra p. 9.

22. Margaret Sullivan, "The Outsize Influence of Cable News," *Washington Post*, 27 May 2019.

23. Ted Koppel, "Don't Expect Trump to Go Quietly," *Washington Post*, 14 January 2019.

24. Ted Koppel, "Olbermann, O'Reilly and the Death of Real News," *Washington Post*, 14 November 2010.

25. Nicholas Confessore and Karen Yourish, "$2 Billion Worth of Free Media for Donald Trump," *New York Times*, 16 March 2016.

26. Aaron Pressman and Danielle Abril, "YouTube's creator economy is bigger and more profitable than ever," *Fortune*, 2 June 2021.

27. David Ingram, "YouTube 2020: Why politics have exploded on the video platform," *NBC News*, 16 September 2020.

28. Alex Thompson, "Trump deploys YouTube as his secret weapon in 2020," *Politico*, 6 September 2020.

29. See generally Adilbeck Madaminov, "All the President's Tweets," *Start It Up*, 24 November 2020; Niall McCarthy, "The End of the Road for Trump's Twitter Account," *Statista*, 11 January 2021; "Social media use by Donald Trump," *Wikipedia*, https://en.wikipedia.org/wiki/Social_media_use_by_Donald_Trump (visited 8 August 2021); Carol D. Leonnig and Dan Lamothe, "How Mattis Reached His Breaking Point—and Decided to Speak Out against Trump," *Washington Post*, 5 June 2020.

30. "Excerpts from Trump's Interview with the *New York Times*," *New York Times*, 1 February 2019.

31. Scott Simon, "Calling the Press the Enemy of the People Is a Menacing Move," *NPR* 4 August 2018.

32. Max Boot, "Dan Coats Was a Casualty of Trump's War on the Truth," *Washington Post*, 29 July 2019.

33. Chris Cillizza, "The 67 Most Stunning Lines from Donald Trump's Epic 2-Hour CPAC Speech," *CNN*, 4 March 2019.

34. 576 US 155 (2015).

35. Andrew Hutchinson, "Facebook Launches New Interview Series Looking at Evolving Shifts in Advertising Approaches," *Social Media Today*, 5 August 2021.

36. Ibid.

37. Valeriya Safronova, "A Private-School Sex Educator Defends Her Methods," *New York Times*, 7 July 2021.

38. Ibid.

39. Cecilia Rodriguez, "New Porn Guide to Classic Nudes in Great Museums: A Controversial Mix," *Forbes*, 25 July 2021.

40. Dorothy Neufeld, "The 50 Most Visited Websites in the World," *Visual Capitalist*, 27 January 2021.

41. "Porn Industry Archives," *Enough-is-Enough*, https://enough.org/stats_porn_industry_archives (visited 8 August 2021).

42. Ibid.

43. Samantha N Sallie, Valentin J E Ritou, Henrietta Bowden-Jones, and Valerie Voon, "Assessing online gaming and pornography consumption patterns during

COVID-19 isolation using an online survey: Highlighting distinct avenues of problematic internet behavior," *PubMed*, 9 July 2021.

44. 521 U.S. 844 (1997).

45. 535 U.S. 234 (2002).

46. Cass Sunstein, *Democracy and the Problem of Free Speech* (New York: Free Press, 1993), p. 215.

47. April Hefner, "Honorable John G. Roberts, Jr., Chief Justice of the United States, Speaks at Belmont University," *Belmont University*, 7 February 2019.

48. 567 US 709, 723 (2012).

49. 564 US 786, 790 (2011).

50. 559 US 460, 482 (2010) (Alito, J. dissenting).

51. Ibid., p. 470.

52. Robert Post and Amanda Shanor, "Adam Smith's First Amendment," *Harvard Law Review Forum* 128 (2015): 165.

53. *Janus v. American Federation of State, County, and Municipal Employees, Council 31*, 585 U.S. ___, 138 S. Ct. 2448, 2501 (2018) (Kagan, J., dissenting) (relying on the First Amendment, the majority ruled public-sector unions cannot charge nonmembers a "fair-share" agency fee).

Endnotes for Prologue

Note: The music that opens the Prologue is from Gilbert Kaplan and the London Symphony Orchestra's 1992 rendition of Mahler's "Adagietto." Without committing ourselves to the Kaplan commentary on the piece, we ascribe our own meaning to his rendition. As we hear it, the rendition both expresses the love of life and the somber anticipation of death.

1. Taken from Sebastian de Grazia, *Machiavelli in Hell* (Princeton, NJ: Princeton University Press, 1989), pp. 38, 393.

2. David Lindley, *The End of Physics: The Myth of a Unified Theory* (New York: Basic Books, 1993), p. 25.

At various points in this work, we refer to James Madison, Madisonian principles, and Madisonian ideals of free speech. By this, we do not necessarily mean to refer to Madison's historical understanding, though, by the same token, we need not formally disavow that understanding. For us what is most important is that such terms have come to connote an elevated and idealized notion of free speech associated with reasoned discourse and civic participation. This "meaning" has frequently been espoused by twentieth-century legal and political thinkers to the point where it has become something of a "tradition" in its own right, whatever its historical lineage may be. For a sample and general discussion of these Madisonian matters, see Gordon S. Wood, "The Founding Realists," *New York Review of Books*, 19 October 1995, p. 58, and Richard K. Matthews, *If Men Were Angels: James Madison and the Heartless Empire of Reason* (Lawrence: University Press of Kansas, 1995).

3. de Grazia, *Machiavelli in Hell*, p. 385. Adapted from Niccolò Machiavelli, *The Mandrake*, in *The Classic Theatre*, vol. 1, ed. Eric Bentley (New York: Doubleday Anchor, 1958), pp. 1, 10.

4. Niccolò Machiavelli, *The Prince*, trans. Harvey Mansfield (Chicago: University of Chicago Press, 1985), p. 61.

5. James B. Twitchell, *Carnival Culture: The Trashing of Taste in America* (New York: Columbia University Press, 1992), p. 251.

6. David Luke, "Thomas Mann's 'Iridescent Interweaving,'" in Thomas Mann, *Death in Venice*, ed. and trans. Clayton Koelb (New York: W. W. Norton, 1994), pp. 195, 201, 204.

Endnotes for Book I: The Paratroopers' Paradox

Note: For additional reference sources pertaining to Book I, see Ronald K.L. Collins and David M. Skover, "The First Amendment in an Age of Paratroopers," *Texas Law Review* 68 (1990):1087–1125; Ronald K.L. Collins and David M. Skover, "Pissing in the Snow: A Cultural Approach to the First Amendment," *Stanford Law Review* 45 (1993):783–806.

1. Louis Forsdale, "Marshall McLuhan and the Rules of the Game," in *Marshall McLuhan: The Man and His Message*, ed. G. Sanderson and F. MacDonald (Golden, CO: Fulcrum, 1989), pp. 169, 173 (quoting Marshall McLuhan, "Educational Effects of the Mass Media of Communication," seminar paper presented at Teacher's College, Columbia University, 1955).

2. Todd Gitlin, *Inside Prime Time* (New York: Pantheon Books, 1983), p. 335.

3. See generally Nielsen Media Research, *1992–1993 Report on Television* (New York, 1993); Gene F. Jankowski and David C. Fuchs, *Television Today and Tomorrow* (New York: Oxford University Press, 1995), pp. 182–183 (TV viewing as percentage of spare time); "NRTC Executive: DirecTV a Big Hit in the Country," *Multichannel News*, 15 December 1994, p. 32 (cable TV); Philip Elmer-Dewitt, "Electronic Superhighway," *Time Magazine*, 12 April 1993, p. 55 (video rentals); Jay Matthews, "One Sure-Fire Hit on TV: Commercials," *Washington Post*, 20 May 1995, sec. D, p. 1 (TV ad expenditures); Verhovek, "New York Bans Sponsored TV from Its Schools," *New York Times*, 17 June 1989, sec. A, p. 1 (commercial viewing by youths).

4. See Stanley Ingber, "The Marketplace of Ideas: A Legitimizing Myth," *Duke Law Journal* (1984):1, 2 nn. 1–2; Vincent Blasi, "The Checking Value in First Amendment Theory," *American Bar Foundation Research Journal* (1977):521, 527–542; Alexander Meiklejohn, *Political Freedom: The Constitutional Powers of the People* (New Haven, CT: Greenwood Press, 1960), pp. 9–28 (self-realization rationale); Thomas Emerson, *The System of Freedom of Expression* (New York: Vintage Books, 1970), p. 6 (self-realization rationale); Martin Redish, *Freedom of Expression: A Critical Analysis* (Charlottesville, VA: Michie, 1984), pp. 20–30 (self-realization rationale); C. Edwin Baker, *Human Liberty and Freedom of Speech* (New York: Oxford University Press, 1989), pp. 47–69 (individual liberty); Steven H. Shiffrin, *The First Amendment, Democracy, and Romance* (Cambridge: Harvard University Press, 1990) (romantic eclecticism).

5. Sybille Bedford, *Aldous Huxley: A Biography* (New York: Carroll & Graf, 1973), pp. 490–491 (in a letter to George Orwell, Huxley maintained: "I feel that the

nightmare of *Nineteen Eighty-Four* is destined to modulate into the nightmare of a world having more resemblance to that which I imagined in *Brave New World.*").

6. Neil Postman, *Amusing Ourselves to Death: Public Discourse in the Age of Show Business* (New York: Viking Penguin, 1985), p. vii. Professor Postman's thought-provoking writings on public discourse do not address the First Amendment issues discussed here. Moreover, and as we point out later, the substance of Huxley's writings may be more relevant to our First Amendment inquiry than to Professor Postman's particular project.

7. Aldous Huxley, *Brave New World and Brave New World Revisited* (New York: Harper & Row, 1965), pp. 29 (BNWR), 58 (BNW).

8. Ibid., p. 29 (BNWR).

9. Ibid., pp. 90, 41 (BNWR).

10. Ibid., pp. 28–29 (BNWR).

11. Ibid., p. 96 (BNWR).

12. Walter Goodman, "And Now, Heeeeeeeer's a Referendum!" *New York Times*, 21 June 1992, sec. H, p. 25.

13. Postman, *Amusing Ourselves to Death*, pp. 78, 87.

14. Quoted on *48 Hours*, CBS, 2 June 1993 (special report on TV talk shows hosted by Dan Rather).

15. James Twitchell, *Carnival Culture: The Trashing of Taste in America* (New York: Columbia University Press, 1992), pp. 201, 195–196.

16. These examples are drawn from ibid., pp. 202, 7, 219, 240.

17. Quoted in Carl Bernstein, "Talk Show Nation," *New Perspectives Quarterly* 11 (Summer 1994):22.

18. Robert Hughes, "Why Watch It, Anyway?," *New York Review of Books*, 16 February 1995, pp. 37, 38.

19. This is the chorus line from the 1967 hit by Sonny & Cher, "The Beat Goes On." From *The Beat Goes On — The Best of Sonny & Cher* (Atlantic Records, 1991).

20. Todd Gitlin, *The Whole World Is Watching: Mass Media in the Making and Unmaking of the New Left* (Berkeley: University of California Press, 1980), pp. 5–13 ("What makes the world beyond direct experience look natural is a media frame.... Media frames are persistent patterns of cognition, interpretation, and presentation, of selection, emphasis, and exclusion, by which symbol-handlers routinely organize discourse, whether verbal or visual."). Admittedly, other forms of communication, such as print, "frame" reality. But television "frames" differ in essential ways: They are more imagistically dramatic; they can instantaneously capture more unprocessed information; and they can divorce information from its natural and larger context in a more visually sensational manner. See Ronald K.L. Collins and David M. Skover, "Paratexts," *Stanford Law Review* 44 (1992):509, 510 n. 5.

21. Oreskes, "America's Politics Loses Way As Its Vision Changes World," *New York Times*, 18 March 1990, sec. A, p. 16.

22. Hughes, "Why Watch It, Anyway?," p. 38.

23. Leo Bogart, quoted in *Media, Democracy and the Information Highway*, ed. Martha FitzSimon (New York: Freedom Forum Media Studies Center, 1993), p. 11.

24. Ted Koppel, quoted in William Safire, *Lend Me Your Ears: Great Speeches in History* (New York: W. W. Norton, 1992), pp. 680–684 (address delivered to the graduating class of Duke University on May 10, 1987).

25. Yaukey, "Newsman Schorr Blasts Politics Warped by TV," *Ithaca Journal*, 15 November 1988, sec. A, p. 3 (quoting from a lecture delivered at Cornell University on November 14, 1988).

26. Neil Postman, *Conscientious Objections: Stirring Up Trouble About Language, Technology, and Education* (New York: Knopf, 1988), p. 169.

27. James Barber, "And Now, Mr. Lincoln, You Have 15 Seconds," *New York Times*, 30 October 1988, sec. 7 (Book Review), p. 36.

28. Huxley, *Brave New World and Brave New World Revisited*, p. 46 (BNWR).

29. Twitchell, *Carnival Culture*, p. 6. Our discussion is informed in part by Professor Twitchell's excellent analysis of the "blockbuster" phenomenon. See ibid., pp. 83–84 (paperbacks), 140–141 (movies and network television), 213–214 (syndication and cable television), 149–152 (videocassette sales), 141–143 (merchandising rights).

30. Ibid., p. 262. Quote taken from Carl Bernstein, "The Leisure Empire," *Time*, 24 December 1990, pp. 56, 59.

31. Gitlin, *Inside Prime Time*, pp. 328–329.

32. Twitchell, *Carnival Culture*, pp. 212, 207.

33. Boyer, "The Shift of Rather," *New York Times*, 6 August 1988, p. 50. See also Boyer, "When News Must Pay Its Way, Expect Trivia," *New York Times*, 2 October 1989, sec. A, p. 19 (warning that "journalists are becoming entertainers").

34. Huxley, *Brave New World and Brave New World Revisited*, p. 26 (BNWR) (Huxley was referring to propaganda generally).

35. For a superb illustration of this point, consider the difficulties encountered by electronic broadcasters in airing programs pertaining to the abortion issue. See Gay, "*Roe vs. Wade* Sells Out, but Did the Advertisers Sell Out to Boycott Threat?" *Variety*, 17 May 1989, p. 1 (although the program was presented in a balanced and non-controversial manner, NBC suffered a substantial loss of revenue even after it reduced advertising rates); Lipman, "Barbara Walters Radio Special on Abortion Shunned by Sponsors," *Wall Street Journal*, 16 June 1989, sec. B, p. 1 (observing that the network was unable to "sign up a single advertiser" because of the program's subject). Many of the same problems confront public television. See Walter Goodman, "Public TV Juggles a Hot Potato," *New York Times*, 3 September 1989, sec. 2, p. 1 ("How can

[public television] serve as a forum for all manner of opinions, including those that are bound to irritate many viewers, yet retain its financial support?"). Indeed, corporations and advertisers employ television-screening agencies to monitor the content of network shows and to ensure that advertising dollars dictate standards for controversial programming. See Bill Carter, "Screeners Help Advertisers Avoid Prime-Time Trouble," *New York Times*, 29 January 1990, sec. C, p. 1.

36. See Collins and Skover, "Age of Paratroopers," pp. 1099–1100 nn. 66–69 (holdings in the cable industry, chase for ad revenues and market shares, and cable programming that mirrors network entertainment shows). See also Ben Bagdikian, *The Media Monopoly* (Boston: Beacon Press, 1992).

37. Stanley Rothman, "The Development of the Mass Media," in *The Mass Media in Liberal Democratic Societies*, ed. Stanley Rothman (New York: Paragon House, 1992), pp. 37, 53; Roderick P. Hart, *Seducing America: How Television Charms the Modern Voter* (New York: Oxford University Press, 1994), pp. 7, 59.

38. Kathleen Hall Jamieson, quoted in Walter Goodman, "All That Piffle on TV? It's Someone Else's Fault," *New York Times*, 21 February 1993, sec. H, p. 37; Howard Kurtz, "Television Has Trouble Bringing Congress's Revolution into Focus," *Washington Post*, 24 January 1995, sec. A, pp. 1, 2.

39. "The Remaking of the Candidate," *Campaigns and Elections Magazine*, May–June 1988, pp. 27, 28 (interview with Michael Sheehan).

40. Howard Kurtz, "A Revisionist's Nightmare," *Washington Post*, 10 June 1993, sec. D, p. 1; Howard Kurtz, "Gingrich Criticizes 'Nit-Picking' Media," *Washington Post*, 10 January 1995, sec. A, p. 7.

41. John Tierney, "Sound Bites Become Smaller Mouthfuls," *New York Times*, 23 January 1992, sec. A, p. 1.

42. Kiku Adatto, "The Incredible Shrinking Sound Bite," *New Republic*, 28 May 1990, p. 20. Reproduced in Kiku Adatto, *Picture Perfect: The Art and Artifice of Public Image Making* (New York: Basic Books, 1993), pp. 2, 25, 171.

43. Ibid., p. 187 n. 7.

44. Tierney, "Sound Bites Become Smaller Mouthfuls," sec. A, p. 1.

45. George Will, "The Uselessness of Debates," *Washington Post*, 11 September 1988, sec. C, p. 7.

46. David S. Broder, "War on Cynicism," *Washington Post*, 6 July 1994, sec. A, p. 19.

47. "The Public Mind: Leading Questions," PBS, 15 November 1989. See also Stuart Hall, "Bill Moyers Holds a Mirror Up to America," *Los Angeles Times*, 12 November 1989 (magazine supplement), p. 4.

48. "The Public Mind: Illusions of News," PBS, 22 November 1989 (statement of Lesley Stahl).

49. Dan Rather, quoted in Elizabeth Kolbert, "Dan Rather Scolds TV News as Pandering to Get Ratings," *New York Times*, 1 October 1993, sec. A, p. 8 (speech to the Radio and Television News Director Association).

50. *Nightline*, ABC, 22 July 1994 (statement of *Los Angeles Times* media critic Tom Rosenstiel). See also Tom Shales, "Chung's Glossy Magazine," *Washington Post*, 25 September 1989, sec. B, p. 1 ("More and more in television, stories that should be treated in documentary fashion end up as TV movies, and stories that would make good TV movies end up as news productions. The line between news and entertainment hasn't just been blurred; everything's gone topsy-turvy.").

51. To examine the current state of public relations art, *Harper's* hired public relations consultants to develop a media strategy for winning over American opinion at the Second Coming of Jesus Christ. The resulting strategies included a staged appearance on *Saturday Night Live*, a media sound bite, a national tour, and a battery of one-minute television commercials announcing the Second Coming. See "He's Back!!!" *Harper's*, 19 April 1989, p. 47.

52. *This Week with David Brinkley*, ABC, 6 November 1988 (emphasis added).

53. Twitchell, *Carnival Culture*, p. 250 (citation omitted).

54. Quoted in *Penguin Dictionary of Modern Humorous Quotations*, ed. Fred Metcalf (1986), p. 248.

55. Bernstein, "Talk Show Nation," p. 24.

56. See Collins and Skover, "Age of Paratroopers," p. 1105 n. 92. See generally *Review of Child Development Research*, vols. 1–7 (Chicago: University of Chicago Press, 1964–1985).

57. Stuart Ewen, quoted in Hall, "Bill Moyers Holds a Mirror Up to America," *Los Angeles Times*, 12 November 1989, p. 4.

58. Twitchell, *Carnival Culture*, p. 195.

59. Cartoon by Jim Borgman, reprinted in *Washington Post*, 27 June 1992, sec. A, p. 19.

60. Carl M. Cannon and Marc Gunther, "From the Campaign Trail to the Talk-Show Circuit," *Philadelphia Inquirer*, 21 June 1992, sec. C, p. 6.

61. Howard Kurtz, "Networks Adapt to Changed Campaign Role," *Washington Post*, 21 June 1992, sec. A, p. 19; Richard L. Berke, "Mixed Results for CBS Rule on Sound Bite," *New York Times*, 11 July 1992, sec. A, p. 7; Editorial, "A Bite in the Right Direction," *Los Angeles Times*, 7 July 1992, sec. B, p. 6; Jim Benson, "Sound Bites May Bite Dust at CBS," *Variety*, 20 July 1992, p. 24.

62. Quoted in *48 Hours*, CBS, 2 June 1993 (special report on TV talk shows).

63. M. Ethan Katsh, "Rights, Camera, Action: Cyberspatial Settings and the First Amendment," *Yale Law Journal* 104 (1995):1681, 1685. See also M. Ethan Katsh, *Law in a Digital World* (New York: Oxford University Press, 1995).

64. Marshall McLuhan and Quentin Fiore, *War and Peace in the Global Village* (New York: McGraw-Hill, 1968), p. 18. According to McLuhan's biographer, he frequently employed the "metaphor he had devised to express what Wyndham Lewis had once taught him: 'The present cannot be revealed to people until it has become yesterday.' McLuhan termed this the 'rearview mirror phenomenon.' People went through life looking into the rearview mirror — seeing the present in terms of the past — instead of paying attention to the reality confronting them." Philip Marchand, *Marshall McLuhan: The Medium and the Messenger* (New York: Ticknor & Fields, 1989), p. 209 (footnote omitted), referencing H. Kenner, *The Pound Era* (1971), p. 436 (quoting Wyndham Lewis).

65. *American Media and Mass Culture: Left Perspectives*, ed. Donald Lazere (Berkeley: University of California Press, 1987), p. 407 (referring to statement by Alvin Gouldner).

66. Simon Lee, *The Cost of Free Speech* (London: Faber & Faber, 1990), p. 3.

67. Meiklejohn, *Political Freedom*, pp. 87, xv–xvi (the first passages quoted were originally written in 1948).

68. George Anastaplo, "Self-Government and the Mass Media: A Practical Man's Guide," in *The Mass Media and Modern Democracy*, ed. Harry M. Clor (Chicago: Rand McNally, 1974), pp. 222, 223–224.

69. Ithiel de Sola Pool, *Technologies of Freedom* (Cambridge: Harvard University Press, 1983), pp. 4, 10. Other noted advocates of nonregulation of the electronic media are Professor Lucas A. Powe Jr. and communications law attorney Jonathan W. Emord. See Lucas A. Powe, *American Broadcasting and the First Amendment* (Berkeley: University of California Press, 1987); Jonathan W. Emord, *Freedom, Technology, and the First Amendment* (San Francisco: Pacific Research Institute for Public Policy, 1991).

70. de Sola Pool, *Technologies of Freedom*, p. 54.

71. George Gilder, *Life After Television: The Coming Transformation of Media and American Life* (New York: W. W. Norton, 1994), pp. 44, 46.

72. Ralph Nader and Claire Riley, "Oh, Say Can You See: A Broadcast Network for the Audience," *Journal of Law and Politics* 5 (1988):1, 6–7 (footnotes omitted).

73. Ibid., pp. 7–9.

74. Ibid., pp. 4, 86.

75. Postman, *Amusing Ourselves to Death*, p. 158.

76. Collins and Skover, "Age of Paratroopers," p. 1119 n. 146; Collins and Skover, "Paratexts," pp. 509–552. For the classicists to deny the proposition noted in the text, they would have to set aside the paradox latent in the war between print and oral traditions. The advent of print raised its own form of the paratroopers' paradox in its time: Orality could not save itself without destroying itself because the word, in order

to be effective, had to "speak" in print. See generally Plato, *Phaedrus*, trans. Alexander Nehamas and Paul Woodruff (Indianapolis: Hackett, 1995), pp. xxxvi–xxxvii and n.34.

77. *The Republic of Plato*, trans. Allan Bloom (New York: Basic Books, 1968), p. 235.

78. Frederick Schauer, "Free Speech and the Demise of the Soapbox," *Columbia Law Review* 84 (1984):558, 565.

79. Gitlin, *Inside Prime Time*, p. 334.

80. Huxley, *Brave New World and Brave New World Revisited*, p. 26 (BNWR).

81. Gilder, *Life After Television*, p. 57; Jankowski and Fuchs, *Television Today and Tomorrow*, pp. 163, 180. Responding to Gilder's arguments in the 1992 edition of his book, Jankowski and Fuchs referred to Gilder's original use of the term "telecomputer" rather than to his later use of "teleputer."

82. W. Russell Neuman, "The Mass Audience," *Media Studies Journal* 5 (1991): 156, 157; W. Russell Neuman, *The Future of the Mass Audience* (Cambridge: Cambridge University Press, 1991), pp. 41–43, 158, 162.

83. This is not to deny, apart from the First Amendment context, the importance of the relationship between media and power. See, e.g., Harold Innis, *The Bias of Communication* (Toronto: University of Toronto Press, 1951), pp. 3–32; C. Wright Mills, *Power, Politics, and People* (New York: Oxford University Press, 1963), pp. 577–598.

84. Huxley, *Brave New World and Brave New World Revisited*, pp. 90–91 (BNWR).

85. Hall, "Bill Moyers Holds a Mirror Up to America," p. 4.

86. The "dialogue" in the text was, in large part, excerpted from a colloquy published in the *Texas Law Review* in 1990. Notes have been omitted where they do not significantly qualify the substantive import of the text. See "Colloquy: The First Amendment and the Paratroopers' Paradox," *Texas Law Review* 68 (1990):1087– 1193. Our colleagues, living and dead, were kind enough to allow us to reprint portions of their replies to our initial work on the paratroopers' paradox. The reader is encouraged to consult the complete colloquy for a richer account of the replies to our arguments.

87. Todd Gitlin, "Blips, Bites and Savvy Talk: Television's Impact on American Politics," *Dissent* (Winter 1990):18, 26.

88. Huxley, *Brave New World and Brave New World Revisited*, p. xix (introduction by Martin Green).

89. Pittman, "We're Talking the Wrong Language to 'TV Babies,'" *New York Times*, 24 January 1990, sec. A, p. 15.

90. Hall, "Bill Moyers Holds a Mirror Up to America, " p. 84 (interview with Bill Moyers).

91. *The Republic of Plato*, p. 194.

Endnotes for Book II: Commerce & Communication

1. *Virginia State Board of Pharmacy v. Virginia Citizens Consumer Council, Inc.*, 425 U.S. 748, 765 (1976). See also *City of Cincinnati v. Discovery Network, Inc.*, 113 S.Ct. 1505, 61 U.S.L.W. 4272, 4277–4278 (1993) (Blackmun, J., concurring).

2. David N. Martin, *Romancing the Brand: The Power of Advertising and How to Use It* (New York: AMACOM, 1989), p. 9.

3. Betsy Frank, vice president of the former Saatchi & Saatchi advertising agency, quoted in Jeff Silverman, "TV's Creators Face a New Caution," *New York Times*, 8 December 1991, sec. 2, pp. 1, 31.

4. Madonna, "Material Girl," from *Like a Virgin* (Sire/Warner Bros. Records, 1990) (written by Peter Brown and Robert Rans).

5. Oliver Wendell Holmes, *Collected Legal Papers* (1920), p. 270.

6. Burt Neuborne, *Free Speech — Free Markets — Free Choice: An Essay on Commercial Speech* (New York: Association of National Advertisers, 1987), p. 19.

7. Charles Panati, *The Browser's Book of Beginnings: Origins of Everything Under (and Including) the Sun* (Boston: Houghton Mifflin, 1984), p. 167; see also Gillian Dyer, *Advertising as Communication* (London: Routledge, 1982), p. 15.

8. Charles Goodrum and Helen Dalrymple, *Advertising in America: The First 200 Years* (New York: Harry N. Abrams, 1990), pp. 14 (first ad), 8 (Easter rule books), 13 (shop signs and colonial newspapers), 17 (pre–Civil War papers), 23 (nationwide informational advertising), 24 (ads for major inventions); Dyer, *Advertising as Communication*, p. 16 ("mercuries"); Michael Schudson, *Advertising, the Uneasy Persuasion: Its Dubious Impact on American Society* (New York: Basic Books, 1984), pp. 180–182 (mass-appeal advertising and mass production); Jules Henry, *Culture Against Man* (New York: Random House, 1963), pp. 17–19 (discussing advertising's efforts to create new needs as mass production outstripped population growth); William Leiss, Stephen Kline, and Sut Jhally, *Social Communication in Advertising* (New York: Routledge, 1990), p. 153 (ad campaigns to sell national brand products); T. J. Jackson Lears, "The Rise of American Advertising," in *American Media*, ed. P. Cook, D. Gomery, and L. Lichty (Washington, DC: Wilson Center Press, 1989), pp. 257–258 (ongoing feud in early twentieth century between "reason-why" and "atmosphere" advertising copywriters and editors).

9. Lears, "The Rise of American Advertising," p. 258 ("Each piece of reason-why copy contained a vigorous sales argument, crammed with facts and pock-marked with dashes, italics, and exclamation points.").

10. Stephen Fox, *The Mirror Makers: A History of American Advertising and Its Creators* (New York: Vintage Books, 1985), p. 50 (emphasis in original). Regarding reason-why copy, Fox has observed: "Instead of general claims, pretty pictures, or jingles, an ad should offer a concrete *reason why* the product was worth buying. Not charming or amusing or even necessarily pleasing to the eye, a good ad was a rational, unadorned instrument of selling."

11. Goodrum and Dalrymple, *Advertising in America*, p. 114.

12. Leiss, Kline, and Jhally, *Social Communication in Advertising*, p. 280. But see T. J. Jackson Lears, "From Salvation to Self-Realization: Advertising and the Therapeutic Roots of the Consumer Culture, 1880–1930," in *The Culture of Consumption: Critical Essays in American History, 1880–1980*, ed. Richard W. Fox and T. J. Jackson Lears (New York: Pantheon Books, 1983), p. 18 (challenging the notion that reason-why advertising originally was more informative than emotive).

13. Leiss, Kline, and Jhally, *Social Communication in Advertising*, pp. 63 (decline of product-information ads after 1920s), 244 (product-image ads), 246–254, 272–274, 291–292 (product-personality ads); Roland Marchand, *Advertising the American Dream: Making Way for Modernity 1920–1940* (Berkeley: University of California Press, 1985), p. 358 (personification of perfumes and cars).

14. David M. Potter, *People of Plenty: Economic Abundance and the American Character* (Chicago: University of Chicago Press, 1954), p. 171; see also Sut Jhally, "Image-Based Culture: Advertising and Popular Culture," *World and I*, July 1990, pp. 507–508 (noting the representations of people who stand for social values in product-image advertising).

15. Charles Revson, quoted in Charles H. Sandage and Vernon Fryberger, *Advertising Theory and Practice* (Homewood, IL: Richard Irwin, 1975), p. 191.

16. Guy Debord, *The Society of the Spectacle*, trans. Donald Nicholson-Smith (New York: Zone Books, 1994), p. 32.

17. James Collins, quoted in Lears, "The Rise of American Advertising," p. 265.

18. Marshall McLuhan, *The Mechanical Bride* (New York: Vanguard Press, 1951), p. v.

19. Schudson, *Advertising, the Uneasy Persuasion*, p. 63.

20. Ibid., p. 50 (emphasis in original).

21. Leo Bogart, *Strategy in Advertising* (Lincolnwood, IL: NTC Publishing Group, 1990), p. 5.

22. Goodrum and Dalrymple, *Advertising in America*, p. 260 (reason-why advertising became less fact-based as product differentiation became more difficult); Schudson, *Advertising, the Uneasy Persuasion*, p. 62 (with the increasing number of advertisements for similar competing products, advertising became less informative as it aimed to be more distinctive and memorable "with a few eye-catching words or pictures").

23. Rosser Reeves, quoted in Goodrum and Dalrymple, *Advertising in America*, p. 45.

24. Ibid.

25. Leiss, Kline, and Jhally, *Social Communication in Advertising*, p. 102; see also Sut Jhally, *The Codes of Advertising* (New York: Routledge, 1987), pp. 127–128 (describing segmentation strategies as "user-centred").

26. Leiss, Kline, and Jhally, *Social Communication in Advertising*, p. 281.

27. Goodrum and Dalrymple, *Advertising in America*, p. 45 (discussing the advent of advertising strategies focused on the audience in response to the "challenge of the identical product").

28. Leiss, Kline, and Jhally, *Social Communication in Advertising*, p. 262.

29. Hal Himmelstein, *Television Myth and the American Mind* (New York: Praeger, 1984), p. 64.

30. Leo Bogart, *Commercial Culture: The Media System and the Public Interest* (New York: Oxford University Press, 1995), pp. 111–113.

31. Bogart, *Strategy in Advertising*, p. 59 (different advertising strategies to reach different target audiences); Schudson, *Advertising, the Uneasy Persuasion*, pp. 51, 64 (examining advertisers' attempts to tailor advertising according to the nature of the product and the target audience).

32. Bogart, *Strategy in Advertising*, pp. 1–2 (figures on daily advertising); Bogart, *Commercial Culture*, p. 335 n. 14 (percentage figures on TV, radio, newspaper, and magazine ad space); Alan Durning, "Can't Live Without It," *World-Watch*, May–June 1993, p. 15 (Postal Service ad mailings); Martin, *Romancing the Brand*, p. 104 (time spent watching commercials); Susan Phinney, "The 27-Inch Mall: Channel Surfers Catch the Big Wave of Home Shopping," *Seattle Post-Intelligencer*, 1 August 1994, sec. C, p. 1; information on file with the Center for the Study of Commercialism, Washington, D.C. (assorted placements of ad messages); see also Julia Reed, "Ads Where You Least Expect Them," *U.S. News and World Report*, 9 March 1987, p. 46 (reporting ads located on standard-sized billboards on trucks, on videocassette tapes, in computer programs, and between songs on rock albums); Suzanne Alexander Ryan, "Companies Teach All Sorts of Lessons with Educational Tools They Give Away," *Wall Street Journal*, 19 April 1994, sec. B, p. 1 (corporate videos in classrooms); Laurie Flynn, "Gauging Ad Audience in Cyberspace," *New York Times*, 29 May 1995, p. 19 (tens of thousands of businesses are running interactive ads on the World Wide Web); Laurence A. Canter and Martha S. Siegel, *How to Make a Fortune on the Information Superhighway* (New York: HarperCollins, 1994); Edward C. Baig, "Is Bigger Better for Philip Morris?" *Fortune*, 8 May 1989, p. 69; see also Alex Kozinski and Stuart Banner, "When Speech Isn't Free," *Philip Morris*, Summer 1991, p. 26. *Philip Morris* magazine was free to its readers, contributing to its vast circulation; Edward J. Whetmore, *Medi-*

america: Form, Content, and Consequence of Mass Communication (Belmont, CA: Wadsworth, 1989), p. 272 (journalism students with careers in advertising); "Robert Cohen Presentation on Advertising Expenditures," *Insider's Report* (New York: McCann-Erickson Advertising Agency, December 1994) (total domestic ad spending at $138 billion in 1993 and estimate of $149 billion for 1994); Jordan Reeves, "Culture Jamming: The New Ad Game," *Adbusters Quarterly*, Winter 1995, pp. 79–80 (advertiser-produced interactive programming); Jay Mathews, "Ad Industry Pledges to Defend Its TV Turf," *Washington Post*, 13 March 1995, sec. D, p. 2 (advertiser response to developing new media technologies).

33. Leiss, Kline, and Jhally, *Social Communication in Advertising*, p. 352.

34. John O'Toole, *The Trouble with Advertising: A View from the Inside* (New York: Times Books, 1985), p. 87.

35. Al Ries and Jack Trout, *Positioning: The Battle for Your Mind* (New York: Warner Books, 1986), pp. 8, 30.

36. Linda Benn, "The Ethics of Advertising," *World and I*, December 1990, pp. 531, 534–535.

37. Dyer, *Advertising as Communication*, p. 80 (noting that these qualities are "often confused with or transferred to the possession of things").

38. Jhally, *The Codes of Advertising*, p. 129 (emphasis in original).

39. Jhally, "Image-Based Culture," p. 510 (quoting an unidentified advertising executive).

40. Jean Baudrillard, "Consumer Society," in *Jean Baudrillard: Selected Writings*, ed. Mark Poster (Stanford, CA: Stanford University Press, 1988), p. 10 ("If we consume the product as product, we consume its meaning through advertising.").

41. Dyer, *Advertising as Communication*, p. 116.

42. Jhally, *The Codes of Advertising*, p. 50.

43. Leiss, Kline, and Jhally, *Social Communication in Advertising*, p. 352.

44. Leo Bogart, *The American Media System and Its Commercial Culture* (New York: Gannett Foundation Media Center, 1991), p. 2.

45. Henry, *Culture Against Man*, p. 50; see also Stuart Ewen, *All Consuming Images* (New York: Basic Books, 1988), p. 265.

46. Torben Vestergaard and Kim Schrøder, *The Language of Advertising* (New York: Basil Blackwell, 1985), p. 167 ("Black is Beautiful"); Marcy Magiera, "Spike Lee's 'Malcolm X' Gets New Kind of Tie-Ins," *Advertising Age*, 13 July 1992, p. 36.

47. The Beatles, "Revolution" (Apple Records single, 1968); see also William J. Dowlding, *Beatlesongs* (New York: Fireside, 1989), pp. 208–209. Interestingly, the same company that used "Revolution" to sell sneakers in 1987 launched a new ad campaign featuring John Lennon's "Instant Karma." Whereas the former commercial stirred up protests from Beatles fans and a lawsuit from Paul McCartney, this effort to

transform Lennon's sound into a sales pitch was undertaken with Yoko Ono's permission and has generated no critical response. See Paul Farhi, "Well, We All Shine . . . Shoes? Is There Any Song Madison Avenue Won't Steal?" *Washington Post*, 22 March 1992, sec. 6, p. 1 ("Advertisers have been grafting popular songs onto ad campaigns for so long that no one complains, even when Aretha Franklin transforms a song that wasn't hers, 'Rescue Me,' into 'Deliver Me' for Pizza Hut.").

48. Whetmore, *Mediamerica*, p. 279 (spruce tree and daisy field ads) (emphasis in original). For an unconventional discussion of the daisy field ad, see Marshall McLuhan, *Culture Is Our Business* (New York: McGraw-Hill, 1970), pp. 180–181.

49. Henri Lefebvre, *Everyday Life in the Modern World*, trans. Sacha Rabinovitch (New Brunswick, NJ: Transaction Books, 1971), pp. 110–123.

50. Henry, *Culture Against Man*, p. 48 (emphasis in original).

51. Ibid., p. 21 (emphasis omitted).

52. Bogart, *Strategy in Advertising*, p. 7.

53. Lears, "From Salvation to Self-Realization," p. 21. Notably, Lears's observation came at least four years prior to the controversy over the commercial use of John Lennon's "Revolution."

54. Henry, *Culture Against Man*, p. 65.

55. *All Things Considered*, National Public Radio, 30 July 1991; see also Stuart Elliott, "Benetton Stirs More Controversy," *New York Times*, 23 July 1991, sec. D, p. 22.

56. *Vanity Fair*, March 1992, pp. 132–133 (dying AIDS victim ad), 130–131 (refugee ship ad); see also Paula Span, "Colored with Controversy," *Washington Post*, 13 February 1992, sec. D, p. 1 (discussing AIDS victim ad); Gary Levin, "Benetton Brouhaha," *Advertising Age*, 17 February 1992, p. 62 (shrouded corpse and armed-soldier ads); *Rolling Stone*, 19 April 1992, pp. 18–19. By 1995, Benetton had changed its advertising practices and abandoned its controversial "language of images" ads, though the imagistic style remains popular in advertising circles. See Marshall Blondsky and Contardo Calligaris, "At Benetton, a Retreat from Revolution," *Washington Post*, 30 April 1995, sec. H, p. 1.

57. "Radio Station Tunes into Controversy with Boards," *Advertising Age*, 20 April 1992, p. 17 ("Father Knows Best" and "Nun Better" ads); Elizabeth Kastor, "'Simple'-Minded: The Ad World Appropriates a Shaker Hymn," *Washington Post*, 22 February 1995, sec. D, p. 1.

58. *Sun-Sentinel* (Palm Beach, FL), 29 March 1991, sec. A, p. 4. Above this statement, the ad read in part: "This Easter, faith shines bright with [Company X's] unique crosses of semi-precious gems surrounded with diamonds. Gifts as beautiful as they are meaningful.... Blue topaz cross, $1,650.... Large rubelite cross, $6,300. Also available in blue topaz, $4,995; peridot, $5,250; green tourmaline, $7,300."

59. *Butler's Lives of the Saints*, ed. Michael Walsh (New York: HarperCollins, 1985), pp. 149–151, 439.

60. Oliviero Toscani, in-house creative director for Benetton, quoted in Levin, "Benetton Brouhaha," p. 62.

61. Judith Williamson, *Decoding Advertisements: Ideology and Meaning in Advertising* (New York: Marion Boyers, 1978), p. 46 (emphasis omitted).

62. Schudson, *Advertising, the Uneasy Persuasion*, p. 210.

63. Lears, "The Rise of American Advertising," p. 263 (quoting an unspecified article in *Judicious Advertising* and James Wallen).

64. Williamson, *Decoding Advertisements*, p. 148 (liquor ad); *Rolling Stone*, 20 October 1988, p. 13 (cologne ad); *Washingtonian*, 9 December 1990, pp. 56–57 (pen ad).

65. Williamson, *Decoding Advertisements*, p. 150 (citations omitted).

66. Bogart, *The American Media System*, pp. 5–6 (advertisers as customers). A. Roy Megary, the publisher of the *Toronto Globe and Mail*, observed: "By 1990, publishers of mass circulation daily newspapers will finally stop kidding themselves that they are in the newspaper business and admit they are primarily in the business of carrying advertising messages." Megary, quoted in Eric Clark, *The Want Makers: Inside the World of Advertising* (New York: Viking Penguin, 1989), p. 317; Leiss, Kline, and Jhally, *Social Communication in Advertising*, p. 102 (audiences as products).

67. Ian Mitroff and Warren Bennis, *The Unreality Industry: The Deliberate Manufacturing of Falsehood and What It Is Doing to Our Lives* (New York: Birch Lane Press, 1989), p. 47 (Saturday-morning cartoons); Stuart Elliot, "Commercial Cartoon Furor Grows," *New York Times*, 5 March 1992, sec. D, p. 1 (full-length programs featuring commercial characters); Sharon Bernstein, "Advocates for Children's TV Air Their Beef with McDonald's," *Los Angeles Times*, 20 December 1991, sec. F, p. 6 ("There's only one thing you think of when you see Ronald McDonald and it's not running to the library for books."); Teri Agins, "Is It a TV Show? Or Is It Advertising?" *Wall Street Journal*, 10 August 1994 (department-store commercial programming); Tom Shales, "'Treasure Island': Prime-Time Travesty," *Washington Post*, 28 January 1994, sec. C, p. 1 (commercial entertainment special).

68. The remarks quoted in the text are drawn from *60 Minutes*, CBS, 12 February 1995 (segment on infomercials hosted by correspondent Morley Safer).

69. Infomercials present a thirty-minute to three-hour commercial as a talk show. In contrast, documercials are advertiser-paid TV "documentaries" that include no explicit invitations to buy products. A video news release is typically a ninety-second "press release," prepared by a public relations firm for local network newscasts, that subtly advances a corporate sponsor's interests without specific identification. Product-placement advertising reaps amounts ranging from $10,000 to $1 million per film for a producer who agrees to include commercial products in the set. (The movie *Total*

Recall [Tri-Star, 1991] projected some 55 product placements for 28 brands.) Advertorials are the print equivalent of infomercials: advertiser-paid stories designed to mimic news stories or editorials. (Advertorials are even mentioned in the tables of contents of some magazines, and other magazines publish "advertiser indexes" to help readers find ads.)

70. Gloria Steinem, the founding editor of *Ms.* magazine, describes the phenomenon of "complimentary copy" in these terms: "Food advertisers have always demanded that women's magazines publish recipes and articles on entertaining (preferably ones that name their products) in return for their ads; clothing advertisers expect to be surrounded by fashion spreads (especially ones that credit their designers); and shampoo, fragrance, and beauty products in general usually insist on positive editorial coverage of beauty subjects, plus photo credits besides. That's why women's magazines look the way they do." Gloria Steinem, "Sex, Lies and Advertising," *Ms.*, July–August 1990, pp. 18–19. Reprinted in Gloria Steinem, *Moving Beyond Words* (New York: Simon & Schuster, 1994).

71. See Paul Farhi, "Disney Blurs the Line Between Ballyhoo and Broadcasting," *Washington Post*, 5 July 1994, sec. E, p. 1 ("Movie News," a Disney commercial promoting its recent releases, "looks just like the entertainment news segment of a TV newscast.").

72. Paul Farhi, "Hard News or Soft Sell?" *Washington Post*, 23 February 1992, sec. H, p. 1.

73. R. Craig Endicott, "Where Those Ad Dollars Go," *Advertising Age*, 20 August 1987, p. 134 (describing Procter & Gamble as "the nation's biggest network TV advertiser, with expenditures of $456.3 million"); Steinem, "Sex, Lies and Advertising," p. 26 (the language quoted in the text is from Ms. Steinem's account). Procter & Gamble once maintained an equally rigid editorial policy for the electronic media in which it advertised: "There will be no material that may give offense either directly or by inference to any commercial organization of any sort. There will be no material on any of our programs which could in any way further the concept of business as cold, ruthless and lacking all sentimental or spiritual motivation." Michael Parenti, *Make-Believe Media* (New York: St. Martin's Press, 1992), p. 186.

74. Starr, quoted in Howard Kurtz, "Media Notes: Treading Lightly on Advertisers," *Washington Post*, 10 July 1991, sec. F, pp. 1, 10.

75. See generally Ronald K.L. Collins, *Dictating Content: How Advertising Pressure Can Corrupt a Free Press* (Washington, DC: Center for the Study of Commercialism, 1992), pp. 32–49 (documenting instances of advertising pressure on editorial content); Bruce Horovitz, "Advertisers Influence Media More, Report Says," *Los Angeles Times*, 12 March 1992, sec. D, p. 2 (discussing examples of news organizations revising or killing stories for fear of upsetting advertisers); G. Pascal Zachery,

"Many Journalists See a Growing Reluctance to Criticize Advertisers," *Wall Street Journal*, 6 February 1992, sec. A, p. 1 (describing editors' responses to advertiser complaints).

76. Nick Coleman, "Stations Give In to Big Advertiser," *St. Paul Pioneer Press*, 5 December 1991, sec. D, p. 1 (describing how members of a Sioux tribe were denied any opportunity to place a paid anti-nuclear-waste spot on three local television stations that regularly run commercials of a power company that plans to build a nuclear waste dump near the tribe's reservation); Ronald K.L. Collins, "Truth in Advertising: The Censors' Control," *Baltimore Sun*, 21 May 1990, sec. A, p. 5 (noting that television network affiliates in six cities rejected a paid political commercial urging boycott of a coffee manufacturer).

77. *New York Times*, 28 April 1991, sec. A, p. 53.

78. Henry, *Culture Against Man*, p. 22.

79. Ewen, *All Consuming Images*, p. 245 (emphasis omitted).

80. Carol Farmer, president of a private consulting firm in Boca Raton, Florida, quoted in Stuart Elliot, "Strategies for Selling More When Shoppers Want Less," *New York Times*, 16 January 1992, sec. D, p. 18; see also Stuart Elliot, "Helping Marketers Adjust to Mood Swings of Consumers," *New York Times*, 10 November 1992, sec. D, p. 21 (analyzing the efforts of advertisers to anticipate the "bungee-like" mood shifts of consumers that are "an overreaction to short-term changes in statistical measures covering important areas like the economy, the environment, health care and crime").

81. Alan T. Durning, ". . . And Too Many Shoppers: What Malls and Materialism Are Doing to the Planet," *Washington Post*, 23 August 1992, sec. C, p. 3 ("Consumerism, no matter how tastefully trimmed with green, is a recipe for ecological decline.").

82. Ewen, *All Consuming Images*, p. 241.

83. Leiss, Kline, and Jhally, *Social Communication in Advertising*, p. 1.

84. Ewen, *All Consuming Images*, p. 32.

85. Baudrillard, "Consumer Society," pp. 53 (premise for human liberation), 48 (citizen's duty) (emphasis in original).

86. Leiss, Kline, and Jhally, *Social Communication in Advertising*, p. 389.

87. Robert B. Westbrook, "Politics as Consumption: Managing the Modern American Election," in *The Culture of Consumption: Critical Essays in American History, 1880–1980*, ed. Richard W. Fox and T. J. Jackson Lears (New York: Pantheon Books, 1983), pp. 143, 155 (*Nation's Business* magazine); John A. Farrell, "The Electronic Election," *Boston Globe*, 13 November 1988 (use of imagery in the Bush and Dukakis campaigns).

88. Michael Wines, "Bush's Campaign Tries Madison Ave.," *New York Times*, 27 May 1992, sec. A, p. 18 ("President Bush's re-election campaign is handing control of

its $40 million-plus advertising program to two Madison Avenue executives with scant political experience."); Dan Balz, "New Clinton Ad Team Combines Political, Commercial Veterans," *Washington Post*, 4 July 1992, sec. A, p. 8 ("Clinton has tapped the firm of Deutsch Inc., a New York company best known for its ads in behalf of IKEA, the Swedish home products retailer."); Steven W. Colford, "Perot Talks to Riney About Campaign Ads," *Advertising Age*, 22 June 1992, p. 1 (reporting speculation as to advertising executive Hal Riney's involvement in the Perot campaign).

89. Balz, "New Clinton Ad Team," p. 8 (quoting Mandy Grunewald, media consultant to the 1992 Clinton presidential campaign).

90. Westbrook, "Politics as Consumption," p. 145.

91. Lee Comegys, "Catch, Catch Can," 30 October 1984, LEXIS, Nexis Library, WIRES File; Martin Schram, "Media Feed Floridians Debate in Morsels," *Washington Post*, 13 March 1984, sec. A, p. 8.

92. *Associated Press v. United States*, 326 U.S. 1, 20 (1945).

93. Bogart, *Strategy in Advertising*, p. 107 ("[Advertising's] importance lies not in having elicited a specific purchase response to a specific ad. The real significance of advertising is its total cumulative weight as part of the culture — in the way in which it contributes to the popular lore of ideas and attitudes toward consumer products."); Schudson, *Advertising, the Uneasy Persuasion*, p. 238 (arguing that advertising fosters "a consumer way of life").

94. 421 U.S. 809, 812 (1975).

95. Michael G. Gartner, *Advertising and the First Amendment* (New York: Priority Press, 1989).

96. Martin H. Redish, "The First Amendment in the Marketplace: Commercial Speech and the Values of Free Expression," *George Washington Law Review* 38 (1971):429, 443–444.

97. *Bates v. State Bar*, 433 U.S. 350, 382 (1977).

98. *Edenfield v. Fane*, 113 S.Ct. 1792 (1993).

99. *Central Hudson Gas & Electric Corporation. v. Public Service Commission*, 447 U.S. 557, 563 (1980).

100. Daniel H. Lowenstein, "'Too Much Puff': Persuasion, Paternalism and Commercial Speech," *University of Cincinnati Law Review* 56 (1988):1205, 1229 (footnote omitted). None of Lowenstein's characterizations has been affected by the Court's more recent commercial speech decisions through the Supreme Court's terms to date.

101. Ronald K.L. Collins and David M. Skover, "Commerce & Communication," *Texas Law Review* 71 (1993):731 n. 178.

102. Eric Barendt, *Freedom of Speech* (Oxford, UK: Clarendon Press, 1985), pp. 57–58 (discussing the approach, recommended by the British Monopolies Commission, of removing any limits on informational advertisements but acknowledging that

"there might in some circumstances be good reasons for inhibiting advertisements designed to create custom[ers]"), 60 (noting that European Convention case law distinguishes "between promotional advertising and commercial speech providing information").

103. Neuborne, *Free Speech*, p. 22.

104. Alex Kozinski and Stuart Banner, "Who's Afraid of Commercial Speech?" *Virginia Law Review* 76 (1990):627, 639 (emphasis added), 640–648 (1990). Kozinski and Banner also offer the following syllogism for justifying First Amendment protection of imagistic advertising: (1) In differentiating commercial from political, artistic, or scientific speech, one cannot inquire into the intent of the speaker according to Supreme Court dictates; (2) lifestyle advertising can be classified as speech proposing a commercial transaction only by inquiring into the intent of the advertiser; (3) therefore, lifestyle advertising cannot categorically be labeled commercial rather than political, artistic, or scientific speech. Succinctly put, this argument depends on a highly formalistic interpretation of the Court's criteria for proposing a commercial transaction. Such an approach belies the obvious: Consumers are likely to recognize as commercial a lifestyle image ad that eschews all express terms inviting them to buy. And pragmatically, since advertising costs are tax deductible, Treasury Reg. §1.162–14 (as amended in 1969), an advertiser would already have told the government in its federal tax return that it engaged in commercial speech. In other words, the government need not inquire as to the advertiser's intent, since it already knows.

105. *Santa Clara County v. Southern Pacific Railroad*, 118 U.S. 394 (1886).

106. Mark Tushnet, "Corporations and Free Speech," in *The Politics of Law: A Progressive Critique*, ed. David Kairys (New York: Pantheon Books, 1982), p. 256.

107. Howard Zinn, *A People's History of the United States* (New York: Harcourt Brace Jovanovich, 1980), p. 255, quoted in Herbert I. Schiller, *Culture, Inc.: The Corporate Takeover of Public Expression* (New York: Oxford University Press, 1989), p. 47.

108. C. Edwin Baker, *Human Liberty and Freedom of Speech* (New York: Oxford University Press, 1989), p. 196.

109. Baudrillard, "Consumer Society," p. 29.

110. Williamson, *Decoding Advertisements*, p. 179.

111. Baker, *Human Liberty*, p. 203 (emphasis added).

112. Baudrillard, "Consumer Society," p. 53.

113. Baker, *Human Liberty*, p. 210.

114. *GQ*, July 1991, pp. 54–55 (advertisement with a recipe for the drink Sex on the Beach); *Rolling Stone*, 8 August 1991, pp. 53, 57 (blue-jeans ad); see also Martha Moore, "Jeans Stretching to Fit All in Flat Market," *USA Today*, 16 August 1991, sec. B, p. 8 (describing the $12 million jeans advertising campaign using stylish drawings); *Glamour*, September 1991, pp. 101–104 (four-page clothing ad).

115. Leiss, Kline, and Jhally, *Social Communication in Advertising*, p. 43.

116. Martin, *Romancing the Brand*, p. 9.

117. O'Toole, *The Trouble with Advertising*, p. 20.

118. Whetmore, *Mediamerica*, p. 279.

119. D. P. Simpson, *Cassell's New Latin Dictionary* (New York: Macmillan, 1968), p. 23 (defining *advertere* literally as "of the senses, thoughts, etc., to direct towards an object").

120. John C. Driver and Gordon R. Foxall, *Advertising Policy and Practice* (New York: St. Martin's Press, 1984), p. 87; see also Dyer, *Advertising as Communication*, pp. 109–110 (discussing studies that conclude that "ads do not act as objective guides to the audience" and that persuasion has a tendency to block rational examination).

121. *Saturday Night Live*, NBC, 27 July 1991 (soft-drink commercial); *Rolling Stone*, 8 August 1991, p. 48 (cigarette ad); *Rolling Stone*, 5 September 1991, inside cover and p. 1 (designer-jeans ad); *GQ*, July 1991, p. 24 (cologne ad).

122. Henry, *Culture Against Man*, pp. 49–50.

123. Williamson, *Decoding Advertisements*, p. 175.

124. *Virginia State Board of Pharmacy v. Virginia Citizens Consumer Council, Inc.*, 425 U.S. 748, 756–757 (1976).

125. *Branzburg v. Hayes*, 408 U.S. 665, 721 (1972) (Douglas, J., dissenting).

126. For an alternative conception of a "free press" subsidized by public tax monies, see C. Edwin Baker, "Advertising and a Democratic Press," *University of Pennsylvania Law Review* 140 (1992): 2097, 2180–2188 (proposing a plan that taxes advertising revenue and returns the tax as circulation revenue, thereby decreasing the media's dependence on advertising). Revised and reprinted in C. Edwin Baker, *Advertising and a Democratic Press* (Princeton, NJ: Princeton University Press, 1994).

127. Walter Goodman, "Pull the Plug on PBS?" *New York Times*, 22 March 1992, sec. H, p. 33 (many public television stations are selling commercial spots, euphemistically called "enhanced underwriting," and are broadcasting documentaries on subject matters related to the products sold by corporate promoters who pay for the production of the documentaries). See also Bogart, *Commercial Culture*, pp. 301–302 (subject to financing pressures, public broadcasting is increasingly dependent on corporate "underwriters"); William Hoynes, *Public Television for Sale: Media, the Market, and the Public Sphere* (Boulder: Westview Press, 1994), pp. 28–34.

128. Neuborne, *Free Speech*, p. 13 (emphasis added).

129. *Saturday Evening Post*, 18 March 1944, p. 65. Quoted in *The Culture of Consumption: Critical Essays in American History, 1880–1980*, ed. Richard W. Fox and T. J. Jackson Lears (New York: Pantheon Books, 1983), p. ix.

130. Jacob D. Fuchsberg, "Commercial Speech: Where It's At," *Brooklyn Law Review* 46 (1980):389, 393.

131. See Bogart, *Commercial Culture*, p. 348 n. 94 (in conjunction with the National Archives, tobacco companies funded advertisements celebrating the Bill of Rights during a "freedom of commercial speech" campaign in 1989 designed to stave off further governmental regulations of tobacco).

132. Admittedly, government has moved incrementally to restrict advertising of products and services that pose the most egregious threats to public health and safety. For example, with industry approval, Congress outlawed cigarette advertising on radio and television in 1969. See generally Federal Cigarette Labeling and Advertising Act of 1969, 15 U.S.C. § 1335 (1988) (effective January 1, 1971). Yet national lawmakers have not banned some $2 billion worth of tobacco advertising and promotions in other media. Larry C. White, *Merchants of Death: The American Tobacco Industry* (New York: William Morrow, 1988), p. 22 (stating that cigarettes are the most advertised product in the United States).

133. Baker, *Human Liberty*, p. 210 (emphasis added).

134. *Adbusters Quarterly*, Summer 1990, inside cover ("Marlboro Country"); *Adbusters Quarterly*, Winter 1989–1990, inside cover ("Smirnoff morning"); "The Tools for Detox," *Adbusters Quarterly*, Summer 1990, pp. 18–19 (TV addiction).

135. Mark Dery, "Oppositional Cultures: A Conversation with Stuart Ewen on Culture Jammers, Social Activism and the New Iconography," *Adbusters Quarterly*, Summer–Fall 1992, pp. 59, 61–62; see also Mark Dery, "Culture Jamming: Hacking, Slashing and Sniping in the Empire of Images," *The Immediast Underground Pamphlet*, no. 2 (Westfield, NJ: Open Media, 1992); Ronald K.L. Collins, "Waging War on Culture Pollution," *Los Angeles Times*, 22 November 1992, sec. M, p. 2.

136. Dery, "Oppositional Cultures," p. 62.

137. See, e.g., Barry Brown, "Magazine's Parody Makes Marketer Absolut-ely Mad," *Advertising Age*, 22 July 1992, p. 42.

138. *Lochner v. New York*, 198 U.S. 45, 75 (1905) (Holmes, J., dissenting).

139. Liva Baker, *The Justice from Beacon Hill: The Life and Times of Oliver Wendell Holmes* (New York: HarperCollins, 1991), p. 415.

140. The "dialogue" in the text was, in large part, excerpted from a colloquy published in the *Texas Law Review* in 1993. Notes have been omitted where they do not significantly qualify the substantive import of the text. See "Colloquy: The First Amendment in a Commercial Culture," *Texas Law Review* 71 (1993): 697–832. Our colleagues were kind enough to allow us to reprint portions of their replies to our initial work on "Commerce & Communication." The reader is encouraged to consult the complete colloquy for a richer account of their replies to our arguments.

141. See Niccolò Machiavelli, *The Prince*, trans. Leo Paul de Alvarez (Irving, TX: University of Dallas Press, 1980), p. 147.

142. "The American Dream," *Miss Saigon* (Geffen Co., 1990).

143. Leiss, Kline, and Jhally, *Social Communication in Advertising*, p. 1 (emphasis omitted).

144. Karl Marx, *Capital*, vol. 1, ed. Frederick Engels, trans. B. Fowkes (New York: Vintage Books, 1977), p. 125.

145. Bogart, *Strategy in Advertising*, p. 107.

146. Bob Garfied, "Ads R Us," *Washington Post*, 26 February 1995, sec. C, pp. 1, 2.

147. Sut Jhally, "Commercial Culture, Collective Values, and the Future," *Texas Law Review* 71 (1993):805, 808.

Endnotes for Book III: Discourse & Intercourse

1. Simon Schama, *Citizens: A Chronicle of the French Revolution* (New York: Knopf, 1989), p. 211.

2. Camille Paglia, *Sex, Art, and American Culture* (New York: Vintage Books, 1992), p. 48.

3. Elizabeth Fox-Genovese, *Feminism Without Illusions: A Critique of Individualism* (Chapel Hill: University of North Carolina Press, 1991).

4. Apparently, a similar term — "pornotopia" — was coined by Steven Marcus in *The Other Victorians: A Study of Sexuality and Pornography in Mid-Nineteenth Century England* (New York: Basic Books, 1964), pp. 216, 268–274. Our use of "porn*u*topia" is not inseparably tied to Marcus's understanding of "pornotopia."

5. See generally U.S. Department of Justice, *Attorney General's Commission on Pornography: Final Report*, vol. 1 (Washington, DC: U.S. Government Printing Office, July 1986), pp. 382–385.

6. This was the nonpictorial book that Chief Justice Burger and four of his colleagues found obscene in *Kaplan v. California*, 413 U.S. 115 (1973). In a few highly publicized but isolated cases, prosecutors have gone after so-called obscene lyrics in rap or rock music. For incisive accounts of governmental and record-industry efforts to censor sexually explicit lyrics, see Marjorie Heins, *Sex, Sin, and Blasphemy: A Guide to America's Censorship Wars* (New York: New Press, 1993), pp. 77–94; Kenneth Masters, "Law in the Electronic Brothel: How Postmodern Media Affect First Amendment Obscenity Doctrine," *University of Puget Sound Law Review* 15 (1992):415–468.

7. See H. Montgomery Hyde, *A History of Pornography* (New York: Farrar, Straus & Giroux, 1964), pp. 40 (*Lysistrata*), 45–47 (*Ars Amatoria*), 54–56 (*Satyricon*), 35 (*Dialogues* and *Deipnosophists*).

8. Ibid., pp. 72 (*Exeter Book*), 65–67 (*Decameron*), 153 (*Index Librorum Prohibitorum*); Walter Kendrick, *The Secret Museum: Pornography in Modern Culture* (New York: Viking Penguin, 1987), pp. 58–59 (*Aretino's Postures*), 100–101 (*Gargantua and Pantagruel*).

9. See Hyde, *A History of Pornography*, pp. 154–155 (Licensing Act of 1662), 156–157 (Edmund Curll), 97 (*Fanny Hill*), 165 (George III); Bernard Arcand, *The Jaguar and the Anteater: Pornography Degree Zero* (New York: Verso, 1993), p. 132 (Charles II); Robert Darnton, *The Forbidden Best-Sellers of Pre-Revolutionary France* (New York: W. W. Norton, 1995), pp. 88 ("Enfer"), 187, 249–299 (*Thérèse philosophe*),

85–114 (*Correspondance d'Eulalie* and other philosophical pornography); Kendrick, *The Secret Museum*, pp. 102–104 (de Sade). The common-law offense of obscene libel was first enforced by the English Court of the King's Bench in the appeal of Edmund Curll's 1725 conviction. See *Dominicus Rex v. Curll*, 2 Strange 789 (1727).

10. *Four Comedies by Aristophanes*, trans. William Arrowsmith, ed. Douglas Parker (Ann Arbor: University of Michigan Press, 1969), p. 70.

11. James C.N. Paul and Murray L. Schwartz, *Federal Censorship: Obscenity in the Mail* (New York: Free Press of Glencoe, 1961), p. 104. See also Edward de Grazia, "Obscenity and the Mail: A Study of Administrative Restraint," *Law and Contemporary Problems* 20 (1955):608.

12. Hyde, *A History of Pornography*, pp. 67, 71. The textual discussion that immediately follows concerning the censorship of *The Decameron* is reported in Paul and Schwartz, *Federal Censorship*, p. 47.

13. See generally Lynn Hunt, ed., *The Invention of Pornography: Obscenity and the Origins of Modernity, 1500–1800* (New York: Zone Books, 1993); Lynn Hunt, ed., *Eroticism and the Body Politic* (Baltimore: John Hopkins University Press, 1991); Schama, *Citizens*, pp. 203–247.

14. See Joan DeJean, "The Politics of Pornography: *L'Ecole des Filles*," in Hunt, *Invention of Pornography*, pp. 109–123.

15. See Schama, *Citizens*, pp. 205, 947 (*Ma Constitution* at Figure 55); Hunt, *Invention of Pornography*, p. 319 (monk at Figure 9–3).

16. Arcand, *The Jaguar and the Anteater*, p. 129.

17. See *Commonwealth v. Sharpless*, 2 Serg. & Rawle 91 (Pa. 1815) (first American common-law obscenity prosecution); Hyde, *A History of Pornography*, pp. 100, 107 (William Haynes), 111 (Henry Hayler); Kendrick, *The Secret Museum*, pp. 11, 242 n. 18 (relying on an *Oxford English Dictionary* reference to C. O. Müller, *Ancient Art and Its Remains; or a Manual of the Archaelogy of Art*, trans. John Leitch [London, 1850]), 134–136 (Anthony Comstock); see also Heywood Broun and Margaret Leech, *Anthony Comstock: Roundsman of the Lord* (New York: Albert & Charles Boni, 1927); *Regina v. Hincklin*, L.R. 3 Q.B. 360, 371 (1868).

18. Theodore A. Schroeder, *Freedom of the Press and "Obscene" Literature* (New York: Free Speech League, 1906); Al Di Lauro and Gerald Rabkin, *Dirty Movies: An Illustrated History of the Stag Film, 1915–1970* (New York: Chelsea House, 1976), p. 43 (*Le Voyeur*); Paul and Schwartz, *Federal Censorship*, pp. 51–137 (obscene mail prosecutions); *Roth v. United States*, 354 U.S. 476 (1957) (Harlan, J., dissenting) (quoting Solicitor General J. Lee Rankin's brief); Linda Williams, *Hard Core: Power, Pleasure, and the "Frenzy of the Visible"* (Berkeley: University of California Press, 1989), p. 90 (Kinsey Institute and Masters & Johnson); Richard S. Randall, *Freedom and Taboo: Pornography and the Politics of a Self Divided* (Berkeley: University of

California Press, 1989), p. 200 (*Deep Throat* and 1960s gross profits); *The Report of the Commission on Obscenity and Pornography* (Washington, DC: U.S. Government Printing Office, 1970) and U.S. Department of Justice, *Final Report* (1986 report); Arcand, *The Jaguar and the Anteater*, p. 42 (SEXTEL and COMPUSEX); U.S. Department of Justice Criminal Division, *Beyond the Pornography Commission: The Federal Response* (Washington, DC: U.S. Government Printing Office, July 1988), p. 6 (1990s gross profits).

19. See, e.g., Michel Foucault, *The History of Sexuality*, vol. 1, trans. Robert Hurley (New York: Vintage Books, 1990), pp. 24–25, 30–31; Kendrick, *The Secret Museum*, pp. 52–53; Arcand, *The Jaguar and the Anteater*, pp. 143–145.

20. Kendrick, *The Secret Museum*, p. 65.

21. Arcand, *The Jaguar and the Anteater*, pp. 56–57 (futility of governmental control); Hyde, *A History of Pornography*, pp. 58–59 (*Body of Evidence*).

22. Editorial, "Beyond the (Garbage) Pale," *New York Times*, 1 April 1969 (discussing explicit portrayal of sexual intercourse on stage) (We assume that the date has no bearing on the editorial message?); Arcand, *The Jaguar and the Anteater*, pp. 172, 173–174.

23. Kendrick, *The Secret Museum*, p. 239.

24. Harry Kalven Jr., *A Worthy Tradition: Freedom of Speech in America*, ed. Jamie Kalven (New York: Harper & Row, 1988).

25. Harry Kalven Jr., *The Negro and the First Amendment* (Chicago: University of Chicago Press, 1966), p. 16.

26. Cass R. Sunstein, *Democracy and the Problem of Free Speech* (New York: Free Press, 1993), pp. 18–21.

27. John Rawls, *Political Liberalism* (New York: Columbia University Press, 1993), p. xix.

28. Sunstein, *Democracy*, pp. 215, 10–11.

29. Consider Cass R. Sunstein, "Words, Conduct, Caste," *University of Chicago Law Review* 60 (1993):795, 808. Professor Sunstein offered an "important qualification" to his argument that sexually explicit speech is low-value expression: Though it may not be "intended and received as a contribution to democratic debate," nevertheless "the development of individual capacities is instrumental to democratic characteristics." At this point, Sunstein dropped a footnote alluding to Alexander Meiklejohn's "extended conception of the political." Ibid., p. 808 n. 48.

30. See Robert Mapplethorpe, *X Portfolio, Jim and Tom, Sausalito* in Richard Bolton, ed., *Culture Wars: Documents from the Recent Controversies in the Arts* (New York: New Press, 1992), p. 321 (urination photos). See Sunstein, *Democracy*, p. 226 (constitutional protection of Robert Mapplethorpe's photography). Here there *could* be some difference between the "obscene" (that which is offensive) and the "porno-

graphic" (that which appeals to prurient interest). For our purposes, it is unnecessary to enter into this thicket. It is enough to observe that in pornutopia the distinction between the obscene and offensive and the pornographic and prurient would largely vanish. In a world of uninhibited sex appeal, little if anything that is sexualized is likely to offend.

31. *Milk Wagon Drivers Union Local 753 v. Meadowmoor Dairies, Inc.*, 312 U.S. 287, 293 (1941).

32. Susan Etta Keller, "Viewing and Doing: Complicating Pornography's Meaning," *Georgetown Law Journal* 81 (1993):2195, 2223.

33. Annette Kuhn, *The Power of the Image: Essays on Representation and Sexuality* (New York: Routledge & Kegan Paul, 1987), p. 44.

34. Elizabeth Cowie, "Pornography and Fantasy: Psychoanalytic Perspectives," in Lynne Segal and Mary McIntosh, eds., *Sex Exposed: Sexuality and the Pornography Debate* (New Brunswick, NJ: Rutgers University Press, 1993), pp. 132, 141–142, 145–146.

35. Joel Kovel, "The Antidialectic of Pornography," in Michael S. Kimmel, ed., *Men Confront Pornography* (New York: Crown, 1990), pp. 153, 161–162.

36. Jerome A. Barron and C. Thomas Dienes, *First Amendment Law in a Nutshell* (New York: West, 1993), p. 91.

37. Donna Tartt, *The Secret History* (New York: Alfred A. Knopf, 1992), p. 155.

38. Susanne Kappeler, *The Pornography of Representation* (Minneapolis: University of Minnesota Press, 1986), pp. 188, 179.

39. Williams, *Hard Core*, p. 46.

40. Nancy Tamosaitis, *net.sex* (Emeryville, CA: Ziff-Davis Press, 1995), pp. 3–4. See also Phillip Robinson & Nancy Tamosaitis, *The Joy of Cybersex: An Underground Guide to Electronic Erotica* (New York: Brady Publishing, 1993).

41. See, e.g., Tamosaitis, *net.sex*, pp. 64–69, 135; Candi Rose and Dirk Thomas, *net.sex* (Indianapolis: Sams Publishing, 1995), pp. 47–91.

42. Susie Bright, *Susie Bright's Sexual Reality: A Virtual Sex World Reader* (Pittsburgh: Cleis Press, 1992), pp. 68, 69 (interview with sci-fi novelist Richard Kadrey).

43. Howard Rheingold, *Virtual Reality* (New York: Summit Books, 1991), p. 348.

44. *The Shorter Oxford English Dictionary*, vol. 1 (Oxford, UK: Clarendon Press, 1993), p. 64.

45. Randall, *Freedom and Taboo*, p. 6 (emphasis added).

46. See U.S. Department of Justice, *The Federal Response*, p. 6 ($10 billion); Gordon Hawkins and Franklin E. Zimring, *Pornography in a Free Society* (New York: Cambridge University Press, 1988), p. 70 (mainstream channels of communication); Michael S. Kimmel, "'Insult' or 'Injury': Sex, Pornography, and Sexism," in Kimmel, *Men Confront Pornography*, pp. 305, 317 (X-rated videos); Hyde, *A History of*

Pornography, p. 35 (Adult Video Association report); John R. Wilke, "A Publicly Held Firm Turns X-Rated Videos into a Hot Business," *Wall Street Journal*, 11 July 1994, sec. A, p. 1 (seventy-five percent adult video sales increase); Charles Oliver, "Defending Pornography: Free Speech, Sex, and the Fight for Women's Rights," *Reason Magazine*, April 1995, p. 63 (1994 rentals); Anne McClintock, "Gonad the Barbarian and the Venus Flytrap" in Segal and McIntosh, *Sex Exposed*, pp. 111, 130 (women renting pornography); Williams, *Hard Core*, pp. 231, 293 n. 1 (*Redbook* magazine survey of 26,000 women). It is unclear to us whether the women represented in the studies engaged in the renting and viewing of pornography at their own or another's behest. Barry Shell, "Internet Top Tens," *Adbusters Quarterly*, Winter 1995, pp. 14–15 (erotic pictures on Usenet).

47. See generally Eric Clark, *The Want Makers: Inside the World of Advertising* (New York: Penguin Books, 1988), pp. 113–123.

48. Giselle Benatar, "Sex and Money," *Entertainment Weekly*, 6 November 1992, pp. 19, 20, 23.

49. For moralists, pornography is the glorification of hedonism, the degradation of the noble in humanity, and the public exposure of private intimacy. Government must regulate to prevent these evils. See, e.g., Harry M. Clor, *Obscenity and Public Morality: Censorship in a Liberal Society* (Chicago: University of Chicago Press, 1969), pp. 6–7.

50. For radical feminists, pornography subjugates, degrades, objectifies, defames, and even rapes and kills women. It is not mere speech but gender inequality and violence and ought to be regulated by government. See, e.g., Catharine MacKinnon, *Only Words* (Cambridge: Harvard University Press, 1993), pp. 38–41; Andrea Dworkin, *Pornography: Men Possessing Women* (New York: E. P. Dutton, 1981), pp. 13–47, 129–198.

51. For liberals and libertarians, pornography is expression that largely impacts the realms of moral autonomy and individual privacy, and government must not therefore regulate such realms. See, e.g., Ronald Dworkin, "Is There a Right to Pornography?" *Oxford Journal Legal Studies* 1 (1981):177, 199, 206; Martin Redish, *Freedom of Expression: A Critical Analysis* (Charlottesville, VA: Michie, 1984), p. 263.

52. For neo-Freudians, pornography is the celebration of the innate human libidinal energy, and government must not regulate to prevent women from becoming the equals of men where the enjoyment of sex — in all its ugly and beautiful forms — is concerned. See, e.g., Cowie, "Pornography and Fantasy," pp. 132–152.

53. For Foucaultians, pornography is discourse about power that is currently male-centered. Government must not intervene to prevent women from forming their own pornographic vision of the erotic life. See, e.g., Williams, *Hard Core*, pp. 229–230.

54. Fox-Genovese, *Feminism Without Illusions*, p. 90.

55. Leon Wieseltier, "Total Quality Meaning," *New Republic*, 19 July 1993, pp. 16, 18. We adapt Mr. Wieseltier's words for our own purposes without expressing any view on his particular topic. Sallie Tisdale, "Against Censorship: A Feminist Case," *Washington Post*, 19 February 1995, Book World, p. 3.

56. In dicta, the *Chaplinsky* opinion defined obscene expressions as constitutionally unprotected because they are "no essential part of any exposition of ideas, and are of such slight social value as a step to truth that any benefit that may be derived from them is clearly outweighed by the social interest in order and morality." 315 U.S. 568, 572 (1942).

57. In *Roth*, the Supreme Court extended "full protection of the [First Amendment] guaranties" to all pornography having "even the slightest redeeming social importance." 354 U.S. 476, 489 (1957).

58. The *Miller* Court declared that a determination of obscenity depended upon the following factors: "(a) whether 'the average person, applying contemporary community standards' would find that the work, taken as a whole, appeals to the prurient interest; (b) whether the work depicts or describes, in a patently offensive way, sexual conduct specifically defined by the applicable state law; and (c) whether the work, taken as a whole, lacks serious literary, artistic, political, or scientific value." 413 U.S. 15, 24 (1973).

59. *Miller*'s "serious literary, artistic, political, or scientific value" prong was revised in *Pope v. Illinois*, 481 U.S. 497 (1987), to impose a "reasonable person" standard on the jury.

60. See generally Sunstein, *Democracy*, pp. 210–211; Edward de Grazia and Roger K. Newman, *Banned Films: Movies, Censors and the First Amendment* (New York: R. R. Bowker, 1982), pp. 359–381 (two of fourteen movies ultimately held obscene from 1973 to 1981); U.S. Department of Justice, *The Federal Response*, p. 49 (of eighty federal obscenity indictments brought in 1987 — the highest number of indictments brought between 1978 and 1987 — fewer than twenty percent resulted in convictions).

61. Fox-Genovese, *Feminism Without Illusions*, p. 105 (footnote omitted).

62. But see *Ginzburg v. U.S.*, 383 U.S. 463 (1966) (pre-*Miller* ruling permitting regulation of "the sordid business of pandering"); *FW/PBS v. Dallas*, 493 U.S. 215 (1990) (Scalia, J., dissenting).

63. Thomas Hobbes, *Leviathan*, ed. Richard Tuck (Cambridge: Cambridge University Press, 1991), p. 459. Originally published in 1651.

64. Georges Bataille, *Erotism: Death and Sensuality*, trans. M. Dalwood (San Francisco: City Lights Books, 1986).

65. See Leo Strauss, *Natural Right and History* (Chicago: University of Chicago Press, 1953), pp. 169, 188–189 (the spirit of political idealism and hedonism). See also Frederick Vaughan, *The Tradition of Political Hedonism: From Hobbes to J. S. Mill* (New York: Fordham University Press, 1982), pp. 68–80; Victor Gourevitch, "The Problem of Natural Right and the Fundamental Alternatives in *Natural Right and His-*

tory," in *The Crisis of Liberal Democracy*, ed. Kenneth Deutsch and Walter Soffer (New York: State University Press of New York, 1987), pp. 30, 36–37; Shadia B. Drury, *The Political Ideas of Leo Strauss* (New York: St. Martin's Press, 1988), p. 135 (liberating hedonism from its apolitical character); C. B. MacPherson, *The Political Theory of Possessive Individualism* (Oxford, UK: Oxford University Press, 1962); Michael Oakeshott, "Moral Life in the Writings of Thomas Hobbes," in *Rationalism in Politics* (London: Methuen, 1962), pp. 248, 251–252. But see Norberto Bobbio, *Thomas Hobbes and the Natural Law Tradition* (Chicago: University of Chicago Press, 1993), pp. 70–71 ("Hobbes never had the slightest hesitation in choosing between the excess of freedom, and the excess of authority.").

66. Catharine MacKinnon, *Toward a Feminist Theory of the State* (Cambridge: Harvard University Press, 1989), pp. 138, 197.

67. See, e.g., *American Booksellers Association v. Hudnut*, 771 F.2d 323, 328–329, 329 nn. 1, 2 (7th Cir. 1985) (Easterbrook, J.), affirmed without opinion, 475 U.S. 1001 (1986). On the matter of just what the *American Booksellers* court "conceded," compare Catharine A. MacKinnon, "Pornography: An Exchange," *New York Review of Books*, 3 March 1994, pp. 47, 48 (arguing in a letter to the editor that the court conceded pornography's harm to women) and Ronald Dworkin, "Reply," *New York Review of Books*, 3 March 1994, p. 48 (arguing the court conceded harm only *arguendo*).

68. *American Booksellers*, 771 F.2d at 328.

69. MacKinnon, *Only Words*, p. 93; Frank I. Michelman, "Conceptions of Democracy in American Constitutional Argument: The Case of Pornography Regulation," *Tennessee Law Review* 56 (1989):291, 307.

70. Thomas Mann, *Death in Venice*, trans. Clayton Koelb (New York: W. W. Norton, 1994), p. 63.

71. Bataille, *Erotism*, pp. 17, 16; Mary Caputi, *Voluptuous Yearnings: A Feminist Theory of the Obscene* (Lanham: Rowman & Littlefield Publishers, 1994), pp. 6, 48.

72. Simon Lee, *The Cost of Free Speech* (London: Faber & Faber, 1990), p. 125.

73. Andrea Dworkin, *Letters from a War Zone* (Chicago: Lawrence Hill Books, 1993), p. 308.

74. Camille Paglia, *Sex, Art, and American Culture*, p. 74 (interview with CNN Television's Sonya Friedman).

75. Catharine MacKinnon, *Feminism Unmodified: Discourses on Life and Law* (Cambridge: Harvard University Press, 1987), p. 174.

76. *Butler v. Regina*, 2 W.W.R. 577, 609, 618 (1992). In *Butler*, the Canadian Supreme Court unanimously upheld its federal pornography law on the grounds of sexual equality.

77. *New Oxford Annotated Bible* (New York: Oxford University Press, 1991), p. 671 (Job 41:11).

78. *Chaplinsky v. New Hampshire*, 315 U.S. 568, 571 (1942). Quoted approvingly in *Roth v. U.S.*, 354 U.S. 476, 485 (1957) (per Brennan, J.).

79. *Winters v. New York*, 333 U.S. 507, 510 (1948).

80. Bob Woodward and Scott Armstrong, *The Brethren: Inside the Supreme Court* (New York: Simon & Schuster, 1979), p. 198.

81. Hobbes, *Leviathan*, p. 48.

82. Madonna, *The Immaculate Collection* (Sire/Warner Brothers Records, 1990).

83. Bolton, *Culture Wars*, p. 309 (photo).

84. Alexander Meiklejohn, "The First Amendment Is an Absolute," *Supreme Court Review* (1961):245, 262.

85. Robert Bork, "Neutral Principles and Some First Amendment Problems," *Indiana Law Journal* 47 (1971):1, 29.

86. *Ginzburg v. U.S.*, 383 U.S. 463, 499 n. 3 (1966) (Stewart, J., dissenting) (quoting brief of U.S. Solicitor General Thurgood Marshall). See briefs of counsel in 16 U.S.L.Ed.2d 1077, 1078 (1966).

87. Frederick Schauer, "Speech and 'Speech' — Obscenity and 'Obscenity': An Exercise in the Interpretation of Constitutional Language," *Georgetown Law Journal* 67 (1979):899, 921–922.

88. John M. Finnis, "'Reason and Passion': The Constitutional Dialectic of Free Speech and Obscenity," *University of Pennsylvania Law Review* 116 (1967): 222, 236.

89. Frederick Schauer, "Response: Pornography and the First Amendment," *University of Pittsburgh Law Review* 40 (1979):605, 607 (emphasis in original).

90. Finnis, "Reason and Passion," pp. 241, 240 (quoting *Ginzburg v. U.S.*, 383 U.S. 463, 470 [1966]).

91. U.S. Department of Justice, *Final Report*, vol. 1, p. 266.

92. Joel Feinberg, *Offense to Others: The Moral Limits of the Criminal Law* (New York: Oxford University Press, 1985), p. 169.

93. U.S. Department of Justice, *Final Report*, vol. 1, p. 266.

94. Frederick Schauer, *Free Speech: A Philosophical Enquiry* (Cambridge: Cambridge University Press, 1982), p. 182 (emphasis in original).

95. Mapplethorpe quoted in Edward de Grazia, *Girls Lean Back Everywhere: The Law of Obscenity and the Assault on Genius* (New York: Random House, 1992), p. 626; Schauer, quoted in ibid., p. 652.

96. Camille Paglia, quoted in Bright, *Susie Bright's Sexual Reality*, p. 73.

97. See Schauer, *Free Speech*, pp. 182–183.

98. Fox-Genovese, *Feminism Without Illusions*, p. 107.

99. 208 U.S. 412 (1908) (upholding state legislation setting a maximum of ten hours' work a day for women employed in factories and laundries).

100. Robin Morgan, "Theory and Practice: Pornography and Rape," in Laura Lederer, ed., *Take Back the Night: Women on Pornography* (New York: William Morrow, 1980), pp. 134, 139.

101. Wendy Kaminer, "Pornography and the First Amendment: Prior Restraints and Private Action," in Lederer, *Take Back the Night*, p. 241.

102. Gloria Steinem, "Erotica and Pornography: A Clear and Present Difference," *Ms.*, November 1978, p. 53.

103. Susan Griffin, *Pornography and Silence: Culture's Revenge Against Nature* (New York: Harper & Row, 1981), p. 111 (emphasis omitted).

104. Andrea Dworkin and Catharine MacKinnon, *Pornography and Civil Rights: A New Day for Women's Equality* (Minneapolis: Organizing Against Pornography, 1988), p. 138 (sec. 1, clause 2).

105. Of course, there are other notable arguments offered by the radical feminists to justify censorship of pornography, including rationales tied to civil equality and critical race theory. See, e.g., MacKinnon, *Only Words*, pp. 45–68. But see Nadine Strossen, *Defending Pornography: Free Speech, Sex, and the Fight for Women's Rights* (New York: Scribner, 1995), pp. 120–141 (sexuality does not equal sexism), 218–247 (lessons from enforcement), 248–265 (censoring porn would not reduce discrimination or violence against women). We confine our discussion to the personal-harm argument because it appears to have received the most public attention and because it has been frequently attacked as largely rhetorical. Finally, we acknowledge that a different set of concerns may arise in the context of gay pornography. See, e.g., Jeffrey G. Sherman, "Love Speech: The Social Utility of Pornography," *Stanford Law Review* 47 (1995):661, 689–705.

106. Ronald Dworkin, "Women and Pornography," *New York Review of Books*, 21 October 1993, pp. 36, 38.

107. Strossen, *Defending Pornography*, p. 249, 251–265. See also "Two Female Lawyers Talk About Pornography," *Charlie Rose Show*, WNET-NY, 19 January 1995 (available on NEXIS) (Strossen: "In point of fact, . . . no such causal connection has ever been shown [between pornography and violence against women], and that is true with respect to all of the studies.").

108. Richard Posner, *Overcoming Law* (Cambridge: Harvard University Press, 1995), pp. 363–364.

109. Fox-Genovese, *Feminism Without Illusions*, p. 95.

110. Edward Donnerstein and Daniel Linz, "Mass Media, Sexual Violence, and Male Viewers: Current Theory and Research," *American Behavioral Scientist* 29 (May–June 1986):601, 618. See also Kent Greenawalt, *Fighting Words: Individuals, Communities, and Liberties of Speech* (Princeton, NJ: Princeton University Press, 1995), p. 109 (questioning the "crime prevention" rationale for prohibiting obscenity).

111. Todd Gitlin, "The Left and Porno," in Kimmel, *Men Confront Pornography*, pp. 102, 103.

112. Kovel, "The Antidialectic of Pornography," p. 167.

113. Wendy Kaminer, "Feminists Against the First Amendment," *Atlantic Monthly*, November 1992, pp. 110, 118.

114. Kappeler, *The Pornography of Representation*, p. 157.

115. Gitlin, "The Left and Porno," p. 104. See also Zillah R. Eisenstein, *The Radical Future of Liberal Feminism* (Boston: Northeastern University Press, 1993), pp. 220–253 (the contemporary capitalist state strives to contain the subversive quality of liberal feminist attacks on society's patriarchal organization).

116. George F. Will, *The Leveling Wind: Politics, the Culture & Other News, 1990–1994* (New York: Viking, 1994), p. 29 (emphasis added). Of course, the statement by Mr. Will could be explained on other grounds.

117. de Grazia and Newman, *Banned Films*, pp. 378–379. The Bob Guccione quotation in note q is found at ibid., p. 148.

118. The "dialogue" in the text was created from: a memorandum letter of January 26, 1995, from Suzanne Singer to the authors; a memorandum letter of February 11, 1995, from David O'Brien to the authors; a transcript of comments on "Discourse & Intercourse" delivered by Elizabeth Fox-Genovese at the annual meeting of the American Political Science Association on September 1, 1994, in New York; a transcript of public remarks by Cass Sunstein, delivered at Harvard Law School on November 13, 1993, in response to the authors' earlier work on pornography, entitled "The Pornographic State," *Harvard Law Review* 107 (1994):1374; and a memorandum letter of March 14, 1995, from Nadine Strossen to the authors. Again, we alert the reader that the "dialogue" is a composite of selected and rearranged excerpts from these sources.

119. Edward Laumann, Robert Michael, and John Gagnon, *The Social Organization of Sexuality* (Chicago: University of Chicago Press, 1995); Robert Michael and Gina Kolata, *Sex in America: A Definitive Survey* (New York: Little, Brown, 1995); Philip Elmer-Dewitt, "Now for the Truth About Americans and Sex," *Time*, 17 October 1994, pp. 62–70. But see Richard C. Lewontin, "Sex, Lies, and Social Science," *New York Review of Books*, 20 April 1995, p. 24, and a letter to the editor by Richard C. Lewontin, *New York Review of Books*, 25 May 1995, p. 43.

120. Cass R. Sunstein, "Porn on the Fourth of July," *New Republic*, 9 January 1995, pp. 42, 44.

121. 403 U.S. 15 (per Justice Harlan, 1971). See note g in Book III.

122. Gitlin, "The Left and Porno," p. 104.

123. Jonathan Rauch, *Kindly Inquisitors: The New Attacks on Free Thought* (Chicago: University of Chicago Press, 1995), p. 17.

Endnotes for Epilogue

1. Adapted from Drew R. McCoy, *The Last of the Fathers: James Madison and the Republican Legacy* (New York: Cambridge University Press, 1989), pp. 371- 372.

2. Friedrich Nietzsche, *Beyond Good and Evil: Prelude to a Philosophy of the Future*, trans. Walter Kaufman (New York: Vintage Books, 1966), p. 93. The Epilogue introduces the complex connections among lying, First Amendment jurisprudence, and political philosophy. In what follows, the Epilogue offers a *sketch* that others may complete in future and more detailed portraits. This is in keeping with our reader-friendly invitation to develop any or all of the points examined in this work, especially our novel cultural approach to the First Amendment.

3. Cass Sunstein, *Democracy and the Problem of Free Speech* (New York: Free Press, 1993), pp. 243–244 (footnotes omitted and emphasis in original) (quoting Jon Elster, "Strategic Uses of Argument," in *Barriers to Conflict Resolution*, ed. K. Arrow et al. [Palo Alto: Stanford University Press, 1993]).

4. Sunstein, *Democracy*, p. 244 (quoting La Rochefoucauld, *Maxims*, trans. L. Tancock [New York: Penguin, 1959], p. 65). It is well to remember that La Rochefoucauld also said: "We are never so ridiculous for the qualities we have as through those we pretend to have." Ibid., p. 54.

5. Sunstein, *Democracy*, p. 244. See also Jon Elster, *The Cement of Society: A Study of Social Order* (Cambridge: Cambridge University Press, 1989), pp. 109, 233–234 (the culture of hypocrisy holds that preservation of social norms may be more important than admission of violations of them).

6. Erasmus, quoted in Sissela Bok, *Lying: Moral Choice in Public and Private Life* (New York: Vintage Books, 1989), p. 168.

7. Loyal D. Rue, *By the Grace of Guile: The Role of Deception in Natural History and Human Affairs* (New York: Oxford University Press, 1994), p. 209.

8. Walter F. Berns, *Freedom, Virtue, and the First Amendment* (Chicago: Henry Regnery, 1965), p. 253.

9. Leo Strauss, *The City and Man* (Chicago: Rand McNally, 1964), p. 102.

10. *The Republic of Plato*, trans. Allan Bloom (New York: Basic Books, 1968), pp. 366–367.

11. Bok, *Lying*, p. 173.

12. *Turner Broadcasting System v. Federal Communications Commission*, 114 S. Ct. 2445, 2462 (1994) (emphasis added). See, e.g., Cass R. Sunstein, "The First Amendment in Cyberspace," *Yale Law Journal* 104 (1995):1757–1804 (defending Madiso-

nian interpretation of *Turner*).

13. Bok, *Lying*, pp. 172–173; Carl Page, "The Truth About Lies in Plato's *Republic*," *Ancient Philosophy Journal* 11 (1991):1, 2.

14. Rue, *By the Grace of Guile*, p. 6.

15. *The Occasional Speeches of Justice Oliver Wendell Holmes*, comp. Mark DeWolfe Howe (Cambridge: Harvard University Press, 1962), p. 178 (quoting Virgil's "Copa Surisca").

16. It may be that the American judiciary sometimes reaches First Amendment decisions consistent with the cultural approach, albeit by circuitous routes. But it is clear that the courts have never openly legitimated such an approach as their modus operandi. Perhaps only the late Justice William O. Douglas (1898–1980) might have expressed some sympathy with the cultural approach. As he wrote in his dissent in *Byrne v. Karalexis*, 396 U.S. 976 (1969), "I think the First Amendment bars all kinds of censorship."

17. *The Standard Edition of the Complete Psychological Works of Sigmund Freud*, vol. 14 (London: Hogarth Press, 1957), pp. 275, 284–285.

18. David Nyberg, *The Varnished Truth: Truth Telling and Deceiving in Ordinary Life* (Chicago: University of Chicago Press, 1993), pp. 5, 2, 105.

19. Rue, *By the Grace of Guile*, p. 207. We have appropriated Professor Rue's argument for our purposes by substituting the word "lie" for his use of the word "myth." See generally note 2.

20. Daniel J. Boorstin, "A History of the Image: From Pseudo-Event to Virtual Reality," *New Perspectives Quarterly* 11 (Summer 1994):16, 19.

21. Louis Forsdale, "Marshall McLuhan and the Rules of the Game," in *Marshall McLuhan: The Man and His Message*, ed. G. Sanderson and F. MacDonald (Golden, CO: Fulcrum, 1989) (quoting Marshall McLuhan, "Educational Effects of the Mass Media of Communication" seminar paper presented at Teacher's College, Columbia University, 1955).

22. From Max Lerner interview with Albert Camus, 1945.

Endnotes for Afterword

1. The "dialogue" in the text was, in large part, excerpted from a Symposium published in the University of Cincinnati Law Review in 1996. Notes have been omitted where they do not significantly qualify the substantive import of the text. See "Noble Lies and the First Amendment: A Symposium on *The Death of Discourse*," *University of Cincinnati Law Review* 64 (1996): 1191-1321. The law review was kind enough to allow us to reprint portions of its issue. The reader is encouraged to consult the complete Symposium for a richer account of the participants' perspectives on our arguments.

2. Alexander M. Bickel, *The Morality of Consent* (New Haven, CT: Yale University Press, 1975), pp. 77–78 (commenting on Justice Wendell Holmes's free speech theory of the marketplace of ideas).

3. *New York Times Co. v. United States*, 403 U.S. 713 (1971).

4. Donald P. Spence, *Narrative Truth and Historical Truth: Meaning and Interpretation in Psychoanalysis* (New York: W.W. Norton & Co., 1982), p. 31.

5. See generally Richard Rorty, *Contingency, Irony, and Solidarity* (New York: Cambridge University Press, 1989).

6. See generally Stanley Fish, *There's No Such Thing as Free Speech and It's a Good Thing, Too* (New York: Oxford University Press, 1994).

7. Stanley Rosen, *Hermeneutics as Politics* (New York: Oxford University Press, 1987), p. 138.

8. Loyal Rue, *By the Grace of Guile* (New York: Oxford University Press, 1994), p. 207.

9. Judith N. Shklar, *Ordinary Vices* (Cambridge, MA: Harvard University Press, 1984), p. 248. See also ibid., pp. 67-78.

10. Dennis F. Thompson, "Hypocrisy and Democracy," in *Liberalism Without Illusions: Essays on Liberal Theory & the Political Vision of Judith N. Shklar*, ed. Bernard Yack (Chicago: University of Chicago Press, 1996) (offering one explanatory interpretation of the passage quoted in the text).

11. See, e.g., *Lorillard Tobacco Co. v. Reilly / Altadis U.S.A. Inc. v. Reilly*, 121 S. Ct. 2404; *Thompson v. Western States Medical Center*, 122 S.Ct. 1497 (2002).

12. Todd Gitlin, *The Twilight of Common Dreams: Why America Is Wracked by Culture Wars* (New York: Metropolitan Books, 1995), p. 214.

13. Todd Gitlin, *Media Unlimited: How the Torrent of Images and Sounds Overwhelms Our Lives* (New York: Metropolitan Books/Henry Holt and Company, 2001), p. 68; Constance L. Hays, "Commercialism in U.S. Schools Is Examined in New Report," *New York Times*, 14 August 2000, sec. C, p. 1 (Channel One figures derived

Bibliography

Books are not absolutely
dead things, but do contain
a potency of life in them.

— John Milton
Areopagitica (1644)

Bibliography for Foreword

Books

Chang, Nancy. *Silencing Political Dissent: How Post-September 11 Anti-Terrorism Measures Threaten Our Civil Liberties*. New York: Seven Stories Press, 2002.

Chomsky, Noam. *9-11*. New York: Seven Stories Press, 2001.

Debord, Guy. *The Society of the Spectacle*. Brooklyn, NY: Zone Books, 1995.

Goldberg, Danny, Victor Goldberg, and Robert Greenwald, eds. *It's a Free Country: Personal Freedom in America After September 11*. New York: RDV Books, 2002.

Lawyers Committee for Human Rights. *A Year of Loss: Reexamining Civil Liberties Since September 11*. LCHR Report. New York: Lawyers Committee for Human Rights, 2002.

Leone, Richard C., and Greg Anrig, Jr., eds. *The War on Our Freedoms: Civil Liberties in an Age of Terrorism*. New York: PublicAffairs, 2003.

Porter, Roy. *Studies in European History: The Enlightenment*. New York: Palgrave Macmillan, 1996.

Redish, Martin. *Commercial Speech as Free Expression: The Case for First Amendment Protection*. New York: Cambridge University Press, 2021.

Reporters Committee for Freedom of the Press. *Homefront Confidential: How the War on Terrorism Affects Access to Information and the Public's Right to Know*. RCFP White Paper, no. 3. Lucy A. Dalglish, Gregg P. Leslie, and Philip Taylor, eds. Arlington, VA: The Reporters Committee for Freedom of the Press, 2003.

Silberstein, Sandra. *War of Words: Language, Politics and 9/11*. New York: Routledge, 2002.

Sunstein, Cass. *Democracy and the Problem of Free Speech*. New York: Free Press, 1993.

Articles*

Collins, Ronald K.L., and David M. Skover. "Paratexts." *Stanford Law Review* 44 (1992): 509–552.

Post, Robert, and Amanda Shanor. "Adam Smith's First Amendment." *Harvard Law Review Forum* 128 (2015): 165.

* Newspaper articles cited in notes are not listed, while notable journal articles are listed.

Bibliography for Prologue

Books

Grazia, Sebastian de. *Machiavelli in Hell.* Princeton, NJ: Princeton University Press, 1989.

Lindley, David. *The End of Physics: The Myth of a Unified Theory.* New York: Basic Books, 1993.

Machiavelli, Niccolò. *The Prince.* Translated by H. Mansfield. Chicago: University of Chicago Press, 1985.

Matthews, Richard K. *If Men Were Angels: James Madison and the Heartless Empire of Reason.* Lawrence: University Press of Kansas, 1995.

Montesquieu. *The Spirit of the Laws.* Translated by T. Nugent, 1750. Edited by D. Carrithers. Berkeley: University of California Press, 1977.

Twitchell, James. *Carnival Culture: The Trashing of Taste in America.* New York: Columbia University Press, 1992.

Williams, C. K. *A Dream of Mind.* New York: Farrar, Straus & Giroux, 1992.

Articles

Luke, David. "Thomas Mann's 'Iridescent Interweaving.'" In Thomas Mann, *Death in Venice.* Edited and translated by Clayton Koelb. New York: W. W. Norton, 1994.

Wood, Gordon. "The Founding Realists." *New York Review of Books*, 19 October 1995, p. 58.

Bibliography for Book I: The Paratroopers' Paradox

Books

Abramson, Jeffrey B., F. Christopher Arterton, and Gary R. Orren. *The Electronic Commonwealth: The Impact of New Media Technologies on Democratic Politics.* New York: Basic Books, 1988.

Adatto, Kiku. *Picture Perfect: The Art and Artifice of Public Image Making.* New York: Basic Books, 1993.

Allen, R., ed. *Channels of Discourse, Reassembled: Television and Contemporary Criticism.* Chapel Hill: University of North Carolina Press, 1987.

Altschuler, Glenn, and David Grossvogel. *Changing Channels.* Urbana: University of Illinois Press, 1992.

Anastaplo, George. *The Constitutionalist: Notes on the First Amendment.* Dallas: Southern Methodist University Press, 1971.

Ang, Ien. *Desperately Seeking the Audience.* London: Routledge, 1991.

Ansolabehere, Stephen, Roy Behr, and Shanto Iyengar. *The Media Game: American Politics in the Television Age.* New York: Macmillan, 1993.

Bagdikian, Ben. *The Media Monopoly.* Boston: Beacon Press, 1992.

Bagehot, Walter. *The Works of Walter Bagehot.* Hartford: Travelers Insurance, 1889.

Baker, C. Edwin. *Human Liberty and Freedom of Speech.* New York: Oxford University Press, 1989.

Barber, Benjamin R. *Jihad vs. McWorld.* New York: Times Books, 1995.

Baudrillard, Jean. *Revenge of the Crystal.* Concord, MA: Pluto Press, 1990.

Bedford, Sybille. *Aldous Huxley: A Biography.* New York: Carroll & Graf, 1973.

Bianculli, David. *Teleliteracy: Taking Television Seriously.* New York: Continuum, 1992.

Bliss, Edward, Jr. *Now the News: The Story of Broadcast Journalism.* New York: Columbia University Press, 1991.

Bliss, Edward, Jr., ed. *In Search of Light: The Broadcasts of Edward R. Murrow 1938–1961.* New York: Knopf, 1967.

Bollinger, Lee. *The Tolerant Society.* New York: Oxford University Press, 1986.

______. *Images of a Free Press.* Chicago: University of Chicago Press, 1991.

Boorstin, Daniel J. *The Image: A Guide to Pseudo-Events in America.* New York: Random House, 1992.

Brand, Stewart. *The Media Lab.* New York: Viking Press, 1987.

Brooks, Tim, and Earle Marsh. *The Complete Directory to Prime Time Network TV Shows: 1946–Present.* New York: Ballantine Books, 1988.

Carey, James. *Communication as Culture*. Boston: Hyman, 1989.

Carter, T. Barton, Marc Franklin, and Jay Wright. *The First Amendment and the Fifth Estate: Regulation of Electronic Mass Media*. Westbury, CT: Foundation Press, 1989.

Chappell, Warren. *A Short History of the Printed Word*. Boston: Nonpareil Books, 1970.

Clanchy, M. T. *From Memory to Written Record*. Oxford: Blackwell, 1993.

Cook, P., D. Gomery, and L. Lichty, eds. *American Media*. Washington, DC: Woodrow Wilson Center Press, 1989.

______. *The Future of News*. Washington, DC: Woodrow Wilson Center Press, 1992.

Cubitt, Sean. *Timeshift: On Video Culture*. New York: Routledge, 1991.

Curran, J., and M. Gurevitch, eds. *Mass Media and Society*. New York: Routledge, 1991.

Curry, R., ed. *Freedom at Risk: Secrecy, Censorship, and Repression in the 1980s*. Philadelphia: Temple University Press, 1988.

Czitrom, Daniel. *Media and the American Mind from Morse to McLuhan*. Chapel Hill: University of North Carolina Press, 1982.

Davis, Douglas. *The Five Myths of Television Power*. New York: Simon & Schuster, 1993.

Debord, Guy. *The Society of the Spectacle*. Translated by Donald Nicholson. New York: Zone Books, 1994.

Denisoff, R. Serge. *Inside MTV*. New Brunswick, NJ: Transaction Books, 1988.

Eisenstein, Elizabeth. *The Printing Press as an Agent of Change*. Cambridge: Cambridge University Press, 1979.

Ellul, Jacques. *The Technological Society*. New York: Knopf, 1964.

Emerson, Thomas. *The System of Freedom of Expression*. New York: Vintage Books, 1970.

Emord, Jonathon W. *Freedom, Technology, and the First Amendment*. San Francisco: Pacific Research Institute for Public Policy, 1991.

Entman, Robert M. *Democracy Without Citizens: Media and the Decay of American Politics*. New York: Oxford University Press, 1989.

Febvre, Lucien, and Henri Jean Martin. *The Coming of the Book*. London: Verso, 1990.

Ferrarotti, Franco. *The End of Conversation: The Impact of Mass Media on Modern Society*. New York: Greenwood Press, 1988.

Fiske, John. *Television Culture*. New York: Routledge, 1987.

______. *Reading the Popular*. Boston: Hyman, 1989.

______. *Understanding Popular Culture*. Boston: Hyman, 1989.

FitzSimon, M., ed. *Media, Democracy and the Information Highway*. New York: Freedom Forum Media Studies Center, 1993.

Fowles, Jib. *Why Viewers Watch*. Newbury Park: Sage, 1992.

Friedman, Lawrence. *The Republic of Choice: Law, Authority, and Culture.* Cambridge: Harvard University Press, 1990.

Friendly, Fred. *Due to Circumstances Beyond Our Control.* New York: Vintage Books, 1968.

Gans, Herbert J. *Popular Culture and High Culture: An Analysis and Evaluation of Taste.* New York: Basic Books, 1974.

Garry, Patrick M. *Scrambling for Protection: The New Media and the First Amendment.* Pittsburgh: University of Pittsburgh Press, 1995.

Gilder, George. *Life After Television: The Coming Transformation of Media and American Life.* New York: W. W. Norton, 1994.

Gitlin, Todd. *The Whole World Is Watching: Mass Media in the Making and Unmaking of the New Left.* Berkeley: University of California Press, 1980.

______. *Inside Prime Time.* New York: Pantheon Books, 1983.

Gitlin, Todd, ed. *Watching Television.* New York: Pantheon Books, 1986.

Goldstein, Norm. *The History of Television.* New York: Portland House, 1991.

Goody, Jack. *Literacy in Traditional Societies.* New York: Cambridge University Press, 1968.

______. *The Interface Between the Written and the Oral.* Cambridge: Cambridge University Press, 1987.

Graham, Fred. *Happy Talk: Confessions of a TV Newsman.* New York: W. W. Norton, 1990.

Grossman, Lawrence K. *The Electronic Republic: Reshaping Democracy in the Information Age.* New York: Viking Penguin, 1995.

Hadden, Jeffrey K., and Anson Shupe. *Televangelism: Power and Politics on God's Frontier.* New York: Henry Holt, 1988.

Hanhardt, J., ed. *Video Culture: A Critical Investigation.* New York: Visual Studies Workshop Press, 1990.

Hart, Roderick P. *Seducing America: How Television Charms the Modern Voter.* New York: Oxford University Press, 1994.

Hartley, John. *Tele-ology: Studies in Television.* New York: Routledge, 1992.

Harvey, David. *The Condition of Postmodernity.* Oxford: Blackwell, 1989.

Havelock, Eric. *The Muse Learns to Write.* New Haven: Yale University Press, 1986.

Himmelstein, Hal. *Television Myth and the American Mind.* New York: Praeger Press, 1984.

Hoynes, William. *Public Television for Sale.* Boulder: Westview Press, 1994.

Huxley, Aldous. *Brave New World and Brave New World Revisited.* New York: Harper & Row, 1965.

Inglis, Fred. *Media Theory.* Oxford: Blackwell, 1990.

Innis, Harold A. *The Bias of Communication.* Toronto: University of Toronto Press, 1951.

______. *Empire and Communications.* Toronto: Press Porcépic, 1986.

Iyengar, Shanto. *Is Anyone Responsible?* Chicago: University of Chicago Press, 1991.

Iyengar, Shanto, and Donald Kinder. *News That Matters.* Chicago: University of Chicago Press, 1987.

Jamieson, Kathleen Hall. *Eloquence in an Electronic Age.* New York: Oxford University Press, 1988.

Jankowski, Gene F., and David C. Fuchs. *Television Today and Tomorrow.* New York: Oxford University Press, 1995.

Katsh, M. Ethan. *The Electronic Media and the Transformation of Law.* New York: Oxford University Press, 1989.

______. *Law in a Digital World.* New York: Oxford University Press, 1995.

Keane, John. *The Media and Democracy.* Oxford: Blackwell, 1991.

Kellner, Douglas. *Jean Baudrillard: From Marxism to Postmodernism and Beyond.* Palo Alto: Stanford University Press, 1989.

______. *Television and the Crisis of Democracy.* Boulder: Westview Press, 1990.

Kottak, Conrad. *Prime-Time Society: An Anthropological Analysis of Television and Culture.* Belmont, CA: Wadsworth, 1990.

Krol, Ed. *The Whole Internet User's Guide and Catalogue.* Edited by M. Loukides. Sebastopol, CA: O'Reilly & Associates, 1992.

Lazere, Donald, ed. *American Media and Mass Culture: Left Perspectives.* Berkeley: University of California Press, 1987.

Lee, Simon. *The Cost of Free Speech.* London: Faber & Faber, 1990.

Levy, Leonard. *Emergence of a Free Press.* New York: Oxford University Press, 1985.

Lewis, Justin. *The Ideological Octopus: An Exploration of Television and Its Audience.* New York: Routledge, 1991.

Logan, Robert. *The Alphabet Effect.* New York: St. Martin's Press, 1986.

Mander, Jerry. *Four Arguments for the Elimination of Television.* New York: Quill Press, 1977.

Marc, David. *Demographic Vistas: Television in American Culture.* Philadelphia: University of Pennsylvania Press, 1984.

______. *Comic Visions: Television Comedy and American Culture.* New York: Routledge, 1989.

Marchand, Philip. *Marshall McLuhan: The Medium and the Messenger.* New York: Ticknor & Fields, 1989.

McKitterick, Rosamond. *The Carolingians and the Written Word.* New York: Cambridge University Press, 1989.

McLuhan, Marshall. *The Gutenberg Galaxy: The Making of Typographic Man.* Toronto: University of Toronto Press, 1962.

______. *Understanding Media.* New York: McGraw-Hill, 1964.

McLuhan, Marshall, and Quentin Fiore. *War and Peace in the Global Village.* New York: McGraw-Hill, 1968.

Meiklejohn, Alexander. *Political Freedom: The Constitutional Powers of the People.* New Haven, CT: Greenwood Press, 1960.

Mellencamp, P., ed. *Logics of Television.* Bloomington: Indiana University Press, 1990.

Mendelsohn, Harold. *Mass Entertainment.* Chapel Hill: University of North Carolina Press, 1966.

Meyrowitz, Joshua. *No Sense of Place: The Impact of Electronic Media on Social Behavior.* New York: Oxford University Press, 1985.

Miller, Mark Crispin. *Boxed In: The Culture of TV.* Evanston, IL: Northwestern University Press, 1988.

Mills, C. Wright. *The Power Elite.* New York: Oxford University Press, 1956.

______. *Power, Politics, and People.* New York: Oxford University Press, 1963.

Minow, Newton, and Craig LaMay. *Abandoned in the Wasteland.* New York: Hill & Wang, 1995.

Mitroff, Ian, and Warren Bennis. *The Unreality Industry.* New York: Birch Lane Press, 1989.

Modleski, T., ed. *Studies in Entertainment: Critical Approaches to Mass Culture.* Bloomington: Indiana University Press, 1986.

Mukerji, C., and M. Schudson, eds. *Rethinking Popular Culture.* Berkeley: University of California Press, 1991.

Nelson, Jacques. *Sultans of Sleaze: Public Relations and the Media.* Berkeley: Common Courage Press, 1989.

Neuman, W. Russell. *The Future of the Mass Audience.* New York: Cambridge University Press, 1991.

Neuman, W. Russell, M. Just, and A. Crigler. *Common Knowledge: News and the Construction of Political Meaning.* Chicago: University of Chicago Press, 1992.

O'Connor, A., ed. *Raymond Williams on Television: Selected Writings.* New York: Routledge, 1989.

Ong, Walter J. *Orality and Literacy.* New York: Methuen Press, 1982.

Orwell, George. *Nineteen Eighty-Four.* Oxford: Clarendon Press, 1984.

Parenti, Michael. *Make-Believe Media: The Politics of Entertainment.* New York: St. Martin's Press, 1992.

Philo, Greg. *Seeing and Believing: The Influence of Television.* New York: Routledge, 1990.

Polenberg, Richard. *Fighting Faiths: The Abrams Case, the Supreme Court, and Free Speech.* New York: Viking Press, 1987.

Pool, Ithiel de Sola. *Technologies of Freedom.* Cambridge: Harvard University Press, 1983.

Poster, Mark. *The Mode of Information: Poststructuralism and Social Context.* Chicago: University of Chicago Press, 1990.

Poster, Mark, ed. *Jean Baudrillard: Selected Writings.* Palo Alto: Stanford University Press, 1988.

Postman, Neil. *Teaching as a Conserving Activity.* New York: Dell, 1979.

______. *Amusing Ourselves to Death: Public Discourse in the Age of Show Business.* New York: Viking Penguin, 1985.

______. *Conscientious Objections: Stirring Up Trouble About Language, Technology, and Education.* New York: Knopf, 1988.

______. *Technopoly.* New York: Vintage Books, 1992.

Powe, Lucas A., Jr. *American Broadcasting and the First Amendment.* Berkeley: University of California Press, 1987.

Powers, Ron. *The Beast, The Eunuch, and the Glass-Eyed Child.* New York: Anchor Books, 1984.

Redish, Martin. *Freedom of Expression: A Critical Analysis.* Charlottesville, VA: Michie, 1984.

The Republic of Plato. Translated by A. Bloom. New York: Basic Books, 1968.

Review of Child Development Service, ed. *Review of Child Development Research.* 7 vols. Chicago: University of Chicago Press, 1964–1985.

Rheingold, Howard. *Virtual Reality.* New York: Addison-Wesley, 1991.

Rothman, S., ed. *The Mass Media in Liberal Democratic Societies.* New York: Paragon House, 1992.

Rushkoff, Douglas. *Media Virus! Hidden Agendas in Popular Culture.* New York: Ballantine Books, 1994.

Schiller, Herbert I. *Culture, Inc.* New York: Oxford University Press, 1989.

Schwartz, Tony. *Media: The Second God.* Garden City, NY: Anchor Press, 1983.

Science, Technology, and the First Amendment. Washington, DC: Office of Technology Assessment, 1988.

Shiffrin, Steven. *The First Amendment, Democracy, and Romance.* Cambridge: Harvard University Press, 1990.

Smolla, Rodney. *Free Speech in an Open Society.* New York: Knopf, 1992.

Sterns, Jane, and Michael Sterns. *Encyclopedia of Pop Culture.* New York: Harper Perennial, 1992.

Taylor, Paul. *See How They Run: Electing the President in an Age of Mediaocracy.* New York: Knopf, 1990.

Tichi, Cecelia. *Electronic Hearth.* New York: Oxford University Press, 1991.

Twitchell, James. *Carnival Culture: The Trashing of Taste in America.* New York: Columbia University Press, 1992.

Ulmer, Gregory. *Teletheory: Grammatology in the Age of Video.* New York: Routledge, 1989.

Weil, Simone. *The Need for Roots.* Translated by Arthur Wills. Boston: Beacon Press, 1952.

Woolley, Benjamin. *Virtual Worlds: A Journey in Hype and Hyperreality*. New York: Penguin Books, 1992.

Wurman, Richard S. *Information Anxiety.* New York: Doubleday, 1989.

Articles*

Ackerman, Bruce. "Constitutional Politics/Constitutional Law." *Yale Law Journal* 99 (1989):453.

Anastaplo, George. "Self-Government and the Mass Media: A Practical Man's Guide." In Harry M. Clor, ed., *The Mass Media and Modern Democracy*. Chicago: Rand McNally, 1974.

Bagdikian, Ben. "The Lords of the Global Village." *The Nation*, 12 June 1989.

Bernstein, Carl. "Talk Show Nation." *New Perspectives Quarterly* 11 (Summer 1994):22.

BeVier, Lillian. "The First Amendment and Political Speech: An Inquiry into the Substance and Limits of Principle." *Stanford Law Review* 30 (1978):299.

Blasi, Vincent. "The Checking Value in First Amendment Theory." *American Bar Foundation Research Journal* (1977):521.

Bork, Robert. "Neutral Principles and Some First Amendment Problems." *Indiana Law Journal* 47 (1971):1.

Collins, Ronald K.L., and David M. Skover. "The First Amendment in an Age of Paratroopers." *Texas Law Review* 68 (1990):1087.

______. "Paratexts." *Stanford Law Review* 44 (1992):509.

______. "Pissing in the Snow: A Cultural Approach to the First Amendment." *Stanford Law Review* 45 (1993):783.

Forsdale, Louis. "Marshall McLuhan and the Rules of the Game." In G. Sanderson and F. MacDonald, eds., *Marshall McLuhan: The Man and His Message.* Golden, CO: Fulcrum, 1989.

Gitlin, Todd. "Blips, Bites and Savvy Talk: Television's Impact on American Politics." *Dissent* (Winter 1990):18.

Greenawalt, R. Kent. "Free Speech Justifications." *Columbia Law Review* 89 (1989): 199.

Hughes, Robert. "Why Watch It, Anyway?" *New York Review of Books*, 16 February 1995, p. 37.

Ingber, Stanley. "The Marketplace of Ideas: A Legitimizing Myth." *Duke Law Journal* (1984):1.

Katsh, M. Ethan. "The First Amendment and Technical Change: The New Media Have a Message." *George Washington Law Review* 57 (1989):1459.

* Newspaper articles and television and radio transcripts cited in notes are not listed, while notable magazine articles are listed.

______. "Rights, Camera, Action: Cyberspatial Settings and the First Amendment." *Yale Law Journal* 104 (1995):1681.

Lerner, Max. "Some Reflections on the First Amendment in an Age of Paratroopers." *Texas Law Review* 68 (1990):1127.

Nader, Ralph, and Claire Riley. "Oh, Say Can You See: A Broadcast Network for the Audience." *Law and Politics Journal* 5 (1988):1.

Neuman, W. Russell. "The Mass Audience." *Media Studies Journal* 5 (1991):156.

O'Brien, David M. "Between the Nightmares of Orwell and Huxley: A Note on the Noble Dream of the First Amendment." *Texas Law Review* 68 (1990):1137.

Post, Robert. "The Constitutional Concept of Public Discourse: Outrageous Opinion, Democratic Deliberation, and *Hustler Magazine v. Falwell.*" *Harvard Law Review* 103 (1990):601.

Redish, Martin. "Killing the First Amendment with Kindness: A Troubled Reaction to Collins and Skover." *Texas Law Review* 68 (1990):1147.

"The Remaking of the Candidate." *Campaigns and Elections* (May–June 1988).

Rubin, Edward. "Television and the Experience of Citizenship." *Texas Law Review* 68 (1990):1155.

Scanlan, John. "Aliens in the Marketplace of Ideas: The Government, the Academy, and the McCarran-Walter Act." *Texas Law Review* 66 (1988):1481.

Scanlan, Thomas. "A Theory of Freedom of Expression." *Philosophy and Public Affairs* 1 (1972):204.

Schauer, Frederick. "Free Speech and the Demise of the Soap-Box." *Columbia Law Review* 84 (1984):558.

Schiller, Herbert I. "Television is a Social — Not a Biological or Technological — Problem." *Texas Law Review* 68 (1990):1169.

Schlender. "Couch Potatoes! Now It's Smart TV." *Fortune*, 20 November 1989.

Secunda, Eugene. "Video News Releases: The Hidden Persuaders Revisited?" Unpublished paper presented at Annual Media Ecology Conference, Saugherties, NY, 8 October 1989.

Sharp, Malcolm. "Crosskey, Anastaplo, and Meiklejohn on the United States Constitution." *University of Chicago Law School Record* 20 (1973):3.

Stewart, Potter. "Or of the Press." *Hastings Law Journal* 26 (1975):631.

Tushnet, Mark. "Decoding Television (and Law Reviews)." *Texas Law Review* 68 (1990):1179.

Bibliography for Book II: Commerce & Communication

Books

Baker, C. Edwin. *Human Liberty and Freedom of Speech*. New York: Oxford University Press, 1989.

______. *Advertising and a Democratic Press*. Princeton, NJ: Princeton University Press, 1994.

Barendt, Eric. *Freedom of Speech*. Oxford: Clarendon Press, 1985.

Barnouw, Erik. *The Sponsor: Notes on a Modern Potentate*. New York: Oxford University Press, 1978.

Bogart, Leo. *Strategy in Advertising*. Lincolnwood, IL: NTC Publishing Group, 1990.

______. *Commercial Culture*. New York: Oxford University Press, 1995.

Bosmajian, Haig. *Metaphor and Reason in Judicial Opinions*. Carbondale: Southern Illinois University Press, 1992.

Canter, Laurence A., and Martha S. Siegel. *How to Make a Fortune on the Information Superhighway*. New York: HarperCollins, 1994.

Clark, Eric. *The Want Makers: Inside the World of Advertising*. New York: Viking Penguin, 1989.

Collier, James. *The Rise of Selfishness in America*. New York: Oxford University Press, 1991.

Collins, Ronald K.L. *Dictating Content: How Advertising Pressure Can Corrupt a Free Press*. Washington, DC: Center for the Study of Commercialism, 1992.

Cook, Guy. *The Discourse of Advertising*. New York: Routledge, 1992.

Crossen, Cynthia. *Tainted Truth: The Manipulation of Fact in America*. New York: Simon & Schuster, 1994.

Debord, Guy. *The Society of the Spectacle*. Translated by Donald Nicholson. New York: Zone Books, 1994.

Driver, John C., and Gordon R. Foxall. *Advertising Policy and Practice*. New York: St. Martin's Press, 1984.

Durning, Alan. *How Much Is Enough?* New York: W. W. Norton, 1992.

Dyer, Gillian. *Advertising as Communication*. London: Routledge, 1982.

Ekelund, Robert, Jr., and David Saurman. *Advertising and the Market Process*. San Francisco: Pacific Research Institute, 1988.

Ewen, Stuart. *All Consuming Images*. New York: Basic Books, 1988.

Fox, R., and T. J. Lears, eds. *The Culture of Consumption: Critical Essays in American History, 1880–1980*. New York: Pantheon Books, 1983.

Fox, Stephen. *The Mirror Makers: A History of American Advertising and Its Creators.* New York: Vintage Books, 1985.

Gartner, Michael G. *Advertising and the First Amendment.* New York: Priority Press, 1989.

Goldfarb, Jeffrey C. *The Cynical Society.* Chicago: University of Chicago Press, 1991.

Goldman, Robert. *Reading Ads Socially.* New York: Routledge, 1992.

Goodrum, Charles, and Helen Dalrymple. *Advertising in America: The First 200 Years.* New York: Harry N. Abrams, 1990.

Hacker, George, Ronald Collins, and Michael Jacobsen. *Marketing Booze to Blacks.* Washington, DC: Center for Science in the Public Interest, 1987.

Henry, Jules. *Culture Against Man.* New York: Random House, 1963.

Himmelstein, Hal. *Television Myth and the American Mind.* New York: Praeger, 1984.

Jacobson, Michael, and Laurie Ann Mazur. *Marketing Madness.* Boulder: Westview Press, 1995.

Jhally, Sut. *The Codes of Advertising.* New York: Routledge, 1987.

Leach, William. *Land of Desire: Merchants, Power, and the Rise of a New American Culture.* New York: Pantheon Books, 1993.

Lears, T. Jackson. *Fables of Abundance.* New York: HarperCollins, 1994.

Lefebvre, Henri. *Everyday Life in the Modern World.* Translated by Sacha Rabinovitch. New Brunswick, NJ: Transaction Books, 1971.

Leiss, William, Stephen Kline, and Sut Jhally. *Social Communication in Advertising.* New York: Routledge, 1990.

Marchand, Roland. *Advertising the American Dream: Making Way for Modernity 1920–1940.* Berkeley: University of California Press, 1985.

Martin, David. *Romancing the Brand: The Power of Advertising and How to Use It.* New York: AMACOM, 1989.

Mayer, Marti. *Whatever Happened to Madison Avenue?* Boston: Little, Brown, 1991.

McCracken, Grant. *Culture and Consumption.* Bloomington: Indiana University Press, 1990.

McLuhan, Marshall. *The Mechanical Bride.* New York: Vanguard Press, 1951.

______. *Culture Is Our Business.* New York: McGraw-Hill, 1970.

Mitroff, Ian, and Warren Bennis. *The Unreality Industry: The Deliberate Manufacture of Falsehood and What It Is Doing to Our Lives.* New York: Birch Lane Press, 1989.

Neuborne, Burt. *Free Speech — Free Markets — Free Choice: An Essay on Commercial Speech.* New York: Association of National Advertisers, 1987.

Ogilvy, David. *Ogilvy on Advertising.* New York: Pan Books, 1983.

______. *Confessions of an Advertising Man.* New York: Atheneum, 1987.

O'Toole, John. *The Trouble with Advertising: A View from the Inside.* New York: Times Books, 1985.

Parenti, Michael. *Make-Believe Media.* New York: St. Martin's Press, 1992.

Potter, David M. *People of Plenty: Economic Abundance and the American Character.* Chicago: University of Chicago Press, 1954.

Rapp, Stann, and Tom Collins. *Maxi-Marketing.* New York: Plume, 1988.

Ries, Al, and Jack Trout. *Positioning: The Battle for Your Mind.* New York: Warner Books, 1986.

Sandage, Charles H., and Vernon Fryberger. *Advertising Theory and Practice.* Homewood, IL: Richard Irwin, 1975.

Schiller, Herbert I. *Culture, Inc.: The Corporate Takeover of Public Expression.* New York: Oxford University Press, 1989.

Schudson, Michael. *Advertising, the Uneasy Persuasion: Its Dubious Impact on American Society.* New York: Basic Books, 1988.

Schwartz, Barry. *The Costs of Living: How Market Freedom Erodes the Best Things in Life.* New York: W. W. Norton, 1994.

Selling America's Kids: Commercial Pressures on Kids of the 90's. Washington, DC: Consumers Union Education Services, 1990.

Shi, David. *The Simple Life: Plain Living and High Thinking in American Culture.* New York: Oxford University Press, 1985.

Shields, R., ed. *Lifestyle Shopping: The Subject of Consumption.* New York: Routledge, 1992.

Shorris, Earl. *A Nation of Salesmen.* New York: W. W. Norton, 1994.

Thompson, William. *The American Replacement of Nature.* New York: Doubleday Currency, 1985.

Tomlinson, A., ed. *Consumption, Identity, and Style.* New York: Routledge, 1990.

Twitchell, James. *Adcult USA: The Triumph of Advertising in American Culture.* New York: Columbia University Press, 1995.

Vestergaard, Torben, and Kim Schrøder. *The Language of Advertising.* New York: Blackwell, 1985.

Whetmore, Edward J. *Mediamerica: Form, Content, and Consequence of Mass Communication.* Belmont, CA: Wadsworth, 1989.

White, Larry C. *Merchants of Death: The American Tobacco Industry.* New York: William Morrow, 1988.

White, Mimi. *Tele-Advertising.* Chapel Hill: University of North Carolina Press, 1992.

Williams, Raymond. *Problems in Materialism and Culture.* New York: Verso, 1980.

Williamson, Judith. *Decoding Advertisements: Ideology and Meaning in Advertising.* New York: Marion Boyers, 1978.

Articles*

Baig, Edward C. "Is Bigger Better for Philip Morris?" *Fortune*, 8 May 1989, p. 69.

Baker, C. Edwin. "Advertising and a Democratic Press." *University of Pennsylvania Law Review* 140 (1992):2097.

Baudrillard, Jean. "Consumer Society." In Mark Poster, ed. *Jean Baudrillard: Selected Writings*. Stanford: Stanford University Press, 1988.

Benn, Linda. "The Ethics of Advertising." *World and I*, December 1990, p. 531.

Bogart, Leo. "The American Media System and Its Commercial Culture." New York: Gannett Foundation Media Center, 1991.

______. "Freedom to Know or Freedom to Say?" *Texas Law Review* 71 (1993): 815.

Coase, Ronald. "Advertising and Free Speech." *Journal of Legal Studies* 6 (1977):1.

Cohen, Robert. "Presentation on Advertising Expenditures." *Insider's Report*. New York: McCann-Erickson Advertising Agency, June 1994.

Collins, Ronald K.L., and David M. Skover. "Commerce & Communication." *Texas Law Review* 71 (1993):697.

Dan-Cohen, Meir. "Freedoms of Collective Speech." *California Law Review* 79 (1991):1229.

Endicott, R. Craig. "Where Those Ad Dollars Go." *Advertising Age*, 20 August 1987, p. 134.

Etzioni, Amitai. "The Moral Foundations of the Marketplace: What Is to Be Done?" *World and I*, December 1990, p. 466.

Fuchsberg, Jacob D. "Commercial Speech: Where It's At." *Brooklyn Law Review* 46 (1980):389.

Howard, Alan. "The Constitutionality of Deceptive Speech Regulations." *Case Western Reserve Law Review* 41 (1991):1093.

Hyman, Michael. "Advertising Ethics: Not an Oxymoron." *World and I*, December 1990, p. 544.

Jhally, Sut. "Image-Based Culture: Advertising and Popular Culture." *World and I*, July 1990, p. 507.

______. "Commercial Culture, Collective Values, and the Future." *Texas Law Review* 71 (1993):805.

Kaiser, Susan B. "Fashion and Popular Culture." *World and I*, July 1990, p. 520.

Kavanaugh, John. "New Time Religion: Accept Consumerism in Your Heart." *Adbusters Quarterly*, Winter 1993, p. 18.

Kowinski, Bill. "Graven Images." *Adbusters Quarterly*, Winter 1993, p. 25.

* Newspaper articles cited in notes are not listed, while notable magazine articles are listed.

Kozinski, Alex, and Stuart Banner. "Who's Afraid of Commercial Speech?" *Virginia Law Review* 76 (1990):627.

______. "When Speech Isn't Free." *Philip Morris*, Summer 1991, p. 26.

______. "The Anti-History and Pre-History of Commercial Speech." *Texas Law Review* 71 (1993):747.

Lears, T. J. Jackson. "The Rise of American Advertising." In P. Cook, D. Gomery, and L. Lichty, eds., *American Media*. Washington, DC: Woodrow Wilson Center Press, 1989.

Levin, Gary. "Benetton Brouhaha." *Advertising Age*, 17 February 1992, p. 62.

Lowenstein, Daniel H. "'Too Much Puff': Persuasion, Paternalism and Commercial Speech." *University of Cincinnati Law Review* 56 (1988):1205.

Magiera, Marcy. "Spike Lee's *Malcolm X* Gets New Kind of Tie-Ins." *Advertising Age*, 13 July 1992, p. 36.

Redish, Martin. "The First Amendment in the Marketplace: Commercial Speech and the Values of Free Expression." *George Washington Law Review* 39 (1971):429.

Reeves, Jordan. "Culture Jamming: The New Ad Game." *Adbusters Quarterly*, Winter 1995, p. 79.

Schauer, Frederick. "The First Amendment as Ideology." *William and Mary Law Review* 33 (1992):853.

Secunda, Eugene. "Infomercials on Network?" *Advertising Age*, 30 November 1992, p. 20.

Shiffrin, Steven. "Listeners' Rights." In Kenneth Karst, ed., *The First Amendment*. New York: Macmillan, 1990.

Smolla, Rodney A. "Information, Imagery, and the First Amendment: A Case for Expansive Protection of Commercial Speech." *Texas Law Review* 71 (1993):777.

Snyder, Steven. "Movies and Product Placement: Is Hollywood Turning Films into Commercial Speech?" *University of Illinois Law Review* (1992):301.

Steinem, Gloria. "Sex, Lies and Advertising." *Ms.*, July–August 1990, p. 18.

Tushnet, Mark. "Corporations and Free Speech." In D. Kairys, ed., *The Politics of Law: A Progressive Critique*. New York: Pantheon Books, 1982.

Zickerman, Jennifer. "Infomercials on the Rise." *Adbusters Quarterly*, Winter 1993, p. 28.

Bibliography for Book III: Discourse & Intercourse

Books

Arcand, Bernard. *The Jaguar and the Anteater: Pornography Degree Zero.* Translated by W. Grady. New York: Verso, 1993.

Aristophanes. *Four Comedies.* Translated by D. Parker. Edited by W. Arrowsmith. Ann Arbor: University of Michigan Press, 1969.

Athenaeus. *The Deipnosophists.* Translated by C. B. Gulick. Cambridge: Harvard University Press, 1937.

Barron, Jerome A., and C. Thomas Dienes. *First Amendment Law in a Nutshell.* New York: West, 1993.

Bataille, Georges. *Erotism: Death and Sensuality.* Translated by M. Dalwood. San Francisco: City of Lights Books, 1986.

Bobbio, Norberto. *Thomas Hobbes and the Natural Law Tradition.* Chicago: University of Chicago Press, 1993.

Bolton, Robert, ed. *Culture Wars: Documents from the Recent Controversies in the Arts.* New York: New Press, 1992.

Bright, Susie. *Susie Bright's Sexual Reality: A Visual Sex World Reader.* Pittsburgh: Cleis Press, 1992.

Broun, Heywood, and Margaret Leech. *Anthony Comstock: Roundsman of the Lord.* New York: Albert & Charles Boni, 1927.

Caputi, Mary. *Voluptuous: A Feminist Theory of the Obscene.* Lanham: Rowman & Littlefield, 1994.

Clancy, C. A., ed. *Pornography: Solutions Through Law.* Washington, DC: National Forum Foundation, 1985.

Clor, Harry M. *Obscenity and Public Morality: Censorship in a Liberal Society.* Chicago: University of Chicago Press, 1969.

Clor, Harry M., ed. *Censorship and Freedom of Expression.* Chicago: Rand McNally, 1971.

Darton, Robert. *The Forbidden Best-Sellers of Pre-Revolutionary France.* New York: W. W. Norton, 1995.

Di Lauro, Al, and Gerald Rabkin. *Dirty Movies: An Illustrated History of the Stag Film, 1915–1970.* New York: Chelsea House, 1976.

Drury, Shadia B. *The Political Ideas of Leo Strauss.* New York: St. Martin's Press, 1988.

______. *Alexandre Kojève.* New York: St. Martin's Press, 1994.

Dworkin, Andrea. *Pornography: Men Possessing Women.* New York: E. P. Dutton, 1981.

______. *Letters from a War Zone.* Chicago: Lawrence Hill Books, 1993.

Dworkin, Andrea, and Catharine MacKinnon. *Pornography and Civil Rights: A New Day for Women's Equality.* Minneapolis: Organizing Against Pornography, 1988.

Dwyer, S., ed. *The Problem of Pornography.* New York: Wadsworth, 1994.

Eisenstein, Zillah. *The Radical Future of Liberal Feminism.* Boston: Northeastern University Press, 1993.

Feinberg, Joel. *Offense to Others: The Moral Limits of the Criminal Law.* New York: Oxford University Press, 1985.

Foucault, Michel. *The History of Sexuality.* Translated by R. Hurley. New York: Vintage Books, 1990.

Fox-Genovese, Elizabeth. *Feminism Without Illusions: A Critique of Individualism.* Chapel Hill: University of North Carolina Press, 1991.

Grazia, Edward de. *Girls Lean Back Everywhere: The Law of Obscenity and the Assault on Genius.* New York: Random House, 1992.

Grazia, Edward de, and Roger K. Newman. *Banned Films: Movies, Censors and the First Amendment.* New York: R. R. Bower, 1982.

Greenawalt, Kent. *Fighting Words: Individuals, Communities, and Liberties of Speech.* Princeton, NJ: Princeton University Press, 1995.

Griffin, Susan. *Pornography and Silence: Culture's Revenge Against Nature.* New York: Harper & Row, 1981.

Hawkins, Gordon, and Franklin E. Zimring. *Pornography in a Free Society.* New York: Cambridge University Press, 1988.

Heins, Marjorie. *Sex, Sin, and Blasphemy: A Guide to America's Censorship Wars.* New York: New Press, 1993.

Hobbes, Thomas. *Leviathan.* Edited by Richard Tuck. Cambridge: Cambridge University Press, 1991.

Hunt, Lynn, ed. *Eroticism and the Body Politic.* Baltimore: Johns Hopkins University Press, 1991.

______. *The Invention of Pornography: Obscenity and the Origins of Modernity, 1500–1800.* New York: Zone Books, 1993.

Hyde, H. Montgomery. *A History of Pornography.* New York: Farrar, Straus & Giroux, 1964.

Kalven, Harry, Jr. *A Worthy Tradition: Freedom of Speech in America.* Edited by Jamie Kalven. New York: Harper & Row, 1988.

Kappeler, Susanne. *The Pornography of Representation.* Minneapolis: University of Minnesota Press, 1986.

Kendrick, Walter. *The Secret Museum: Pornography in Modern Culture.* New York: Viking Penguin, 1987.

Kimmel, Michael, ed. *Men Confront Pornography.* New York: Crown, 1990.

Kuhn, Annette. *The Power of the Image: Essays on Representation and Sexuality.* New York: Routledge & Kegan Paul, 1985.

Laumann, Edward, Robert Michael, and John Gagnon. *The Social Organization of Sexuality*. Chicago: University of Chicago Press, 1995.

Lederer, Laura, ed. *Take Back the Night: Women on Pornography*. New York: William Morrow, 1980.

Lederer, Laura, and Richard Delgado, eds., *The Price We Pay*. New York: Hill & Wang, 1995.

Lee, Simon. *The Cost of Free Speech*. London: Faber & Faber, 1990.

MacKinnon, Catharine. *Feminism Unmodified: Discourses on Life and Law.* Cambridge: Harvard University Press, 1987.

______. *Toward a Feminist Theory of the State.* Cambridge: Harvard University Press, 1989.

______. *Only Words.* Cambridge: Harvard University Press, 1993.

MacPherson, C. B. *The Political Theory of Possessive Individualism.* Oxford: Oxford University Press, 1962.

Mann, Thomas. *Death in Venice.* Translated by Clayton Koelb. New York: W. W. Norton, 1994.

Marcus, Steven. *The Other Victorians: A Study of Sexuality and Pornography in Mid-Nineteenth Century England.* New York: Basic Books, 1964.

Michael, Robert, and Gina Kolata. *Sex in America: A Definitive Survey.* New York: Little, Brown, 1995.

Paglia, Camille. *Sex, Art, and American Culture.* New York: Vintage Books, 1992.

Paul, James C. N., and Murray L. Schwartz. *Federal Censorship: Obscenity in the Mail.* New York: Free Press of Glencoe, 1961.

Posner, Richard A. *Overcoming Law.* Cambridge: Harvard University Press, 1995.

Randall, Richard. *Freedom and Taboo: Pornography and the Politics of a Self Divided.* Berkeley: University of California Press, 1989.

Rauch, Jonathan. *Kindly Inquisitors: The New Attacks on Free Thought.* Chicago: University of Chicago Press, 1995.

Rawls, John. *Political Liberalism.* New York: Columbia University Press, 1993.

Redish, Martin. *Freedom of Expression: A Critical Analysis.* Charlottesville, VA: Michie, 1984.

Report of the Commission on Obscenity and Pornography. Washington, DC: U.S. Government Printing Office, 1970.

Rheingold, Howard. *Virtual Reality.* New York: Summit Books, 1991.

Robinson, Phillip, and Nancy Tamosaitis. *The Joy of Cybersex: The Underground Guide to Electronic Erotica.* New York: Brady, 1993.

Rose, Candi, and Dirk Thomas. *net.sex: The Complete Guide to the Adult Side of the Internet.* Indianapolis: Sams Publishing, 1995.

Schama, Simon. *Citizens: A Chronicle of the French Revolution.* New York: Knopf, 1989.

Schauer, Frederick. *Free Speech: A Philosophical Enquiry.* Cambridge: Cambridge University Press, 1982.

Schroeder, Theodore. *Freedom of the Press and "Obscene" Literature.* New York: Free Speech League, 1906.

Segal, Lynne, and Mary McIntosh, eds. *Sex Exposed: Sexuality and the Pornography Debate.* New Brunswick: Rutgers University Press, 1993.

Stan, Adele M., ed. *Debating Sexual Correctness: Pornography, Sexual Harassment, Date Rape, and the Politics of Sexual Equality.* New York: Delta Books, 1995.

Strauss, Leo. *Natural Right and History.* Chicago: University of Chicago Press, 1953.

Strossen, Nadine. *Defending Pornography: Free Speech, Sex, and the Fight for Women's Rights.* New York: Scribner, 1995.

Sunstein, Cass. *Democracy and the Problem of Free Speech.* New York: Free Press, 1993.

Tamosaitis, Nancy. *net.sex.* Emeryville: Ziff-Davis Press, 1995.

Tartt, Donna. *The Secret History.* New York: Alfred A. Knopf, 1992.

U.S. Department of Justice. *Attorney General's Commission on Pornography: Final Report.* Washington, DC: U.S. Government Printing Office, 1986.

U.S. Department of Justice Criminal Division. *Beyond the Pornography Commission: The Federal Reponse.* Washington, DC: U.S. Government Printing Office, 1988.

Vaughan, Frederick. *The Tradition of Political Hedonism: From Hobbes to J. S. Mill.* New York: Fordham University Press, 1982.

Will, George F. *The Leveling Wind: Politics, the Culture and Other News, 1990–1994.* New York: Viking, 1994.

Williams, Linda. *Hard Core: Power, Pleasure, and the "Frenzy of the Visible."* Berkeley: University of California Press, 1989.

Woodward, Bob, and Scott Armstrong. *The Brethren: Inside the Supreme Court.* New York: Simon & Schuster, 1979.

Woolley, Benjamin. *Virtual Worlds: A Journey in Hype and Hyperreality.* New York: Penguin Books, 1992.

Articles*

Benatar, Giselle. "Sex and Money." *Entertainment Weekly*, 6 November 1992, p. 19.

Bork, Robert. "Neutral Principles and Some First Amendment Problems." *Indiana Law Journal* 47 (1971):1.

* Newspaper articles cited in notes are not listed, while notable magazine articles are listed.

______. "What to Do About the First Amendment." *Commentary* 99 (1995):23.

Donnerstein, Edward, and Daniel Linz. "Mass Media, Sexual Violence, and Male Viewers: Current Theory and Research." *American Behavioral Scientist* 29 (May–June 1986):601.

Dworkin, Ronald. "Is There a Right to Pornography?" *Oxford Journal of Legal Studies* 1 (1981):177.

______. "Women and Pornography." *New York Review of Books*, 21 October 1993, p. 36.

______. "Reply." *New York Review of Books*, 3 March 1994, p. 48.

Finnis, John M. "'Reason and Passion': The Constitutional Dialectic of Free Speech and Obscenity." *University of Pennsylvania Law Review* 116 (1967):222.

Gourevitch, Victor. "The Problem of Natural Right and the Fundamental Alternatives in *Natural Right and History*." In K. Deutsch and W. Soffer, eds. *The Crisis of Liberal Democracy*. New York: State University Press of New York, 1987.

Grazia, Edward de. "Obscenity and the Mail: A Study of Administrative Restraint." *Law and Contemporary Problems* 20 (1955):608.

Kaminer, Wendy. "Feminists Against the First Amendment." *Atlantic Monthly*, November 1992, p. 110.

Keller, Susan Etta. "Viewing and Doing: Complicating Pornography's Meaning." *Georgetown Law Journal* 81 (1993):2195.

MacKinnon, Catharine. "Pornography as Defamation and Discrimination." *Boston University Law Review* 71 (1991):793.

______. "Crimes of War, Crimes of Peace." In S. Shute and S. Hurley, eds. *On Human Rights: The Oxford Amnesty Lectures 1993*. New York: Basic Books, 1993.

______. "Pornography: An Exchange." *New York Review of Books*, 3 March 1994, p. 47.

Masters, Kenneth. "Law in the Electronic Brothel: How Postmodern Media Affect First Amendment Obscenity Doctrine." *University of Puget Sound Law Review* 15 (1992):415.

Meiklejohn, Alexander. "The First Amendment Is an Absolute." *Supreme Court Review* (1961):245.

Michelman, Frank. "Conceptions of Democracy in American Constitutional Argument: The Case of Pornography Regulation." *Tennessee Law Review* 56 (1989): 291.

Oakeshott, Michael. "The Moral Life in the Writings of Thomas Hobbes." In *Rationalism in Politics*. London: Methuen, 1962.

Schauer, Frederick. "Response: Pornography and the First Amendment." *University of Pittsburgh Law Review* 40 (1979):605.

______. "Speech and 'Speech' — Obscenity and 'Obscenity': An Exercise in the Interpretation of Constitutional Language." *Georgetown Law Journal* 67 (1979):899.

Sherman, Jeffrey G. "Love Speech: The Social Utility of Pornography." *Stanford Law Review* 47 (1995):661.

Steinem, Gloria. "Erotica and Pornography: A Clear and Present Difference." *Ms.*, November 1978, p. 53.

Sunstein, Cass. "Words, Conduct, Caste." *University of Chicago Law Review* 60 (1993):795.

______. "Porn on the Fourth of July." *New Republic*, 9 January 1995, p. 42.

"Where Do We Stand on Pornography?" *Ms.*, January–February 1994, p. 32.

Wieseltier, Leon. "Total Quality Meaning." *New Republic*, 19 July 1993, p. 16.

Bibliography for Epilogue

Books

Berns, Walter. *Freedom, Virtue, and the First Amendment.* Chicago: Henry Regnery, 1965.

Bok, Sissela. *Lying: Moral Choice in Public and Private Life.* New York: Vintage Books, 1989.

Elster, Jon. *The Cement of Society: A Study of Social Order.* Cambridge: Cambridge University Press, 1989.

Gilbert, A., ed. and trans. *The Letters of Machiavelli.* Chicago: University of Chicago Press, 1961.

Marchand, Philip. *Marshall McLuhan: The Medium and the Messenger.* New York: Ticknor & Fields, 1989.

McCoy, Drew R. *The Last of the Fathers: James Madison and the Republican Legacy.* New York: Cambridge University Press, 1989.

Nietzsche, Friedrich. *Beyond Good and Evil: Prelude to a Philosophy of the Future.* Translated by Walter Kaufmann. New York: Vintage Books, 1966.

Nyberg, David. *The Varnished Truth.* Chicago: University of Chicago Press, 1993.

The Republic of Plato. Translated by Allan Bloom. New York: Basic Books, 1968.

Rue, Loyal. *By the Grace of Guile: The Role of Deception in Natural History and Human Affairs.* New York: Oxford University Press, 1994.

Standard Edition of the Complete Psychological Works of Sigmund Freud. London: Hogarth Press, 1957.

Steiner, George. *After Babel: Aspects of Language and Translation.* New York: Oxford University Press, 1975.

Strauss, Leo. *The City and Man.* Chicago: Rand McNally, 1964.

Sunstein, Cass. *Democracy and the Problem of Free Speech.* New York: Free Press, 1993.

Articles

Boorstin, Daniel J. "A History of the Image: From Pseudo-Event to Virtual Reality." *New Perspectives Quarterly* 11 (Summer 1994):16.

Cahn, Edmund. "Justice Black and First Amendment 'Absolutes': A Public Interview." *New York University Law Review* 37 (1962):549.

Page, Carl. "The Truth About Lies in Plato's *Republic.*" *Ancient Philosophy Journal* 11 (1991):1.

Bibliography for Afterword

Books

Benjamin, Walter. *Illuminations*. Translated by H. Zohn. Edited by H. Arendt. New York: Schocken Paperback, 1969.

Bickel, Alexander M. *The Morality of Consent*. New Haven: Yale University Press, 1975.

Ellul, Jacques. *Perspectives on Our Age*. Translated by J. Neugroschel. Edited by W. Vanderburg. New York: The Seabury Press, 1981.

Fish, Stanley. *There's No Such Thing as Free Speech and It's a Good Thing, Too*. New York: Oxford University Press, 1994.

Gitlin, Todd. *The Twilight of Common Dreams: Why America Is Wracked by Culture Wars*. New York: Metropolitan Books, 1995.

______. *Media Unlimited: How the Torrent of Images and Sounds Overwhelms Our Lives*. New York: Metropolitan Books/Henry Holt, 2001.

Jacobson, Michael F., and Laurie Ann Mazur. *Marketing Madness: A Survival Guide for a Consumer Society*. Boulder, CO: Westview Press, 1995.

Meiklejohn, Alexander. *Political Freedom: The Constitutional Powers of the People*. Westport, CT: Greenwood Publishing Group, 1979.

Rorty, Richard. *Contingency, Irony, and Solidarity*. New York: Cambridge University Press, 1989.

Rosen, Stanley. *Hermeneutics as Politics*. New York: Oxford University Press, 1987.

Rue, Loyal. *By the Grace of Guile*. New York: Oxford University Press, 1994.

Schwartz, Barry. *The Costs of Living: How Market Freedom Erodes the Best Things in Life*. New York: W.W. Norton, 1994.

Shklar, Judith. *Ordinary Vices*. Cambridge: Harvard University Press, 1984.

Spence, Donald P. *Narrative Truth and Historical Truth: Meaning and Interpretation in Psychoanalysis*. New York: W.W. Norton, 1982.

Articles*

Collins, Ronald K.L., and David M. Skover. "New 'Truths' and the Old First Amendment." *University of Cincinnati Law Review* 64 (1996):1295.

Drury, Shadia B. "Lying and Politics." *University of Cincinnati Law Review* 64 (1996):1227.

* Newspaper articles cited in notes are not listed, while notable journal articles are listed.

Hariman, Robert. "Machiavelli at the Fair." *University of Cincinnati Law Review* 64 (1996):1237.

Nietzsche, Friedrich. "On the Pathos of Truth." In Reinhold Grimm and Caroline Molina, eds., *Philosophical Writings*. Translated by B. Armstrong. New York: Continuum, 1995.

Nyberg, David. "Noble Lies, Narrative Truths, and the Art of Voice: Thoughts on Pragmatic Language and the First Amendment." *University of Cincinnati Law Review* 64 (1996):1203.

Rue, Loyal. "After the Death of Discourse." *University of Cincinnati Law Review* 64 (1996):1277.

Stivers, Richard. "Technology, Discourse, and Truth." *University of Cincinnati Law Review* 64 (1996):1259.

Thompson, Dennis F. "Hypocrisy and Democracy." In Bernard Yack, ed., *Liberalism Without Illusions: Essays on Liberal Theory & the Political Vision of Judith N. Shklar*. Chicago: University of Chicago Press, 1996.

Discography

Music oft hath such a charm to make bad good, and good provoke to harm.

— William Shakespeare
Measure for Measure (1604)
act 4, sc. 1, lines 14–15

Bartoli, Cecilia. "Sposa Son Disprezzata" by Vivaldi. *If You Love Me*. London Records compact disk 436 267-2, 1992.

Boublil, Alain, and Claude-Michel Schonberg. "The American Dream." *Miss Saigon*. Original cast recording. Geffen Records cassette M5G 24271, 1990.

Madonna. "Material Girl." *The Immaculate Collection*. Sire/Warner Brothers compact disk 9 26440-2, 1990.

Mahler, Gustav. "Adagietto." *Symphony no. 5*. London Symphony Orchestra conducted by Gilbert Kaplan. Innovative Music Productions compact disk GKS 1001, 1992.

Mouret, Jean-Joseph. "Rondeau." *First Symphonic Suite*. From The Greatest Hits of 1720. Philharmonica Virtuosi of New York conducted by Richard Kapp. Columbia Records MX 34544, 1977.

Mozart, Wolfgang Amadeus. "Introit." *Requiem*. Berlin Philharmonic conducted by Herbert Von Karajan. Deutsche Grammophon compact disk 2GGA 419867, 1987.

Rolling Stones. "Parachute Woman." *Beggar's Banquet*. ABKCO compact disk 7539, 1986.

Sade. "No Ordinary Love." *Love Deluxe*. Arista compact disk EK 53178, 1992.

Simon, Paul. "You Can Call Me Al." *Graceland*. Warner Brothers cassette 25447-4, 1986.

About the Book & Its Design

This is a book about discourse in America. More specifically, it is about discourse and the First Amendment. It is a work as much concerned with opening a new discourse as with heralding the death of an old one. For that reason, the work is more a book of questions than answers, more of ideas than ideologies, and certainly more of dialogue than monologue.

This discussion of the culture of free speech in America examines three of the major categories of popular expression — electronic visual entertainment, mass advertising, and pornography. Where the First Amendment is the touchstone, why are such forms of expression valued? Is it because they actually further Madisonian ideals such as reasoned decisionmaking, civic participation, social dissent, or self-realization? If so, do such high values comport with the tastes of modern culture? In other words, is the First Amendment what the elite few say or rather what the popular masses do? To ask these questions is to cast the First Amendment in a bold new light — if only by way of divulging the pomp and hypocrisy surrounding free speech jurisprudence. This last matter — exposing deliberate lies — is the focus of the final segment of the book. Hence, the First Amendment question of our times is essentially: Can we live without lies, even worthy ones?

A note on the text: This book is interactive and multimedia at times, much as the *Phaedrus* was in antiquity. In a literary and philosophical sense, then, it is a book yearning to be unbound.

The Death of Discourse is a collaborative effort, one that underscores the relationship between style and substance, indeed between art and expression.

For this reason, the authors thought it essential that *they* select a graphic artist. After several months of research, they approached Bruce Mau, who read the text and discussed the project with them. Mr. Mau then agreed to produce the book, working in conjunction with the authors.

Bruce Mau is a graphic designer from Toronto. Among other works, he has designed books for Zone Books, most notably the *Fragments for a History of the Human Body* series. In his work with Zone Books, he has designed books for authors such as Guy Debord, Georges Bataille, Michel Foucault, and Gilles Deleuze.

Mau collaborated with Rem Koolhaas on *S,M,L,XL* (Monacelli Press, 1996). The book's publication was preceded by a Koolhaas exhibit at the Museum of Modern Art in New York. Mr. Mau also did the graphic design work for the pop art sculptor Claes Oldenburg's latest book, *Large-Scale Projects* (Monacelli Press, 1995).

Bruce Mau has done graphic art work for the Whitney Museum of Art in New York, the Getty Center for the History of Art and the Humanities in Santa Monica, and the MOCA in Los Angeles.

The authors ventured to Canada where much of the collaborative and conceptual work for the design of the cover and text were done with Bruce Mau and his assistant Chris Rowat assuming the role of producers.

About the Authors

Ron Collins and David Skover are friends.

Ron lives in the East, David in the West.

They have been writing together for more than three decades. Their work is a joint effort, with David manning the keys and Ron pacing.

Ron, who grew up in Southern California, is a retired law professor. David, who grew up in Wisconsin, is an emeritus law professor at Seattle University.

Both are law graduates. Ron went to law school at Loyola in Los Angeles, David at Yale in New Haven.

Both clerked for appellate judges—Ron for Justice Hans A. Linde of the Oregon Supreme Court (and later as a judicial fellow for Chief Justice Warren Burger of the United States Supreme Court), and David for Judge Jon O. Newman of the United States Court of Appeals for the Second Circuit.

In a prior life, David sang in professional operatic and musical theater productions. He adores the works of Mozart, Verdi, Puccini, and Wagner, and admires the music of Stephen Sondheim.

Ron likes to probe Plato, Camus, and Wittgenstein. He is the editor of *Attention*, a journal on the life and legacy of Simone Weil, and the editor of *First Amendment News*, a weekly blog on free speech.

Ron and David have published eight books together, among which are *The Trials of Lenny Bruce: The Fall & Rise of An American Icon* (Sourcebooks, 2002), *On Dissent: Its Meaning in America* (Cambridge University Press, 2013), *The Judge: 26 Machiavellian Lessons* (Oxford University Press, 2017), and *Robotica: Speech Rights and Artificial Intelligence* (Cambridge University Press, 2018). They have also coauthored numerous scholarly articles in journals such as the *Harvard*, *Stanford*, and *Michigan Law Reviews* and in *The Supreme Court Review*.

Index

The most accomplished Way of using Books at present, is twofold: Either first, to serve them as some Men do Lords, learn their Titles exactly, and then brag of their Acquaintance. Or Secondly, which is indeed the choicer, the profounder, and politer Method, to get a thorough Insight into the Index, by which the whole Book is governed and turned, like Fishes by the Tail. For, to enter the Palace of Learning at the great Gate, requires an Experience of Time and Forms; therefore Men of much Haste and little Ceremony, are content to get in by the Back-Door.

— Jonathan Swift
A Tale of a Tub (1704)
section vii